CW00558117

GRIMOIRES

GRIMOIRES
A HISTORY OF MAGIC BOOKS

OWEN DAVIES

OXFORD
UNIVERSITY PRESS

OXFORD
UNIVERSITY PRESS

Great Clarendon Street, Oxford OX2 6DP

Oxford University Press is a department of the University of Oxford.
It furthers the University's objective of excellence in research, scholarship,
and education by publishing worldwide in

Oxford New York

Auckland Bangkok Beunos Aires Cape Town Chennai
Dar es Salaam Delhi Hong Kong Istanbul Karachi Kolkata
Kuala Lumpur Madrid Melbourne Mexico City Mumbai Nairobi
São Paulo Shanghai Taipei Tokyo Toronto

Oxford is a registered trade mark of Oxford University Press
in the UK and in certain other countries

Published in the United States
by Oxford University Press Inc., New York

A catalogue record for this title is available from the British Library

Library of Congress Cataloging in Publication Data

Data available

Typeset by SPI Publisher Services Ltd, Pondicherry, India
Printed in Great Britain
on acid-free paper by
Clays Ltd, St Ives plc

ISBN 978-0-19-920451-9

1 3 5 7 9 10 8 6 4 2

ACKNOWLEDGEMENTS

My parents, brother, sister, and Céline have been as supportive as ever in the writing and researching of this book. My mother and her sister also helped with translation. Thanks also to the following for their interest and advice or for providing sources and generously answering my queries: Willem de Blécourt, Ronald Hutton, David Lederer, Dave Evans, Soili-Maria Olli, Manfred Tschaikner, Caroline Oates, Francesca Matteoni, Steven Wood, Matthew Green, Rowland Hughes, Stephan Bachter, Éva Pócs, Lisa Tallis, Jason Semmens, Laura Stark, María Tausiet, Hugh Sadleir, Johanna Jacobsen, Benedek Lang, Helen Boak, Enrique Perdiguero, Ane Ohrvik, Cecile Dubuis, and Tom Johnson. In collecting the source materials for this book I particularly appreciated the helpfulness of Jacques Pons (Archives Départementales des Landes), Evelyne Bacardatz (Archives de Bayonne), and Simone Shepherd (ACIJ publications officer). I am also thankful for the valuable comments on an early typescript of the book provided by my publisher's anonymous reviewer, and for the patience and suggestions of my editors at Oxford University Press, Luciana O'Flaherty and Matthew Cotton.

CONTENTS

LIST OF ILLUSTRATIONS

LIST OF PLATES

I came to the gate, where some dozen or so of devils were playing tennis . . . in their hands they held rackets of fire; but what amazed me still more was that books, apparently full of wind and rubbish, served them for tennis balls, a strange and marvellous thing.

—Cervantes, *Don Quixote*, Chapter 70, trans. John Ormsby

INTRODUCTION

What are the most dangerous books in the world? Some might nominate the founding texts of our major religions, which through misinterpretation and manipulation have led to the suffering of millions over the centuries. Others might point to defining modern political works such as Karl Marx's *Das Kapital*, Hitler's *Mein Kampf*, or Chairman Mao's *Little Red Book*. Fiction can also gravely offend public sensibilities, as we have seen in recent decades with book burnings of the *Satanic Verses* and *Harry Potter* novels. But for many down the millennia and across the globe no books have been more feared than grimoires: then again, no books have been more valued and revered.

'Grimoire' has a familiar ring to many people, particularly following the popularity of such 'teen witch' dramas as *Buffy the Vampire Slayer* and *Charmed*, but few people are sure what it means, and my computer spellchecker certainly does not know what to make of it. Put simply, then, grimoires are books of conjurations and charms, providing instructions on how to make magical objects such as protective amulets and talismans. They are repositories of knowledge that arm people against evil spirits and witches, heal their illnesses, fulfil their sexual desires, divine and alter their destiny, and much else besides. Grimoires are books of magic, then, but not all books of magic are grimoires, for as we shall see, some magic texts were concerned with discovering and using the secrets of the natural world rather than being based on the conjuration of spirits, the power of words, or the ritual creation of magical objects. The derivation of 'grimoire' is not entirely certain. In the early nineteenth century it was suggested that it came from the Italian 'rimario', a book of rhymes or Bible verses. It more likely derives from the French word 'grammaire', which originally referred to a work written in Latin. By the eighteenth century it was being widely used in France to refer to magic books, perhaps because many of them continued to circulate in Latin manuscripts at a time when most other publications were in French. It was used as a figure of speech to denote something that was difficult to read or impossible to understand, such as, 'it is like a grimoire to me'.[1] It was only in the nineteenth century, with the educated resurgence of interest in the occult, that it began to enter general English usage.

Defining the meaning of magic is a far trickier task. For all the time, paper, and intellectual energy spent on trying to do so, there is no overarching answer. Any useful understanding must be tied to the cultures of the people being studied in specific periods and places.[2] The boundary between religion and magic is certainly never clear-cut and changes over time and in relation to different religious belief systems. This will become clear in the first chapter. What is worth stating now is that grimoires never represented the totality of people's experience and knowledge of magic in the past. There are numerous charms, spells, and rituals that were passed down orally through many generations, and were only recorded in writing by folklorists and antiquarians in the nineteenth century. Furthermore, women have always been as important as men in the recorded history of magical practice, yet because of their restricted access to literacy, they play only a minor role in the story of grimoires until the sixteenth century.

Grimoires exist because of the desire to create a physical record of magical knowledge, reflecting concerns regarding the uncontrollable and corruptible nature of the oral transmission of valuable secret or sacred information. This urge to provide a tangible magical archive dates right back to the ancient civilization of Babylonia in the second millennium BCE. But grimoires also exist because the very act of writing itself was imbued with occult or hidden power. 'A book of magic is also a magical book,' as one historian of the subject has observed.[3] As this suggests, I am concerned with the history of books and not just the magic they contained. It is important to understand their meaning and social significance, and to consider the endless attempts by religious and secular authorities to censor and suppress them. In this sense, grimoires represent much more than magic.[4] They tell us about fundamental developments in history over the past two thousand years. To understand their past is to understand the spread of Christianity and Islam, the development of early science, the cultural influence of print, the growth of literacy, the social impact of slavery and colonialism, and the expansion of Western cultures across the oceans.

This story concerns the spread of written magic from the ancient Middle East, through Europe and then across the Atlantic, but it is important to highlight that other venerable literary cultures also enshrined their magical knowledge in writing and considered writing magical. India's literary heritage, in particular, was a major influence across much of south Asia. The various Batak ethnic groups of Sumatra, for instance, have long had a semi-literate culture, perhaps for a millennium and more. Their alphabet is based on the Brahmi script, the earliest examples of which have been found in Southern India, dating to the third century BCE. Writing was primarily a tool of magic for the Batak, preserving their magical tradition more faithfully than oral transmission. The art of writing was largely the preserve of the *datu* or priest-magician, who recorded it in magic books (*poestaha*)

inscribed on the inner bark of the *alim* tree and folded like an accordion.[5] The
literary magic of the East also influenced the West through early trading links.
Magic squares consisting of a grid of numbers of astrological, metaphysical, or
mystical significance are thought to have spread westwards from China in the late
first millennium thanks to Persian and Arab traders. The magic square also became
an integral element of Indian magic, perhaps around the same time as papermak-
ing was introduced there from China in the eighth century. One of the earliest
surviving Indian expositions of the art was a book of mathematics written in 1356.
Other elements of astrological magic also filtered from India into the writings of
Islamic Arab and Persian scientists and magicians.[6]

Books can be magical without actually containing magic. In the past, uneducated people identified certain physical attributes of books, such as large size,
venerable appearance, and contents full of unfamiliar signs, figures, and languages
as indicative of magical purpose. Practitioners of magic sometimes displayed books
which matched these characteristics in their consulting rooms to give the impression that they were adepts in the occult arts, even though the texts had nothing to
do with magic. Some books were also used as protective talismans.[7] The most
obvious example is the Bible, which people placed under their pillow to protect
them from witches and evil spirits, or touched when swearing oaths. It was also
used in popular divination. By placing a key at certain passages in the Bible,
binding and then suspending it, the divine power enshrined in the 'good book'
would make it turn in response to the name of a thief. The Bible was obviously
not a grimoire, but the power of the words, stories, psalms, and prayers it
contained, as well as its holiness as an object, made it the most widely used
magic resource across the social and cultural spectrum over the past thousand
years. Passages written on scraps of paper were used as healing charms, and the
psalms were read for magical effect. So as we shall see, in the Christian world the
Bible has always been thought a necessary companion of the grimoire, and both
were required to make magic.

It is no wonder, then, that as Christianity spread across the European colonies
natives wondered whether the Bible was the occult source of power of the white
colonizers. Amongst the peoples of parts of Africa, South America, the Caribbean,
and the South Pacific, anthropologists have found a widespread notion that the
white man deliberately withheld the full power of Christianity in order to keep
them in a state of subjugation. This was not necessarily achieved by restricting
literacy, but by deliberately withholding some of the *true* Bible and therefore the
complete key to wisdom, knowledge, and consequently power.[8] In the Caribbean
today, for instance, the Bible is considered by some as an African divine text
appropriated and controlled by Europeans. When asked why he accepted the
Bible but not Catholicism, a worshipper of the Trinidadian spirit religion of

Orisha explained, 'The Bible came from Egypt; it was stolen by the Catholics who added and removed parts for their own purposes.'[9] As we shall see, such notions proved fertile ground for the spread of grimoires that purported to contain these missing parts. The notion that sacred knowledge has been withheld was not just a product of colonial tensions. The Bible, as we know it, is the result of a highly selective and political process of compilation. The elements that make up the Bible were chosen from a diverse range of biblical texts. Yet the Church never managed to suppress those apocryphal biblical gospels, histories, stories, and events dismissed and excluded from the official Bible story. This alternative literary biblical tradition became the source of numerous magical traditions that continue today.

A grimoire is defined by the writing it contains, but the act of writing can itself be magic and certain words can have active properties independent of the holy or magical text in which they are written. Their power could be stimulated by the ritual use of specific inks and blood. Across the world from antiquity to the present we find the notion, for example, that the writing in sacred texts was imbued with physical divine power that could be utilized by eating or drinking it. In Numbers 5 in the Old Testament it is instructed that a woman suspected of adultery could be brought to a priest who would make her undergo the ordeal of bitter water: 'And the priest shall write these curses in a book, and he shall blot them out with the bitter water. And he shall cause the woman to drink the bitter water that causeth the curse.' If she is guilty 'the water that causeth the curse shall enter into her, and become bitter, and her belly shall swell, and her thigh shall rot: and the woman shall be a curse among her people.' If innocent the divine written curse would not be activated.

The ingestion of holy writing was normally employed for healing purposes. In medieval Europe sacred words were written on bread or cheese to be swallowed by the sick. Some medieval religious manuscripts bear the signs of having been rinsed with water so that some of the ink washed off and could therefore be drunk. The seventh-century Book of Durrow, an illuminated manuscript of the Gospels, is a good example. In the seventeenth century it was dunked in water by Irish farmers to produce a sacred medicine for curing sick cattle. In parts of Islamic West Africa passages of the Koran written out in ink are similarly washed and drunk to cure disease and witchcraft. Amongst the Berti of northern Darfur, the *fakis* (Koranic teachers and healers) write certain verses from the Koran on a wooden slate, using a pen made from a millet stalk and ink made from a mix of soot and gum Arabic. The water is then washed off into a small bowl or bottle for clients to drink either at once or in small doses throughout the day. As part of their graduation ceremony the Batak *datu* made his students inscribe an incantation, dictated by him, on bamboo held over a heap of boiled rice. The scratchings produced by inscribing fell onto the rice, and the ritual was completed when the boys ate the rice and with it 'the soul of the writing'.[10]

If writing was so important to grimoire magic what was the effect of the print revolution from the late fifteenth century onwards? Magicians had no personal influence over the creation of print grimoires, could not imbue them with power through the ritual use of materials. The printed book was not integral to the magic, rather a record of it. Magicians were merely purchasers of a product.

The importance of print was its role in democratizing literary magic.[11] The presses could produce copies in far greater numbers and far more quickly than scribes, and so the knowledge of the learned few became available to the expanding literate masses. While print drained power from the grimoire in terms of its magical integrity, it also empowered it through growing access and social influence. Furthermore, print did not usurp the role of manuscript; the magic latent in the words contained in print grimoires could be reactivated through transcription. Neither did print cheapen the aura of grimoires. It is true that the power of literary magic was in part invested in the restricted access to literacy, which is one reason why the history of grimoires needs to be sensitive to gender inequalities. Until the twentieth century the literacy rates of women lagged far behind men. Yet, as we shall see, even in the age of mass-produced grimoires and near universal education there was a widespread perception that the ability to read was not the only requirement for using them. The qualities of the magician remained important. Whether by birth right, geography, or piety only certain people were thought to have the innate power to possess and perform grimoire magic on the behalf of others. So even when grimoires were available to everyone not everyone could use them safely and effectively.

To end this brief introduction let me pose some riddles. What links Chicago to ancient Egypt, Germany to Jamaica, and Norway to Bolivia? How did a Swede become the greatest wizard in America? What did Rastafarians and Alpine farmers have in common? Who is the 'Little Albert' famed from Canada to the Indian Ocean? And how did a poor crossing-sweeper from Ohio become a feared mythical spirit in the Caribbean? Grimoires provide all the answers. They not only reflected the globalization of the world but helped shape it. The key to their extraordinary influence lies back in the ancient world of the Middle East, which is where our journey now begins.

Chapter One

ANCIENT AND MEDIEVAL GRIMOIRES

The modern history of ancient and medieval magic is vast and often inaccessible to the non-expert, yet there is much to catch the imagination and challenge our understanding of religion and society in past eras. While European grimoires were largely a product of the medieval period their inspiration lies much further back in the religions of the ancient civilizations of the Near and Middle East. In the eastern Mediterranean the religious traditions of paganism, Judaism, Christianity, and later Islam rubbed off on each other despite the obvious antagonisms in terms of competing political influence. How medieval scholars understood that distant past and reconstructed it, often wrongly, was as important to the history of magic as the magical knowledge actually passed down during the first millennium.

The cross-fertilized intellectual culture of the Middle East was introduced to most of Europe during the Middle Ages, at a time when the Continent has often been portrayed as being in the grip of a bigoted and zealous Church, a period of religious intolerance with the Crusades against Islam, the setting up of Inquisitions, and pogroms against the Jews. This portrayal is far from being completely unjustified, yet the medieval era was also an age of extraordinary scholarly collaboration and understanding between different religions and cultures. The writings of the pagan ancient Greeks, Romans, and Egyptians were translated and pored over, and churchmen travelled across Europe to immerse themselves in the Arabic sciences and Jewish mysticism taught in the schools of Spain and southern France. Magic was seen as an aspect of science as well as religion, and its roots were traced back thousands of years through the wider reconstruction of the history of written knowledge. So to understand the origins of the grimoire we must explore the ancient world through the prism of the medieval intellectual mind.

Ancient masters of magic

The ancient Greeks and Romans believed that the priests of a Persian tribe, the Magi, were the first practitioners of magic, taught to them by their founder Zoroaster. The 'wise men from the East' who came bearing gifts for the baby Jesus were their representatives. According to the naturalist and military man Pliny the Elder, writing in the first century CE, 'without doubt magic was first invented over there in Persia by Zoroaster . . . But it is not established whether there was just one man of this name or whether there was another one afterward too.' He went on to report that the Greek mathematician Eudoxus calculated that Zoroaster lived six thousand years before the death of Plato. That would put the age of Zoroaster and the birth of magic to around 6347 BCE. But Pliny went on to make a distinction between the invention of magic and when it was first written down. As far as he could discover, the first man to do that was a Persian magician and astrologer named Osthanes, who accompanied King Xerxes in his failed war with Greece (480 BCE), and in the process 'scattered, as it were, the seeds of the hideous craft along the way, infecting the world with it'.[1]

In Jewish, Christian, and Islamic traditions, which were ultimately influenced by Babylonian myth, the origins of magic books were dated to the age before the great Flood. While some Hebrew and Samaritan texts ascribed writings to the first man Adam, in late antiquity and the medieval period Enoch (Idris in Arabic) was more generally believed to be the inventor of books. As is evident from fragments of the famed Dead Sea Scrolls, found in caves around Qumran near the Dead Sea in the mid-twentieth century, purported *Books of Enoch* containing astronomical, astrological, and angelic lore were circulating at the time of Jesus. According to one medieval account, Enoch's great-grandson Noah received his understanding of medicine from a book of knowledge given to him by the archangel Raphael. It was a book that had been concealed in a cave since the time of Adam. Enoch read it there and learned the art of astronomy, while Noah found in it advice on constructing the Ark. Another tradition relates how the angel Raziel communicated to Noah a secret book containing the art of astrology, which was then written on a sapphire that Noah kept in a golden chest that he brought with him in the Ark. This was subsequently inherited by his son Shem. A surviving astrological tract called the *Treatise of Shem* dates to sometime in the late first century BCE or early CE.[2]

So, according to this biblical chronology, the earliest works on the occult sciences were those studied by Enoch. The first book of conjuration and magic, though, is associated with Noah's sons Shem and Ham (Cham in Latin). Histories of the lives of Noah's sons outside the Old Testament were mutable and sometimes conflicting. In some accounts Ham wrote down the secrets of his demonic magic on metal plates and stone tablets before the Flood, buried them, and then returned to them once the waters had subsided. Others, such as the first Bishop of Norwich (d. 1119), thought his magic book was secreted in the Ark: 'the ark was of small compass; but yet even there Ham preserved the arts of magic and idolatry.' In some medieval texts Zoroaster is the son of Ham and in others he *is* Ham. According to the twelfth-century scholar Michael Scot, in his history of astrology and astronomy, Zoroaster was the inventor of magic, but he was descended from Shem, and it was Ham who invented the art of divination with the help of demons. Ham then taught it to his son Canaan who wrote down the secrets of the art in thirty volumes, which were burned after he was killed in battle. As to the lasting heritage of Noah's sons, one commentary recorded the belief that Japhet was the father of all Europeans, Shem the heir to Africa, while the pagan peoples of Asia, and tellingly, the Egyptians, descended from Ham.[3]

Although Persia was seen as the source of magic, the people of the ancient civilization of Chaldea, part of Babylonia, were also renowned for their astrological and magical abilities. Zoroaster was sometimes referred to as a Chaldean. In archaeological terms too, the Sumerian-inspired cuneiform writing of the Akkadians, one of the peoples of the Mesopotamian region, represent the first major repository of written magic spells and conjurations, though their secrets were only deciphered in the nineteenth century. In Uruk, one of the world's earliest cities, and now part of Iraq, excavations of houses dating from the fifth and fourth centuries BCE turned up cuneiform clay tablets containing a series of magic rituals and incantations. They were, it seems, the private libraries of well-known scribes and exorcists.[4] By the birth of Christ, though, it was the later civilization of Egypt that was seen by Greeks, Romans, Christians, Jews, and later Muslims, as the centre of magic and the home of the most adept magician priests. According to the Jewish Talmud, nine-tenths of the world's sorcery resided in Egypt.[5] It was the place of pilgrimage for all those who desired to learn the magical arts. It was believed in later antiquity that even famous Greek philosophers such as Plato and Pythagoras had been instructed in wisdom and occult knowledge by Egyptian priests. Centuries after his death, those who subscribed to the teachings of Pythagoras continued to be suspected of dabbling in magic.[6] Most of the early physical evidence for ancient Egyptian magic derives from burial goods, amulets, stone monuments, and inscriptions on metal and clay tablets and bowls. They remind us that we should not think of literary magic only in terms of the written page. While books were principally used as records, the power of written words was effected through their transcription on to ritual or protective objects.

The first identifiable phase in the development of the grimoire occurred during the Hellenistic period, when Egypt was under Greek rule for three hundred years following Alexander the Great's conquest of the country in 332 BCE This was a fertile period of cultural and religious exchange, with the Egyptian priesthood learning and using Greek and the Greeks imbibing Egyptian religion and magic. One result of this fusion was the founding of the great Library of Alexandria, which attracted scholars from all over the Greek world. Another was the Coptic writing system constructed from the Greek alphabet and Egyptian phonetics. More to the point, thanks to the amazing nineteenth-century archaeological discoveries of what are known as the Graeco-Egyptian papyri, we can see how the magic tradition that would later spread across Europe was largely a product of cultural exchange in Hellenistic Egypt. These papyri date from the late first century BCE to the fifth century CE, thus mostly from the period of Roman rule, and are written in Greek, Demotic Egyptian, and Coptic rather than the hieroglyphic magic associated with Egyptian temples and burial monuments. They contain a fascinating mix of Egyptian, Greek, and Jewish religious influences, and there is considerable debate about how much and which of the spells and conjurations are truly Egyptian in origin. There are distinct differences between the magic they contain and that found in the earliest magical inscriptions and papyri from the time of the pharaohs. While the latter are primarily concerned with health and protection, the Graeco-Egyptian papyri manuscripts are much more focused on the desires and ambitions of the magician, with magic used for financial gain, social success, and sexual conquest. The summoning of visions of deities to impart occult knowledge or divine the future was also a major component of the ritual magic of the later period.[7]

In biblical chronology Moses is calculated by theological scholars to have lived sometime between the fifteenth and thirteenth century BCE—long after the Flood. This prophet, miracle worker, and leader of the Hebrew slaves out of Egypt had an eventful life by all accounts, but there are two episodes that bear directly on the grimoire tradition. The first was his and Aaron's titanic magic contest against the Pharaoh's wizards, during which, as told in Exodus, he turned the rivers and pools of Egypt into blood and summoned up a plague of flies. The second was his reception of the Torah and the two tablets bearing the Ten Commandments during his revelation on Mount Sinai. The former sealed the tradition of Moses the magician while the latter was the source of myths regarding the divine transmission of more secret knowledge than is mentioned in the Torah and Old Testament.

According to the New Testament (Acts 7:22) 'Moses was learned in all the wisdom of the Egyptians, and was mighty in words and in deeds.' In an Egyptian context, wisdom was taken in antiquity to mean occult knowledge and this comment represents a more general belief at the time that Moses had learned the art of magic during his time in Egypt—he was after all born there and brought up in Pharaoh's household. The Greek pagan Celsus, writing in the second century CE, asserted that the Jews were much addicted to the sorcery taught them by Moses. It was certainly the case that by the time of Jesus their reputation as magicians had grown to a similar level to that of the Egyptians. During Roman rule there is evidence of Jewish magicians being sought out, and they could be found in the entourage of high Roman officials. Jewish elements can also be found in numerous charms in the Graeco-Egyptian papyri.[8]

It was, however, fundamental to the identity of Jewish religion, and important to Christianity, that a clear distinction was made between the 'portents and miracles' of Moses and the 'sorcery' of Egyptian wizards. The gods worshipped by the latter, and the assistance they sought from 'corrupt angels' and demons, were vanquished by the superior powers of the one God acting through Moses. In the process clear water was put between the cultures of Judaism and Egypt, both of which were represented in the life of Moses.[9] Yet from the late medieval period onwards, Christian occult philosophers, mystics, and magicians began to redefine Moses as an Egyptian rather than a Jew, presenting him as a repository of Egyptian wisdom and magic. Later he would come to be seen as a great African wonder-worker in African-American popular religion.[10] Moses meant many things to many people.

The Jewish Torah, or Pentateuch as Christians refer to the five scrolls or books that make up the first part of the Old Testament (Genesis, Exodus, Leviticus, Numbers, Deuteronomy), was dictated to Moses by God. But did he receive more wisdom than the Jewish and Christian priests revealed? Over the millennia many people have certainly thought so. Two surviving magic papyri from around the fourth century CE are entitled the 'hidden book of Moses called "eight" or "holy"', and 'Unique or Eighth Book of Moses'. They mention other lost Mosaic texts, namely the *Key of Moses*, *Archangelical Teaching of Moses*, *Secret Moon Book of Moses*, and *Tenth Hidden [Book of] Moses*.[11] The *Eighth Book of Moses* provides ritual for meeting the gods and instructs:

> Now when the god comes in do not stare | at his face, but look at his feet
> while beseeching him, as written above, and giving thanks that he did not
> treat you contemptuously, but you were thought worthy of the things
> about to be said to you for correction of your life. You, then, ask,
> 'Master, what is fated for me?' And he will tell you even / about your

star, and what kind of demon you have, and your horoscope and where you may live and where you may die.

There were also less elevated spells such as to 'put down fear or anger' which involved writing a magic sign on a laurel leaf and showing it to the sun, saying 'I call on you, the great god in heaven, [strong] lord, mighty IAŌ OYŌ IŌ AIŌ OYŌ, who exist; protect me from all fear, from all danger that threatens.'[12]

If there is an *Eighth Book* it stands to reason that a *Sixth* and *Seventh Book of Moses* might also have been in circulation at the time. We only know about the *Eighth Book* from the archaeological discovery and translation of the papyri in the nineteenth and twentieth centuries. Yet, intriguingly, by the late eighteenth century a manuscript claiming to be the *Sixth* and *Seventh Books of Moses* was circulating in Germany. Whoever wrote it would have been unaware of the existence of a purported *Eighth Book*, but was no doubt conscious of rumours and claims of the discovery of other lost Mosaic texts. In 1725, for instance, a book was printed in Cologne claiming to contain 'the newly found books of secrets of Moses'.[13] Three centuries earlier, manuscripts of simple, practical magical receipts written in a mix of Hebrew, Aramaic, and gibberish, were circulating in Europe bearing the title the *Harba de-Mosha* or *Sword of Moses*, though a work of the same name was known as early as the eleventh century. One version provided a spell for how to walk on water without getting one's feet wet, allowing the magician to mimic a miracle attributed to Jesus.[14] As we shall see later in the book, though, it was the *Sixth* and *Seventh Books of Moses* that would have the greatest influence on the modern world of magic and religion.

Hermes Trismegistus was the other central figure in historic conceptions of ancient Egyptian magic, and the next great reputed author of occult books in this survey of the dubious lineage of magic. In his most mythical guise he was a conflation of Thoth, the ibis-headed Egyptian god of Wisdom, and the Greek god Hermes (equated with the Roman Mercury). Thoth was thought to be the inventor of writing and mathematics and therefore the patron God of scribes and administrators. As the founder of the written word it stood to reason he was also a supreme master of magic. His merging with Hermes took place during the Hellenistic period and the result, Hermes Trismegistus the 'thrice great', was, as one historian has remarked, 'more than the sum of his parts'.[15] But we need to be careful not to present this version of Hermes as being the only one. In an Islamic tradition dating to at least the ninth century there are three people identified as Hermes. The first was Enoch/Idris, the founder of astrology who, by carving his occult scientific knowledge on a temple, preserved the wisdom of the antediluvian world for future mankind. The second lived in Egypt or Chaldea after the Flood and taught Pythagoras, and the third was a great physician who lived in Egypt and wrote books on alchemy and poisonous animals. In some accounts he was also a contemporary of Moses.[16] Disentangling the various identities when reading ancient and medieval references to Hermes is not an easy task.

The third-century BCE Egyptian historian and priest Manetho reckoned there were an impressive 36,525 books of Hermes. Several centuries after his death Manetho was given the spurious authorship of one of these, the *Book of Sothis*, which was essentially a chronicle of Egyptian Kings purportedly inscribed in sacred characters by Trismegistus before the Flood.[17] Another estimate from the same era mentioned the more modest number of 20,000 works, others mere tens and hundreds rather than thousands.[18] Several surviving medieval and early modern Hermetic occult texts were purportedly copies of works by another ancient mage named Toc or Toz Graecus (Toz the Greek). A work attributed to him on the creation of magical images, rings, and mirrors through the divine influence of Venus was described as an 'evil book' by one medieval scholar. As to the background of Toz Graecus, as one variant spelling of his name 'Thot' suggests, he may have been one and the same as Hermes Trismegistus, but by the medieval period confusion had arisen and a separate identity created. In some later grimoires, however, he was sometimes referred to as Ptolomaeus Graeccus and described as a disciple of Solomon. As a seventeenth-century Latin grimoire entitled 'A commentary by Toz Graecus, philosopher of great name' explained, its contents were the summation of all Solomon's knowledge, which he wrote down in a book for his son Rehoboam, who buried it in his tomb in an ivory casket. When Toz discovered it he wept with frustration at his inability to understand it, until an angel revealed its secrets to him.[19] What was this fabled book?

The Solomon we are talking about, of course, is the Old Testament King, the son of David, who completed his father's work of building the Holy Temple in Jerusalem in which the Ark of the Covenant was housed. In biblical chronology it is calculated that he ruled Israel during the tenth century BCE. The account of him in the Old Testament refers to his wisdom as being 'greater than all the wisdom of Egypt'. He was the source of 3,000 proverbs and over a thousand songs, and knew the secrets of plants and animals better than any man. There is no biblical intimation of Solomon as being a great magician, but his reputation for astrology and knowledge of the spirit world seems to have circulated in the Near East and Egypt by the second century BCE. It is the first-century Jewish historian Josephus who presents us with the first clear representation of Solomon the magician, telling how Solomon had written 3,000 books including ones containing incantations and exorcisms to heal demon-induced sickness. The first actual magic book attributed to him, the *Testament of Solomon*, was written in Greek sometime during the first five centuries CE and probably originated in Babylonia or Egypt.[20] The earliest surviving papyri excerpts from it date to the latter end of this period.

There is no evidence, as some scholars have suggested, that the Greek version borrowed from an earlier Jewish Solomonic book of magic. It was only centuries later that copies appeared in Hebrew, Arabic, and Latin.

The *Testament* is essentially a tale of how demons hampered the construction of the Temple by plaguing Solomon's favourite workman. Heeding Solomon's prayers for help, the angel Michael presented to him a magical ring from God. Engraved upon it was the Seal of Solomon that had the power to bind demons, and was depicted in later grimoires as variously a pentagram, hexagram, or circular symbol, while in Russia it was associated with the SATOR AREPO word square.[21] The latter was a magic palindrome, examples of which have been found dating back to Roman times, including amongst the ruins of Pompeii. It was usually written as follows:

SATOR
AREPO
TENET
OPERA
ROTAS

Numerous translations have been proposed to explain its meaning, but none are entirely satisfactory. The fact that the letters were also reformulated to spell PATER NOSTER twice, arranged in the form of a cross, might suggest it was of Christian origin. In several medieval Near Eastern churches one or more of the words in the square were given to the shepherds who visited the infant Jesus.[22]

Through the power of the ring, thirty-six or more demons were compelled to appear and identify themselves to Solomon, telling him their evil powers, and how they could be controlled by writing down certain words. So the demon *Autothith* stated that he caused grudges and fighting but could be banished by writing down 'Alpha' and 'Omega', the First and the Last. The dirty swine *Agchoniōn* explained that he lay among the swaddling-clothes of babies causing mischief. He fled when a diminishing form of the word 'Lycurgos' was written on a fig leaf: 'Lycurgos, ycurgos, curgos, yrgos, gos, os'. Armed with this knowledge, Solomon sealed some of the demons up in vessels like genies in a bottle, while others were put to work building the temple using their superhuman powers to speed up the work. Solomon lost his divinely bestowed power after becoming besotted by a foreign woman. He was told by the priests of her land that he could not sleep with her until he had made a sacrifice to the god Moloch. This he did and subsequently committed further idolatry by building temples to two other gods, Baal and Rapha. The *Testament* ends with Solomon saying he wrote down his account for the benefit of others who might be inspired and aided by his knowledge, but warned off the path to his own ultimate downfall, 'So that you may find grace forever and ever.'[23]

There is no doubt the *Testament* was used as a grimoire rather than merely read as a cautionary religious or mystical text. A medieval version in the British Library includes additional annotations by its owner to supplement and facilitate its use for performing exorcisms.[24] The list of demons and their powers would become a staple of later grimoires. During the medieval period other magic texts ascribed to Solomon also began to appear. The renowned thirteenth-century scientist and friar Albertus Magnus of Cologne noted that five necromantic books ascribed to Solomon were circulating at the time.[25] One of them with a long shelf life was the *Almandal*, surviving examples of which in German and Latin date to the fifteenth century. The title of this straightforward guide to the ritual invocation of angels refers to an Arabic word for a wax tablet altar on which the magician engraves divine names and the seals of Solomon with a silver stylus. To heighten the anticipation of the reader, and to ensure the magician knew they had conjured up the correct celestial visitor, descriptions were provided of how the angels would appear. The angel of the second altitude revealed himself as a three-year-old child in a radiant red garment, face, and hands blood red with the fire of divine love, wearing a crown of wild roses. The angelic encounter would clear the mind of the magician, he would be overwhelmed by love and affection, and humbled by the angel's assurances of redemptive friendship.[26]

Despite being condemned by some medieval commentators the *Ars Notoria* or *Notary Arts* was another similarly benign Solomonic work rather than a demonic grimoire.[27] Its rationale was based on a passage in 2 Chronicles in the Old Testament where Solomon asks God:

> Give me now wisdom and knowledge, that I may go out and come in before this people: for who can judge this thy people, that is so great? And God said to Solomon, Because this was in thine heart, and thou hast not asked riches, wealth, or honour, nor the life of thine enemies, neither yet hast asked long life; but hast asked wisdom and knowledge for thyself, that thou mayest judge my people, over whom I have made thee king: Wisdom and knowledge is granted unto thee; and I will give thee riches, and wealth, and honour, such as none of the kings have had that have been before thee, neither shall there any after thee have the like.

Surviving early copies, of which over fifty exist for the period 1300–1600, contain prayers with words purporting to be Chaldean, along with Greek and Hebrew, and various occult signs and geometric figures revealed to Solomon by an angel as he prayed one night. Through employing these in conjunction with purification rituals, the magician, like Solomon, could request the angels, saints, Christ even, to bestow divine knowledge regarding the seven liberal arts of medieval education—namely grammar, rhetoric, and logic (the verbal arts), and arithmetic, music, geometry, and astronomy (the mathematical arts).[28] The *Ars Notoria* also held out the prospect of experiencing ecstatic visions, and obtaining fast-track means of becoming an adept in science and learning languages. Those who used it were not inspired by greed or the manipulation of others for money, political power, and sex. It was the first Solomonic text to be put into print, with a Latin edition appearing around 1600, though it did not contain the *notae* or occult signs and figures found in the earlier manuscripts.

The most enduring, influential, and notorious Solomonic book, the *Clavicula Salomonis* or the *Clavicule* or *Key of Solomon*, was a true grimoire. The earliest versions of the text were written in Greek in the fifteenth century and bore the titles *Magical Treatise of Solomon* or the *Little Key of the Whole Art of Hygromancy, Found by Several Craftsmen and by the Holy Prophet Solomon*. By the time they were translated into Latin and Italian in the following century the term *Clavicula* was being used. Although some manuscripts again claimed that they were translations from Hebrew there is no substantive evidence for a Hebrew version before the seventeenth century.[29] There is no one definitive version of the *Clavicule* but, along with conjurations to command and control the 'Angels of Darkness', manuscripts usually contained rituals and symbols for personal rather than spiritual well being, such as to provoke love, punish enemies, become invisible, and deal with thieves. We shall encounter its use again and again in the next chapter.

The New Testament, while rich in miracles, exorcisms, and magic, did not provide any notable future grimoire authors. Yet there are two figures from the Gospels and the Acts of the Apostles that had the potential to join Enoch, Moses, and Solomon. One was Simon Magus and the other Jesus. We are introduced to the former, a Samaritan, in Acts 8 where it is written:

> But there was a certain man, called Simon, which beforetime in the same city used sorcery, and bewitched the people of Samaria, giving out that himself was some great one: To whom they all gave heed, from the least to the greatest, saying, This man is the great power of God. And to him they had regard, because that of long time he had bewitched them with sorceries.

This is an extract from the King James edition of the New Testament, produced in the early seventeenth century, and interpreting the references to magic, witchcraft, and sorcery it contains is fraught with problems due to the distortions of incorrect and imprecise translation. Furthermore, the choice of words was shaped by the conceptions and perceptions of the translators. The use of the term 'witch' and 'witchcraft' in early modern vernacular Bibles provided an important justification for the witch trials. Yet the meaning of the original Greek words usually referred to diviners and poisoners rather than people who performed *maleficium* or harmful acts of magic to kill, injure, or ruin their neighbours and their goods, which is how witchcraft was usually defined in the early modern period. Likewise it has been suggested that poor translation generated an inaccurate portrayal of Simon as a base magician.[30]

Over the next four centuries after Jesus' death, Christian propagandists further besmirched Simon Magus's reputation. It was said he used semen and menstrual blood in his incantations. The second-century sect known as the Simonian Gnostics, which was believed to have been founded by Simon Magus, was denounced as being addicted to magic. By the fourth and fifth centuries he was no longer just a magician and Gnostic but was being denounced as the father of all heresies.[31] A host of apocryphal accounts of Simon Magus circulated in medieval Europe, such as his demonic ability to fly, his conjuring up of vicious dogs to attack the apostle Simon Peter, and his ability to render himself invisible.[32] Medieval Irish legends tell of the druid Mog Ruith who, along with his daughter, travelled to the Middle East to learn magic from Simon Magus. His apprenticeship lasted between six and thirty-three years, and one of the great feats he learned was that of flying using a magic wheel, which he used to attack the apostles. In one legend it was Mog Ruith, carrying on the diabolic work of his master, who beheaded John the Baptist.[33]

The portrayal of Simon Magus served the purpose of creating the antithesis of Jesus. Both were seen as miracle workers in their own lifetimes. Some Jewish and pagan critics dismissed Jesus as a magician, a necromancer even, just as Christians later dismissed Simon Magus. The pagan author Celsus argued that Jesus had visited Egypt to learn magic.[34] Jesus' feats were not as showy as the apocryphal ones of Simon Magus, or Moses for that matter, but he nevertheless performed the mechanics of practical magic if not the ritualistic aspects of it. He cured merely by uttering words such as 'arise' and 'be clean', and applied saliva to cure the deaf and blind. He cast out demons. His initial fame rested on these activities. Yet Jesus' motives are portrayed as pure and his miracles effected through faith, whereas Simon Magus, as the archetypal magician, was arrogant, sinful, vain, motivated by base desires, and his magic all artifice and demonic. There is evidence, nevertheless, that care was taken about how and which of Jesus' miracles were included in the New Testament, particularly in Matthew, so as not to present them as magical in comparison with the healing magic practised at the time.[35] The authors of the New Testament also performed a more subtle balancing act in comparing Jesus with King Solomon. In light of the appearance of Christ, the reputation of Solomon as the wisest man ever and forever needed qualifying. So Jesus is also referred to as the 'son of David', and the emphasis on Jesus the healer and caster out of demons demonstrated that he was not a second-rate Solomon.[36]

In the Bible and the apocrypha neither Jesus nor Simon Magus are particularly associated with *written* sources of occult knowledge and wisdom, in contrast with Enoch, Moses, and Solomon. There are no stories of how secret books were buried, hidden, or handed down for future generations. This is one reason why grimoire traditions did not accrue around them over the centuries. There are more obvious reasons why Jesus remained untainted of course, blasphemy and heresy being two, but considering the reputation of Simon Magus in the medieval period it is still surprising that he was not widely associated with grimoires. The influential German abbot, occultist, and bibliophile Trithemius (1462–1516), who we shall meet again in the next chapter, apparently owned a magic book called the *Book of Simon the Magician*, which presumably referred to Magus.[37] A Hebrew manuscript entitled the *Book of the Key of Solomon* (*Sepher Maphteah Shelomoh*), which dates to no earlier than the late seventeenth or eighteenth century and was probably translated from Italian, contains a Satanic conjuration called 'The Operation of Simon Magus'. It instructs that the magician stand in the middle of a magical circle, and say three times, neither more nor less, these words:

> I adjure you, O Lucifer, and all thy associates, by the Living God, by the Angels above and below, by So and So, and in the name of A and B, &c.; I furthermore adjure you by Belzebuk, your Lord; I moreover adjure you by Satan, in whose hands are the Keys of Gehinnom. I adjure you by Lucifer, your King; I adjure you by the mighty deep; I adjure you by the Law of the Lord, that you shall have no power to stand in the air, nor beneath the air; nor on the earth, or beneath the earth; nor in the water, or under the water; nor in the heavens, or beneath the heavens; nor in any place of the world; but that thou shalt come forthwith unto this place, thou, O Lucifer, with thy associates, or that thou shalt send three of thy servants, who shall tell me the truth concerning all that I shall inquire of them, in the name of AGLA, AGLAJI, AGLTA, AGLAUT, AGLTUN, and in the name of ALPHA, V, HE, VJV, JUD, HE, MAHL, ALIHAI, ELOKIM, ZEBAOTH, ELYON, &c.[38]

But the fact that we shall hardly mention him again in the rest of our journey confirms that his reputation had a minimal influence in the history of literary magic. Grimoire authorship was generally associated with figures known for their wisdom, knowledge, or Christian piety, even if the latter was achieved through the renunciation of prior sinful magical practices. In this context a Magus grimoire was a contradiction in terms for it could only be a work of evil, and therefore indefensible by those magicians who believed they were acknowledging the glory of God through their rituals and invocations.

Burning books

It is obviously a matter of religious belief whether Hermes, Ham, Zoroaster, Solomon, or Moses existed or performed miracles let alone received and wrote books. What is certain is that by the fourth century BCE books of spells and charms written on papyrus were being produced.[39] It was papyrus, made from the pith of the wetland plant of the Nile Delta, that enabled the production of books, if we define a book as a portable series of written leaves or sheets joined together—which certainly does not apply to clay, wooden, or stone tablets. Papyrus books consisted of glued sheets, sometimes up to tens of feet in length, which were rolled around a rod.[40] Writing on papyrus required the use of inks, and this led to new magical notions based on their constituents. Ink containing myrrh, a resinous plant sap, was specified for some charms, for instance, and blood was sometimes intermingled, as in a dream spell that required the blood of a baboon, the sacred animal of Thoth-Hermes.[41] The one significant disadvantage of papyrus was that it was flammable.

By the early years of Christianity numerous such magic books or rolls were in circulation in the eastern Mediterranean amongst Jews, pagans, and Christians. We have archaeological evidence for this as represented by the Graeco-Egyptian and Coptic papyri. They were evidently sufficiently influential for the early Church to launch a series of campaigns against grimoires and other occult literature. Magic was explicitly associated with paganism, and in the struggle for religious and political dominance the Church saw magic books as sources of religious corruption that tarnished Christians and hampered the conversion of pagans. The Church was by no means a trendsetter in burning books in the name of religion. The pagan Roman authorities had kept a close eye on undesirable literature that threatened state control of religious worship.

Their primary concern was the practice of divination, which also had political and military implications. In 186 BCE, for instance, the senate requested the Roman magistrates to round up and burn books of soothsaying. Over a century and a half later 2,000 books of divination were said to have burned on the orders of Emperor Augustus. Some religious and philosophical works fared no better. In 181 BCE a buried chest of books purporting to be the work of Pythagoras were turned to ashes on the orders of the senate. Further east, Antiochus Epiphanes, king of the Seleucid Empire, which was a relic of Alexander the Great's conquest that stretched from Turkey to Turkmenistan at its height, ordered the seizure and burning of Jewish religious texts in 168 BCE. Christians were also the target of imperial suppression, with the Roman Emperor Diocletian's edict of 303 CE ordering the destruction of all copies of the Scriptures.[42]

But it is the Church that most determinedly went after magic books. The most well-known and earliest case concerns St Paul's conversion of the Ephesians to Christianity. As related in Acts 19, many of the Jews and Greeks of Ephesus, a city now in Turkey, famous for its Temple of the goddess Artemis, 'used curious arts [and] brought their books together, and burned them before all men: and they counted the price of them, and found it fifty thousand pieces of silver.' Ephesus had a reputation as a centre of magic in the Hellenistic and Roman world, and the term *Ephesia grammata* (Ephesian letters) was given to mysterious non-Greek and non-Latin words, supposedly engraved on the statue of Artemis, which were thought to have 'evil-averting' magical properties and were used in magic inscriptions and curse tablets.[43] A silver piece or drachma was equivalent of a day's wages at the time so, whether the New Testament story is factual, the intention was to show the value placed on the magic books in circulation in the city. Some Bible scholars have suggested that those who handed over their magic books were newly converted Christians destroying the last vestige of their old religion, though the dominant interpretation is that it was Jews and pagans who handed them over as an act of conversion to the new faith. Either way the sheer number of books involved, if the details are to be believed, suggest that grimoires were not only in the possession of the professional magicians and healers but were kept in many homes.[44]

Saint John of Chrysostom, the late-fourth-century archbishop of Constantinople, recalled how one day during his childhood in Antioch, an important city and early home of Christianity in Anatolia (part of modern Turkey), he witnessed soldiers launch a dragnet for books of sorcery and magic. One magician was captured but before his arrest managed to fling his unbound manuscript into a river. While on their way to church John and a friend saw something floating in the water which they at first thought was a linen cloth. On closer inspection they realized it was a book and fished it out, only to find to their horror that it contained magic.

> There were we congealed with fear. For who would have believed our story that we had picked it up from the river, when all were at that time, even the unsuspected, under strict watch? And we did not dare to cast it away, lest we should be seen, and there was a like danger to us in tearing it to pieces. God gave us means, and we cast it away, and at last we were free for that time from the extreme peril.[45]

Such round-ups were evidently unsuccessful. A severe campaign against pagans in the city launched in the mid-sixth century turned up more magic books. They were still being used by pagans in the countryside as well. In the life of Saint Theodore (d. 613) of Galatia, Anatolia, there is an account of an unbaptized village magician who owned magic books that he used to deal with spirits and conjure up clouds of locusts for a fee.[46] In mid-fifth-century Egypt, Shenoute, the abbot of the Coptic White Monastery in the Theban desert, instituted a ruthless policy of destroying the signs of pagan worship. When he and his followers vandalized the shrine of a local notable they found and burned a library of sacred texts that Shenoute believed also contained magic books, and they likewise destroyed the library of a group of idol worshippers in the village of Pneuit.[47]

It was clear to the Church authorities, though, that magic was not just a pagan problem, even if magic was deemed pagan. In the 480s the Church in Beirut launched an investigation into magic being practised by law students in the city. At the centre of the allegations was a Christian from Thebes named John Foulon.[48] While in Beirut he had become infatuated with a chaste woman who resisted his attempts at wooing. Together with several fellow students, he decided to use magic to call up a demon by sacrificing an Ethiopian slave he owned. They were found out before they could complete the ceremony and the slave reported his master's actions. When John's house was searched several grimoires were found in a box hidden under a seat. One of the investigators, Zacariah of Mytilene, later described how: 'In the books were certain drawings of perverse *daimones*, barbaric names, and harmful, presumptuous commands replete with arrogance and quite fit for perverse *daimones*. Certain of the incantations were attributed to Zoroaster the *magus*, others to Ostanes the magician, others yet to Manetho.' Foulon confessed and blamed the student ethos in the city for his descent into magic, naming several other students of his acquaintance who practised the art. A fire was then lit and he cast his books into it. Not long after, some of those on the list, including pagans, were caught. One of them named George of Thessalonike was reported after asking a scribe to make a copy of his grimoire. As Zacariah recalled, 'the entire city was in a state of uproar because [the students] were spending their time studying magic books instead of applying themselves to law.' As well as this town–and–gown tension there was also fighting in the streets as one of the suspected magicians, a pagan, drafted in some roughs to disrupt the house searches being conducted by the authorities. These tactics seemed to be partially successful for grimoires were found in only two homes including George's. Once the street violence had died down the magic books were publicly burned in a great bonfire in one of the city's public squares.

As various ordinances, edicts, and laws show, the Church had concerns that not only fickle students but its own priests were prone to being led astray. A Church canon issued in Alexandria, perhaps during the late fourth or early fifth century, ordered that clergy hand over to the civil authorities any of their sons found studying books of magic.[49] It was in this period, 386 to be precise, that a Spanish bishop, Priscillian of Avila, was condemned to death for allegedly practising sorcery and consorting with depraved women in nocturnal revels. The following century a group of bishops investigated the activities of some suspected heretics in Tarragona, Spain, amongst them a wealthy priest named Severus, who possessed three large magic books. He had been travelling to one of his estates when he was ambushed by robbers. They took his books and intended to sell them in the town of Ilerda, but fearing they were heretical handed them over to the town's bishop, Sagittius. He kept two for himself and sent the other to his superior after cutting out those sections 'which contained the shameful and sacrilegious learning of magical spells'. Severus was brought before his bishop Syagrius for questioning. He claimed that the books had belonged to his late mother and he knew nothing of their contents. This rather lame excuse convinced Syagrius, who returned the book in his possession, and Severus subsequently bought back the other two volumes from Sagittius. At this point a monk named Fronto stepped in to accuse Severus and a female relative of heresy. It all got very messy with Fronto organizing a lynch mob at one point. A council of seven bishops was convened and they decided to snuff out the case before it became even more of an embarrassment. The three magic books were burned, and when Fronto protested about the termination of the investigation he was beaten senseless by one of the bishops.[50]

Over the next few centuries Church authorities from across the Christian world issued repeated warnings. In 694, for instance, the Council of Toledo issued an edict stating 'it is not permitted for altar ministers or for clerics to become magicians or sorcerers, or to make charms, which are great bindings on souls. And we declare that those who practise this will be ejected from the Church.'[51] Edicts and canons piled up as the Church pushed its boundaries northwards to the pagan lands of Scandinavia and the eastern Baltic, and they increasingly focused on the laity rather than the clergy. By the end of the millennium, with Christianity having been the sole religion across much of Europe for several centuries, paganism and its ambivalent demons of the natural world had long ceased to be relevant. In their stead demonic fallen angels and their ruler Satan increasingly came to be associated with magic and its practitioners. New enemies of Christ were formed and in the process many more books were destined to burn in the age of Inquisitions.

The medieval mix

While the Church was ultimately successful in defeating pagan worship it never managed to demarcate clearly and maintain a line of practice between religious devotion and magic. The medical manuals known as leechbooks, which were produced by the clergy or monastic communities of late Anglo-Saxon England, are a good example. They were based principally on classical medicine but also contained spells for healing and protection. How else was one to deal with malicious elves for instance?[52] Some of the charms were Christianized versions of pagan healing verses. While most of the spells included in these medical manuscripts were enacted orally, in other words their written form served only as a record, textual amulets were clearly an integral part of tenth- and eleventh-century medicine as practised by clergy and literate lay folk. They consisted of exorcisms and prayers asking for help and protection, sometimes interspersed with magical holy names in Greek, Latin, and Hebrew. Apocryphal celestial letters purporting to be messages sent from God and delivered in writing by angels were also popular.[53] This is just the sort of material that made up a lot of the content of the grimoires denounced by the clergy. It was the context in which they were recorded and used, and by whom, that determined whether they were considered acts of sinful magic or pious devotion. For the common people such distinctions were largely irrelevant.

To further complicate things, not all magic was condemned outright by all theologians. While magic had only negative connotations for some, a clear intellectual division developed during the medieval period between natural magic and demonic magic or necromancy. Natural magic rested on the premise that interconnecting hidden or occult natural forces existed in God's universe that could be tapped by humans. So plants, animals, and precious stones, for instance, were composed of compounds and substances that could and did have curative and protective properties, but some were also imbued with hidden essences and powers influenced and activated by other unseen forces such as astral emanations from stars and planets. The occult properties of some plants and animals were encoded in their appearance. God had given them a signature identifying the sympathy they had with other living things. So the mandrake root, which had a roughly humanoid shape, was invested with human sentience. It was thought that it screamed and cried when pulled out of the ground, cursing those who disturbed it. A particularly contentious area of natural magic concerned the possibility that humans and their souls could influence others. Could women harm people by merely looking at them? Could thoughts and desires be projected?[54] These were all ancient conceptions, but in the medieval period the boundaries of natural magic were renegotiated, and justifications had to be found if those magical properties deemed natural were not to be confused with demonic magic and condemned as anti-Christian.

If magic was not natural then it was either fraudulent pretence, illusion, or enacted through the power of demons. In the medieval period the term necromancy, originally a means of divination by summoning the dead, began to be used to describe such demon conjuring. This came about because of the theological view that the raising of the dead was a divine miracle beyond human influence. The supposed spirits of the dead who appeared to the magicians of antiquity and the Bible were in reality demons in disguise. Similarly, those medieval magicians who practised what they believed to be the pious act of ritually contacting angels were accused of vanity and much more. The very act of conjuration was an open invitation to demonic gatecrashers. Magicians had no control over the spirit world and believing they could do so through magic was a denial of God's omnipotence. The word 'nigromancy' also appears in medieval documents. This was a variant spelling of necromancy, but it came to have its own meaning as 'black magic'.

As written magic developed in Europe new traditions developed in relation to the use of parchment. Papyrus was not a native plant in Europe of course and rolls were expensive to import. So as we know from Roman archaeology, bark, and wooden and wax tablets were commonly used as portable writing surfaces. Ritual curses and spells deposited at shrines were also incised on metal sheets, while ephemeral charms were created by writing on plant leaves. Parchment, which is thinly stretched animal skin, usually from sheep, goats, and calves, was already used for writing in the Near East during the third century BCE and began to be increasingly adopted in the Mediterranean world a couple of centuries later. It was more flexible and durable than papyrus and both sides could be written on. Pages could be stitched together to make books, which were easier to consult than rolled up scrolls. Religious considerations also shaped how parchment was used and conceived. It was never adopted in Hindu and Buddhist Asia where the idea of using butchered animals was offensive. Jewish religious laws regarding clean and unclean animals also dictated that parchment for ritual purposes was not to be made from the likes of camel, pig, and hare. From at least the medieval period onwards deerskin parchment would come to be preferred for Jewish amulets.[55] Christians did not share these concerns and restrictions and the parchment book became the medium through which the Bible spread across Europe. It was only superseded by paper made from linen rags in the fifteenth century, a transition sealed by the rise of printing. Still, parchment retained its special status for use in drawing up legal charters and religious documents, and in magical practice.

Medieval grimoires sometimes specified that virgin or unborn parchment should be used for making copies and writing out amulets. The former was made from animals that had not yet reached sexual maturity, while unborn parchment was made from the amniotic sac of aborted animal foetuses. The reason for their use was to ensure the purity of the grimoire or charm; in effect it was an act of sympathetic magic that cleansed the written word from the impurity of thought or action of the magician. It was sometimes specified that the magician should personally induce the abortion or cut out the uterus from dead animals to ensure that no external agencies contaminated the process. The use of ink consecrated by a priest further enhanced the act of writing magic. In the age of paper this ritual rationale meant that right into the modern period some magicians continued to use parchment to make manuscript grimoires and amulets even when paper was a much cheaper option.

The magic of the first millennium, as we know it from surviving written texts, was primarily a mix of Greek, Egyptian, Babylonian, and Jewish influences. Medieval grimoires reflect this, but new traditions also developed as scholars and theologians reconceptualized and reconstructed, sometimes falsely, the cultures, philosophies, and beliefs of the ancient world. While the magical reputations of the likes of Pythagoras were based on well-worn accusations levelled back in antiquity, other great intellectual figures of the distant past became the subject of new medieval legends—no one more so than the Roman poet Virgil (70–19 BCE). Why he came to generate so many tales of conjuring capers in the medieval period is difficult to fathom. He was said to have built an enchanted palace in Rome, carried off the daughter of a Babylonian Sultan, and founded a school of magic in Naples. As to the source of his powers, one legend stated that he obtained them from a book found beneath the head of the fabled Greek centaur Chiron. Gervase of Tilbury, writing in the early thirteenth century, related that an Englishman had gone to Naples to excavate Virgil's grave. His body was found perfectly preserved and under his head were books including the *Ars Notoria*. Other medieval tales tell how he possessed Solomon's book of necromancy or that of one Zabulon, a Greek or Babylonian prince who had invented necromancy and astrology 1,200 years before Christ.[56] Virgil's magical reputation would spread further during the early sixteenth century when popular books recounting his feats of 'witchcraft and negromancye' were printed, and in Naples legends of Virgil as a magician continued to circulate into the eighteenth century.[57] It is no wonder, then, that Virgilian grimoires circulated in the early modern period.

The Greek-Egyptian astronomer and geographer Ptolemy, who lived in the second century CE, also had his name put on works of talismanic magic a thousand years after his death.[58] But no classical writer accrued more spurious texts than the philosopher Aristotle (384–322 BCE). The most notable was the *Secretum secretorum* (*Secret of secrets*), which consisted of Aristotle's apocryphal correspondence with his former pupil Alexander the Great while he was fighting in Persia. It was translated into Latin from Arabic texts in the twelfth and thirteenth centuries and contained advice on talismanic magic. His name was also put on several works claiming to reveal Hermes Trismegistus's secrets of astral magic.[59] In later centuries, though, Aristotle would come to be more associated in popular culture with less esoteric publications on fortune-telling and sexual advice.[60] The classical grimoire tradition, as perceived by medieval chroniclers and romance writers, may have been spurious, but the medical and divinatory writings of some Greek and Roman authors were enduring influences on manuscript and print magic. Pliny the Elder's *Natural History*, for instance, a monumental compilation of information regarding the natural world, was particularly well mined by compilers of grimoires and works on natural magic. Amongst the descriptions of medicinal plants, animals, and gemstones were numerous examples of their hidden properties and efficacy as amulets. The line of transmission of some of this classical knowledge to the West stemmed from the religious and scientific cultures of Arab Islam.

The Muslim Moors of North Africa swept across the Iberian peninsular during the eight century brushing aside the forces of the numerous fractious Christian kings in the region. By the beginning of the eleventh century the Moorish Caliphate had, itself, divided into some twenty feuding kingdoms whose rulers were just as likely to ally themselves with the slowly encroaching Christian kings of northwestern Spain as with their fellow Muslim rulers. These competitive relations seem to have inspired a flourishing of Arabic scholarship and science in the major Moorish cities, such as Saragossa, Córdoba, and Seville. Impressive royal libraries of Arabic culture and learning were assembled, and amongst them were works on medicine, alchemy, astrology, and astronomy. These were eye-openers to inquisitive western and northern European Christian scholars, providing new access to the revered knowledge generated during the Hellenistic rule of the Near East.

In terms of European grimoires, perhaps the most important Arabic influence concerned the interest in and practice of astral magic.[61] This was based on the notion that the powers emanating from the planets and stars could be channelled into talismans and images through the agency of named spirits and angels at astrologically propitious moments. Prayers were used to beseech and praise the actions of the spirits rather than to command or compel them as in the conjurations of the *Clavicule of Solomon* and the like. An example of how astral magic could be harnessed is found in a fifteenth-century grimoire in the Bavarian State Library:

> During the fifth day hour one should make an image to tame wild beasts, such as lions, bears, wolves, and any other wild and harmful beasts. At this hour cast an image of the animal of the sort you wish to control or tame, and on the head of the image carve the name of the animal, and on the chest the name of the hour and the name of the lord of the hour, and on the stomach the seven names of the first hour, and fumigate the image with Indian wood and with red sandalwood, and bury the image in a place of your choosing, and with the Lord's help aiding you, you will see that all those animals will be turned to your will.[62]

The idea that divine and astral spirit forces could be harnessed by magical means dates right back to the beginnings of recorded magic. It was practised in ancient Babylonia, and Jewish and Indian influences can also be found in the Arabic works.[63] So the Moorish tradition brought to Spain was a fusion of Near Eastern cultural contacts, which for the first time filtered into the Western formulation of natural magic.

Very few Christian European scholars could read Arabic though. So during the twelfth century the centres of Spanish Moorish learning instigated a boom in the translation of the hitherto largely untapped wealth of Arabic learning into Latin. The centre of this profound exchange of literary religious, scientific, and magical knowledge was the city of Toledo in central Spain.[64] It had been captured from the Moors in 1085 by Alfonso VI of Castile, who declared himself 'the king of the two religions'. While many of the Muslim elite left, Arabic scholarship continued amongst Moors who had converted to Christianity and amongst Christians who had been culturally 'Arabized' after several centuries of Moorish rule. The city was also home to Jewish intellectuals fluent in Arabic. The impetus to translate works into Latin came from the interests of the one intellectual community in the city that contained few Arabic readers, the French-dominated clergy running the cathedral and the numerous wandering scholars who travelled to stay with them. Amongst them was the Norfolk clergyman Daniel of Morley. Sometime in the late twelfth century he set out for the Continent 'for the purposes of study'. Unimpressed by his stay in Paris he set his sights on Toledo. 'I hastened with all speed,' he wrote, 'that I might attend the lectures of the wisest philosophers of the world.' He returned to England with a valuable collection of books.[65] And so it was through such networks, and the demand of European universities for insight into Arab knowledge, that new works on magic began to percolate through the Continent.

Of the various Arabic astrological and magic texts to circulate in Europe as a consequence of this flourishing intellectual culture the *Picatrix* was the most influential.[66] Known in Arabic as the *Ghāyat al-Hakīm* (*The Aim of the Sage*), the *Picatrix* seems to have been written by an Arabic scholar in Spain around the middle of the twelfth century. We do not know his identity though it was falsely attributed by some to a well-known Spanish Arab mathematician. A century later it was translated into Spanish and then into Latin under the orders of the Christian king of Castile, Alfonso the Wise. It was a compilation of instructions on astral magic describing how to make astrological talismans by drawing into them the power of the presiding spirits of the planets and stars. The rituals of conjuration for doing this required the magician to wear elaborate apparel including helmets and swords. Animal sacrifices were involved such as a white dove to propitiate Venus and a black billy goat to honour Saturn. The *Picatrix* did not advocate demonic magic, but it is understandable why it was denounced as a work of necromancy by some over the next few centuries. Its author boasted of having compiled it from 224 books. Be that as it may, it was obviously culled from various Arabic astrological, alchemical, magical, and Hermetic texts written in the Near East during the ninth and tenth centuries, and ultimately derives from Greek, Syrian, Persian, and even Indian influences. Based on similar sources, a book of charms and magic number squares called the *Shams al-ma'arif* (*Illumination of Knowledge*), written in the thirteenth century by a famed magician named Ahmad bin Ali al-Buni (d. 1225), went on to become the most influential magic book in Arabic popular culture, but never permeated the European tradition to the extent of the Latin translation of the *Picatrix*.[67]

While historians now recognize medieval Toledo as an extraordinarily enlightened centre of multicultural scholarship, for centuries afterwards it had a disreputable reputation as the hub of necromancy. The French priest and writer Hélinand of Froidmont, who died in the 1220s or 1230s, observed for instance that clergymen seeking instruction found the liberal arts in Paris, the law in Bologna, medicine in Salerno, and demons in Toledo.[68] The city's reputation for black magic was spread across northern Europe not only through such clerical condemnation but also through the popularity of French and German romance literature in which Toledo and its magicians were represented as a potent source of supernatural power in tales of chivalric adventure.[69] As to the reality, in 1234 a necromancer from Toledo was apparently found teaching magic in Maastricht.[70] The Italian monk Francesco Maria Guazzo, writing in the early seventeenth century, recounted the cautionary legend of the friar and physician Blessed Giles (d. 1265) of Santarém, Portugal. This vice-ridden scion of a rich family, while on his way to study at Paris, fell in with a demon in human disguise who persuaded him to visit a vast cavern in Toledo. Here he met demons and their worshippers, and signed a pact with the Devil. For the next seven years he 'deeply studied the Black Arts and Magic' before eventually seeing the error of his ways.[71] The legend of a cave in Toledo where magic had been practised for centuries, and where a powerful grimoire lay hidden, seems to have developed in the late medieval period.[72] One of the stories written by Don Juan Manuel, a fourteenth-century Spanish nobleman from the province of Toledo, who unusually wrote in Castilian rather than Latin, concerns a deacon from Santiago who becomes a pupil of a great magician of Toledo called don Yllán who has an underground library and workshop. The deacon eventually becomes Pope and ungratefully threatens to imprison his old master for practising sorcery.[73]

The Toledo legend was developed and given further legitimacy in the seventeenth century by the historian Cristóbal Lozano. He wrote a fantastical account of how during the Roman period there existed under the city a vast subterranean palace of Hercules where magic was studied and practised. This occult under-world collapsed and for centuries lay buried until, according to Lozano's take on history, in 1543 the archbishop of Toledo organized an excavation and found an altar decorated with bronze statues. A loud noise was heard when they entered and some of the party died of fright. The archbishop ordered that the entrance be sealed once more to prevent its evil manifestations from spreading. One source of the legend is the archaeological remnants of a short subterranean passage flanked by two Roman columns, which was probably intended to act as nothing more magical than a sewer or drain.[74] Similar stories circulated regarding the city of Salamanca, where the second oldest university in Spain was founded in 1218. The earliest reference to a cave-school of magic there is from a French chronicle from the mid-fifteenth century. It is clear that Salamanca, by now considered the major centre of learning, was deliberately or mistakenly associated with the old Toledo Hercules legend. It proved enduring. The Jesuit theologian Martín Del Rio (1551–1608), who studied at the university, wrote,

> I have read that, as a result of the Moorish occupation of Spain, the magical arts were virtually the only subjects being taught in Toledo, Seville and Salamanca. When I was living in Salamanca, I was shown a secret vault which had been blocked off with rubble on the orders of Queen Isabella. It was a place where forbidden knowledge was taught.[75]

As Del Rio's account indicates, the great age of Arabic-inspired magic in Spain was thought to have been effectively suppressed by King Ferdinand and his wife, Isabella, the monarchs who forged a united Spain during the late fifteenth and early sixteenth centuries. The credulous twentieth-century witchcraft historian, Montague Summers, who believed wholeheartedly in the legends regarding Toledo and Salamanca, expressed great satisfaction that the monarchs had rooted out 'these horrible and ill-famed schools', these 'abominations'.[76] In fact, Ferdinand and Isabella, who sanctioned the setting up of the first permanent Inquisition, endorsed the forced conversion of Muslims and ordered the expulsion of the Jews, putting an end to a rich history of religious, cultural, and scientific collaboration.

The other important meeting place of Arabic and European scholarship was Constantinople. The city was the seat of the Byzantine Roman Empire, and in the twelfth century, after a long period of dwindling influence, it experienced a resurgence, in part due to its trading links with Venice and also the money generated from the large numbers of Crusaders and other Westerners it attracted. Art and architecture flourished. It was here, in 1169, that the *Kyranides*, a book of natural magic containing a mix of charms, amulets, and medicine, was translated into Latin from a Greek text on the orders of the Byzantine Emperor Manuel

Comnenus. An ancient Persian king purportedly wrote it, though it probably dates to no earlier than the first few centuries CE. Some copies stated the Greek version was a translation from the Arabic, but this is unlikely even though Arabic versions apparently circulated. The *Kyranides* became the most notorious work of magic in medieval Constantinople, as is evident from several trials heard by the city's Eastern Orthodox Church Synod in 1370. A copy was found amongst a number of magic books, including one full of demonic invocations and spells, packed in boxes in the house of one Gabrielopoulos. He was possibly a monk and doctor, and was evidently a major figure in the dissemination of grimoires in and around the city.[77] Italian manuscript versions also circulated further west, and in the seventeenth century several print versions were produced in German and English.

The importance of Hebrew scholars in the translation of Arabic texts has already been noted, and now we must turn to the influence of Jewish magic on European tradition. The importance of the Torah in the formation of the founding myths of grimoires is clear, as is the influence of Jewish magic in the Graeco-Egyptian papyri. As with Christian and Arabic magic, though, the medieval period heralded new developments as well as a continuation of traditions from antiquity. Once again, the heady intellectual world of medieval Spain was centre stage.

During the twelfth century some Spanish Jewish intellectuals became particularly interested in astral magic, for instance, incorporating it into their theologies and philosophies of medicine. Through the Jewish scholarly community it subsequently permeated more widely in Europe, with astral magic being included in the medical syllabuses of the universities of Montpellier and Bologna.[78]

As to the circulation of Jewish grimoires in medieval Europe the picture is less clear. We know how prominent Jewish magic was in Egypt in late antiquity, and it was a considerable influence on the later Arabic tradition, but determining what was available in the medieval period is, for the moment, a matter of guesswork, as much research remains to be done.[79] The now well-known *Book of Raziel*, for instance, first appeared as a unified text in a version printed in Amsterdam in 1701, though its various treatises on magic and mysticism clearly derive from a much earlier period. The most notorious Jewish grimoire, the *Sefer ha-Razim* or *Book of Mysteries*, was pieced together from a series of fragments by a rabbinic scholar in the 1960s.[80] It is related to the *Book of Raziel* and likewise purports to consist of knowledge revealed to Noah by the angel. Amongst its numerous spells and angelic conjurations is the following piece of necromancy:

> If you wish to consult a ghost, stand facing a tomb and recall the names of
> the angels of the fifth camp, holding in your hand a new glass bowl
> containing oil and honey mixed together, and say thus:

'I adjure you, O Spirit, Ram-bearer, who dwells among the graves upon the bones of the dead, that you will accept from my hand his offering, and do my will by bringing me N son of N who is dead. Raise him up so that he will speak to me without fear, and tell me the truth without deception. Let me not be afraid of him, and let him answer whatever question I need to ask him.'

'Ram-bearer' is a Greek term for Hermes, and other linguistic and textual evidence suggests the original work was probably composed in Palestine sometime in the fifth or sixth century CE. It is, according to one expert, 'the first attested Jewish grimoire' in the sense that it is the first example of a Hebrew book of black magic akin to the necromantic works of the Christian medieval world.[81]

There is certainly no lack of evidence for medieval Jewish magic, though, and in recent years work has finally begun on exploring the amulets, spells, and conjurations found in the Cairo *Genizah*, one of the most important repositories of ancient and medieval Jewish literature. A *genizah* is a hiding place and the one housed in the Ezra Synagogue in Cairo, which was founded in 882, contained tens of thousands of pages of papyri and parchment on Jewish theology, philosophy, and much else besides, providing important insights regarding both Jewish and Egyptian cultures in the region. The Cairo *Genizah* had been known about in the West since the mid-eighteenth century, but its literary treasures only began to be explored late in the following century when they were dispersed to libraries across Europe and America. By piecing together the fragments from the *Genizah* and comparing them with European Jewish manuscripts of the medieval and early modern periods, which is just how the *Sefer ha-Razim* was reconstructed, historians are showing the interplay of Arab and Judaic magical traditions.[82]

The discovery of a Hebrew magic manuscript in the Cairo *Genizah* that was probably written in eleventh-century southern Italy is just one indication of how the exchange of esoteric ideas flowed both ways across the Mediterranean at the time. The most influential example of this was the development of the Jewish mystical interpretation of the Torah known as Kabbalah, which emerged in twelfth-century Provence before developing further in the Spanish cities. While Kabbalah was underpinned by complex theological and philosophical debates generated amongst European Jewish scholars, its practical application was more directly shaped and influenced by the fusion of occult traditions in Spain, and Arabic astral magic in particular. Put very simply, practical Kabbalah was based on the premise that Hebrew was the language spoken by God, and as such the letters of the Hebrew alphabet were connected to God through divine emanations. So too were the secret names of God transmitted orally to Moses and which provided a key to the written Torah. The magical potential of this obviously appealed to magicians, whether Islamic, Jewish, or Christian. By using combinations of Hebrew letters and 'secret' names of the divinity they could enhance the power of talismans and more directly communicate with the angelic world. Such was the symbolic allure of the appearance of Hebrew characters that in some European grimoires words and characters were invented that looked like Hebrew but in fact had no recognizable meaning.

Of all the numerous Jewish holy names for God, Tetragrammaton became the most widely used and recognizable in the European magic tradition. It was, in fact, a Greek translation of the Hebrew name 'YHWH' (Yahweh). Jewish religious laws forbade its pronunciation, and in writing other than in the Holy Scriptures, it was usually indicated by abbreviations or signs. Although European clergymen condemned a legend that Jesus owed his miraculous powers to sur-reptitiously learning it from the Temple in Jerusalem, the word 'Tetragrammaton' was frequently used in medieval Christian charms and amulets, and subsequently filtered into the popular magic of Europe and beyond through grimoires.[83]

For our final, albeit minor ingredient in the medieval grimoire cooking pot we need to look northwards to Scandinavia, where Christianity only supplanted paganism in the tenth and eleventh centuries. Grimoires or *galdrabœkr* were clearly a part of the magical tradition of medieval Iceland. They are referred to in Church statutes and other ecclesiastical writings, and also appear in a fourteenth-century story of a student using his master's magic book to raise a storm.[84] What they consisted of we can only surmise from later surviving examples from the sixteenth century. On this basis we can assume the medieval books were based heavily on the literary magic found elsewhere in Europe at the time, with the special addition of runic symbols. Runes were the alphabet of the cultures of northern Germany and Scandinavia, and were brought to England and elsewhere by invading Anglo-Saxons and Vikings. They seem to have developed during the first few centuries of the first millennium, though their use was gradually supplanted by Latin as Christianity spread across the region. Perhaps before, but certainly after Chris-tianity was established, runes accrued magical properties. In the mid-fourteenth century a Norwegian archbishop issued warnings about the use of 'runes, black magic and superstition', and as we shall see in the next chapter, people in Iceland were executed for the harmful use of runes during the period of the witch trials.[85] By this time they also served a cryptographic purpose in the magical tradition. This is most evident from several runic versions of the SATOR AREPO word square found in medieval Swedish and Norwegian manuscripts.[86]

Runes were largely restricted to Scandinavian grimoires but they have also been found in a magic book from southern Germany, and even more intriguingly from a fourteenth-century manuscript of Italian provenance which is now in the British Library.[87] The latter work bore the heading 'this book belongs to the spiritual works of Aristotle, and it is the book *Antimaquis*, which is the book of the secrets of Hermes.' It is essentially a work of Arabic astral magic related to the *Picatrix* and also contains spells for invisibility and love. The 'runae', as the scribe calls them, are used as a cryptic means of writing the names of planetary spirits, just as pseudo-Hebraic or Chaldean characters were used in other grimoires. Their depiction and their names are so garbled and corrupt that little sense can be made of them, though it is clear that the original author of the manuscript had some knowledge of the runic alphabet. As such the manuscript represents a rare counter-flow of magical knowledge from north to south.

Saints, popes, and meddling monks

At this point readers might be thinking, with some justification, that there was not much distinctly Christian about the literary magic of Europe. How could medieval magicians profess to be true Christians? Well, Christian prayers and blessings were also integral to the magic contained in grimoires. Christ, Mary, and the apostolic saints were all appealed to for protection from harm, while apocryphal accounts of encounters between New Testament figures were the basis for charms that endured right into the present century. The sign of the Cross, holy water, and consecrated paraphernalia were important defences against inadvertently conjuring up demons. Although a blasphemous act, the Mass was used in some conjurations, and was notoriously inverted and perverted in the lurid confessions of tortured witches and in reality by some debauched necromancers in the early modern period. The Church also inspired a new generation of bogus grimoire authors. We have seen how in the early centuries of Christianity the clergy and even bishops came under suspicion for practising magic, and from the medieval period onwards the finger of accusation also pointed higher up the hierarchy at popes and saints. What does this tell us? That ordination, piety, and power were no safeguards against the suspicions and jealousies generated by successful career advancement, wealth, and political influence. I will begin, though, with a saint who probably never existed.

Saint Cyprian of Antioch is a legendary third-century Christian martyr who, through confusion with the very real Cyprian of Carthage (martyred in 258 CE), came to have an enduring reputation as a magician and grimoire author.[88] The conflation occurred in Christian writings as early as the late fourth century. The Spanish poet Prudentius related how Cyprian practised magic spells 'amid the tombs to raise passion in a wife and break the law of wedlock'.[89] By the medieval period the story of Cyprian the magician had developed into three books telling his conversion, confession, and martyrdom, with Greek, Latin, Syriac, Coptic, and Arabic manuscripts circulating across Europe and the Near East. In his confession Cyprian tells of how he had, as a child, been devoted to Apollo and been introduced to the mysteries of Mithras. On Mount Olympus he saw bands of demons and the armies of the gods. He later travelled to Egypt and Babylonia where he was instructed in Chaldean magic, alchemy, and astrology. He returned to Antioch a great magician revered by the local pagans. His road to Christianity began when he was asked by a client to use his magic to force a Christian woman named Justa to accept his amatory advances. Cyprian called up a demon using his books of magic. Justa's virginal Christian armour repelled the demon's assaults. Stronger demons were conjured up but they too failed. Incensed by the impotence of his magic, Cyprian vented his frustration on the people of the city until he realized that nothing could beat the sign of the Cross and so renounced his magic and paganism. In his confession he recalled how he wrote to the bishop, and 'brought the books of sorcery unto him while all the honourable men of the city were present, and I burned them with fire.'[90] He subsequently rose to be bishop, before he and Justa (now Latinized to Justina) were tragically martyred. This legend of Cyprian the magician was reinforced in the early modern period by its allegoric use by poets and dramatists. The English Renaissance physician and astrologer Anthony Ascham wrote a poem about 'Sanct Cipriane, the Grett Nigromancer', and the famed seventeenth-century Spanish dramatist Pedro Calderón was also inspired by the story.[91]

It is not surprising that spells and charms attributed to Cyprian also circulated from early on in the Near East. An eleventh-century Coptic love spell consists of a first-person confession by Cyprian relating his attempt to use his magic against Justa, and includes a conjuration to an angel rather than a demon that begins, 'Yea, I adjure you, O Gabriel: Go to N. daughter of N. Hang her by the hair of her head and by the lashes of her eyes. Bring her to him, N. son of N., in longing and desire.'[92] 'Scrolls of Cyprian' were worn as talismans in Armenia into the modern period, with an account of his life and times appearing in a popular Armenian book of protective 'prayers for all occasions' printed in Constantinople in 1712. The prayer was also a component of a common early-modern Ethiopian Christian magic book known as the *Arde'et* or *The Disciples*.[93] In the West, the prayers of Saint Cyprian were used in love magic, but while Trithemius apparently owned a demonological treatise bearing his name, it was only in the late eighteenth century that Cyprian grimoires began to circulate widely in parts of Europe. One late-nineteenth-century Spanish grimoire, for instance, related how in the year 1001 a German monk named Jonas Sufurino, librarian of the monastery of Brooken, conjured up the Devil on a mountaintop one night and was given a copy of Cyprian's magic book as reward.

The *Sworn Book of Honorius*, which first appeared in the first half of the thirteenth century, has nothing to do with the Emperor Honorius. According to the earliest Latin manuscripts it was written by one Honorius of Thebes, son of Euclid—presumably the fourth-century CE Greek mathematician of that name who lived in Alexandria, and whose work was first translated into Latin in the twelfth century. It tells how it originated from the meeting of a general council of 811 Masters of Magic from the main centres of the occult arts, Naples, Athens, Toledo, and Thebes. They nominated Honorius to preside over the compilation of all their magic books into one text, three copies of which were to be made. Only the godly and faithful who had sworn an oath and been tested for the space of a year were to be allowed access to it. The reason for the endeavour was the magicians' fear that the pope and his cardinals, envious and diabolically inspired, were planning a campaign to suppress them and burn their books.[94] The *Sworn Book* represented, then, a radical challenge to the Church. As to the magic it contained, which Honorius declares follows the precepts of Solomon, the surviving manuscripts consist of a series of prayers, some in a nonsensical mix of purported Chaldean and Hebrew, spirit names, circles, and stars. By following its lengthy instructions magicians would be able to have a vision of God, hell, and purgatory, and obtain countless treasures and knowledge of all science.

Move forward a few centuries to the late 1600s and we find manuscripts circulating amongst Parisian magicians bearing the title *Grimoire du Pape Honorius*. They were not direct copies of the surviving fifteenth-century versions it would seem, but similar enough. Somewhere along the way the Theban Honorius with his Egyptian aura was supplanted by the crusading Italian Pope Honorius III (1148–1227). In the late eighteenth century the widespread circulation of a cheap printed version of the *Grimoire* sealed this new tradition. One nineteenth-century historian of magic suggested that the attribution was a deliberate act of vengeance orchestrated by persecuted medieval magicians who desired to place responsibility for their diabolic crimes on the papacy.[95] Maybe the association was to do with Honorius III's failed Crusade to capture Egypt or because of his protection of the Knights Templar, who, in the early fourteenth century, were accused of sorcery and worshipping a diabolic idol named Baphomet. Then again, perhaps the enterprising scribe who first penned the *Grimoire du Pape Honorius* in the second half of the seventeenth century was ignorant of the legend of the Theban magician, and the only Honorius he or she knew was of the papal kind.

Honorius III was not the only medieval pope to get an unwarranted magical makeover. A similar fate befell Leo III, who presided over the Vatican between 795 and 816. A protective letter that he purportedly sent to Charlemagne, the first Holy Roman Emperor, was circulating in manuscript by the early sixteenth century, and in the late seventeenth century this was used as the basis for a French manuscript magic *enchiridion* or handbook. One example entitled the *Clavicule de l'enchiridion du Pape Leon* contained exorcisms as well as instructions on how to conjure treasure and how to create pentacles or amulets usually involving a five-pointed star or pentagram. A less necromantic version was printed several decades later.[96]

While Honorius's reputation was apparently an invention of the seventeenth century, there were other popes about whom magical reputations circulated widely in scholarly circles back in the medieval period, but who did not have the ignominious honour of having grimoires named after them in later centuries. The most renowned or notorious of these was Gerbert, Pope Silvester II, whose short pontificate lasted between 999 and 1003. Rumours of his dabbling in the black arts were circulating from at least the twelfth century when the English chronicler William of Malmesbury, in listing Gerbert's impressive breadth of scientific knowledge, mentioned that he knew 'the art of calling up spirits from hell' and had used the 'art of necromancy' to discover hidden treasures in Rome. One rumour suggested that he fled from his study of magic in Toledo after stealing his master's grimoire. Over the next few centuries, legends of his relations with the Devil also developed so that by the Protestant Reformation Silvester's reputation was sufficiently besmirched for Catholic historians to try and rehabilitate his papacy.[97] In the case of Pope Boniface VIII (d. 1303), rumour and legend added to the political machinations that led to his posthumous trial between 1303 and 1311 on charges of demonic magic amongst other crimes. He was accused of having three demons under his control and a ring containing a spirit. One witness testified that he had seen Boniface drawing a magic circle in his garden, sacrificing a cockerel within it, and then dripping its blood on a fire while reading out a demonic conjuration from a grimoire.[98]

The stories of magic-wielding popes were seized upon with relish by Protestant Reformers in the sixteenth century and amplified for propaganda purposes. The mathematician John Napier (1550–1617) declared that twenty-two popes had been 'abominable Necromancers' who had bound themselves to the Devil and used their magic powers to accrue power and wealth. The names of some of this tarnished twenty-two were listed in the preface to a pamphlet on the trial of an English folk magician in 1566. The aim was to link the perceived contemporary plague of sorcery and witchcraft with the Catholic past. So Pope Alexander VI was described as a 'horrible Sorcerer' who 'gave hymselfe body and soule' to 'wicked Sprites and Divels', while Pope Gregory the VII (Hildebrand) was 'a great Sorcerer and Nigromancer'. John Bale, a friar turned Protestant reformer, concluded that the magic of the popes far exceeded that of the 'soothsayers of Egypte'.[99] The question arises why some popes were later chosen as spurious grimoire authors and others were not. Maybe Silvester and Hildebrand did not attract grimoires for the same reason as Simon Magus. For Protestants, and some Catholics, they had besmirched reputations for diabolism, whereas the names of Leo and Honorius could be used to promote the legitimacy of magic.

While the medieval and Reformation stories of necromantic popes and early saints were mostly fictions turned into dubious facts, there is ample evidence that the medieval clergy were the main practitioners of magic and therefore the owners, transcribers, and circulators of grimoires. Monasteries were certainly important repositories of magic books. During the first half of the fourteenth century, for example, a collection of over thirty magic texts were donated to St Augustine's Abbey, Canterbury, by at least five different monks. Later in the same century the impressive book collection of Friar John Erghome, which, at some 300 volumes, was one of the largest personal libraries in the country at the time, became part of the library of the Austin Friars at York. It included magic works attributed to Solomon, the *Sworn Book of Honorius*, and an influential Arabic work on astrology by the ninth-century astrologer and scientist al-Kindi.[100] We should not think of monks as cloistered away from the wider community. Many friars served as parish priests as well as preachers, and so there was plenty of opportunity to share their privileged access to magic books with the educated laity. Over and over again in the trials of monks involved in treasure hunting escapades we find them working together with the likes of schoolmasters and clerks.

The universities of Europe were the other main centres of grimoire production and consumption. William of Auvergne, who was bishop of Paris in the early twelfth century, recalled how while a student he had seen and handled some of the magic books available in the city.[101] In the medieval period universities were essentially religious institutions but they provided a fertile social environment in which clergy and lay scholars intermingled, debated, and pushed boundaries, particularly in the fifteenth century when the university training of medical and legal professions became increasingly separated from ecclesiastical control. Many students never actually graduated but attained enough education and working knowledge of Latin to obtain administrative jobs such as clerks. In the year they spent at university, and in the humming social and intellectual world of the cities, there was ample opportunity to consult books of magic. The rather shaky Latin of some surviving medieval grimoires suggests that this group of scholars were significant players in the circulation and practical use of magic books.[102] They were part of what has been called the 'clerical underworld' of magic. This was inhabited by monks but also a range of minor clergy, parish priests, and curates who did not necessarily have a university education, and may not have been well versed in theology niceties, but who possessed enough knowledge of Church ritual and exorcism to employ grimoires.[103]

Considering the clergy had a near monopoly on access to grimoires, at least until the fifteenth century, it is understandable that clerics who wrote about magic, or who were associated with the major scholarly centres of the occult sciences, would accrue unjustified reputations as being the *authors* of grimoires. The Scottish clergyman scientist and astrologer Michael Scot (1175–c.1232) was a critic of magic, but as he was canon of Toledo Cathedral during the height of the translation boom in the city, was proficient in Hebrew and Arabic, and translated some of the works of Aristotle, rumour later had it that he had also picked up the secrets of necromancy during his stay. It seems that the first magic books bearing his name circulated around Europe in the fifteenth century. The German abbot Trithemius possessed a book of demonological invocations attributed to Scot which instructed how to conjure up familiar spirits.[104] A sixteenth- or seventeenth-century grimoire in the John Rylands Library, Manchester, is entitled *Michael Scot's Magic Book*. By this time his transformation into an adventurous wizard had filtered into popular legends and tales in his homeland of Scotland and further afield.[105]

A generation on, the famed English scientist and Franciscan friar Roger Bacon (c.1214–94), who criticized Scot for not understanding the sciences, suffered a similar fate after his death.[106] Bacon believed that books falsely ascribed to Solomon 'ought all to be prohibited by law', and grumbled at those who 'put famous titles upon their works and impudently ascribe them to great authors in order to more powerfully allure men to them'.[107] He would be turning in his grave to know that by the mid-sixteenth century John Bale could list numerous Latin occult manuscripts attributed to Bacon, including such suggestive titles as *De necromanticis imaginibus* and *Practicas magiæ*. Around 1527 a priest named William Stapleton borrowed a book called the *Thesaurus Spirituum* from a vicar to help him magically find treasure. Although not listed by Bale, surviving manuscripts of the same name, though of later date, were also attributed to Bacon. Another seventeenth-century Baconian grimoire, entitled the *Necromantia*, includes instructions for conjuring up the spirits of the dead.[108] His spurious magical reputation further developed and spread through a play written in 1592, and a very popular cheap book called *The famous historie of Fryer Bacon Containing the wonderfull things that he did in his life*, which went through numerous reprints during the seventeenth century. In this Bacon, who learns the occult arts while at Oxford University, is presented as a good-natured comic-hero with a love of using his magic to make moral points. Things get more serious towards the end though. He pits his wits in a magic contest with a rival German conjuror named Vandermast where they stand in their magical circles a hundred feet apart and call up mythical creatures to do battle on their behalf. *The famous historie of Fryer Bacon* concludes with Bacon repenting his use of magic. He calls together his friends, students, and scholars to announce:

> I have found that my knowledge hath been a heavy burthen and hath kept down my good thoughts: but I will remove the cause which are these Books; which I do purpose here before you all to burn. They all entreated him to spare the Books, because in them there were those things that after ages might receive great benefits. He would not hearken unto them, but threw them all into the fire, and in that flame burnt the greatest learning in the world.[109]

Turning to the Continent, one of the most notorious of the bogus grimoires attributed to medieval scholars was the *Heptameron* of Peter d'Abano, an Italian who studied at the University of Paris in the second half of the thirteenth century.[110] His numerous real works included discourses on medicine, physiognomy, poisons, and the celestial sciences. It was the latter interest that got him into trouble with the Inquisition. The only times he briefly discussed magic in his numerous works was with the aim of distinguishing it from the honourable study of astrology. His interests overlapped with natural magic but otherwise there is no evidence to suggest he had anything to do with the *Heptameron*, which is concerned entirely with the ritual preparations for composing a magic circle and conjuring the angels. It would appear that, compared to Bacon, a longer period elapsed before d'Abano became associated with grimoires, for the earliest verifiable evidence of the *Heptameron* is in the mid-sixteenth century.[111] As we shall see in the next chapter, another manuscript attributed to d'Abano called the *Lucidarius* was found in the hands of several Italian treasure seekers. This was presumably a version of the *Lucidator*, a work that d'Abano probably did write, and which contains discussion on the art of geomancy. This was a form of divination based on the interpretation of lines or dots marked on the ground or on parchment.

Of all the magical works falsely attributed to medieval theologians and scientists none was more enduringly influential and widespread than those bearing the name Albertus Magnus (*c.*1193–1280). This German Dominican friar, one-time Bishop of Cologne, and author of numerous highly respected scientific works, attracted the title 'The Great' in his own lifetime. Who better to promote a book of magic? Latin manuscripts of the *secrets of Albert* or *experiments of Albert* appeared during or shortly after his lifetime. They included some information from Albertus's actual work on minerals, but most of it was culled from Pliny and a pseudo-Aristotle. It was not a grimoire but rather a work on the 'science of magic'. This was at least how one compiler defined it in defending it against accusations of evil. In other words it was a book of natural magic and medicine like the *Kyranides*, of which the compiler was aware. But it came to be seen over the centuries as a dangerous grimoire by those who condemned it without reading it, and no doubt many who bought one of the many print versions produced across Europe from the early sixteenth century onwards were left a little disappointed. Still, if for fun you wanted to see people standing around with the appearance of having camel's heads, then the *secrets of Albert* was the book for you, advising the lighting of a lantern anointed with the animal's blood.[112]

Using magic

While for some the attraction of magic held out the possibility of such lofty aims as learning languages and the secrets of nature, many owners of grimoires, particularly necromantic ones, had much baser motives on their minds, mostly concerning money and sex. Priests and monks made up many of the cases of treasure hunting investigated by the Inquisitions and ecclesiastical courts in the late medieval period. Treasure hunting did not require magic, and the activity was not in itself heretical or 'superstitious', but tradition held that many buried treasures were guarded by ghosts and spirits. Who were you going to call? Why the priests and monks who had access to the grimoires which instructed on how to conjure, exorcize, and control them. In England, in 1466, Robert Barker of Babraham, Cambridgeshire, was brought before his bishop to answer for having in his possession 'a book, and a roll of the black art containing characters, circles, exorcisms and conjurations; a hexagonal sheet with strange figures; six metal plates with diverse characters engraved; a chart with hexagonal and pentagonal figures and characters, and a gilded wand.' These were to be used to conjure up a spirit that would direct him to hidden gold and silver. He was sentenced to public penance, walking around the marketplaces of Ely and Cambridge in bare feet and carrying his books and magical paraphernalia, which were subsequently burned in Cambridge marketplace. Across the other side of Europe the fifteenth-century astronomer Henry the Bohemian, a member of the Polish royal household, was charged in 1429 with possessing necromantic books and finding buried treasure with the aid of demons. He confessed, probably under torture, that he and several companions, two of whom were professors at Krakow University, used books to conjure up treasure in the royal zoological garden.[113]

In 1517 Don Campana, a Modenese priest and treasure hunter, confessed that 'he once had a book, called *Clavicula Salomonis*, and another book, called *Almandel* and some other booklets and writings with many love magic instructions, and he said he burned them all.'[114] Love magic was, indeed, as common a use of grimoires as treasure hunting in the period. The aim was either to entice or coerce someone into having sex, enhance the sexual experience, or ensure a long-lasting sexual relationship.[115] Such binding magic could be achieved using a variety of practices, from potions based on natural magic, to image magic and necromancy. In Carcassonne, in southwestern France, a monk named Pierre Recordi was sentenced to life imprisonment after confessing under torture to attempting to have control over women by offering to the Devil wax puppets containing his saliva and the blood of toads. In the same town in 1410 a notary named Geraud Cassendi was tried by an inquisitor for attempting to debauch women by invoking demons using a magic book and gold scrapings from an image of the Virgin.[116]

The flip side of love magic was ensuring that people could not have sex.[117] The *Picatrix* was a useful source in this respect, providing advice for both causing and curing magically inspired impotence. The following example of astral image magic for the purpose comes from a manuscript attributed to Ptolemy:

> When you wish to bind a man or woman, make an image of a man whose feet are raised to the heavens and whose head is in the ground. This should be made of wax, saying 'I have bound N. son of such-and-such a woman, and all his veins, until he does not have a man's desire.' After that, bury the image in his path, and he will not use a woman for as long as the image lasts. And it is said by some that this image is made under the second decan of Aries.[118]

Sex, inheritance, and political power were major preoccupations of Europe's aristocracy, and accusations of love magic and poisoning were prominent in the increasing number of cases of heretical magic concerning royal courtiers that were heard during the fourteenth century.

The medieval clergy and nobility did not have a complete monopoly on grimoires. Although, as we shall see in the next chapter, the spread of magic books down the social scale is clearly evident from the sixteenth century onwards, there are already signs of democratization towards the end of the medieval period. There is an account in French chronicles of a poorly educated sorcerer, Arnaud Guillaume, who in 1393 attempted to cure the king of witchcraft. He carried with him a grimoire called *Smagorad*, which gave him power over the stars and planets. It was said to have been a copy of a book given to Adam by an angel. A surviving German-language manuscript of the *Almandal* was included along with advice on horticulture and medicine in the commonplace book of a late fifteenth-century Augsburg merchant called Claus Spaun. His own annotations to the text suggest that he had experimented with its angelic invocations. He added further practical astrological guidance as to the appropriate angel to call upon, and made numerous insertions insisting that the magus should kneel devoutly.[119]

Women had always been major consumers of literary magic, as the many written amulets for childbirth attest, but examples of women owning or using grimoires is scant before the sixteenth century.[120] In Roman antiquity there are allusions to the fact that some high-class prostitutes were literate and so could have possessed and written magic books containing the love magic and binding spells that were their stock-in-trade. The Roman poet Horace imagined his prostitute-witch creation, Canidia, possessing books of incantations, and there is no reason to assume that the small minority of literate women at the time were *less* likely to use grimoires than literate men.[121] There are a few late medieval examples of women having access to grimoires if not owning them. In 1493 Elena Dalok was brought before a London ecclesiastical court charged with being a common slanderer, professing to be able to magically induce rain, and for saying she owned a book that told her of things to come.[122] This may have been an idle boast, but, if true, her book sounds more like an astrological or prophetic text rather than a grimoire. More convincing evidence comes from a trial six years later in Italy. Bernardina Stadera, who was denounced in 1499 for being a 'charmer, conjurer and procuress', was accused, along with her lover, a priest, of reading demonic invocations from a manuscript she had borrowed from some friars of Modena. She deposed that one of the friars had:

> a book of paper, handwritten, with a white leather binding, of average size, which he lent to her. She kept that book for six months, meaning to copy what was in it, even though she never did because she had been very busy. She anyway read that book many and many times, and found how to make images and in what way they have to be baptised by a priest to make people love each other, as well as how to curse the mass by saying, 'You're lying in your throat' when the priest says, 'May the Lord be with you,' as she thinks. There was also a conjuration which included the names of many saints, mixed with several names of demons.[123]

The mistress of a French conjuring monk testified that she had heard him loudly reciting passages from a grimoire, and on one occasion she accompanied him to a hill where he undressed and disappeared behind a bush with his magic books for an hour. She could not tell what he was up to. As with all confessions extracted under the inquisitorial laws of medieval Europe, we need to be very cautious about taking such statements at face value. When in 1370 an illiterate woman named Benvenuta Mangialoca confessed that her father-in-law had instructed her how to invoke demons using 'a big book' she had almost certainly been subjected to torture.[124]

It can be assumed, then, that due to the high level of female illiteracy, and the physical and social restrictions on women's access to books, very few possessed grimoires, though some clearly knew of and had access to them. The masculine nature of medieval literary magic was also reinforced in the pages of grimoires, in which there is a strong emphasis on sexual purity and abstinence, reflecting the clergy's vow of celibacy. The *Sworn Book of Honorius* instructed that it was not to be given to women. Rituals often advised that the magician should not associate with the opposite sex while preparing for conjurations and invocations, and that they were to be kept away from ritual paraphernalia. At the same time, many of the spells were to entice and impress women, while invisibility spells also often had prurient aims. Either way, grimoire magic was clearly masculine in its emphasis on the sexual self-control of the male magician and the sexual conquest of women. That is not to say that this misogynistic emphasis was mirrored in the actual *use* of written magic—as we shall see in the next chapter.[125]

Despite numerous clerical and secular condemnations of magic in the medieval period, attempts to suppress grimoires and their users were sporadic, ad hoc rather than systematic. In 1277 the Bishop of Paris issued a condemnation of 'books, rolls, or booklets containing necromancy or experiments of sorcery, invocations of demons, or conjurations hazardous for souls.' Still, this was one of only a few official condemnations of forbidden books issued by the University of Paris that explicitly referred to magic.[126] In other words, other heretical texts were of more immediate concern at the time. We do know that the medieval inquisitions, which were instituted in the late twelfth century, and set up wherever and whenever outbreaks of heresy were suspected, periodically found and burned books of magic. In his manual for inquisitors the Spanish Dominican friar and grand inquisitor Nicholas Eymeric (1320–99) recounted reading and burning numerous grimoires confiscated from magicians, including works attributed to Solomon and Honorius.[127] The extent to which the authorities were successful in suppressing their circulation is very difficult to assess. Many were obviously burned by the Roman and Orthodox Churches, while others were destroyed by their fearful owners. Although numerous books of natural and astral magic no doubt ended up in the flames, it is likely that necromantic works fared far worse.

Does the uneven pattern of surviving grimoires reflect the relative success of the Church authorities and the reach of the inquisitions in different parts of Europe? It could explain why the libraries of central Europe contain very few explicitly demonic grimoires. Maybe such works also circulated less in the region because copyists and collectors were more nervous about transmitting demonic invocations and conjurations.[128] We also need to bear in mind that many late medieval grimoires were destroyed during the campaigns against witches and magicians in the sixteenth and seventeenth centuries, the ruthlessness of which also varied from country to country.

In 1258 Pope Alexander IV instructed inquisitors 'not to intrude into investigations of divination or sorcery without knowledge of manifest heresy involved'. The crime of magic was otherwise to be dealt with by ecclesiastical courts and the secular authorities. Acts of sorcery and divination that savoured of 'manifest heresy' were defined as 'praying at the altars of idols, to offer sacrifices, to consult demons, to elicit responses from them'.[129] Definitions of both heresy and magic were by no means hard and fast in the period, and as this papal instruction indicates, a lot of magic was not heretical but merely 'superstitious' or rooted in sinful 'erroneous' beliefs. But the definition of magic as heresy became increasingly all embracing from the late fourteenth century onwards. The long-standing but socially restricted concern over the ritual magic used by clergy and courtiers began to extend to more popular, non-literary forms of harmful magic or sorcery. Increasingly all magic came to be redefined as heretical in that it was all believed to be inspired by an ominously encroaching Devil. Grimoires, with their complex ceremonial invocations and conjurations, were no longer the only keys to demonic magic. With heretical magic unbound from the book, women increasingly became the focus of authoritarian concern. Before 1350 over 70 per cent of those accused of magic in the courts were men, but during the early fifteenth century between 60 and 70 per cent were female.[130] Here lies the origin of the witch hunts of the sixteenth and seventeenth centuries, when across much of Europe the legislature ensured that the poor, the illiterate, and women supplanted the privileged, erudite male owners of grimoires as the greatest magical threat to Christian society.

CHAPTER TWO

THE WAR AGAINST MAGIC

The late fifteenth and early sixteenth centuries heralded three profound and interlinked events in European history that can be explored through the story of grimoires: the rise of print, the Protestant and Catholic Reformations, and the witch trials. For some, the Devil lay behind all these momentous events. Printing was described as a 'black art' and books as 'silent heretics'. The success of the Reformation was heavily dependent on the power of the printed page, with Martin Luther being the most published author of the era. For him and other Reformers printing was a 'divine' and 'miraculous' gift. For the papacy Luther was the Devil's spawn and the presses a sewer of satanic propaganda. The English Catholic clergyman Rowland Philipps warned, 'we must root out printing or printing will root out us.'[1] For the Church, the Reformation was further confirmation of growing suspicions of a sustained attack by the Devil on Christian Europe. A series of heresy and witch trials in the Alps during the second half of the fifteenth century had fuelled concerns. These were born out by the increasing number of German and Swiss states that rejected Rome and become Protestant from the 1520s onwards. The Catholic Church launched its counter-offensives. The Italian Inquisition was instituted in 1542 primarily to stem the Protestant threat and the books that carried the heresy across the Alps. It followed the model of the Spanish Inquisition and its regional tribunals, which had already been combing the Spanish territories for other heretics for over sixty years.

For the new Protestant Churches of northern and central Europe the corruption of the old Church was portrayed as a sign of the arrival of the Antichrist in the guise of the Pope. Pre-millennial tension was a major condition of the age.

The Devil was active everywhere and theologians thought they had discovered an ever-expanding cohort of his earthly army consisting principally of poor women. The product of endless neighbourly rumour and suspicion, the popular conception of the village witch was transformed into the greatest of satanic threats through the theological reasoning of educated demonologists. And it is no coincidence that the rise of the witch trials during the early sixteenth century occurred in the same period that print was becoming a major cultural force. It was demonological books that spread the ideas and fears of this diabolic witchcraft conspiracy, and it was the printed pamphlets detailing their execrable crimes that penetrated far into the conscientiousness of the general population. The English lawyer and printer John Rastell, writing in 1530, was not wrong when he described the advent of print as having 'been the cause of great learning and knowledge | and hath been the cause of many things and great changes | & is like to be the cause of many strange things here after to come.'[2]

The laws against witchcraft instituted across Europe during the first half of the sixteenth century were not just concerned with harmful witches: all magic, whether good or bad, was considered the tool of the Devil. Some demonologists, both Protestant and Catholic, asserted that 'good witches' or cunning-folk, in other words those who practised magic to help people by removing spells, detecting stolen goods, and much else besides, were even worse than 'black' witches. This was because the victims of witches did not become lost souls, whereas the clients of cunning-folk, by resorting to magic, risked damnation by being complicit in the Devil's works. So the secular and religious authorities were most keen to suppress all magical practitioners. While the common people shared their enthusiasm for the extermination of witches, they were not, however, so keen to see cunning-folk on the end of a rope, dismembered, or burned to death.

Magic was an ambivalent force but a necessary one in most people's lives, which is why printers, at considerable risk, soon saw the market potential. In 1528 the warehouse of one Seville printer contained amongst its stock 8,000 printed sheets of *nóminas*, a thousand of which were hand-coloured. These consisted of prayers and names of the saints used as protective talismans. *Nóminas* had circulated on paper and parchment, and their appearance in print at such an early date demonstrates how printers were quick to capitalize on 'superstitious' popular religion.[3] One of the most popular was the prayer of St Cyprian. As early as 1498 copies were being printed and sold in Spain, and they appeared in Italy not long after. That it was being used in a magical rather than a devotional religious sense, independent of the clergy, is evident from the fact that the Church banned it several decades later.[4] As we shall see, these tentative attempts to assuage the popular thirst for magical aid were the first steps in the history of print's slow but sure grip on the magical tradition. They also mark the beginning of authoritarian attempts to stop this democratic process.

The Renaissance mage

The Renaissance has been defined by the development of humanism, and the enthusiasm for the discovery and rediscovery of the intellectual world of the ancient Romans and Greeks. As one historian has commented, 'In the Renaissance, the "new" meant the "old," the very old.'[5] It was supported by the patronage of a new wealthy urban elite, and spread through the medium of print. However, there was nothing particularly revolutionary about the Renaissance in intellectual terms, and historians are now increasingly emphasizing that the flowering of the Renaissance emerged from branches of medieval scholarship. So where does that leave the notion of Renaissance magic? There was no 'rebirth' of magic, no great break with the past, but rather a continuation and development of medieval ideas about the secrets encoded in ancient texts, be they pagan, Jewish, Islamic, or Christian, and the possible role that magic could play as an adjunct of Christian theology.[6]

Nevertheless, there were some significant developments in the magic tradition during the Renaissance. One was the spread of Hermeticism in western European thought. The *Corpus hermeticum* were a group of Greek religious and philosophical texts written in the first few centuries after Christ. Although clearly influenced by Greek philosophy, they were thought to encapsulate the far more ancient thoughts of Hermes Trismegistus. We have seen that Hermetic writings were known in medieval Europe, but their intellectual relevance was boosted massively when, in 1460, a Byzantine monk brought a version of the *Corpus* to Florence, where it was translated into Latin by Marsilio Ficino (1433–99) and published in 1471.[7] As a consequence, Ficino became a central figure in the world of intellectual occultism. His conception of magic was hugely influential, and the lynchpin of the intellectual magic traditions of the early modern period based on the Neoplatonic concept of a universe in which all things were interconnected by spiritual bonds. The other significant development of the Renaissance, which would have more of an influence on the development of future grimoires than Hermeticism, was the spreading influence of Kabbalah in European magical thought. The mystical system of Kabbalah that developed in medieval Spain had been percolating into Christian magic before the late fifteenth century, but it was its espousal by another Florentine philosopher and natural magician, Pico della Mirandola (1463–94), that introduced it to a new readership and led to renewed engagement with its occult promises.[8] Johannes Reuchlin, a German humanist scholar and expert in Greek and Hebrew, further advanced its influence north of the Alps. In 1490 he travelled south and visited Pico—a sign of the developing European network of occult philosophers.

The resurgent interest in Hermeticism and Kabbalah would also act as inspiration for Rosicrucianism. During the early seventeenth century several curious German publications appeared claiming the existence of an occult fraternity founded by a fifteenth-century German knight named Christian Rosenkreutz who was an adept in Hermetic and Kabbalistic magic. His followers, the Brotherhood of the Rosy Cross, were dedicated to a spiritual reformation of society through magical principles. There is no evidence that the Brotherhood existed, but the pamphlets generated considerable interest and were quickly translated into other languages. While some, such as the Jacobean playwright Ben Jonson, poked fun at the 'Chimera of the Rosie Crosse, Their Charmes, their Characters, Hermetticke Rings',[9] others took the story seriously. We shall encounter the Rosicrucians again with regard to the esoteric Freemasonry movements of the eighteenth and nineteenth centuries.

Much has been written on the nature of Renaissance magic, and its role in the development of science, but what I want to focus on here is the way in which natural magic and its practitioners were caught up in the authoritarian view that all magic, whether witchcraft, natural magic, celestial magic, or spirit conjuration, was demonic in origin and intent. It was the notoriety generated by these associations that led later generations to associate the misrepresented reputations of the great Renaissance magicians with sinister conjuration. In the process, the sixteenth-century heirs to the Florentine magicians became the new generation of bogus grimoire authors, joining the biblical magicians, medieval popes, and saints in the occult firmament.

The most important of the Renaissance era magicians in this story was the German humanist scholar Heinrich Cornelius Agrippa von Nettesheim (1486–1535).[10] He was a well-travelled young man due to his military service and his spirit of intellectual adventure, and studied at the universities of Cologne and Paris. He was interested in the occult from an early age, reading the work of that other famous inhabitant of Cologne, Albertus Magnus. He also studied the works of the Italian Renaissance mages, and when, around 1511, he found himself in Italy on military business he took the opportunity to further his knowledge on Kabbalah and Hermeticism. The German Benedictine abbot Johannes Trithemius (1462–1516) was another important influence closer to home.[11] Trithemius had experimented with drawing benign spirits into crystals, and his most well-known magical work *Steganographia* (*Secret writing*), which was written around 1499 but only published in Frankfurt in 1606, posited the existence of an occult code that would enable communication with spirits and angels. Trithemius possessed and pored over the key medieval magical manuscripts in circulation at the time. Through his writings elements of the medieval grimoires, which otherwise remained unpublished until the modern era, found their way into print. Agrippa dedicated his own opus *De occulta philosophia*, later known as his *Three Books of Occult Philosophy*, to Trithemius. It contained a rich distillation of the celestial wisdom to be gained through the practice of natural magic, ceremonial angelic communication, and Kaballah, and the occult sympathies that united the material and elemental worlds. He had written a draft of this around 1510 but he only had it published in Antwerp in 1533. By this time he had, like other prominent Renaissance mages, already publicly disavowed and condemned such 'vain sciences' as Kabbalah, magic, and alchemy, along with a more extreme denunciation of astronomy, geometry, and arithmetic. This makes his decision to publish his early views rather curious.

The impressively named Philippus Aureolus Theophrastus Bombatus von Hohenheim (1493–1541) was a German-speaking contemporary of Agrippa. Paracelsus, as he was thankfully better known, was a Swiss physician whose experiments and ideas regarding medicine, alchemy, astrology, and celestial magic were hugely influential across Europe.[12] Very few of his writings were published in his lifetime, and, as with Agrippa's *Opera*, the corpus of works bundled together and edited after his death probably contains some that he did not write.[13] *Of the supreme mysteries of nature*, translated into English in 1655, may or may not be one such pseudo-Paracelsian work. Its contents certainly reflected Paracelsus's views on the division between good and bad magic. It contained instructions on how to create a series of metal lamens engraved with occult symbols and secret words of power, each effective against specific medical conditions. 'Characters and Seals have likewise in them wonderful virtue, which is not at all contrary to nature, nor superstitious,' he explained. Conjuration was another matter altogether, and in *Of the supreme mysteries* 'Ceremonial Nigromancers' are denounced as 'arch-Fools, and ignorant men of no worth!' All conjurations 'are against God, and are contrary to his word'.[14]

Despite their denunciations of 'vain' and demonic magic Agrippa and Paracelsus became the two most reviled and misrepresented magicians of the era, and the subject of numerous published attacks. Slanderous and fictitious stories circulated about their satanic activities. By the end of the sixteenth century the legend that Agrippa kept a demonic familiar in the shape of a black dog was widely believed. The followers of Paracelsian medicine constantly had to fend off accusations that he was 'a magician and an impostor who had dealings with demons'.[15] The evil reputations of both men circulated far and wide. An English pamphlet written in 1631 by a Buckinghamshire parson attacking the concept of the weapon-salve, a sympathetic magic technique attributed to Paracelsus whereby wounds were healed by treating the offending weapon with the patient's blood, became a wider attack on the two occult philosophers. Paracelsus was declared to be 'a Witch and Conjurer' and Agrippa's books of occult philosophy denounced as being 'stuffed with Conjurations of the divell'.[16]

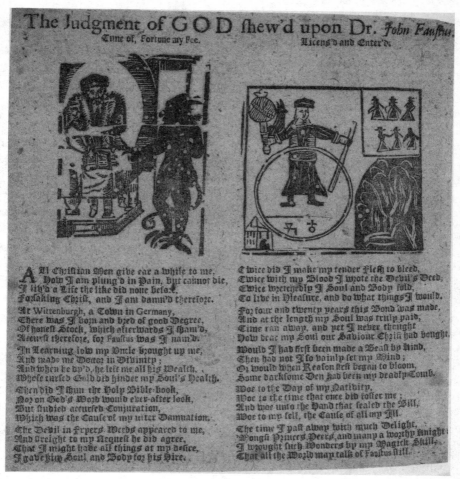

Fig. 1 Dr Faustus depicted in seventeenth-century literature.

The diabolic reputations and legends surrounding both men were further coloured by association with the hugely popular legend of Dr Faust or Faustus and his tragic relations with the Devil. An itinerant magician named Georg Faust certainly existed, though his sketchy history has been obscured by confusion with other men bearing the same surname.[17] He was a contemporary of Agrippa and Paracelsus who developed a reputation for diabolic magic in several German states in his own lifetime. Complaints about him pop up here and there in the books and letters of humanists and occult philosophers of the period. The earliest reference to Faust is in a letter written by Trithemius in 1507, in which he is also identified as one Georgius Sabellicus, 'who dares to call himself the prince of necromancers, is a vagrant, a charlatan, and a rascal'. In 1513 the humanist Konrad Muth wrote that he had heard one Georg Faustus bragging at an inn about his prowess as a fortune-teller. Martin Luther made a reference to him in 1537. After his death, around 1539–40, perhaps in Luther's Wittenberg, Faust became a magnet for a variety of old legend motifs of magical escapades and diabolic pacts that transmitted orally and in print around central and northern Europe.

The crucial step in the demonizing of Faust was the publication in German in 1587 of a book regaling stories of his mischievous magical career; how he conjured up and made a pact with Devil, and ultimately ended up being torn to pieces by his satanic master—a fitting end, of course, for all those who dabbled in the magical arts. The 1587 Faust book fed on the popularity of *teufelsbücher* or Devil's books in German popular culture during the second half of the sixteenth century. They sold in their thousands, and were mostly Protestant in authorship. Both humorous and scary in tone, they related and depicted the Devil's many ways of exploiting and ruining sinners. One of them published in 1553, *Der Zauber Teuffel* (*The Devil of Magic*), which contained a woodcut of a magician conjuring in a circle, directly influenced the 1587 Faust book. Such literature was not unique to the German states, and so it is no surprise that the sensational tale of Faust was soon translated into other languages, and disseminated widely in learned and popular culture. The legend's enduring influence was further sealed by the Faust plays of Christopher Marlowe and Goethe.[18]

Agrippa, Paracelsus, and Faust may have been contemporary magicians but they were very different characters, with divergent and antagonist positions regarding the nature and practice of magic. Yet the three of them were tarred with the same diabolic reputation, and all three would have their names associated with grimoires of the darkest magic. Faust's time would come in the eighteenth century. It was the name of Agrippa that found itself on the title page of the first true grimoire of the print age.

New wave, old waves

The first edition of *The Fourth Book of Occult Philosophy*, in Latin, was produced in Marburg in 1559, and another edition appeared in Basel six years later.[19] Subsequent editions were often printed in the *Opera*, a collation of real and spurious works by Agrippa, along with the *Heptameron*, and *Ars Notoria*.[20] Although a former pupil of Agrippa named Johan Weyer would later protest that the *Fourth Book* had nothing to do with his late master, for demonologists it was the real thing, the proof that Agrippa had been deep in diabolic magic all the time.[21]

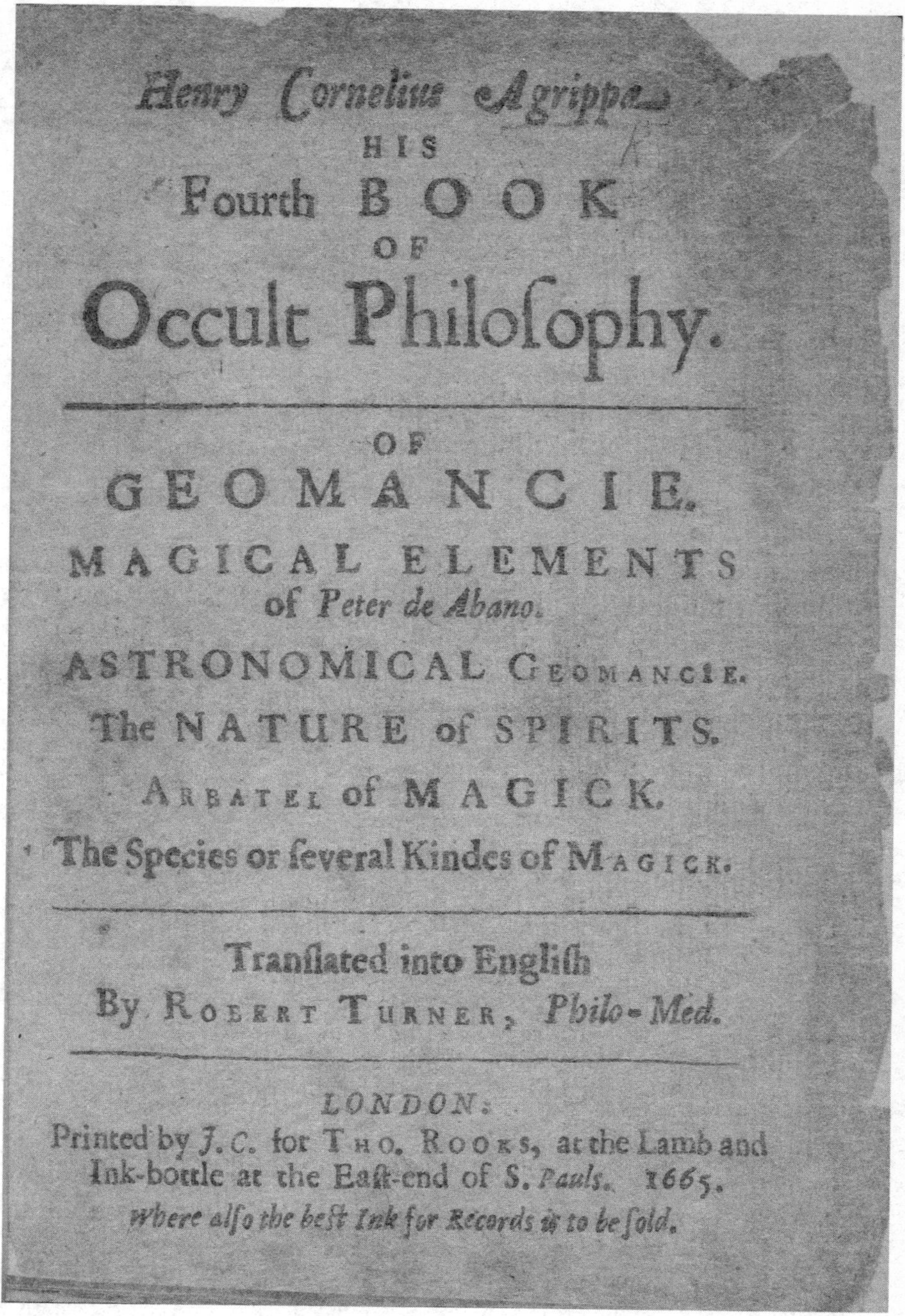

Henry Cornelius Agrippa

HIS

Fourth BOOK

OF

Occult Philosophy.

OF

GEOMANCIE.

MAGICAL ELEMENTS
of *Peter de Abano*.

ASTRONOMICAL GEOMANCIE.

The NATURE of SPIRITS.

ARBATEL of MAGICK.

The Species or several Kindes of MAGICK.

Translated into English
By ROBERT TURNER, *Philo-Med.*

LONDON:
Printed by *J.C.* for THO. ROOKS, at the Lamb and
Ink-bottle at the East-end of S. *Pauls.* 1665.
Where also the best Ink for Records is to be sold.

FIG. 2 First English edition of the *Fourth Book of Occult Philosophy*.

Copies quickly began to circulate across Europe. The Elizabethan mage John Dee owned the 1559 edition and brought it with him during his travels around central Europe in 1583.[22] By the late 1580s manuscript versions were passing through the hands of less well-connected Italian magicians. A Neapolitan treasure hunter named Michele Navarra purchased a copy amongst a bundle of magical manuscripts he bought for the considerable sum of thirty-eight ecus of gold. Another Neapolitan was found with a copy along with a manuscript of *Clavicule of Solomon*.[23] One of the charges against a young man prosecuted in Normandy in 1627 included the possession of a grimoire and 'asking a student for a book by Agrippa'.[24]

The first English version only appeared in 1655, published by the Cambridge educated astrologer-physician Robert Turner. Scholarly magicians would have already obtained a Latin edition, and so the purchasers of the English text were probably a mix of the intellectually curious and professional astrologers and cunning-folk. Its swift notoriety is evident from a 1678 pamphlet attacking ignorant 'ass-trologers', 'piss-prophets', and 'starr-wizards'. The author described the standard consulting-room decor and accoutrements of such people, advising, 'let your Table be never without some old musty *Greek* or *Arabick* author, and the 4th book of *Cornelius Agrippa's Occult Philosophy*, wide open, to amuse spectators.' A decade or so later the clergyman Richard Baxter recorded, 'I had a very Godly Friend, that a Week ago told me, that he read Cornelius Agrippa's *Occulta Philosophia*, and read the same Words that he saith will raise Devils.' This was almost certainly the *Fourth Book*, and as his conscientious friend avowedly detested the book, 'nothing appeared to him'. The son of a minister who came to see Baxter in a state of terror was less fortunate. He had also read a book of conjurations to make the Devil appear; he duly did, urging the young man to slit his throat.[25]

The *Arbatel* was another work included in editions of Agrippa's *Opera*, and it appeared in the English edition of the *Fourth Book of Occult Philosophy*. It was concerned with the hierarchy, nature, and governance of the spirit world, and what the spirits could teach mankind. According to the *Arbatel*, between the years 1410 and 1900 the ruling prince of spirits was Hagith who had 4,000 legions of spirits under his command. He possessed the knowledge to convert copper into gold, so he was a spirit alchemists were likely to be familiar with. Following on from Hagith's reign, Ophiel is the current governor of the spirit world. He also has alchemical powers, but can also make men live to three hundred, and more modestly he can cure the dropsy. Although editions of the *Arbatel* appeared bearing dates in the early sixteenth century, the first edition, in Latin, was actually printed in Basel in 1575. German translations were soon circulating in manuscript form, usually attributing it to Paracelsus. As to its real author we know nothing, though he was clearly learned in medieval and Renaissance magic and a follower of Paracelsus and Hermeticism. There was also a degree of invention as well as heavy borrowing. It included spirit names unknown in the previous literature that would find their way into popular grimoires of the eighteenth and nineteenth centuries.[26]

The publication of the *Arbatel* in Basel scandalized the town's theologians. The pastor Simon Sulzer denounced it from his pulpit. Calls were made for the printer to be punished, though there is no evidence that any other action was taken.[27] In 1617 senior members of the Protestant University of Marburg investigated the curriculum being taught at the town's school by the Paracelsian and Rosicrucian schoolmaster Philipp Homagius and his colleague Georg Zimmermann. A search of their lodgings revealed copies of the *Arbatel* printed in editions of Agrippa's *Opera*, and it transpired that they had even intended to introduce the *Arbatel* as a school textbook. In his own copy Homagius noted, 'I wrote this and was happy to complete it on 4 May 1617. This book deals with the way how to evoke spirits, and how we may obtain our familiar spirits; amongst their tasks it is to provide longevity and to prolong life by 300 years.' A copy was also found on a student who was so absorbed in it that for more than a year and a half after having been expelled he did not attend any lectures, 'nor was he inclined to do so'.[28]

This first wave of print grimoires emanated from Protestant German and Swiss publishing centres such as Frankfurt and Basel. The long arms and beady eyes of the papal censors did not reach these Protestant areas. The notoriety of the Germanic mages, Trithemius, Faust, Agrippa, and Paracelsus, would have also generated a keen regional audience. But such occult works were not only of interest to practical magicians and the simply curious. A strong mystical, spiritual tradition emerged in Protestantism during the sixteenth century, most notably expressed in the influential writings of the Lutheran visionary Jacob Boehme (1575–1624), but also evident in numerous other small Protestant sects, such as those that made their way to America during the late seventeenth century. The Neoplatonic discourses on the angelic and spiritual hierarchies contained in the *Arbatel*, *Heptameron*, *Book Three* and *Fourth Book of Occult Philosophy*, and the *Steganographia*, and the keys they provided to direct celestial communication, appealed to the prophetic and revelatory aspects of Protestant theology.

It would be going too far, though, to claim that print revolutionized the European grimoire tradition at this period. It certainly introduced influential new texts into the canon, significantly increased the pool of available magical knowledge, and heightened authoritarian concerns over their dissemination and influence. Yet the continued power and influence of handwritten manuscripts is clearly evident from the fact that, across much of Europe, the number of Latin and vernacular copies of the classic medieval grimoires which remained unpublished in the early modern period multiplied many times. Many handwritten copies of printed works like the *Fourth Book* also circulated. It has been said that the reason for this was because printed editions had no intrinsic value, as high magic required the ritualized transcription and consecration of each individual grimoire.[29] This is undoubtedly a significant factor, but increasing numbers of users were not earnest seekers of magical enlightenment assiduously carrying out the stipulated fastings, consecrations, and other preparations. They just wanted quick-fix conjurations, and the basic details on what to say and where to say it. Manuscripts still held an aura for these people, and their clients in particular, but ultimately there was no intrinsic difference between print or manuscript versions in using the conjurations they contained. The fact is that demand for print conjurations outstripped supply and so manuscripts continued to be produced in their thousands.[30]

We get a good idea of the most popular of the old texts from Inquisition trials concerning the search for buried treasure. In Sicily, which was under Spanish rule and therefore the jurisdiction of the Spanish Inquisition, we find that the *Clavicule of Solomon* and the *Lucidarius* of Peter D'Abano circulated quite widely, and treasure-seeking priests such as one Antonio Panayno, investigated in the 1630s, were instrumental in facilitating the diffusion of such grimoires.[31] A manuscript called the *Gabala Regnum* and the *Clavicule* were found hidden amongst the mathematical books of a southern Italian treasure hunter and surveyor prosecuted twice in the 1680s named Nicodemo Salinaro. He told an acquaintance that they could not only help find treasure but make a man invisible and help him to 'obtain grace'.[32] In the 1590s a fraternity of Capuchin friars from Verona were found to be circulating several prohibited books on magic amongst themselves, including the *Clavicule of Solomon* and the *Centum Regnum (One Hundred Kings)*.[33] The latter, which appeared variously as the *Forty Three, Fifty,* or *Hundred Kings,* consisted of a list of the principal spirits and their powers, in the tradition of the *Testament of Solomon*. It was evidently a popular grimoire in Italy at the time, as was noted by several Italian inquisitors. A copy was also found in the occult library of a Maltese notary condemned as a heretic in 1574.[34]

In 1579 the Venetian Inquisition uncovered a five-man team of treasure hunters led by a nobleman, Giulio Morosoni, who was advised and aided by a former professor of theology named Father Cesare Lanza. The group made lengthy preparations including the collection of several magic books, amongst them a copy of the *Clavicule of Solomon* solemnly consecrated by Cesare Lanza, Agrippa's *De occulta philosophia,* the *Lucidario* of d'Abano, an unnamed work attributed to Roger Bacon, and *The Forty-Three Kings of Spirits* (a version of the *Centum Regnum*). One of the team, a former friar and priest, Gregorio Giordano, described the latter to the Inquisitors: 'there was written there on each page the name of a spirit, its powers, its characters, and the methods of conjuring it . . . and among other things there was one who said after his name "I am the God of Treasure".[35] Not all the team took seriously the solemnity of the ritual magic employed by Cesare. One of them told the tribunal that during the consecration of one grimoire Cesare 'drew the large knife with the right hand and recited the psalm *Exurgat Deus* with such vehemence that it seemed he wanted to cut all the spirits into pieces in that one act, whereupon I wanted to start laughing; I was dying with laughter so that I could hardly contain myself.' It is possible, of course, that this dismissal of ritual conjuration was an attempt to mitigate his criminal involvement.[36]

In Italy the *Clavicule of Solomon* was clearly the most ubiquitous and widely circulated grimoire. In early modern Venice versions were available not only in Latin and Italian, but French, English, and German, or a combination of them. The same holds true for Spain, and the copy confiscated from a priest in Gran Canaria in 1527 shows that wherever the Spanish clergy were to be found so to was the *Clavicule*.[37] That other medieval hit, the *Picatrix*, circulated less widely, basically because it provided little practical help in conjuring and controlling demons. The *Book of Honorius* was popular amongst the practical magicians and diabolic dabblers of late-seventeenth-century Paris, but otherwise it was nowhere near as widespread as the *Clavicule*.

It is important to point out that in the manuscript grimoire tradition few works were ever quite the same. There was no founding text, no print template for the *Clavicule* for instance. Over the generations copyists added their own personal touches, taking bits out, adding information from other sources. Apart from the rare cases where copies were kept by the authorities rather than burned, whenever the *Clavicule* or other well-known grimoire is mentioned in a trial record we usually have little idea as to what it contained or looked like. Some clearly followed the template of the learned medieval examples. Others might have the name of Solomon on them but were basically magic scrapbooks, compilations of practical magic for dealing with witches, causing rain, seducing women, and the like, culled from manuals of exorcisms, orations, prayers, and oral sources of knowledge. Some were large, imposing leather-bound parchment tomes, while others were cheaply bound paper volumes, pocket-sized for ease of carrying and so that they could be hidden up a sleeve by itinerant cunning-folk.[38] Similarly, the trial records do not always distinguish between Agrippa's *Occulta philosophia* and the *Fourth Book*, or make clear whether they were a print or manuscript version.

Innovation and invention continued to occur in the manuscript tradition during the early modern period. When in 1627 an Italian Benedictine monk named Stefano Peranda fled his abbey after hearing he had been denounced to the Inquisition he left behind in his cell a manuscript entitled *Zecorbeni seu clavicula Salomonis*.[39] As the title suggests, and as two eighteenth-century manuscripts called *Zekerboni* in the French *Bibliothèque de l'Arsenal* show, although the title was novel the contents were basically another variation on the *Clavicule*.[40] Although it never became a major player, a small number of copies circulated outside of Italy by the end of the century. As well as the French examples, in 1674 the English antiquarian John Aubrey translated and transcribed an Italian manuscript *Zecorbeni*, which is now in the Bodleian Library. It has been suggested that Aubrey may have tried out some of its contents.[41]

The most interesting aspect of the *Zekerboni* is that the French copies stated that they were written by an early seventeenth-century Milanese doctor and occultist named Pierre or Pietro Mora. Attributing books to mythical doctors was part of the grimoire tradition, of course, but in this case it was only in the twentieth century that the mysterious Mora was given a dubious history by Montague Summers, a widely read author of populist works on the history of witchcraft and magic. Employing his love of the Gothic, Summers provided a lurid two-page account of 'this mysterious and menacing personage' who apparently confessed to the Inquisition that he was 'the Grand Master and preceptor of a band of Satanists, who with infernal malice were leagued to spread the pestilence by all means they could devise'. This account was then taken up by other historians, with one concluding from Summers' account that Mora 'must have been a Satanist'.[42] In fact there is no evidence of a Milanese medical man of that name having been executed in Milan for plague-spreading at the time. There was, however, a barber-surgeon named Giovanni Giacomo Mora who was executed in 1630 after confessing under torture to being part of a plague-spreading conspiracy. Summers seems to have mixed up the two Moras, and then invented the diabolic element, for Mora was never questioned by the Milanese authorities about satanic worship or magical practices.[43]

As I indicated earlier, manuscript grimoires, particularly those that increasingly circulated in popular culture, often consisted mostly of the bricolage of oral and print sources of practical occult knowledge rather than conjurations and endless spirit descriptions. Astrological almanacs became hugely popular in the seventeenth century, and their lists of good and bad days, weather forecasts, and useful proverbs seeped deep into the agricultural world of the common people, and were scribbled into the pages of grimoires. Another very popular print genre was the 'secrets of secrets' whose natural magic mixed with the demonic in manuscript and later print grimoires. Well known in the medieval period, and with their contents relying heavily on ancient Greek, Roman, and Arabic texts, these expositions of the hidden wonders of nature embodied both the intellectual Renaissance fascination with ancient wisdom and fired and informed the popular imagination of an expanding readership. They were works of magic only in the sense that they revealed the secret powers of plants, animals, stones, and the mysterious workings of natural processes that might otherwise be deemed the result of the magical actions of magicians or the world of spirits. One popular print example was a version of the *Kyranides*. A seventeenth-century English edition entitled *The Magick of Kirani King of Persia* contained such priceless information as 'A Weezle's Tongue dried, and worn in ones shooes, makes all his Enemies to be mute,' and 'For an Alopecia, or falling of the hair; Apply the ashes of little Frogs with Tar.' Frog was also good for the reverse process, so if you want a painless alternative to waxing, 'burn the skin of a Frog, and put it into the water of the Bath.'[44]

In the print age, the medieval book of secrets falsely attributed to Albertus Magnus would prove the most enduring, influential, and pervasive, finding a following across the western hemisphere where it was known to many as the *Grand Albert*. Several new publications also emerged with similar commercial success, though without the lasting notoriety of the Albertus book. The greatest challenger was the *Secreti* of Alessio Piemontese. First printed in Italian and Latin in the 1550s, and obviously created to build on the success of Albertus, the preface told how Piemontese, a fictional but not unrealistic archetype of the Renaissance occult scholar, had gathered his secrets of medicine and nature from his travels across Italy and the Middle East. Over the next two centuries various editions appeared in English, German, Dutch, French, Spanish, and Polish.[45] Amongst these false and fictional authors the work of the very real Giambattista Della Porta (1535–1615) stands out. This Italian polymath spent a lifetime exploring the natural world and occult philosophy.[46] Like Paracelsus he denounced spirit conjuration but unlike Agrippa he never disavowed natural magic. For his pains he was constantly harassed by the Italian Inquisition. His most celebrated work *Magia naturalis* or *Natural Magic* first appeared in 1558 and subsequently went through at least twenty editions. Unlike Albertus and Piemontese, *Natural Magic* was intended explicitly for an intellectual readership. While it contained much that was similar to the others it also provided learned discourses on subjects like optics, and has been characterized by one historian as reading 'like a manifesto for a new scientific methodology: that of science as a venation, a hunt for "new secrets of nature."'[47] Nevertheless, with a title containing magic, the ignorant and suspicious were quick to make assumptions about dealings with the darker arts, and although far from it, *Natural Magic* was sometimes considered a work of diabolic magic rather than of scientific endeavour.

Almanacs and books of secrets may have seasoned the grimoire recipe, but the most influential occult products of the print age, exorcism manuals, were often endorsed by the Catholic Church—at least at first. There had always been lay exorcists practising a wide range of oral means of dispossession. But the Church's lack of control over the performance of exorcisms was thoroughly exposed in the seventeenth century by the proliferation of lay exorcists and maverick clergymen.

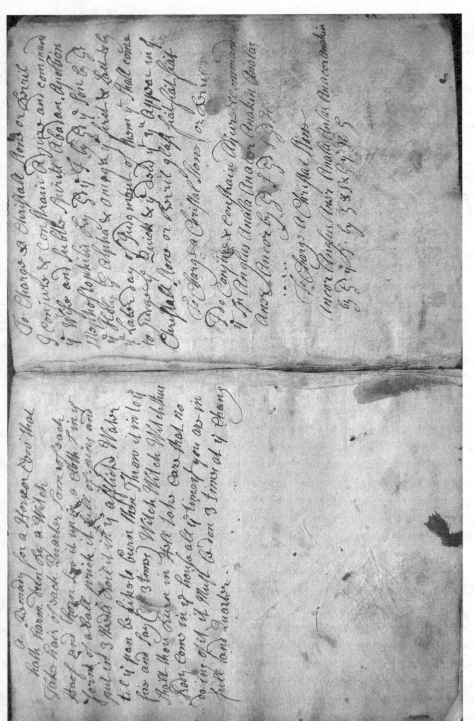

Fig. 3 Notebook of the early eighteenth-century Yorkshire cunning-man Timothy Crowther, containing a mix of conjurations, axioms, weather-signs and astrological calculations.

Catholic Bavaria proved fertile ground for such men and women. One such practitioner was a pastor named Johann Weiss, the son of a parish priest, who was charged by the secular authorities in 1579 with practising magic. Weiss had been in the business of exorcizing people, many of whom believed they were driven insane by being possessed by the purgatorial spirits of stillborn children. On being apprehended Weiss was ordered to hand over a suspicious book ostensibly thought to contain blessings for good weather and exorcisms, but which it was suspected contained more. It could not be found and Weiss claimed he had lost it.[48] As this case suggests, and others confirm, a key reason for the proliferation of such unofficial exorcism was the increasing public access to the many exorcism manuals in Italian and Latin pouring off the presses of Bologna, Milan, and Venice during the late sixteenth and early seventeenth centuries.

The practice of exorcism, which was condemned by the Protestant churches, was an excellent propaganda tool for the Catholic Church. In his book on the evils of witchcraft, the French judge and demonologist Henri Boguet included several chapters aimed at those who mocked the exorcisms of the priesthood. It contained a series of accounts of how French Calvinists (Huguenots) found themselves powerless in the face of witchcraft and demonic attack, and ended up having to resort to the Catholic clergy for succour.[49] Without the power of exorcism the Protestant clergy had no place on the battlefield against the Devil and his minions. Yet, as Protestant theologians never tired of pointing out, there was little or no difference between exorcism and conjuration, as both involved talking to Devils. The difference depended on whether one accepted the holy power invested in the ordained priest.

Conjurations were often no more than tweaked versions of the official rites of exorcism, so it is no wonder that the printed exorcism manuals resembled magic books in some respects. The *Practica of Exorcists*, for example, written by a Franciscan and published in 1586, discussed how the exorcist could communicate with the demonic spirits in order that their names could be written down above an image of a demon drawn on paper, which should then be burned. *The Hammer of the Demons* (1620) by another Franciscan, Alexander Albertinus, consisted of passages of Scripture mixed with prayers and conjurations to command and expel demons. The most influential author of exorcism manuals at this time was the Franciscan exorcist Girolamo Menghi, some of whose various popular works were also published in Frankfurt. He produced a series of books with titles like *The Devil's Scourge* and the *Club against Demons*, some of which were produced in pocket versions, ideal for itinerant lay and ordained exorcists. As inquisitorial and ecclesiastical records show, in such hands his manuals were used as grimoires for such purposes as treasure seeking and curing impotency.[50] In 1643, for instance, a monk named Zorzi used a copy of *The Devil's Scourge* to conjure up rather than banish demons and also to consecrate talismans for winning at gambling.[51] The mid-seventeenth-century exorcism manuals of Candido Brugnoli were central to the magical practices of a popular Brazilian exorcist and Carmelite friar, Luis de Nazaré, who was charged by the Inquisition in the 1740s. Brugnoli attacked the practice of touching the female genitalia and breasts during exorcisms, but that is exactly what Nazaré did, even going so far as to copulate with the possessed. The Inquisition banished him to a remote monastery for five years, forbade him from forever exorcizing again, but allowed him to remain a priest.[52]

Several of these exorcism manuals, including Menghi's, were belatedly added to the papal *Index* in 1709, but by this time the Church had been complicit in spreading the magical use of exorcisms at the same time as its courts were attempting to suppress lay and ecclesiastical 'superstition'.[53]

Print culture also influenced the magic tradition through more subtle pathways. A good example of this is the way in which fairies were incorporated into both the ritual conjurations of Tudor English grimoires and the literary culture of the early modern stage.[54] In several English sixteenth-century manuscripts we find the names of fairies among the demonic and spirit names included in Solomonic conjurations. As one twentieth-century scholar with a jaundiced view of Continental magical traditions put it, 'It is an extraordinary experience to follow the dark trail of ritual magic from the Continent (and notably from Germany) to England, and to find oneself escaping from puerility and squalor into poetry, fairy-tales and romance.'[55] This highly subjective description was coloured more by the fairy-lore prominent in Elizabethan and Jacobean drama than any uniquely poetic quality in English grimoires of the period. The key link between the two literary traditions was the figure of Oberon, king of the fairies, who was to be found onstage in Shakespeare's *A Midsummer's Night Dream* and Ben Jonson's *Oberon, the Fairy Prince*.

Similar sounding spirits had been mentioned in early sixteenth-century Church court records. In 1510 a priest named James Richardson was accused of preparing a lead tablet inscribed with the image of a spirit named Oberion. Eighteen years later a treasure-seeking monk named William Stapleton confessed to having heard from a friend that the parson of Lesingham and Sir John of Leiston had conjured up three spirits named Andrew Malchus, Inchubus, and Oberion.[56] By the late sixteenth century surviving grimoires show that Oberion had become firmly identified as a fairy rather than one of the legions of other spirits and demons. A magic manuscript in the Folger Shakespeare Library includes Oberion amongst a list of eighty-two spirits, and states, 'he teacheth a man knowledge in phisicke and he sheweth the nature of stones herbes and trees and of all mettall. he is a great and mighty kinge and he is kinge of the fairies. he causeth a man to be Invissible. he showeth where hiding treseuer is and how to obtain the saime.' An early-seventeenth-century manuscript in the Bodleian Library provides instructions on how to conjure up the fairies and how to call Oberion into a crystal.[57]

The influence of Oberon and his transformation into the king of the fairies in the English grimoire and literary tradition was primarily influenced by the translation and printing in 1534 of a French romance called *Huon of Bordeaux*, in which a fairy king is shrunk to the size of a small child by a curse. The figure of Oberon subsequently developed through the interplay of print and manuscript literature. The playwrights' conception of ritual magic was influenced by their knowledge of manuscript grimoires, and, in turn, stage plays fed back into magical culture, exciting interest in calling up the fairies. It is surely the work of Shakespeare and Jonson, and their portrayals of Queen Mab, queen of the fairies, which influenced the subsequent reference to her in conjurations. She is mentioned in a seventeenth-century magical manuscript in the British Library, and the astrologer William Lilly recalled meeting a magician named Mortlack who professed to call upon Queen Mab via his crystal ball.[58] Pathways were also opened between literary and oral cultures of magic. The Revd Thomas Jackson, writing in 1625, recalled that during his ministry he questioned a parishioner, 'an ignorant soule', who he knew 'to have beene seduced by a teacher of unhallowed arts, to make a dangerous experiment'. When asked whether he thought the Devil was at work in a ritual involving the watching of fern seeds, he replied 'No; it is in the keeping of the *King of Fayries*, and *he* I know will doe me no harme.' The name of the King escaped him, however, so Jackson 'remembred it unto him out of my reading in *Huon of Burdeaux*'.[59]

Democratization

As historians quite rightly revise the 'newness' of Renaissance occultism, the real revolution has gone largely unremarked—the democratization of high magic.[60] Print was a key factor in the trickle down of literary magic, as was the growing dissemination of vernacular manuscripts, but both developments were fuelled by an expanding market for literary magic. But who made up this new readership?

If monks were the grimoire masters of the medieval period, in the sixteenth century they were in competition with the parish clergy. The shockingly poor level of education and professionalism of many priests was no secret on the eve of the Reformation. The pattern of clerical education in 1500 was by no means uniform, but in the Netherlands only 20 per cent of the clergy were university-trained and the situation was little better in northern German states. At the same time literacy had increased in wider society, highlighting more starkly the educational poverty of the priesthood. Church court records from across western and southern Europe reveal numerous complaints from parishioners about lax, womanizing, and drunken village priests.

The image of such dissolute and ignorant clergymen was a favourite of late-fifteenth- and early-sixteenth-century cartoonists and satirists like Erasmus. The widespread criticism of the parish clergy was certainly a contributory factor in the discontent that fomented the Protestant Reformation. Church authorities in newly Reformed states knew that the success of the Reformation depended on a clergy that was educated and conscientious, and surveys and court records showed they were not in generous supply. In 1551 the Bishop of Gloucester, England, found 168 priests in his diocese could not even repeat the Ten Commandments properly.[61]

The Reformation heralded a major change in the educational status of the parochial clergy, though it took several decades to get going and recruitment was initially sluggish.[62] A programme of clerical retraining and education was at the heart of the strategies of the main Protestant churches. A Danish Church Ordin-ance of 1627 required all prospective Lutheran ministers to obtain a university degree. A study of ministers in the Lutheran German duchy of Brunswick-Wolfenbüttel reveals that, by 1630, 80 per cent were university-trained, though not necessarily obtaining degrees in theology. In England by the same date the vast majority of Anglican clergymen were also university graduates.[63]

The Catholic Church eventually responded to criticism from both within and without, launching its own reformation of clerical piety and behaviour. While the Spanish Crown had forced an overhaul of the clergy in the late fifteenth century, it was the decrees of the Council of Trent, deliberating between 1545 and 1563, which launched a major renewal of the pastoral activities of the Church. The need for these Tridentine reforms of clergy and laity was evident to any conscientious senior clergyman. When, for instance, the Archbishop of Brindisi-Oria toured his diocese in southern Italy two years after the Council of Trent, he found that in the town of Francavilla there were nine priests who kept concubines and the arch-priest could barely read or write. Of nine magical practitioners mentioned two were clergymen. A survey of the Inquisition records for Modena revealed that the clergy were defendants in 20 per cent of the trials for 'superstition' between 1580 and 1600.[64] A key Tridentine measure was the setting up of seminaries dedicated to the education and re-education of the priesthood. The pace of reform was uneven across Catholic Europe. In the German Catholic prince-bishopric of Münster, for instance, a seminary was only instituted in 1626 but it was at least successful in producing highly educated priests fluent in Latin and trained in the art of preaching.[65] In France the old criticisms about the clergy were still plentiful in the early seventeenth century.[66]

What has this to do with grimoires? The fact that by the early seventeenth century the majority of clergy had access to university or monastic libraries as part of their training meant that they had more opportunity to consult and transcribe works on the occult sciences. Furthermore, a better-educated parish clergy also meant a clergy better able to read, understand, and employ the ritual conjurations contained in grimoires. While even semi-literate Catholic clergy had an advantage in the magical market through their exploitation of consecrated items and their ordained status, the ability to exploit literary magic and employ the numerous Latin exorcism manuals now available—as well as fully understand the Latin Vulgate—would have further enhanced their status amongst the laity. A better educated priesthood did not mean a better paid priesthood. There had been a significant increase in the number of parish priests in some parts of Europe, and while the wealth of the secular clergy varied widely many were poor and poorly trained. It is no wonder, as one historian has suggested, that many members of this 'ecclesiastical proletariat' were tempted to use their educational advantage to explore the money-making possibilities of magic.[67]

The sixteenth century also saw the expansion and opening up of other professions, such as schoolteachers, doctors, lawyers, and military men, which generated new circles of educated magical adepts.[68] A good example of this comes from the Maltese Inquisition's investigation in 1582 of how a local doctor named Galeazzo Cademusto came to transcribe a book of necromancy. It transpired that a Neapolitan schoolteacher owned the original copy. On being sentenced to a spell in the galleys, he had passed it on to his pupil, the brother-in-law of a lawyer.[69] With regard to the ownership of grimoires and the practice of literary magic the medical profession were, perhaps, the most influential after the priesthood. Until the second half of the seventeenth century astrology was a widely accepted and practised component of the medical sciences, and was sometimes a gateway to experimentation in the magical arts. This is clearly evident from the lives of several well-known English astrologer-physicians. Copies of medieval texts such as the *Picatrix* were found in the libraries of the likes of Simon Forman and Richard Napier.[70] Versions of the *Clavicule* also circulated, though sometimes under other titles. A disreputable Tudor astrologer-physician named Gregory Wisdom inherited a mysterious book from his father described as a 'book in English called the Practice of Dammell'. It no longer survives but a manuscript of Solomonic conjurations from the period begins with the similar rubric 'Here beginneth the book which is called the Dannel'.[71]

The diaries of Simon Forman (1552–1611), a very successful London astrologer-physician, who had his books confiscated on a couple of occasions, provide a rare insight into how such men considered and dabbled in spirit conjuration alongside their more respectable occult pursuits. Forman possessed manuscripts of the *Ars Notoria*, *Picatrix*, and *Liber Raziel*, and made copies of several of them. In the late 1580s he began in earnest to contact spirits, and in 1590 noted that he 'wrote a bocke of nigromanti' and had 'entred a cirkell for nicromanticall spells'. He made at least one other copy of his grimoire, presumably to enhance its power. He even dreamed about magic books and in one he 'was sore trobled about hiding of my bocks'.[72]

By no means all early modern astrologers were magicians. The astrological and magical arts were not inseparable, and some astrologers condemned magic outright and not just conjuration. Nevertheless, many theologians suspected otherwise and 'scientific' astrologers were vulnerable to accusations of sorcery. In 1622 Patrick Sinot, an Irish Professor of Rhetoric at the University of Santiago, was accused of possessing books of necromancy containing magical signs, circles, and characters, though the evidence suggests his library was purely astrological and perhaps Kabbalistic. Similarly in 1608 the Catalonia tribunal charged the astrologer Joseph Sala with practising sorcery and incantations, though the only forbidden book they found was a copy of an influential treatise by the thirteenth-century Italian astrologer Guido Bonatti.[73]

The clearest sign of the democratization process was the possession of magic books by artisans, tradesmen, apothecaries, and craftsmen, men who, in the early modern period, usually had an education and an increasing degree of social and geographical mobility. This is exemplified by a magical healer named Nicolas Noel le Bragard, from the town of Nancy, in eastern France. In 1593 he told his prosecutors, no doubt under torture, how he came to practise magic. Bragard had begun his working life as a cobbler, and then been a soldier. He was educated and knew a little Latin. He said he knew nothing of magic books until one day he saw an acquaintance, one of the town's gatekeepers, with 'a book containing various recipes, such as to find lost property, to have oneself loved by and to enjoy women, and others he did not well remember, which made him envious to acquire that science.' He tore several pages out of the book but desired to know more. A soldier of his acquaintance possessed another such book but would not lend it to him. Then he came across a woman who owned some old magic books and papers kept in a chest. He bought them from her, transcribed them and then sold them on to a gentleman. He also claimed to have seen a book entitled *D'occulta philosophia*, which he said he thought was the *Fourth Book*. He had tried out a variety of magical rituals contained in his grimoires for 'enjoying a woman', detecting stolen property, and finding treasure, but the results had been generally disappointing.[74]

In 1623 the authorities in Moulins, a town in central France, arrested and interrogated a similar character named Jean Michel Menuisier who stood accused of witchcraft and making a tacit pact with the Devil. He was a practising magician in his fifties who, after having been sentenced to banishment in 1604 for invoking evil spirits, said he had travelled in England, Germany, and Spain, where he stayed in Toledo—a fact that immediately aroused suspicion. During a visit to Vienna he had purchased a magic phial containing a spirit named Boël, which he consulted to know occult secrets and therefore help his clients. As well as practising illegal medicine he confessed that with an accomplice, an apothecary called Sanglant, he had called up spirits and angels including Raphael to find lost treasures. The lengthy transcript of his interrogation reveals how the authorities were preoccupied with finding out his knowledge of grimoires. He admitted to possessing a copy of Agrippa's *Opera*, and was questioned whether he was familiar with the *Fourth Book of Occult Philosophy*. Asked whether he knew Latin he replied in the negative. His interrogator repeatedly brought up the names of grimoires evidently of most concern to the authorities. Did Menuisier use the *Elementa magica* of 'pitri de appono' (Peter d'Abbano)? No. What about a book called the *Arbatel*? Not that either, though in further evidence he or Sanglant admitted to knowing four invocations from it. The *Ars Notoria*? No. He was clearly well versed in grimoire magic though, and confessed his knowledge of the *Clavicula Salomonis* and was asked about the *Salomonis Lemegethan*. He had also used a virgin parchment manuscript called the *Philippus Attinius onorius* consecrated to an angel named Avenel. This was obviously a copy of the *Sworn Book of Honorius* for in reference to it Menuisier mentioned the assembly of all the magicians in Athens. Towards the end of his interrogation he explained that when magic had been taught publicly in Toledo the Spanish Jews had assigned the authorship of magic books to St Paul, St Barnabé, St Leon, Charlemagne, and Albert le Grand, as well as to Abel, Enoch, and Abraham. Menuisier was hung and burned for his crimes.[75]

Vernacular grimoires also penetrated further down the social scale, though rarely to labourers and unskilled workers for reasons of cost and literacy. Sheep and cattle herders had a particular reputation for medical skills and magical powers due in part to their solitary, peripatetic lifestyle, and close relationship to the natural and therefore the occult world.[76] In Normandy there were a series of trials involving shepherds accused of stealing the Eucharist for magical purposes and other magical practices.[77] A wedding prank in Rouen had dire consequences when the bride's brother, a shepherd, decided to put on a public performance of the ligature, a well-known impotence spell involving the knotting of a piece of cord. As part of the mock ritual his accomplice, a pharmacist named Etienne Moreau, then made a show of counteracting the ligature with magic read from a grimoire. The authorities got wind of what had happened and arrested Moreau. They found in his possession 'a bad book containing many recipes and magical signs', a paper covered with strange symbols, and 'four pieces of virgin parchment containing invocations of evil spirits'.[78]

While herders were not high up the list of literate occupations in the early modern period, and occupationally they did not usually require any education other than the ability to count, the literate shepherd was a figure of respect. The vegetarian and mystic Thomas Tryon (1634–1703) learned to read from shepherds, and having tended sheep in his childhood he noted the wisdom of the shepherd over the learned gent. The 'Shepherd and Husbandman understand something of Nature; but most of the Learned are departed from the simple ways of God in Nature, putting out their own Eyes, and then boasting what Wonders they can see with other Mens.'[79] The memoirist and one-time excise officer John Cannon recalled how during his childhood in the late seventeenth century he had befriended a self-taught shepherd who introduced him to the magical arts of conjuring spirits and possessed occult books including Agrippa's *Occult Philosophy*, most likely the *Fourth Book*.[80]

There is no doubt that across Europe more and more women had access to book knowledge considered to be the rightful preserve of men. Protestantism may have encouraged the limited education of girls, but the general educated consensus was that their reading material should be restricted much more than men's. In certain circumstances women and books were seen as a toxic mix. This is certainly apparent in the realm of medicine. Women had always played an important role as simple healers, and it was accepted that they had some natural medical instincts in terms of midwifery, though that was being undermined at the time by the professionalization of the medical establishment. The idea of women of humble origin practising medicine informed by literary texts was far less acceptable. This was undoubtedly increasingly happening, though, and the rather sparse evidence of it suggests that female healers were usually obtaining their book knowledge from male practitioners. Amongst the few cases of magical healers prosecuted in eastern France we find one illiterate woman who said a surgeon for whom she worked gave her a large piece of paper containing pictures of various herbs.[81] Consider Tempel Anneke, a healer and diviner from near the city of Brunswick, in the Lutheran state of Lower Saxony, who was beheaded and burned in 1664 after being tortured into confessing to diabolic witchcraft. Anneke, a widow living with her farmer son, had been to school and could read. Her medical knowledge derived from several herbal books in her possession, from shepherds and cowherds, and from her mother who had been a maid to a barber and medical man.[82]

Similar pathways of transmission also enabled women to access grimoires. In 1739 a treasure-hunting schoolmaster's daughter, who lived near Stuttgart, confessed that a Capuchin monk had shown her a book written by Jesuits that provided instructions on how to summon a 'treasure man'.[83] Anne Bodenham, a Wiltshire cunning-woman executed for witchcraft in 1653, claimed to have been instructed in the ways of ritual magic from her time as the servant to the notorious and influential Jacobean astrologer-physician John Lambe, who was murdered by a London mob in 1628. Another seventeenth-century English cunning-woman claimed to have obtained her treasure-seeking knowledge from William Lilly.[84] Whether this was true or not, the point is that they felt it necessary to broadcast their relations with well-known male practitioners and the access that had given them to literary magic. Some prostitute-magicians also had opportunities to draw on the grimoires possessed by their regular clients. Take, for example, Gioanna La Siracusana, who had a relationship with the Maltese military engineer Vittorio Cassar, who, during the early seventeenth century, balanced his lay membership of the Order of St John with rakish behaviour and magical practices. Cassar possessed several prohibited magic manuscripts including the *Clavicule of Solomon* and a work by Peter d'Abano, which he said he had obtained from a brass-worker and friend in Messina. He had also learned Arabic from a Moorish slave who had offered to teach him astrological invocations and necromancy. Gioanna, who claimed she was illiterate, said she knew Cassar had books and writings on magic and kept them in his home, but said she did not know what they contained. Once Cassar got wind of the Inquisition's interest in his activities he hid his books and sent Gioanna to Naples on a trip so that the inquisitors would not be able to interrogate her.[85] This was a wise decision. Women were thought less able to resist the wiles and seductions of devils, and their mere propinquity to grimoires was enough to entangle them in Satan's web. In Cotentin, Normandy, in 1599, a governess named Thérèse de Brye claimed to be persecuted by spirits. On one occasion she said a demon in the form of a big black man had come down the chimney and mistreated her. The suspicion that she was not a victim to be pitied but mixed up in diabolic sorcery was confirmed when it was found she had been in contact with a *Clavicule de Solomon* and a text called *livret des Cavernes de Tolède* (*Little Book of the Toledo Caves*).[86]

With grimoires increasingly filtering down to the social level of cunning-folk, who provided numerous magical services to assuage the illnesses, fears, misfortunes, and desires of the general populace, it is not surprising that literary magic came to be an increasingly important component of popular magic. The contents of some of the grimoires with their Latin, Greek, and Hebrew names were only partially understood by many cunning-folk, who mostly came from the artisan, craftsmen tier of society. So in the early modern period the great grimoires of ritual magic were often not being used for ritual conjuration but as sources for symbols, phrases, and lists of holy and demonic names. Cunning-folk took extracts and snippets to construct written protective charms for popular consumption. In the process they took elements of learned magic out of their ritual context and repackaged them for completely different purposes. In sixteenth-century Venice, for instance, scraps of paper or parchment with brief conjurations, symbols, circles, and pentacles taken from the *Clavicule* were commonly possessed as protective talismans.[87]

Demonologists and debunkers

Concerns about the dangerous spread of grimoires were expressed by intellectuals from across Protestant and Catholic Europe. King James I and VI of England and Scotland warned the readers of his *Dæmonologie* against the evils of the *Fourth Book of Occult Philosophy*.[88] The French judge Jean Bodin denounced Agrippa's work, real and false, as the 'detestable poison of witchcraft'.[89] Writing in 1595 another French witch hunter, Nicolas Rémy, stated that 'Agrippa, Pierre d'Abano and Picatrix, three masters in damnable magic, have left more prescriptions than is necessary for the good of men.'[90] Amongst his warnings to pastors about 'superstitious' practices, the German Protestant theologian Josua Arndius (1626–86) included the use of blasphemous books of magic ascribed to Solomon.[91] The Jesuit theologian Martín Del Rio believed the spread of grimoires generated two types of implicit diabolic pacts. The first occurred 'when someone knowingly and willingly uses those superstitious signs usually employed by magicians, which he gets either from books or from conversations with magicians'. The second when 'people who, in good faith, read superstitious books, thinking they are by reputable philosophers and physicians.'[92]

Still, there was no unanimous agreement that the possession of grimoires constituted an act of heresy. Del Rio stated that bishops did not have authority to burn magic books. They were to be handed over to inquisitors to judge whether they were heretical rather than merely blasphemous. This sometimes led to acrimonious disputes. In the 1520s the Archbishop of Toulouse clashed with the Inquisition over the right to try a doctor and suspected sorcerer named Nicolas de Beaumont. At issue was whether Beaumont's alleged sorcery was truly heretical and therefore under the jurisdiction of the Inquisition. Under Canonical Law heresy constituted a transgression of the articles of Faith and the sacraments of the Church. Not all acts of magic fitted this. Beaumont had been found with books of magic and diabolic invocations, pieces of mandrake, and small human figurines. To the Inquisition this certainly smacked of explicit Satanic relations—an obvious heresy. But the Archbishop's lawyer argued that there was a distinction between adoration of the Devil and his invocation. Beaumont's paraphernalia indicated the latter, which did not constitute a heresy unless a pact could be proven. Unfortunately we do not know the ruling of the adjudicating *Parlement* of Toulouse.[93]

Demonological discourses sometimes provide historians with valuable insights into the content and use of grimoires. As Del Rio explained in his *Investigations into Magic*, he decided to bring 'to light some of the most abstruse material from the books of the magicians themselves, thus revealing their vanity, their perfidy, and their madness'.[94] Without the religious authority of someone like Del Rio, discussing magic, even with the intent of exposing its worthlessness, could be interpreted as an act of reinforcing and spreading magical knowledge. Jacques Ferrand's medical discourse on the cause, diagnosis, and cure of *melancholie erotique*, or lovesickness, which was published in 1610, fell foul of the Church in this way. As part of his survey Ferrand, a respected physician and lawyer, provided numerous details of spells and charms used to cause impotency, provoke love, and other related matters. Although he condemned such practices as a matter of course, he was denounced ten years after its publication by the Toulouse Church tribunal for teaching occult abominations and perniciously spreading magic, and copies of his book were ordered to be burned.[95]

Those demonologists who expressed scepticism regarding the reality of witch-craft, and concern over the innocent lives being wasted by the zealotry of witch hunters like Del Rio, Bodin, and Rémy, could be equally vitriolic in their detestation of grimoires and the users of grimoires. In his *De præstigiis dæmonum*, first published in 1563, Johann Weyer (1515–88), a Protestant Dutch physician and former pupil of Agrippa, devoted a chapter to identifying and denouncing the three principal printed grimoires of the period. Considering his close relationship with Agrippa, he unsurprisingly attacked the spurious *Fourth Book of Occult Philosophy*, describing it as 'pure nonsense, an undone broom with straws scattered everywhere. You can make nothing of it, even if you are an enthusiastic student of this vanity.' The *Heptameron* of Peter d'Abano was described as a 'pestilential little book', which 'should be consigned to Vulcan, among the books that may not be read', while the *Arbatel* was dismissed as 'full of magical impiety'.[96] In order to demonstrate the fallacy of charms, spells, exorcisms, and talismans, Weyer described various formulae, rites, and rituals against witches, demons, and ill-health. This, along with his Protestantism and scepticism, attracted considerable opprobrium from Reformed as well as Catholic demonologists. The Catholic Church forbade his book, and the likes of Jean Bodin accused him of spreading magic. There was an element of verifiable truth in this. The 1583 edition of *De præstigiis dæmonum* included an appendix called the *Pseudomonarchia daemonum*, which was a catalogue of the hierarchy of demons, their powers, and the means of adjuring them to appear. This was essentially a version of the manuscript lists of demons that circulated, like the *Liber centum*, though without any signs or characters. It derived from a manuscript seen by Weyer called the 'Book of the Offices of Spirits', a copy of which Trithemius had in his library. Weyer also mentions seeing an 'abominable manuscript which richly deserved to be burned' in the home of an influential nobleman.[97] Whatever the original source, this first printed list of demons represented a valuable magical resource, and circulated amongst learned spirit conjurers.[98]

A slightly altered English version of *Pseudomonarchia* was published a year later by the Elizabethan sceptic Reginald Scot in his attack on the fallacies of witchcraft, magic, and the Catholicism he believed inspired them. Scot, a rather unusual demonological writer in that he was not a clergyman, lawyer, or physician, propounded a rationalist view of religion that went beyond Weyer's own more cautious view on diabolic intervention. Yet Scot's *Discoverie of Witchcraft* was a treasure trove of magical information, providing spells, Catholic prayers, exorcisms, charms, talismans, and rituals on how to communicate with angels, demons, and the spirits of the dead. There were detailed instructions on conjuring up treasure and how to enclose a spirit in a crystal. One of Scot's main sources was a manuscript grimoire written in red and black ink entitled 'Secretum secretorum, The secret of secrets'. It was evidently used by two cunning-men rather than an occult philosopher. At the beginning of the book was the statement that it was 'invented and devised for the augmentation and maintainance of their living, for the edifieng of the poore, and for the propagating and inlarging of Gods glorie'.[99] So Scot produced what amounted to the first grimoire printed in the English language, and while he did so to prove the worthlessness of its contents he unwittingly ended up democratizing ritual magic rather than undermining it. Not long after its publication, the practical magic and protective Catholic prayers it contained were being transcribed and incorporated into manuscript grimoires.[100] The *Discoverie's* role as a grimoire was further deliberately enhanced by the addition of a 'Discourse on Devils and Spirits' to an edition printed in 1665. During the eighteenth and nineteenth centuries copies of the *Discoverie* were being used as source books by cunning-folk and, as we shall see in a later chapter, there is evidence that treasure hunters in America also employed it.[101]

The witch trials

The evidence of the witch trials does not support the demonologists' worries concerning the explicit relationship between grimoires, witchcraft, and diabolism. From a historical perspective this is hardly surprising. The vast majority of those prosecuted and executed for witchcraft were innocent of the crimes they were alleged to have committed. Furthermore, the practices of those guilty of actually attempting harmful magic, the vast majority illiterate, were mostly reliant on the store of oral knowledge regarding image magic and the like: books were not required to perform simple *maleficium*. That said, books were found on a small percentage of the relatively few cunning-folk who found themselves prosecuted for witchcraft under harsh secular laws, rather than appearing before ecclesiastical courts that dealt with the lesser crime of 'superstition'. There are a couple of cases in the Scottish trial records. One of them was a healer named Bartie Patersoune, who used herbal remedies, healing waters, and charms to cure sickness and counter bewitchment. Some of these spells and remedies were written in a manuscript which contained a SATOR AREPO word square, occult diagrams, and symbols. He was executed in 1607 for 'the crime of sorcery and witchcraft, in abusing of the people with charms and diverse sorts of inchantments, and ministering, under the form of medicine, of poisonable drinks'.[102] In the Swedish witch trial records there are also very few references to magic books. Likewise, a study of the records in the Alpine Jura region revealed 'practically no traces anywhere...of magicians taking their recipes directly from books'. In other parts of eastern France a few cases have been found. There was a doctor from Gray, Franche-Comté, charged in 1606 for, amongst other crimes, having books of magic in his house, and a former executioner of Neuchâtel who in 1668 admitted copying 'charms and diabolical practices' from a Gothic-lettered printed book dated 1602.[103] This was almost certainly a German edition of Agrippa's *Opera*.

The one place in Europe where grimoires did feature prominently in the witch trials was Iceland. Around 134 trials are known to have occurred in this former Danish territory, and nearly a third of them involved grimoires, written spells, or runes and symbols derived from them.[104] Those fortunate enough not be executed were flogged while the pages of their magic manuscripts were burned under their noses.[105] As surviving examples from the period show, the grimoires being used in this northern outpost of European culture consisted of a very distinctive blend of Continental magic, with borrowings from Solomonic texts and the like, and the Nordic runic tradition. There are even some references to Norse pagan deities. Take, for example, the runic farting spell found in a seventeenth-century *galdrabók* or grimoire that had evidently passed through several generations. It instructed the reader to write a series of runic symbols in blood on white calfskin,

> which are to afflict your belly with great shitting and shooting pains, and all these may afflict your belly with very great farting. May your bones split asunder, may your guts burst, may your farting never stop, neither day nor night. May you become as weak as the fiend, Loki, who was snared by all the gods. In your mightiest name Lord God, Spirit, Creator, Óðinn, þór, Savior, Freyr, Freyja, Oper, Satan, Beelzebub, helper, mighty God, you who protect your followers Uteos, Morss, Nokte, Vitales.

In 1656 Jón Jónsson, who was burned to death for sorcery along with his father, admitted carving such farting runes and sending them to a girl. A search of their houses turned up some grimoires and magical writings, and amongst the crimes for which they were convicted Jónsson confessed to using a Solomonic sign to cure one of his calves that had been afflicted by the Devil.[106]

Another distinctive aspect of the Icelandic experience is that only ten of the 128 people known to have been tried by the island's highest court were women.[107] This is extraordinary considering that in Denmark and Norway, and in Iceland's southern neighbour, Scotland, the vast majority were female.[108] One explanation for this emerges from a comparison with Finland where the majority of accused were also men, in contrast with trials in the homeland of its Swedish rulers. Maybe the Norwegian settlers who came to Iceland from the late ninth century onwards brought with them strong elements of the male shamanic cultures of the Saami, which continued to shape the magical tradition of Finland and northern Scandinavia into the early modern period.[109] We need to be clear though, that although accusations of simple harmful witchcraft (rather than full-blown Continental diabolism) were usually the basis of the accusations in Iceland, most of those accused were not witches but rather cunning-folk or *fjölkynngisfólk* ('wise people'). The shaman connection may have some mileage, but Iceland's magic was based much more on literary magic than that of the 'shamanistic', spirit-inspired traditions of Finland. So why did book magic assume such importance?

Iceland had one of the most impressive literacy rates in early modern Europe, thanks in part to the comparative ease with which the Lutheran church controlled and educated a small, albeit dispersed population. The enduring relevance of the island's impressive medieval literary tradition of the sagas and poetry has also been cited as an influence.[110] Maybe the strength of the grimoire tradition rests on this successful programme of education, and the consequent ability of the vast majority of men on the island to explore and exploit literary magic for personal as well as commercial gain. On several occasions in the seventeenth century school pupils were expelled for dabbling with grimoires.[111] Then again, literacy rates were equally impressive in Sweden, and as we have seen magic books were comparatively uncommon in the trials there. So, the importance of rune magic, effective through the act of depiction, may have also generated a strong tradition of writing magic in Icelandic popular culture. For both reasons, when neighbourly accusations of witchcraft formed, the involvement of literary means of inflicting harmful magic would more likely be suspected than elsewhere in Europe's villages.

The first person to be sentenced for witchcraft in Reformation Iceland was a minister named Oddur Gottskálksson, who was found guilty of rape supposedly inspired by the magic contained in grimoires found in his possession. Over a century later the Reverend Árni Jónsson fled the country and sailed to England after six parishioners accused him and another man of practising harmful magic.[112] Across Europe, clergymen are similarly occasionally to be found amongst those accused of witchcraft. In western France the fear of priests employing an impotence spell known as the *nouement de l'aiguillette* (knotting of the cord) during marriage ceremonies was deeply engrained in popular culture. In 1632 a clergyman of Azay-le-Brûlé was repeatedly accused of the crime by a frustrated married couple, and in 1650 another priest was charged with the crime and for demanding fees for countering the spell. A few years later a priest took out a defamation suit after similar accusations.[113]

It did not take much for such accusations to become full-blown cases of witchcraft attracting judicial interest from ardent witch hunters. So it is not surprising that a clutch of French witch trials concerned the French priesthood and their grimoires. The French judge Pierre de Lancre gave considerable thought to the problem of these 'witch priests'. He had tried five of them himself in southwest France and noted that three others had fled to Spain and Navarre before he could get his hands on them. He also related the trial of Pierre Aupetit, a village priest in Limousin, who in 1598 confessed under torture to attending a witches' sabbat: 'he took a certain book there that he read, a book he had later burned, fearing the authorities. The book was written as a printed text, with strange words that he did not understand at all.'[114] In 1603 a scandalous Normandy priest named Godevent was sentenced to be hanged and burned. Amongst his crimes were the use of a magic mirror for finding lost goods, the possession of a booklet of twelve to fifteen pages used for countering spells, and a virgin parchment inscribed with magical characters and invocations to call up devils.[115] Another sensational trial concerned Louis Gaufridy, the priest of a parish near Marseille, who was executed in 1611 for 'kidnapping, seduction, impiety, magic, witchcraft and other abominations'. The case was one of several scandalous French possession and exorcism cases involving nuns, where the accusations of witchcraft were caught up in a swirl of political and religious intrigue. One of the nuns, the daughter of a local nobleman, speaking on her own behalf and that of the twenty-four demons tormenting her, identified Gaufridy as the witch responsible for her plight. These demons told her exorcists that Gaufridy kept a library of magic books in his rooms. Acting on this diabolic tip-off, his premises were searched but nothing suspect was found. Later, languishing in prison, he confessed to trying to wed the nun to the Devil and of attending a witches' sabbat. As to his alleged magic books, he said he had burned the one he owned and the ashes could still be found in the grate.[116]

Suspicious minds

The democratization of grimoires through the circulation of print and vernacular manuscripts, the growth of literacy, and social mobility occurred despite the concerted attempts to control the book trade. As early as 1475 the Pope gave a licence to the University of Cologne to censor printers, publishers, authors, and readers.[117] This tendency accelerated rapidly during the Reformation period, with secular and religious authorities across Europe producing lists of prohibited books to prevent the spread of heresies and limit the influence of non-Christian religions. By far the most influential, though, were the papal *Indexes of Prohibited Books* produced from 1559 onwards. The 1559 *Index* followed a Venetian list produced five years earlier in banning works of geomancy, hydromancy, pyromancy, and necromancy, but then broadened out to cover all magic arts along with chiromancy, physiognomy, and other branches of divination. Of those books specifically mentioned, the most pertinent to our study were the *Clavicule of Solomon*, already condemned in the Venetian *Index*, the books of Hermes, and the works of Agrippa. A 1586 papal bull of Sixtus V further reinforced the censorship of books on judicial astrology.[118] As one historian has pointed out, though, these published *Indexes* were probably counter-productive in that they served to inform and excite public interest in the very books of magic they were meant to suppress.[119] It is possible that the booming market for the *Clavicule* in early modern Italy was fuelled in part by its explicit mention in the *Indexes*.

In 1559 the Spanish Inquisitor General Don Fernando de Valdés ordered the publication of the first of numerous Spanish editions of the *Index*, which followed the papal template closely and included eight Latin works on astrology, Kabbalah, and the occult sciences.[120] The Spanish Inquisition generated the reputation as being the most ruthless persecutor and censor of books. Some early historians have depicted it as being so influential that it retarded Spanish intellectual life until the nineteenth century.[121] But it was not as effective as some have depicted it, as some inquisitors pointed out at the time.

During the first few decades of its existence the Spanish Inquisition was mostly concerned with rooting out heresy amongst *conversos*—that is, Jews converted, mostly forcibly, to Christianity. For the inquisitors the possession of Jewish texts was a sure sign that *conversos* were secretly practising Judaism, and so a ruthless campaign of rooting out and burning such books was instituted. As records show, their owners secreted them down wells and buried them in gardens in order to evade the Inquisition and the neighbours who spied for it. Yet despite all their attentions the Inquisition could not prevent Jewish texts being smuggled in from Italy and the Netherlands.[122] While the Italian Inquisition was primarily set up to counter the threat of Protestantism from over the Alps, it also targeted Jews and their books. In 1553 many thousands of Hebrew works were destroyed in an orgy of book burning across the Italian states. Fifteen years later in Venice, a major centre of Jewish publishing, the authorities instituted another round-up and burned thousands more copies of the Talmud and other Jewish texts. This occurred despite the fact that the *Index of Prohibited Books* issued in 1564 had permitted the Talmud, albeit in an expurgated form and as long is it was not explicitly entitled the Talmud.[123]

The campaign against Jewish books was not only about the heresy of converted Jews secretly practising Judaism, but also about their perceived and real magical activities. For many Christians as well as Jews, Hebrew words were in themselves thought magical, and so for Catholic and Protestant theologians they were obvious pollutants of the Christian faith. In 1529 the Spanish Franciscan Martín de Castañega warned,

> It is vanity, lack of faith, superstition, and even a judaizing trick to use the name of the ancient Hebrew in Catholic and Christian invocations as if the old names were worth more than the new ones. They are especially dangerous for those with little knowledge, because they may say other unknown and diabolical words with those Hebrew and Greek ones.[124]

In fact, to expunge potent Hebrew holy names from the Christian vocabulary would have required the censoring of many Catholic exorcisms. The Hebrew magic word AGLA, for example, which is an acrostic of the phrase 'You are mighty forever my Lord', was used in numerous Catholic exorcisms, including those of Menghi, as well as being a common magical name in grimoires. It was this synergy that inspired Martin Luther to lump together and denounce the 'word magic' of witches, Muslims, Catholics, and Jews.[125]

Suspicions about the use of Hebrew texts emerged in the early seventeenth-century French court intrigue that led to the execution for witchcraft of Léonora Galigaï, one of Maria de Medici's ladies-in-waiting. Her friendship with a Portuguese Jewish doctor and occultist named Philothée Montalto was considered highly suspect. It was alleged that she had talked at length with him regarding the magic and talismans contained in Hebrew 'grimoires' that had been found at his home. She denied the charge but to no avail.[126] There were, of course, Jewish cunning-folk just as there were Christian and Islamic ones, each using their respective religious texts for healing, divination, and making protective charms. Written amulets have been described as constituting 'the most powerful elements of Jewish magic'. Their contents were not necessarily Kabbalistic. They usually referred to the angels, and contained biblical quotes, pentacles, hexagrams, *zahlenquadrats* or magic squares, and pentagrams. Here is one brief example that was to be written on parchment in order to win favour:

> Hasdiel at my right, Haniel at my left, Rahmiel at my head, angels, let me find favour and grace before all men, great and small, and before all of whom I have need, in the name of Yah Yah Yah Yau Yau Yau Yah Zebaot. Amen Amen Amen Selah.[127]

They were, then, very similar to non-Jewish written charms, but the fact they were written in Hebrew was their unique selling point for Christians. In 1643

Domenico Temponi told the Venetian tribunal that a Jew had taught him that to find hidden treasure he should write Hebrew words on a piece of paper and place it under the wing of a white cockerel.[128] Where Jews were allowed to practise their faith, as in the Venetian ghetto, Christians also consulted them. Take Isacco Levi, for instance, a Venetian Jew accused by several Catholics of detecting stolen property by magical means. One said he had seen in Levi's room books of magic including a work by the medieval Spanish mystic Raymond Lull, the Proverbs of Solomon, and most curiously a Kabbalistic manuscript attributed to Pope Urban VIII. Levi was also accused of making copies for sale. The Inquisition called in a converted Jew to assess the content of the books and manuscripts they confiscated from Levi, and he concluded that none of them were openly magical.[129]

A Jew practising magic was not heresy but a converted Jew doing likewise was a quite different matter, and of great interest to the Inquisition. One who came to their attention was a poor, restless convert called Giovanni Battista Bonaventura, who was tried for heretical blasphemy in 1632. He had converted to Islam before then converting to Christianity, leaving his Jewish wife in the ghetto. Giovanni was another of those many men dissatisfied with their modest place in life and who desired a way to instant wealth. Before his baptism he had confessed to the officiating priest that he had wanted to find treasure, and handed over a basketful of magic books and writings to be burned. He also admitted to owning some 'little books' in Hebrew on astrology, dreams, and medicine. Fortunately the Inquisition decided he was no heretic and he was given a spiritual rather than corporal punishment for his religious vanities.[130] The Spanish Inquisition continued to keep its eye on such people right to the end of its existence. In 1776 the Barcelona tribunal investigated a weaver named Juan Soler accused of being a 'heretic, stained with Judaism because of the Hebrew words he combines with conjurations'.[131]

Moriscos, that is, converted Moors, were another heretical 'enemy within' that preoccupied the Spanish Inquisition in particular. The possession of any sort of Arabic texts led to suspicions of secret Islamic worship. The tribunal of Saragossa alone investigated nearly one hundred *moriscos* for carrying *alherces* on their person. These were small pieces of paper or parchment containing verses from the Koran that served as protective talismans.[132] Whether this proved they were practising Islam is another matter, for Spanish Christians also employed *alherces*. Due to its geographic position and naval importance in the Mediterranean, Malta was another region where Arabic magic permeated Christian society. There were around 3,000 Muslim slaves on the island at the end of the sixteenth century, due largely to the crusading activities of the knights of the Order of St John. The Italian-run Maltese Inquisition kept a close eye on their contact with islanders. Muslim slaves were in particular demand by the island's treasure seekers. Islam was outlawed and so the only ones ostensibly practising were the enslaved or crypto-Muslims who risked persecution from the Inquisition. During the early seventeenth century the Canon of the Mdina Cathedral dug up part of his basement believing former Jewish occupants had buried a treasure under his house. Finding nothing he followed the advice of a Cypriot Greek that he should consult a certain Muslim galley-slave. The slave brought a book with him and began to read from it as he paced the basement. His consultation revealed that to obtain the treasure the ritual sacrifice of a black hen was required. After handing over some valuables, the Canon eventually realized he was being defrauded. Unfortunately for the clergyman the Inquisition got to hear of what had been going on.[133]

For the Catholic Church, Protestantism may have been a diabolic heresy but it was not seen as inherently magical. Yet the authoritarian control of printing in the Mediterranean was closely tied to the Protestant threat, and Spanish disquiet over the leaky Pyrenees shaped enduring perceptions of the source of illicit magic and grimoires. In 1569 an inquisitor in Catalonia remarked, 'an inquisitor is needed here in order to frighten the people from France.'[134] The concerns were justified to a certain degree. During the second half of the sixteenth century numerous Frenchmen sought work across the border in Spain, particularly in Catalonia and Aragon. Amongst them were numerous print workers, many of whom were trained in the major publishing centres of Lyon and Geneva, which also happened to be centres of Calvinism. The authorities' fears were also exacerbated by reports of concerted efforts to flood the country with Reformist literature, such as the testimony of a Catholic merchant in 1568 that he had seen large numbers of Protestant books stacked in Lyon awaiting transit to Spain. On the western side of the Pyrenees the situation also caused considerable concern. In 1609 the abbot of Urdax in the Basque region complained that on the route from Bayonne in southwestern France right down to Pamplona there was not one Inquisition agent in position to examine the mule caravans for heretical books.[135]

It should be noted that the French authorities on the other side of the Pyrenees were hardly inactive themselves. In 1547 the archdiocese of Toulouse instructed clergy and civil officials to visit all booksellers in the city, and between 1530 and 1560 the *Parlement* of Toulouse charged some forty people with possessing heretical books. The authorities were particularly suspicious of anyone associated with Geneva, and a royal edict of 1551 instructed that those bearing books from Calvin's city were to be prosecuted 'as heretics and disturbers of public peace and tranquillity'.[136]

Protestantism was not the only heresy the Spanish authorities feared from the north. Over the centuries inquisitors dealt with numerous French magicians and treasure hunters. In 1511 a priest named Joan Vicente and three conspirators were tried for sorcery by the Saragossa tribunal. Vicente, who was originally from

Perpignan, a French town at the base of the eastern Pyrenees, was in possession of a copy of the *Clavicule of Solomon* and other magical manuscripts. They had been transcribed by a notary named Miguel Sánchez from books Vicente said were from Rome. One of them was a work called the *Clavicule of Virgil*, which contained the characters of a hundred demons and the method of conjuring them. The magicians managed to burn their magic books and manuscripts before the Inquisition got their hands on them, and Vicente and Sánchez later escaped from prison. The frustrated inquisitors burned them in effigy instead.[137] In 1668 a French Franciscan was condemned to three years reclusion by the Saragossa tribunal for possessing forbidden books and treasure hunting. At the end of the century the Inquisition tortured and questioned a young *morisco* healer named Jeronimo Espinel from the village of Torrellas, who had been engaged in exorcizing the possessed. He claimed he 'had read much in Castilian universities, including the Pentacles of Solomon'. More to the point, he had also acquired magical knowledge from two Frenchmen who aided him in finding buried treasure.[138]

Concerns over the spread of witches and magicians from France reached fever pitch in 1609 when a major witch hunt was launched in the neighbouring Basque French region of the Pays de Labourd. One of the two judges who zealously pursued the investigation, Pierre de Lancre, described how witches 'were fleeing in great numbers both by land and sea . . . and the crowd at the frontier grew larger by the hour. They professed to be travelling pilgrims on the way to Santiago.' Two French agents were sent into Spain to try and find and arrest one suspected female ringleader of the witches. The local inquisitors, although fairly sceptical regarding the accusations against the fleeing French witches, were concerned that this foreign invasion would still 'do great harm' to the realm.[139]

The fear of magical traffic was not all one way. Throughout the sixteenth and seventeenth centuries French demonologists had blamed foreigners, Savoyards and Italians in particular, with introducing and spreading the plague of witchcraft and sorcery across the kingdom. The French lawyer Jean Bodin (1530–96) identified one such source of diabolic infection. 'In the year 1568,' he declared, 'the Italians and Spaniards going to the Low Countries carried notes full of sorceries that had been given them as guarantees against all misfortunes.'[140] He was referring to what is known as the Spanish Road, the hugely important military and trade route running down eastern France to northwestern Italy, which was crucial for fuelling the Spanish military occupation of the Low Countries. Such suspicions over foreigners and the viral texts they carried were born out by cases such as that reported in a pamphlet in 1610. It related how the *Parlement* of Bordeaux had arrested four itinerant Spaniards, three men and a woman, for being magicians and witches. The group had apparently wandered all over Italy,

Flanders, and France offering their services, and stood accused of killing livestock and harming crops. When the authorities searched their bags they found 'several books, characters, notes, wax, knives, parchments and other items used in magic'. They said they had learned their magical arts in Toledo.[141] As we have seen, tensions across the southwestern border were high at the time due to the witch hunt carried out by de Lancre. While the Spanish authorities were concerned about witches fleeing in their direction, de Lancre warned of the Spanish *saludadores* or cunning-folk coming the other way to make money from curing witchcraft. This was compounded by the many Moors making their way across the Pyrenees after a mass expulsion in 1609. De Lancre described one *saludador* named Dom Pedro who was active in the region around the town of Bayonne. 'I don't know if he was one of them, or whether the Great Moor Satan had left him in this country to take advantage of its people,' he said. Dom Pedro managed to evade the French authorities and de Lancre pondered whether 'he returned to Spain to tell the other *saludadores* that it would do them no good to come to France.'[142]

The Inquisitions clearly failed to control the flow of magic manuscripts. In fact they circulated more widely then ever before. A decree of the Congregation of the Holy Office issued in 1573 ordered the burning of all books of magic confiscated and archived by the tribunals because the numbers of them were becoming unmanageable.[143] This fact in itself shows how the Church was losing the battle. They were, however, pretty effective in controlling the development of the printing industry, in Spain in particular. Yet the restrictions merely led to a flourishing Spanish language publishing industry outside the country and the development of smuggling operations that funnelled large numbers of forbidden Spanish books produced by printers in France, Germany, and the Netherlands.[144] In Italy, which was not a unified country and therefore had no centralized secular authority other than the Papacy, it was one thing for the Church to issue edicts about inspecting and suppressing booksellers but they were not necessarily carried out with any real conviction by the various city-states and principalities. In Venice, for instance, the printed works of Agrippa could be purchased to order from booksellers who used their contacts abroad to smuggle in copies. One such Venetian book dealer, Pietro Longo, had previously worked in Basel and Strasburg. In 1586 he obtained a work by Agrippa for a Bolognese visitor to Venice, and admitted to giving another Agrippa to a nobleman, and a book by Peter d'Abano to a ducal secretary. His son in England was one of his suppliers. Longo paid a terrible price for trading in such books and was drowned on the orders of the Inquisition in 1588.[145] Such harsh punishment evidently did not work as a deterrent. Several Venetian occult booksellers were investigated in the 1640s, including Boniface Cabiana who was reported to deal 'in C. Agrippa and a book with little signs and secret circles'.[146] Furthermore, Italy and Italians seem to have been an important source of the Agrippan works and grimoires that circu-lated in Portugal in the period.[147]

The legacy of the Inquisitions is evident from the fact that while the boom in populist publishing during the eighteenth century led to a massive proliferation of cheap grimoires, little was produced in Italy or Spain: the flow of books was decidedly from north to south. In Protestant countries and in Catholic areas where the Inquisition did not operate, the ecclesiastical and secular authorities had a much harder time in controlling the expansion of illicit magic publishing.

Loving it

Towards the end of the sixteenth century the Inquisitions' attentions began to shift away from heresy towards 'superstition' and moral crimes. Both of these were embodied in the activities of prostitutes who not only engaged in illicit sexual behaviour but also used and traded in magic.[148] Some offered to ensure the gambling success of their clients. In 1627 one man testified to the Venetian tribunal that a prostitute had told him how to conjure the soul of Judas to reveal the names of the victors in a forthcoming election.[149] But it was love magic that generated the most concern. As one inquisitorial manual explained:

> To make men come to their dwellings they perform many sortileges [acts of sorcery]. They sweep the hearth, they cast salt in the fire, they bless beans, they tie ribbons into knots while they are at Mass. And while making these knots they pronounce unknown words, but lascivious and most indecent against this holy sacrifice.[150]

Finding out what these 'unknown words' were and where they learned them was one of the tasks of the inquisitors. An ordinance of the Milan tribunal in 1605 listed as a particularly female problem the profane use and false attribution of prayers to Saint Daniel, Saint Martha, Saint Cyprian, Saint Helen, and others.[151] The prayer to Saint Martha to provoke love was particularly widespread across the Mediterranean during the sixteenth and seventeenth centuries. Legend had it that, after Christ's Ascension, Martha, who was the sister of Mary Magdalene and Lazarus, travelled across the sea to Tarascon in Provence, where she killed a fearsome dragon called la Tarasque and introduced Christianity to the people.[152] The nature of the prayer's content was revealed during an inquisitor's visit to New Granada (Trinidad) in 1568, where he investigated the activities of a magical practitioner named María de Medina. She possessed a written copy, which ran:

My Lady Saint Martha, worthy you are and saintly. By my Lord Jesus Christ you were cherished and loved; by my Lady the Virgin Mary you were hosted and welcomed. To the mount of Talarçon you went and beheld the live serpent; with your hyssop of water you sprinkled it and with your holy girdle you bound and delivered it unto the people. Just as this is true, bring so-and-so unto me, who was the person she desired to come to her, calm, placid, and bound of hand and foot and heart so that he should love me and call me his lady and take pleasure in no one, if not me.[153]

Literacy rates for women remained stubbornly low in Spain and Italy. A study of the early modern Inquisition records of Toledo indicates that some 87 per cent of women were illiterate over the period, and a similar figure has been estimated for women in sixteenth-century Italy.[154] But women, even illiterate women, were evidently taking advantage of literary magic and print culture, servicing both a female and a literate male clientele in the love magic market. This is most evident from the lively trade in *cartas di voler bene*, as they were known in Italy. These were pieces of paper or parchment on which prayers, spells and magical symbols were written and their power was activated by it touching the person desired.[155]

A study of prostitutes investigated by the Inquisition in Modena reveals that although magical orations and charms were learned orally and, as one said, were kept 'always in her heart', those who could read were thought to be the most skilled in the art of love magic. Written copies accrued more potency than those held in oral memory, while those recorded in books were more efficacious than charms written on loose sheets. In 1600 a noted female love magician was described as reading from a big book with 'a black cover, which is full of incantations and secrets'. One prostitute said the prayer she had written on a piece of paper was less effective than another possessed by a courtesan who obtained hers from 'a book in which there are lots of these things'.[156] At the top of this hierarchy of texts was print, and the Modena tribunal heard several cases of prostitute love magicians requesting printers to produce versions of the prayers they knew. This may have been in part to render their power more potent, but the sale of such mass-produced prayers also proved an excellent money-spinner.

There were many female love magicians who were not prostitutes of course, and one of the most well known in mid-seventeenth century Venice was Laura Malipiero, who ostensibly obtained an income running a boarding house. When Inquisition agents searched her premises they found written spells and herbal books, but it was the several copies of the *Clavicule of Solomon* in various stages of completion, which included sections on 'sacrifices for spirits and how to sacrifice', that most interested them. Although Laura said she could not read and that they belonged to one of her lodgers, it is likely that this entrepreneurial woman was involved in the city's thriving black market in grimoires. Another well-known Venetian cunning-woman, Lucia Barozzi, possessed a parchment protective charm containing pentacles, circles, and the names of spirits, and had many copies made to sell on to clients.[157]

So the high rates of illiteracy were not a barrier to the *exploitation* of literary magic, but the vast majority of grimoires still continued to rest in the hands of men rather than women. The illiterate could make play of possessing grimoires, deal in them, and have charms copied from them for resale, but they could not, without aid, actually employ much of the magic they contained. The male dominance of treasure hunting, for instance, has more to do with the lack of most women's ability to *read* grimoires than any engrained gendered division of magical practice in society.

The Devil's book

When questioned by the Inquisition, Father Cesare Lanza, the treasure hunter we met earlier, spoke freely about what he saw as the diminished power of ancient, high magic, and made the telling comment, 'Today a lowly little woman does more than all the necromancers accomplished in the ancient world. Moreover there is not a person who is not wearing some kind of charm with characters.'[158] Maybe he was thinking in terms of the role women evidently played in simple folk magic, but Lanza was speaking at a time when the witch persecution was in full swing, and demonologists found in the witch trials ample evidence that women were more prone to the temptations of the Devil—the inspiration for all magic.

Across Europe many accused witches confessed, often but not always under torture, that they had made a pact with the Devil. This was what the authorities wanted to hear as it confirmed their theological fears of a global satanic conspiracy. Judging from the evidence of the confessions, which were usually shaped by the leading questions of judges and magistrates, there were several ways in which the pact was sealed. Being seduced into sex with the Devil was common for female witches, and the act of the Devil making a secret, indelible mark on the body of his servants was also widely assumed regarding witches of both genders. In parts of England the adoption of suckling spirit familiars became another vehicle of perpetuating satanic relations.[159] The concept of the written pact between witches and the Devil has received less attention from historians, and yet throws up interesting questions about contemporary views of women, literacy, and books.

The trial evidence shows clearly that the learned and popular conception of the witches' written pact was distinct from that of the classic Faustian pact. The latter, an almost exclusively literate male crime, was an act of ritual magic involving the drawing up of a contract by the pact maker that was then presented to the Devil. The usual scenario regarding primarily female witches was a reversal of this process, in that it was the Devil who presented a book or parchment to potential witches and tempted them to sign it. In other words the witch was not the instigator in this pact and there was no bargaining involved. As with sex, the Devil seduced women into signing it.

The signing of the Devil's book or parchment is a comparatively uncommon means of pact-making in the trial records of Continental Europe. The most influential example, and one repeated by several seventeenth-century demonologists, concerned the charge against fourteen women executed for witchcraft in the papal territory of Avignon in 1582: 'that [so] the Father of Lies should have a care to delete and obliterate you from the book of life you did at his direction and command with your own hands write your names in the black book there prepared, the roll of the wicked condemned to eternal death'.[160] As this suggests, then, the Devil's book is basically an inversion of the biblical notion of the Book of Life mentioned in the Old Testament and most prominently in Revelations in the New Testament.[161] So while the Book of Life is a record of all the righteous elected to salvation by God, or contains the names of those for whom Christ died, the Devil's book is a ledger of damnation. One's name cannot be in both.

Most women at the time were illiterate, so the act of signing the book would have limited this diabolic strategy. The English clergyman Richard Bernard (1568–1641), who was heavily influenced by Continental demonological writings, observed that the Devil's pact was 'uttered either by word of mouth, of such as cannot write; or in writing by others'.[162] There were ways around the literacy problem. The Devil could offer a helping hand of course. In 1645 a Norfolk woman confessed that the Devil in the guise of a tall black man conversed with her one moonlit night and cut her hand with a penknife; she wrote her name in his book with the blood, her hand being guided by him.[163] Just as with legal documents at the time, the illiterate could also sign themselves with a cross. One of the women accused at Salem said the Devil in the guise of a black man 'brought a book & she touched it with a stick that was dipt in an ink horne & it made a red mark'.[164] In English cases it is mostly the Devil who actually puts the names of the witches in his book, the physical link required to seal the pact being enacted by writing with the witches' blood. Anne Leach confessed that the Devil drew blood from under her tongue with which he wrote her name on a piece of paper, while Margaret Wyard said he fetched blood from her thigh and wrote on a paper with it. Intriguingly we find a similar preponderance of such accounts in the witch trials of eighteenth-century Hungary. One woman prosecuted in 1746 described how the Devil dressed in a blue caftan 'hit her in the nose, with the blood issuing from there he entered her name in a book', and another accused witch said the Devil entered her name in his book 'with a pen dipped in blood from her little finger'.[165]

Parts of eastern Hungary were Calvinist and it is possible that if such cases were mapped on to the region's confessional map, they might confirm a direct connection between the Devil's book and Calvinism. It is certainly the case that most examples of written witch pacts in England were recorded during the Puritan ascendancy of the Civil War period, and in particular during the East Anglian witch hunt orchestrated by the puritan witch-finder Matthew Hopkins between 1645 and 1647. It is likely the written pact became more prominent at this time due to the Puritan parliamentary emphasis on signing or marking oaths and covenants, such as the Protestation Oath of 1641, the Vow and Covenant of 1643, and the Solemn League and Covenant of 1644. Those who took these oaths or covenants were required to swear them aloud and then sign their names or put their marks in columns on a parchment, roll, or book containing the oath or covenant. For this reason they are important documents for assessing literacy rates at the time.[166] While these covenants were inspired by national political agendas they represented personal commitments, symbolizing individual battles with conscience, and the tormentor Satan. Those who broke them were repeatedly warned of God's judgement. It is understandable, then, that in Puritan-influenced popular cultures at this time entering into 'a solemn league' with the Devil would be conceived as much in terms of a written as a sexual pact.[167]

Although the Devil's book was not a grimoire the two were easily conflated in the minds of the suspicious, particularly with regard to women. If, as some demonologists believed, the mere possession of grimoires constituted an implicit pact, the Eve-inspired curiosity of women would more likely lead them to explicit relations with the Devil. This notion is evident from the 1653 trial of the Wiltshire cunning-woman Anne Bodenham. To impress her clients she made a lot of the fact that she possessed books of magic. These were used to help her clients, but once she was accused of witchcraft the possession of occult works became associated with the Devil's book. Languishing in gaol she wearily confessed that she had a red book which 'was written half over with blood (being the names of witches that had listed themselves under the Devil's command)'.[168]

Colonial fears

One might have thought that controlling the circulation of forbidden books would have proved a much easier task in the Spanish and Portuguese colonies. Yet right from the beginning the censors faced serious difficulties in suppressing the influx of prohibited literature, which arrived not only via Spanish and Portuguese ships but also traders from France and the Low Countries, the main sources of illicit Spanish publications. An inventory of books to be shipped by a dealer in Seville to Mexico in 1600 included works by Della Porta, Albertus Magnus, Alexis Piemontese, and Paracelsus. While none of the titles were explicitly magical in nature, these were names that would have immediately aroused the suspicion of any ecclesiastical censor.[169] Furthermore, colonial ecclesiastical libraries that housed forbidden books were frequently robbed.[170] Those with good social standing did not need to go to such lengths as they could apply to consult the libraries on pious or legitimate scientific grounds. The doctor Cristóbal Méndez, tried for sorcery by the Mexican Inquisition in 1538, testified that he had learned the art of making silver and gold astrological medallions for health and fortune from books he had read in the cathedral library in Mexico City.[171]

A permanent Inquisition was never established in the Portuguese colony of Brazil, so a Visitor General was sent there to try cases three or four times on lengthy visits between 1591 and 1650. The first couple of visits were motivated primarily by concerns over the activities of *conversos* and, to a lesser extent, the influence of Protestantism and Islam. But dozens of cases of magic and 'superstition' were also heard. A detailed study of trials in the Brazilian province of Pernambuco between 1590 and 1810 reveals that of 692 crimes heard by the Inquisition 57 concerned witchcraft and magic, but only 3 concerned the possession of prohibited books. Most concerned Portuguese colonists rather than indigenous peoples or African slaves. Cases of female love magic were prominent, along with witchcraft and magical healing. Seven people came forward to denounce one Maria Gonçalves, for instance, who they accused of carrying the bones of hanged criminals to protect herself from the authorities, and with speaking with demons.[172]

On the other side of the continent, in Peru, the Spanish set up a tribunal in Lima, which tried some three thousand people or so during its existence. Twelve per cent of them concerned magic and 'superstition', mostly involving the lowest strata of society, including slaves and poor women, particularly midwives and prostitutes, amongst whom written and oral prayers to Saint Martha were popular.[173] Several monks were investigated for making diabolic pacts. In the 1580s printed and manuscript books of chiromancy were found on a priest named Fernando de Cuevas, chaplain of the city's Carmelite convent. Its most famous defendant was the famed Spanish sailor and explorer Pedro Sarmiento (1532–92), the author of *The History of the Incas*, and one-time captive of Walter Raleigh's fleet. He found himself hauled before the Lima tribunal on several occasions. One time he was accused of having books of magic and prayers that allowed him to invoke the Devil, and on another occasion of possessing magic rings and magic ink which made love letters irresistible to their female readers.[174] A Neapolitan named Jerónimo de Caracciolo was also accused of possessing books of magic. But the only concrete evidence of the use of a grimoire in Peru concerns an embroiderer, Diego de la Rosa, who was accused of necromancy in 1580.[175] He possessed a manuscript in his own handwriting 'with many characters, Greek and Hebrew letters and other evil things', which he had lent to others to make copies. Its contents contained a familiar blend of spells and conjurations to attract women, fly through the air, become invisible, and find hidden treasure. The pig-tailed de la Rosa's other crime was spending too much time with native Indian witch doctors who instructed him in the use of magical herbs.

In terms of the flow and quantity of forbidden books in circulation in the Spanish Americas it was the Mexican censors who had the most work to do in stemming the tide. A fascinating insight into the challenge they faced is provided by the story of the library of Melchor Pérez de Soto, a Mexico City architect arrested by the Inquisition in 1665, charged with practising astrology and sorcery, and owning prohibited books on the subject. The Inquisition confiscated 1,592 volumes, which meant that Pérez de Soto must have had one of the most extensive private libraries in the colony, particularly for someone of a relatively modest social position. A fifth of his books consisted of fables, novels, poetry, treatise on language, and the like, mostly in Spanish but also some in Latin, Italian, Portuguese, and French. Books on mathematics, astronomy, military science, architecture, medicine, religion, and history formed a major part of the rest of the collection. As to the charges against him, he certainly possessed numerous learned discourses on astrology, two works on physiognomy, and an early sixteenth-century treatise on alchemy.

While still under investigation Pérez de Soto was killed by his prison cellmate. The Inquisitorial censors sifted meticulously through his books, identifying those that could be returned to his widow, those that needed to be expurgated, and those that were to be confiscated and destroyed. Most of the expurgated volumes were works of astronomy. The censors identified ten works that required further investigation. One of them was della Porta's book on cryptography, *De occultis literarum notis*. They probably suspected that it contained information similar to that in his *Natural Magic*. Of the books clearly forbidden there were several on judicial astrology, but none were titles that contained conjurations. Some were withheld because they committed the offence of not stating the date, publisher, and place of publication, while others were published in such heretical places as Amsterdam. An Italian edition of Piemontese's *Secrets* caused some consternation to the censors as only the Spanish edition was listed in the Spanish *Index*, while a book falsely attributed to Peter d'Abano led to some head scratching.[176]

Less innocent was the library and activities of Pedro Ruiz Calderón, who arrived in Mexico over a century before Pérez de Soto's tragic experience with the Inquisition. Ruiz Calderón, a priest, was a boastful chap and a charlatan who sometimes passed himself off as a papal legate or inquisitor. On his arrival in Mexico in the late 1530s he had been quick to broadcast his vaunted skills in the art of magic. Rumour had it that he could make himself invisible, that he could magically transport himself to Spain and back at will, and that he had power over women. Regarding the latter, his powers of invisibility came in handy while fleeing cuckolds. He said he accrued much of his knowledge during a sojourn in the Levant where he had trained amongst wizards and received lessons in Chaldean, Hebrew, and Greek. Then there was a further trip to Germany to take an apprenticeship in alchemy, and on to Paris to learn how to cast out demons. Ruiz Calderón had brought his library of occult works with him, one of which he claimed contained the signature of the prince of Devils which he had obtained in Italy during a brief descent into Hell. In the somewhat claustrophobic world of colonial Mexico it was perhaps inevitable that such boasting would soon attract the attention of the Inquisition. In 1540 Ruiz Calderón was arrested and his books confiscated. As in Pérez de Soto's case, the censors closely scrutinized them. As befitted a priest, there were pious works and breviaries, Dominican sermons and philosophical works. They also found a copy of Albertus Magnus's *Secrets*, an exorcism manual, and a book by the thirteenth-century scientist and alchemist Arnold de Villanova, probably the *Treasure of Treasures*. Apparently no identifiable grimoires were found, and certainly not the one containing the Devil's signature—much to the inquisitors' disappointment. Ruiz Calderón got off fairly lightly, being sentenced to banishment in Spain and prohibited from saying Mass for two years. Immediately after the sentencing, however, he had to be taken to hospital. As the concluding paragraphs of his trial records note, this irrepressible and foolish boaster continued to regale his fellow inmates with stories of his magical accomplishments and told of other books of magic in his possession that had not been confiscated.[177]

Despite suspicions and accusations most of the occult books in the early colonies seem to have been divinatory rather than magical, with almanacs and learned astrological treatises circulating quite widely across Spanish America.[178] This may help explain the surprisingly few cases of magical treasure hunting heard by the overseas Inquisitions. Ruiz Calderón certainly boasted of his ability to discover pre-conquest treasures and claimed several conquistadors had hired his services for this purpose. In 1622 the Lima tribunal heard the case of two men accused of using sorcery to uncover treasure hidden in Inca burial grounds.[179] But otherwise Diego de la Rosa is a rare case. He confessed to using his grimoire during an expedition to uncover a treasure that a native Indian had informed him was buried in a mountain together with the entrails of an Inca chieftain. De la Rosa dressed in a ceremonial white tunic with a green stole, and used incense, wax candles, and four pomegranate wands during the conjuration, but to no avail.[180] A recent major study of witchcraft and magic in colonial Brazil also notes magical treasure hunting as an uncommon activity. The author recounts the case of an eighteenth-century slave and magical healer from Rio de Janeiro named Domingos Álvares who the Inquisition exiled to the Algarve in 1744. Only once settled in Portugal did Domingo begin to specialize in detecting legendary buried treasures attributed to the Moors, and conducting spirit conjurations while wearing a white sheet.[181]

In the English colonies of North America a commercial book trade also began with the arrival of the first settlers. Bibles and pious works obviously predominated, but university-educated men also brought over larger collections of scientific and philosophical works, and hidden amongst them occult texts slipped their way into the new territory. Indeed, the first governor of Connecticut, John Winthrop Jr (1606–76), a practising alchemist, possessed a wide range of esoteric works. Emigrating from England in 1631 he brought over with him some 1,000 volumes, and continued to build up his collection in his new home, most notably obtaining some books owned by John Dee.[182] There were also books on Paracelsian medicine, Rosicrucianism, and astrology amongst the many tomes on theology and personal piety in the library of the wealthy Virginian clergyman Thomas Teackle (d. 1696). He owned the alchemist Thomas Vaughan's, *Magia Adamica* (London, 1650), John Heydon's *The Rosie Crucian infallible axiomata* (London, 1660), and 'Magica natur', which was probably a copy of Porta's *Natural Magic*.[183]

Just as in the Spanish and French colonies, the authorities in New England tried to control the book trade to prevent the Puritan population from being contaminated by the ungodly literature that they saw as plaguing England. To this end the Massachusetts General Court empowered four ministers to 'allowe or prohibit printing'.[184] It was easy at first to control the nascent American print industry, but once again censoring the flow of books from abroad proved an impossible task without instigating a ruthless stop-and-search policy. Profane chapbooks containing light-hearted romances, ballads, and the like were no doubt carried in the packs of emigrants and traded by sailors, as were astrological almanacs and divination manuals. Mention of such texts cropped up occasionally in the witch trials of New England. Literary occult knowledge could also be transported in the mind as well as on the page. During her trial in 1669, for example, Katherine Harrison of Wethersfield, Connecticut, a wealthy woman who had arrived in America around 1651, said she had learned fortune-telling from reading 'Mr Lilly's book' while living in England.[185]

Astrological and other divinatory guides were not grimoires, but in the puritanical environment of early colonial America the possession or knowledge of any book with occult content could generate suspicions of something more satanically sinister. The blurring of devilish magic and astrology in the minds of the religious authorities was made worse by the likes of the New Haven reprobate John Browne, who was tried in 1664 for 'pretending as if he had some art to rayse the divell'. From the detailed account of his trial it would appear he did not, but nevertheless had fun scaring an acquaintance, Eliakim Hitchcock, by pretending to do so by drawing up a horoscope. Hitchcock told Brown he did not think that could be done, but Brown swore it was possible but threw his astrological figures in the fire saying that the Devil would have come otherwise and torn the house to pieces.[186] The danger of such conflation is all too apparent from reading the evidence against Dorcas Hoar, who was caught up in the Salem witch trials of 1692.

The Revd John Hale testified that twenty years or so earlier, stories had circulated that Dorcas was a fortune-teller and possessed a book on palmistry. Hale confronted her about it, telling her 'it was an evill book & evill art.' Much to his satisfaction she renounced such practices, but some years later the wicked book apparently made its appearance again. Hale's daughter, Rebecca, said that she knew Hoar had been involved in thefts from the house but had not told him of it because Hoar 'was a witch & had a book' by which she could divine whether she told her father. Rebecca said that she had seen Hoar's book, '& there were many streaks & pictures in it by w'ch (as she was told) the said Hoar could reveale secretes & work witchcrafts.' Thomas Tuck confirmed that he had also seen the book 'w'th streaks & pictures'. So a simple work on palmistry, through fear, rumour, and ignorance, had become a grimoire. The Reverend now launched a hunt for this evil presence. He strongly believed that witches made their pacts by signing a Devil's book. Some in his community who were plagued by diabolic spectres said the book was 'represented to them (as to them it seemed) with threatnings of great torments, if they signed not'.[187] Hoar's husband admitted that his wife had borrowed the book from a lodger named John Samsons but had returned it some twenty years earlier. Hoar questioned Samsons, who said he had owned a book on palmistry when he lived with the Hoars but had sold it at Casco-Bay many years earlier.[188] No doubt Hale experienced a sense of frustration of such proof being beyond his grasp.

So did grimoires circulate in early colonial popular culture? Were they being used as they were back in England? In Essex County a servant girl was accused of threatening another that 'shee had a book in which she could read and call the divill', and in 1652 a man was accused of saying he had made contact with the Devil after 'he read in a book of magic'.[189] These are likely to have been idle threats or slanderous comments rather than proof that manuscripts of spirit conjuration were being read. Despite the strong puritanical influence over early settlers it would seem that it only took a little more than a generation or so for cunning-folk and fortune-tellers to become firmly established in America.[190] Yet, at least until the last years of the seventeenth century, there is little evidence that they possessed anything more than divinatory works. It was the fear that diabolic grimoires were circulating, rather than the reality, that nurtured the prominence given to the concept of the Devil's book during the devastating Salem trials of 1692.

Around fifty of those accused of witchcraft during the Salem episode confessed to signing the Devil's book to seal their pact, forty of them women.[191] It has been suggested that this preoccupation related to authoritarian concerns over the recent growth of America's printing presses and the production of explicitly astrological almanacs from the 1680s onwards.[192] We can find an analogy for this in the eighteenth-century Hungarian witch trial material. One woman who confessed to pacting with the Devil described how the Devil wrote her name in a book 'that looked like an almanac'.[193] At the same time, the popular conception of signing a Devil's book might also have been influenced by the New England Indian land speculation bubble of the 1680s, during which many people had the experience of signing land purchases with the Native Americans, who some saw as diabolic agents. One Salem woman told how the Devil in the guise of a 'Tawny man' or Indian, had presented her with a piece of birch bark, 'and she made a mark with her finger by rubbing off the white Scurff'.[194] Further analogies have also been made with the popular experience of frontier traders' account books in which customers' credit and debt were recorded. This echoes the register-like nature of the Devil's book and the spiritual debtors who signed it.[195] Indeed, it was recorded of one of the Salem suspects that the Devil temped her with a 'Book, somewhat long and thick (Like the wast-books of many Traders', butt bound and clasp't, and filled not only with the Names or Marks, but also with the explicit (short) Covenants of such as had listed themselves in the Service of Satan'.[196]

Because of their religion and their social status, seventeenth-century New England colonialists had a significantly higher literacy rate than those in the country they left—around 60 per cent male literacy compared to less than 40 per cent in England.[197] For the same reasons they had a more intimate and complex relationship with literary culture. The Devil's book was a sign of the times. In the early 1690s the puritan preoccupation with the ever-present Devil mixed toxically with authoritarian fears over the influence of profane popular literature, particularly on women. It seems likely that this was coupled with popular anxieties raised by the experience of signing—not oaths of allegiance as in Civil War England, but speculative legal and financial documents. Even at this early stage the commercial was evidently a match for the spiritual impulse in American society.

A rude shock

Fears over the aristocratic use of magic to plot against monarchies had been a factor in the rise of witchcraft, but at the dawn of the so-called Enlightenment sensational evidence of the widespread use of magic and grimoires in the court of Louis XIV sealed its decriminalization in France. Towards the end of the seventeenth century the worst of the excesses of the witch hunts were over in Western Europe thanks to increasing judicial circumspection about the evidence required to prove the crime. The trials ended earlier in France than most of the Continent. The last person to be sentenced to death for witchcraft by the *parlement* of Paris, one of nine regional legal jurisdictions in the country which oversaw justice in most of northern France, occurred as early as 1625, and only a trickle of cases were heard after that. Trials and executions took place in greater numbers and later elsewhere in the country, and in the early 1670s the central government in Paris was required to intervene in the affairs of other *parlements* to ensure that rigorous judicial procedures were applied in cases of witchcraft.[198] It was all the more shocking, then, when the royal court was exposed as being the country's hotbed of diabolic activity.

In 1678 the lieutenant general of the Paris police, Nicolas de la Reynie, began to uncover circumstantial evidence of a plot to poison Louis XIV. For a couple of years Reynie had been investigating the activities of poisoners following the scandalous case of the Marquise de Brinvilliers, who was beheaded for poisoning her brothers to get her hands on the family fortune. The more the Paris police delved into the murky world of the supply and administration of poisons in the capital the more it became clear that the trade was part of a wider, thriving network of professional magical practice. Furthermore, it was not only humble Parisians who resorted to the homes of fortune-tellers and cunning-folk. Several practitioners accrued considerable prosperity and influence thanks to the aristocratic demand for their illicit services. Amongst those caught up in the affair was the famed general the Duc de Luxembourg, and one of Louis XIV's mistresses, Madame de Montespan, who was at the centre of the web of suspicions. Male courtiers were particularly enticed by the magicians' promises of great wealth accrued through alchemy, gambling, and treasure hunting. While female aristocrats also shared these interests, they also supported a thriving trade in love powders and potions to ensure the faithfulness of their husbands or lovers. The modern-day obsession with plastic surgery also had its venerable parallels, with magical cosmetics and medicine being purchased to improve complexions and to enlarge breasts. As well as feeding aristocratic greed and vanity, the magicians also provided such sinister services as the disposal of unwanted babies, giving rise to the title 'angel makers', and providing poisons or 'inheritance powders' to do away with detested husbands, family members, and rivals.[199]

This sordid world of magic was first revealed to Reynie in all its grotesqueness by the confessions of two sorceresses. One was a tailor's wife named Marie Vigoureux and the other the widowed wife of a horse dealer, Marie Bosse. As they began to talk under interrogation and out of revenge, a close-knit underworld of magicians, fortune-tellers, shepherd herbalists, chemists, and magicians emerged, and as the police round-up escalated so the grimoires confiscated from their houses began to pile up in police headquarters. A grimoire called the *Enchiridium* was most frequently mentioned in the police records, and its identity is confirmed by one interrogation where the '*Enchiridium Leonis papæ*' was mentioned.[200] Over forty priests were arrested and it would seem that magic books circulated widely among them. Numerous grimoires and magical manuscripts were found in the home of the elderly debauched priest Étienne Guibourg, who confessed to performing black masses using the stomach of a naked woman as an altar, and was also accused of sacrificing babies. One of the books in his library was entitled *Conjuration du mirroires magique* and there were also numerous papers detailing rituals for summoning the demon Salam.[201] Grimoires were by no means restricted to the clergy and their male accomplices. While Bosse could only write her name and nothing more, several grimoires were found amongst the papers of her more educated arch rival La Voisin, amongst them *The Book of the Conjurations of Pope Honorius*, which contained a series of spells for gambling.[202] A female magician named Catherine Trianon, who lived together 'as man and wife' with another cunning-woman, was described as having more learning 'in the tip of her finger' than others acquired in a lifetime. When her house was searched in 1680 twenty-five manuscript volumes on the occult sciences were found.[203]

The Affair of the Poisons was a rude shock to the French body politic. In 1682 Louis XIV ordered the promulgation of a new law to suppress all those 'who follow the vain professions of fortune-tellers, magicians, or sorcerers or other similar names'. Strict regulations regarding the sale of poisons were instituted. The language of the Edict of 1682 also made it clear that magic was a pernicious belief rather than a real diabolic force. By banishing magicians and their ilk the Edict aimed to protect 'many ignorant and credulous people who were unwittingly engaged with them'. The crime of witchcraft was not explicitly mentioned, but the new law effectively ended the likelihood of further trials under its old definition. Over the next few decades legislation would gradually appear elsewhere in Europe reflecting this fundamental shift from magicians as diabolic criminals to magicians as frauds. Grimoires were no longer instruments of heresy but immoral manuals of superstition. In a sense this revised intellectual attitude towards magic was a return to that of the early medieval period, before the rise of the witch trials. Then again the Enlightenment was about to cast new light upon grimoires and those who used them.

ENLIGHTENMENT AND TREASURE

T he European Enlightenment is often portrayed as heralding the victory of reason and rationalism over magic and superstition. The spirit world of Neoplatonism was vanquished and the clockwork Universe ticked for the educated. The age of miracles was over and the Devil chained to hell. The crimes of witchcraft and conjuration were redefined as a delusion and a fraud. It was the age of the Lunar Society in Britain, of Linnaeus in Sweden, of Kant in Germany, and Rousseau in France. Literacy was increasing across much of western and northern Europe, and the guiding light of rationalism penetrated further and further into the minds of the masses through the increased provision of schooling and that defining Enlightenment publishing institution—the newspaper. But all is not what it seems.

The witch trials were by no means over. They continued in some German states and Switzerland well into the second half of the eighteenth century. In Scandinavia people continued to be executed and imprisoned for writing pacts with the Devil. The Inquisitions of southern Europe investigated hundreds of cases of suspected magic. Across Europe magical treasure seekers were prosecuted. For many, educated and illiterate, the Devil and his minions were a continual threat to body and soul. In late-eighteenth-century Germany a Catholic priest named Johann Joseph Gassner (1727–79) attracted considerable fame and criticism for exorcizing thousands of people whose illnesses he believed were demonic. The controversy he provoked has been described as 'one of the largest and noisiest arguments of the whole German Enlightenment'.[1]

The eighteenth century was also the age of roving occult adventurers, notorious across Europe in their own lifetimes, men who earnestly explored magic and at the same time exploited the credulity of others in such matters—men like the Sicilian Giuseppe Balsamo, better known as Count Cagliostro (1743–95).[2] Balsamo had educated himself in Western and Arabic magic and astrology whilst serving as an apprentice to a monk and experimental chemist named Father Albert. Expelled from his monastic apprenticeship, and back on the streets of Palermo, Balsamo made use of his occult knowledge, selling magical amulets and exorcizing evil spirits. He fled the city after having duped a wealthy silversmith named Vincenzo Marano into believing he could conjure up a treasure buried by the Moors. Many more occult adventures followed on his tours across Europe, including the sensational boast that he had dined with the spirit of Voltaire.[3]

Of even more enduring fame was the Venetian Giacomo Casanova (1725–98), in many ways a true representative of the Enlightenment. Alongside his many accomplishments as a lover, artist, writer, translator, and gambler, there was magic. Like Cagliostro, he had amused himself by playing the magician, once attempting to obtain a treasure buried in the cellar of a house in Cesena, Italy. He concocted an account of how Pope Gregory VII had intended to conjure it up but died before doing so, informing his client that 'During a night with a full moon, a learned magician can raise the treasure to the surface of the earth by placing himself in the middle of the magical circle called maximus.'[4] His route to influence in France owed much to his professed skills as an alchemist and magician. Amongst the magic books he innocently lent to a spying emissary of the Inquisition were the *Picatrix*, *Key of Solomon*, and *Zekerboni*. It was partly on the basis of his impressive knowledge of magic that the Austrian nobleman Count Waldstein, a major patron of art and science in central Europe, employed Casanova as his librarian during the adventurer's last years.

Both Cagliostro and Casanova were involved in what some might consider another counter-Enlightenment development in eighteenth-century educated society: the rise of Freemasonry. The origins of modern Freemasonry are a fascinating and complex mix of the mundane and the occult. There is no doubt, though, that ritual magic and alchemy were strong influences on many of those who joined the various Masonic lodges formed across Europe and America during the eighteenth century. The private library of the English Rosicrucian and Freemason General Charles R. Rainsford (1728–1809) demonstrates the wide-ranging occult interests of some members. During his travels and dealings he accumulated manuscript grimoires in German, Latin, Italian, and French, including Solomonic works and the *Picatrix*.[5]

The booming publishing industry in western Europe, which produced newspapers and pumped out books aimed at the education and moral improvement of the masses, also fed the thirst for literary magic amongst a rapidly expanding readership. Obscurantism, the authoritarian impulse to restrict access to knowledge, was alive and well but increasingly difficult to maintain. While the Mediterranean Inquisitions continued to exert considerable control, elsewhere the secular and religious censors fought a losing battle. Nowhere was this more evident than in France and its genre of chapbooks known as the *bibliothèque bleue*.[6] During the first half of the eighteenth century around one million copies of these cheap publications were being produced a year. They encompassed a huge range of sanctioned and illicit subjects. Amongst the romances, practical guides to gardening and cooking, lives of the saints, and pious reflections, we find the darkest secrets of magic laid bare.

Vive le grimoire!

After the Affair of the Poisons and the round-up, execution, and imprisonment of some of Paris's most notable magicians, the authorities turned a deliberate blind eye to the magical underworld, leaving the 1682 Edict underemployed. It was no doubt considered unwise to open up another can of worms that might implicate the French court. Out of a total of 188 different books seized by the Paris police between 1678 and 1701 only three concerned magic.[7] Under the auspices of Marc-René de Voyer d'Argenson, who succeeded Reynie as lieutenant general of the Paris police force in 1697, the number of confiscations would increase significantly. The new chief of police reignited the campaign against the *faux sorciers*, inspired by concerns over their influence on the streets rather than in the boudoirs of the rich. In 1702 d'Argenson wrote a report on the problem addressed to the King in which he explained how the fortune-tellers and magicians who plagued the capital were a serious threat to public order.[8] As a consequence, the police cast their net far wider than they did during the Affair of the Poisons. Between 1700 and 1760 at least 300 such people were either prosecuted or reported to the Paris police.[9] Amongst them was the usual range of male and female treasure hunters, diviners, dealers in magical talismans, and diabolists. Grimoires circulated widely amongst them and the police found copies in the hands of priests, prostitutes, abortionists, chemists, labourers, and tradesmen—a more diverse social range than that apparent from Reynie's investigations. Many of their owners had settled in the capital from all over France, and there was a fair sprinkling of foreigners, particularly Italians but also Germans and Swiss.[10] Some were more far-flung migrants such as one who changed his name regularly but was commonly known as the 'Turc', and dressed like an Armenian. He claimed to be a master of the spirit world, sold love powders, and wielded a magical staff covered with what were thought to be Hebraic characters.[11]

In 1711 a woman named Dequin was put in the Bastille for 'ruining several bourgeois under the pretext of discovering for them a pretended treasure that she said was guarded by spirits'. The arresting officer found a parchment on her full of magical characters, which she said was her sole source of subsistence.[12] Several 'evil books' containing magical characters and spells were confiscated from a twenty-year-old adventurer named Tirmont who was accused of treasure hunting and corrupting young girls.[13] In 1702 the man with the biggest reputation amongst the *faux sorciers* in the city was a carpenter named Louvet, a man 'deep in the science of the grimoire', who lived in the Rue du Four. The police reported that he was rarely to be found with saws and hammers, instead making a healthy living by treasure hunting and arranging pacts with the Devil. His clique consisted of a coachman, a fruiterer, a baker, and his wife.[14] There were those who made a living providing such characters with grimoires. One mentioned in d'Argenson's report was a man named Jemme, who the police believed was a relative of the marquis d'Ambreville. This rogue had left his wife and children and taken up with a prostitute. He also sold consecrated Solomonic pentacles and triangles drawn on virgin parchment. Another was Le Beau, a master tailor, who sold grimoires signed by spirits.[15]

From the records the *Clavicule of Solomon* emerges as the most influential grimoire amongst the Parisian mages. Whether it had grown in popularity since the Affair of the Poisons, or the police were just more detailed in their examination of the magic books they confiscated is difficult to say. The *Grimoire du Pape Honorius* was the next most popular magic book. In 1701 we find a diabolist doctor named Aubert de Saint-Étienne boasting that he possessed copies of both grimoires. These he used on numerous occasions to call up the Devil. During one satanic session with a fellow pact addict, he apparently chopped off the head of a cat and buried the body in a cellar. They put the head in a pot with seven broad beans, one placed in each opening in the head, accompanied by the utterance of various conjurations and the sprinkling of holy water.[16] This ritual for invisibility could be found in versions of the *Clavicule*. The *Enchiridion Leonis Papæ*, Latin print versions of which had been available for a while, was also popular. In 1745 a police search of the papers of a well-known disreputable clergyman, the abbé Le Valet de Rocheblanche, uncovered 'L'Enchiridion du pape Léon, a treatise of magic in Latin, and different magical characters traced on different pieces of paper'.[17] The police also confiscated a grimoire entitled '*les vertus admirables des Psaumes de David*', which its owner, a magical healer named Radeville living in le faubourg de St Denis, was intending to consecrate to the spirit Marcas. In his report d'Argenson described one of the 'psalms' dedicated to the spirit Prince Jesnu, the purpose of which was to protect against fire and bleeding.[18] An obscure text that also cropped up several times in police investigations was dedicated to a spirit named Membrock or Manbrok. It was reported that in 1700 the treasure hunter L'abbé Le Fevre, a Capuchin monk who had fled his monastery in

Compiègne, baptized a grimoire in the name of Manbrok. This act was performed in the church of Noyen-sur-Seine, a village southeast of Paris. A circle was made around the altar with blessed chalk, and Mass was performed on three successive nights. La du Castel, a Parisian seller of love potions, was also much occupied with attempting to conjure up a spirit named 'Membrok', presumably one and the same as Manbrok.[19]

One wonders whether some of these grimoires confiscated on the orders of d'Argenson found their way into the vast library of his grandson, the marquis Marc Antoine René de Voyer d'Argenson, which formed the basis of the great French national library the *Bibliothèque de l'Arsenal*. Amongst this bibliophile's collection of manuscripts were four versions of the *Clavicule of Solomon*, one copy each of the *Enchiridion du Pape Léon* and the *Grimoire du Pape Honorius*, the *Armadel*, and one attributed to 'Tosgrec', in other words Toz Graecus, the fabled author of several medieval occult books.[20]

The vibrant magical world of early-eighteenth-century Paris was well known to Laurent Bordelon (1653–1710), satirist and chaplain of St Eustache in Paris.[21] He mixed in the intellectual and aristocratic circles that were in Louis XIV's favour after the Affair of the Poisons. At a more humble level he must have heard rumours about the various treasure-hunting clergymen operating in the city. One presumes that it was, in part, this that led him to write, shortly before his death, a humorous critique of the belief in witchcraft, magic, divination, and apparitions based around the opinions and adventures of Monsieur Oufle—Oufle being Le Fou ('the fool') spelt backwards. Constant reading of 'superstitious books' had tainted Oufle's mind, and made him exceedingly credulous on matters regarding the supernatural. His belief in magic was also transmitted to his sons. One of them was a timid priest too honest to turn to magicians. The other, a bank worker, was, however, seduced by the prospect of obtaining the great riches held out by conjurers and astrologers: 'When they spoke to him of Devils that could find treasures, his mouth watered so much that he would not send them away.'[22] Bordelon dedicated a chapter to listing the books in Oufle's library, the best part of which consisted of the works of well-known witch-hunters such as the *Malleus Mallificarum*, Bodin's *De la démonomanie des sorciers*, and Boguet's *Discours des sorciers*. These rubbed alongside several grimoires—the books that such demonologists as Bodin and Boguet denounced and burned. Oufle owned the *Grand* and *Petit Albert*, the *Enchiridion*, *Clavicule of Solomon*, and a grimoire that carried a signature of the Devil at the end. By including both genres in Oufle's library Bordelon was making the point that they were essentially the same in the sense that they were founded on credulity and fanned pernicious superstition. Despite such mockery and the vigilance of the Paris police, France was set to become the European centre of grimoire production, with global cultural consequences.

It was during the late seventeenth and early eighteenth centuries that the cheap, simple literary format known as the *Bibliothèque bleue* expanded in France. For a fraction of the price the wealth of practical occult knowledge contained in the manuscripts so treasured by the Parisian magicians became available to all but the poorest in society. Tens of thousands of *Bibliothèque bleue* grimoires circulated around the country over the next century and a half.[23] The main centres of production were Troyes, Rouen, and Paris, and so distribution of the *Bibliothèque bleue* was widest in central and northern France until the expansion of publishing in the nineteenth century. This was also the area of the country that experienced the biggest increases in literacy during the eighteenth century.[24] It must be remembered also that many people in France at the time spoke languages and dialects other than French, and, therefore, the popular influence of this cheap literature varied widely from region to region.

The role of *colporteurs* or peddlers was certainly crucial to the spread of grimoires around the country. They were not mere salesmen though. In their packs they carried knowledge—knowledge from other places, other worlds. They had a reputation for knowing a thing or two about magic and medicine, born partly of their possession of grimoires and almanacs, partly because of the mystique that accrued to them as strangers from unknown lands. *Colporteurs* from Oisans, at the foot of the Alps, for instance, were known throughout France for the mountain herbs they offered for sale.[25]

The popularity of the *Bibliothèque bleue* was a headache for the secular and religious authorities. Laws were instituted and reinforced to suppress literature considered politically and religiously pernicious, and to monitor the activities of *colporteurs*. It is not surprising, then, that the publishers of grimoires were loath to identify themselves. A favourite ruse was to hide behind the fictional publishing company of Beringos Fratres of Lyon, whose premises were located 'at the sign of Agrippa'.[26] This was a tradition that stretched back to the publication of French editions of Agrippa and pseudo-Agrippan works during the sixteenth and seventeenth centuries. Most grimoires were given bogus dates of publication and spurious places of publication like Rome or Memphis. These served the dual purpose of frustrating the censors and giving the grimoires an aura of venerable authority and foreign mystery. They also make it impossible for the historian to date them accurately.

The earliest magic book in the *Bibliothèque bleue* genre was the *Grand Albert*. It may have been available in printed versions for nearly two centuries, but as part of the *Bibliothèque bleue* its publication generated fresh concerns. In 1709 state censors listed it as a book to be condemned and confiscated, along with a raft of populist religious works printed in Rouen.[27] Soon, though, the *Grand Albert*'s little brother, the *Petit Albert*, a true grimoire, would rise to even greater notoriety. It

SECRETS
MERVEILLEUX
DE LA
MAGIE NATURELLE
ET
CABALISTIQUE
DU
PETIT ALBERT,
Traduits exactement sur l'Original Latin,
Intitulé:
ALBERTI PARVI LUCII
LIBELLUS
DE
MIRABILIBUS NATURÆ ARCANIS.
Enrichi de Figures mystérieuses, & de la
manière de les faire.
Nouvelle Édition corrigée & augmentée.

A LION,
Chés les Héritiers de BERINGOS Fratres,
à l'Enseigne d'Agrippa.
M DCC LI.

FIG. 4 Edition of *Le Petit Albert*, title page.

was not attributed to Albertus Magnus, though, but instead to one Albertus Parvus Lucius. The earliest reference I have found to a magical text of this name is in d'Argenson's report of 1702, in which it is noted that the principal grimoire of the magician Radeville was 'Le petit Albert ou le paysan'.[28] This was presumably a manuscript and one wonders whether it, or a variant of it, was the origin of the first mass-produced version. An edition of the *Petit Albert* is thought to have appeared in Geneva in 1704, though the earliest known French edition was published in 1706 under the imprint of Beringos Fratres.[29] As Bordelon's account of Monsieur Oufle's library suggests, by 1710 the *Petit Albert* had already become a notorious and successfully popular grimoire in the Paris region. In 1714 a travelling salesman named Ponce Millet, who hawked cloth, clothing, and books around northeastern France, gave a copy of the *Petit Albert*, at three livres quite an expensive book, to his brother-in-law in the Champagne region.[30] Over the next few decades its influence spread all over France. A *colporteur* arrested in Languedoc in 1745, for instance, was found to be in possession of several copies.[31] It is somewhat ironic that these early copies of the *Petit Albert* are now so rare that they fetch upwards of a thousand pounds.

The *Petit Albert* contained a mix of mundane and magical knowledge. There were the practical tips common to *secrets of secrets*, such as how to fortify wine and make vinegar, and medical advice for bad stomachs, urinary problems, fever, bad breath, and the like. Then there were patriarchal occult tips regarding the control of females, such as how to know whether a woman is chaste, how to make women dance naked, and how to prevent women from talking lewdly with someone. There were charms to ensure success at fishing, such as taking three limpet shells, writing on them in blood the words 'JA SABAOTH', and throwing them in the water. It also contained planetary talismans and number squares, and recipes for magical perfumes. Its most notorious piece of magic concerned the making of the Hand of Glory, which allowed thieves to enter houses at night without being caught by stupefying the inhabitants. It instructed the reader to cut the hand off a criminal who had been gibbeted, wrap it in a burial sheet, then squeeze all the blood out of it. The hand was to be kept in an earthen pot for fifteen days along with a preservative mix including saltpetre, salt, and pounded peppercorns. It was then to be dried by the heat of the sun or in an oven. The mummified hand was to be used to hold a candle made from the fat of a hanged man and virgin wax in a manner illustrated by a woodcut. Variants of this gruesome magical object were known about and apparently put into practice during the seventeenth century, but it was the *Petit Albert* that generated the nineteenth- and twentieth-centuries fascination with the tradition.[32]

Bibliothèque bleue editions of that favourite magic book of the Parisian conjurers, the *Grimoire du Pape Honorius*, first appeared towards the end of the eighteenth century. Some of its contents were copied straight from the *Petit Albert*, including details of the Hand of Glory. Where it differed markedly from the *Petit Albert* was the series of spirit conjurations it contained, which were evidently taken from one of the numerous manuscript versions of the *Grimoire* in circulation. One sign of this is the two conjurations it contains to command a spirit named Nambrot, which is presumably one and the same as the spirit Membrock or Manbrok summoned by early-eighteenth-century Parisian magicians. The basis of the book's popularity was its utility for treasure hunting, providing 'pentacles to discover treasures' and conjurations to deal with the spirit world. The *Petit Albert* contained some discussion on the location of buried treasures, and the salamanders, gnomes, and spirits said to guard them, but little practical advice.[33] The author of the *Grimoire du Pape Honorius* clearly saw a gap in the market.

The *Bibliothèque bleue* version of that other Parisian favourite, the *Enchiridion Leonis Papæ*, also appeared in the same period.[34] It contained the usual simple healing charms, a version of the apocryphal Abgarus letter, and, in the earliest editions, a set of rather handsome colour engravings of talismans and instructions on constructing pentacles. Its defining content, though, was its series of talismanic protective prayers. Some versions of the *Petit Albert* recommended the prayers in the *Enchiridion* to those confronted by spirits when digging for treasure.[35] But there were prayers for more mundane purposes, such as the following to ward off foxes:

> Say three times a week: in the name of the Father +, and of the Son +, and of the Holy Ghost +. Foxes and Vixens, I conjure you, in the name of the virgin and saint, as Our Lady was pregnant, that you will neither take nor scatter any of my birds, my flocks, that is to say cocks, hens or chickens, nor eat their nests, nor suck their blood, nor break their eggs, nor do any harm to them, etc.

Another to be 'hard', and perhaps meant to counter impotency, was diabolic:

> Write on two pieces of paper, with your blood, that which follows: Ranuc +, Malin +, Fora consummatum est, in te confedo, Satana +; swallow one of them, and carry the other around the neck.

During the late eighteenth and early nineteenth centuries the *Grimoire du Pape Honorius* and the *Enchiridion* were joined by such familiar works as *Les véritables clavicules de Salomon* and the *Oeuvres magiques d'Henri Corneille Agrippa*, as well as other more minor titles. In terms of popular influence, though, all these were overshadowed by the *Grand grimoire*, which was the first explicitly diabolic mass-market grimoire. While the first edition has usually been dated to 1702—before the *Petit Albert*—its absence from early-eighteenth-century sources suggests that a *Bibliothèque bleue* edition published around 1750 was the first, or at least the most influential. The *Grand grimoire* was sensational and dangerous in that it gave explicit instructions on how to call up and make a pact with the Devil's prime minister in Hell, Lucifugé Rofocale. Satan had given Lucifugé powers over all the riches and treasures in the world, and so for French treasure hunters he was the most important of spirits. The *Grand grimoire* provided all the instructions, conjurations, and advice required to seal the pact. The 'Great Call' of Lucifugé began:

> Emperor LUCIFER, master of all the rebel spirits, I beg you to favour me in the call that I am making to your grand minister LUCIFUGÉ ROFO-CALE, desiring to make a pact with him; I beg you also, prince Beelze-bub, to protect me in my undertaking. O count Astarot! Be favourable to

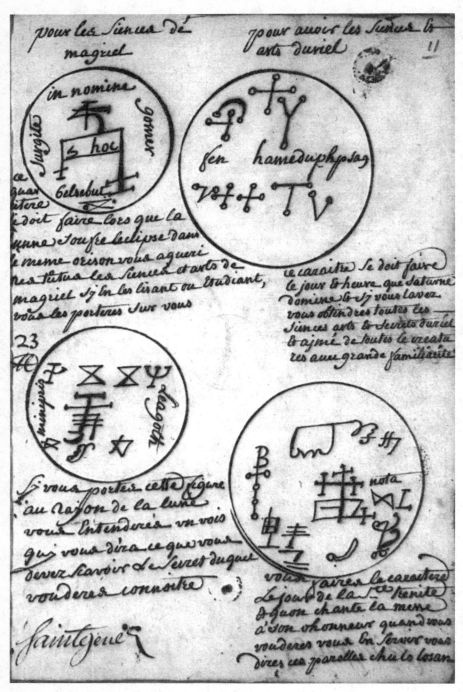

FIG. 5 *Les véritables clavicules de Salomon.* Eighteenth-century manuscript.

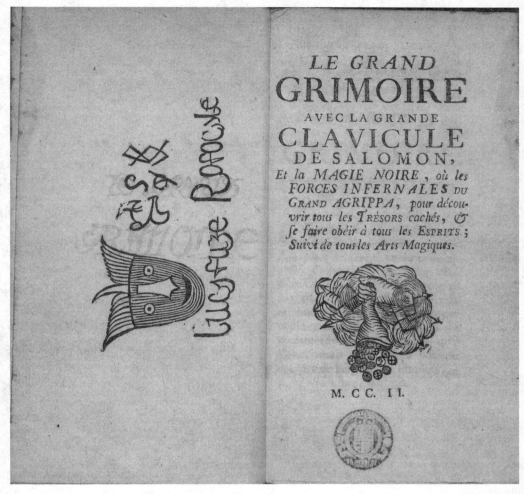

FIG. 6 *Le grand grimoire*. Eighteenth-century imprint.

me, and make it so that this night the grand LUCIFUGÉ appears to me in human form, and without any bad odour, and that he accords to me, by the pact that I am going to present to him, all the riches I need.

The *Grand grimoire* was not only a manual for diabolic communication; the mere possession of it came to be seen as an act of pact-making. In 1804, the same year that Napoleon crowned himself Emperor, a trial in Amiens deliberated on the case of a man found with a grimoire, most likely the *Grand grimoire*, with which he said he could call up the Devil by merely touching it. A government official opened the book in public to demonstrate that this was absurd nonsense.

When the Devil failed to appear the man exclaimed that the official must be a more skilful magician than he to so silence Satan.[36] The founders of the French Republic espoused the advancement of rationalism, and the state's anticlericalism was inspired, in part, by a desire to banish the 'superstitions' promoted by the Catholic Church. The scene in the Amiens court could be seen as representative of the process of popular enlightenment and dechristianization some associated with the Republic. On the other hand, it could also be seen as indicative of a wave of superstition unleashed by the Revolution. People faltered from the true path of Christian piety and moral sensibilities, leading to an era when blasphemous magic flourished. Several clergymen writing in the 1790s claimed the Revolution was a diabolic Freemason conspiracy. For one evangelical campaigner, a century and a half later, the publication in the early nineteenth century of a new version of the *Grand grimoire* under the title of the *Dragon rouge* was symptomatic: 'After the French revolution in 1789, a revolution aimed at dethroning God and enthroning the goddess of reason, this particular book, The Fiery Dragon, became a sinister substitute to the Bible in some French magic circles.'[37] But while magic certainly remained as strong a force in popular culture as it had done in the years before and after the revolutionary period, for the vast majority of Frenchmen and women the Church also maintained its grip on the masses.[38]

The *Dragon rouge* went on to match the *Petit Albert* for notoriety. Writing in the mid-nineteenth century, the historian Charles Nisard described its 'monstrous' and 'bizarre' figures as 'breathing an atmosphere filled with fire, sulphur and bitumen'. It also inspired a work of the same title that was, in fact, an attack on its pernicious influence and that of other cheap grimoires.[39] While the *Petit Albert* had gained its influence through the travels of the *colporteurs*, the *Dragon rouge* profited from the growth of High Street bookshops during the nineteenth century. One commentator, writing in 1861, noted sadly that it was on open sale in the shop windows of Paris, 'to the great scandal of those who think we are progressing'.[40] Other sources confirm that booksellers had no qualms about openly selling and advertising such magical merchandise. In 1818 the avid bibliophile Thomas Frognall Dibdin was sold a copy of the *Dragon rouge* during an antiquarian tour of France and Germany. While visiting Nancy he asked a bookseller and printer if he 'had any thing old and curious?' The bookseller explained that he had once possessed a splendid medieval missal, then handed him a copy of the *Dragon rouge*, saying, 'see, Sir, is not this curious? . . . buy it, and read it—it will amuse you—and it costs only five sous.' Dibdin purchased two copies, partly it seems, because he found the frontispiece image of the Devil intriguing. The bookseller informed him that he regularly sold hundreds of copies to the country people.[41] In October 1823, the year that a very successful edition of the *Dragon rouge* was produced in Nîmes, a religious periodical published in its 'case of conscience' section a letter that had recently been received by a Parisian bookseller

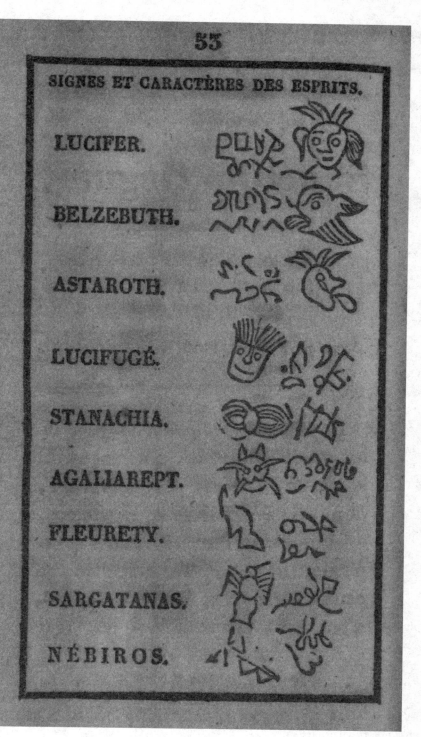

FIG. 7 List of devils and spirits from *Le dragon rouge* (early nineteenth-century edition).

from a correspondent in Normandy.[42] It explained how one of his friends had been to the man's bookshop with a soldier garrisoned at Versailles, and bought a copy of the *Dragon rouge*. The bookseller had told them that he could obtain other more powerful works including a French version of Girolamo Menghi's sixteenth-century exorcism manual *Le Flagellum dæmonum* and the *Clavicule of Solomon*. The correspondent went on to request one such book that would punish evildoers, avowing that he would travel many leagues to obtain it. Needless to say, the pious editor of the clerical periodical denounced the interest in and supply of grimoires.[43]

A spin-off from one of the conjurations in the *Dragon rouge* was *La poule noire*, the first known edition of which appeared in 1820. Its popularity was due to the treasure conjuring ritual of the same name which was notorious in eighteenth-century France. There were several variations of the tradition. One required the releasing of a black hen at the treasure site and then sacrificing it. Another consisted of the sacrifice of a black hen at a crossroads or cross around midnight in conjunction with a conjuration to call up the Devil. His eminence would, in return, proffer a black hen that laid gold or silver eggs. Rumour had it that the wealth of the influential French banker Samuel Bernard (1651–1739) was due to his possession of one such black hen.[44] There is no doubt that the ritual was practised, as was revealed during the trial in 1775 of a winegrower named Jean Guillery and several accomplices. These fraudsters gulled at least two men with the promise of a *poule noire* that laid money. In one instance they began by asking their dupe, a man named Fortier, to write his name on a book owned by an accomplice named Macret, which Fortier described as a grimoire full of strange figures. They led him to a cross in the countryside around the village of Pithiviers, near Orléans. Macret gave his grimoire to Guillery, and following its instructions they spread out a napkin at the foot of the cross. Then, sixty steps from it they drew a circle on the ground in which Fortier was ordered to stand until told otherwise. Guillery placed Fortier's money on the napkin, got down on one knee in supplication, and said 'I greet you, my master.' On saying this, a hen appeared on the napkin, but when Guillery repeated his salutation to the Devil it disappeared along with the money. Meanwhile one of the accomplices rolled around on the ground pretending to be possessed. Guillery walked back to Fortier who remained in the protective circle and informed him that the Devil had snatched the money, and it would require more money to go through the ritual again to procure the *poule noire*. Fortier complied, and after they all said a neuvaine (reciting the same prayer nine days in a row) they went through the whole charade once more. Several of the gang were sentenced to be pilloried, whipped, branded, and banished. One was tied to the pillory post in the public square in Pithiviers on three consecutive market days wearing a paper with the words 'Swindler by false magic'.[45]

Who else purchased the thousands of grimoires being produced? We cannot assume that it was only the literate. The mere possession of non-diabolic grimoires was thought by some to have a protective function. When, in 1815, a vintner and herbal healer named Pierre Belloc was arrested at a Bayonne inn for practising false medicine, they found on him a copy of the *Enchiridion Leonis papæ*. He said he had bought it from a soldier 'who assured him that it would shield him from falling ill and being killed'.[46] Those who could read we can divide into the merely curious and the practitioners. Amongst the former during the mid-eighteenth century was an adventurous, itinerant master glassier named Jacques-Louis Ménétra. His copy of the *Petit Albert* joined a modest list of books we know he also owned, namely the Bible, a spiritual text, and two works by Rousseau. There is no indication in Ménétra's confessional journal that he dabbled in magic, and he was clearly sceptical of the spirit world, so we can only assume that the rumours surrounding the *Petit Albert* intrigued him.[47]

As to the practitioners, we should not presume that they were all interested in conjurations and spells, as most *Bibliothèque bleue* grimoires also contained simple, pious healing charms and natural recipes. In one edition of the *Grimoire du Pape Honorius* we find the following charm for ringworm, which, like numerous others for minor ailments, is based on apocryphal biblical events:

> Saint Peter, on the bridge of God, sat down; Our Lady of Caly came there, and asked him: Peter, what are you doing there? Lady, it is for the hurt of my master that I placed myself there. St Peter, you will remove it; to Saint Ager you will go for it; you will take the holy ointment of the mortal wounds of our Lord; you will grease them and you will say three times: Jesus Mary. It is necessary to make the sign of the cross three times over the head.[48]

Charms such as these for staunching blood, toothache, snakebites, eye complaints, and the like were normally only efficacious when employed by those thought to possess a special gift for charming. So even though the *Bibliothèque bleue* grimoires and the *Médecin des pauvres*, a popular nineteenth-century chapbook of healing charms, were available to all for a few pennies, not everyone could use them.[49] As French anthropologists, folklorists, and sociologists have shown, many charmers did not practise other forms of magic and were devout churchgoers. Spirit conjuration and making women dance naked were not for them. They were, however, for the more unscrupulous cunning-folk.

In 1776 François Duthil, known familiarly as Minette, a former miller of Cernoy, east of Beauvais, was tried for a series of frauds practised over a couple of decades on the inhabitants of the villages and towns of Picardie. Much of his professed power lay in his grimoires. These were small enough to be kept in his pocket, which suggests that they were members of the *Bibliothèque bleue*. One of his victims, a young woman named Agnès de Larche, whom he made pregnant and then abandoned, testified that he

> always had two books with him, which he took great care to hide. He read often from one of the two, and said to me, sometimes crying, 'this book is the cause of our misfortune.' When we entered a town, he hid one of them in his trousers, and gave the other one to me to hide; and when we were ready for bed, he placed them under the mattress, saying to me they were grimoires, and that, if they found them on him, they would not honour him with hanging, but that he would be burned.[50]

Whether Duthil's emotional outbursts were an act is impossible to say. If genuine, then it may have been the case that Duthil had employed one of them, perhaps the *Grand grimoire*, to make a pact with the Devil. He certainly played on his professed familiarity with the Lord of Darkness. He told one of his victims, a labourer named Toussaint Demont, whom, over a period of two years, he swindled out of most of his money with repeated attempts to conjure hidden treasure, that the Devil had written to him regarding its location. Agnès testified that when she informed Duthil she was pregnant 'he told me only that the Devil was tormenting him so that I would give up my child to him, and continually requested me to consent to this sacrifice.'[51] This sounds like a wickedly cynical ruse to destroy the troublesome illegitimate child. In August 1776 Duthil was branded and sent to the galleys for life.

The folklore and trial records of the nineteenth century show how firmly cemented the *Bibliothèque bleue* grimoires had become in the fabric of France's tradition of popular magic. The reputations of cunning-folk depended on them. During the trial in Agen of a wise woman named Rose Pérès in 1829, for instance, it was heard how as part of her ritual for curing the child of a rich peasant she laid down in front of him 'with a grave and mysterious air, the well-known book of *Petit Albert*'. Around the same time a couple of magicians defrauded an old woman near Niort after impressing her with their copies of the *Dragon rouge*, *Petit Albert*, and *Grand grimoire*. Later in the century a witness at the trial of a disreputable sorcerer named Gaucher testified that he was afraid of him because 'he told me he owned the *Petit Albert* and other books, which enabled him to do anything he liked.'[52] The vast majority of those consulting cunning-folk in the early modern period would have known nothing of the titles of the grimoires displayed to impress them. The possession of books, particularly large ones, or manuscripts with arcane symbols, was enough to convince that they were adepts in the occult arts. The spread of literacy and popular literature meant that, by the mid-nineteenth century, the *Petit Albert*, *Grand Albert*, and *Dragon rouge* were household names. To say one had the *Petit Albert* was shorthand for saying one was deep in magic.

Feeling their spiritual authority challenged by the widespread influence of the *Bibliothèque bleue* grimoires, the clergy launched a counter-offensive aimed at demonizing them. They spread the message that those who possessed or even desired such books, let alone used them, were committing a grave blasphemy. Reading was a dangerous act.[53] A perusal of the folklore collections of the late nineteenth and twentieth centuries suggests the clergy met with considerable success. In 1884, for instance, a letter in *The Times* recalled a conversation with a woman in Tours: 'She spoke of the "Petit Albert" with the utmost horror, and told me that the priests said that merely to look into it was a great sin, and that the devil had the power to seize any one while in the act of reading it.'[54] A study of witchcraft beliefs in twentieth-century Languedoc found that such statements were made repeatedly by those interviewed. When asked about the *Petit Albert*, one person said, 'It is forbidden to talk about it, the Church has forbidden it. It is a dangerous book.' When another told his grandmother, 'I am going to buy the Petit Albert,' she replied, 'You are mad! It is forbidden by religion . . . It will make you ill.'[55]

The influence of the *Bibliothèque bleue* grimoires stretched far beyond the French border. France's southern neighbours tried to stem the tide. The *Petit Albert* was added to the Spanish *Index of Prohibited Books* in 1782, and twenty-two years later the 1800 edition of the *Grimoire du pape Honorius* was also included.[56] But the *Index* was a fairly redundant tool of censorship by now. In 1820 a Florence bookseller was openly offering French editions of the *Petit Albert* and *Grand Albert*, despite their presence on the *Index*, as well as recent editions of *Le Grand grimoire* and *Le Dragon rouge*.[57] In the absence of similar chapbook grimoires in Italy, publishers there turned to the French genre, and in 1868 the *Dragon rouge* was translated into Italian as *Il Vero drago rosso*. By this time it had already permeated German magic under the title *Der wahrhaftige, feurige Drache* (*The true, fiery Dragon*). To the north, French grimoires became engrained in the magical traditions of the British Channel Islands and parts of the Low Countries. In 1854 it was estimated that in the Ardennes region alone as many as 400,000 chapbook grimoires were in circulation—surely an exaggeration, but nevertheless indicative of how much they had infused into the popular consciousness.[58]

Satan's Alpine seat

France may have been the centre of European grimoire printing, but for many southern European Catholics during the late seventeenth and eighteenth centuries, Geneva was the capital of diabolic magic, joining Salamanca and Toledo in the geography of occult learning. As trial records show, people travelled to Geneva from across France, Spain, and Italy in search of magic books and familiar spirits. The city was a major centre of publishing, but its occult reputation was due primarily to it being a centre of Protestantism, the heartland of Calvinism. From a Catholic point of view it was consequently portrayed as a wellspring of diabolic heresy, a place where the Devil reigned amongst his Protestant disciples. For Italians it was the nearest influential state free from the reach of the Catholic Church.

In 1744 one Nicolas Lambert played what he called a 'good trick' on some visiting Italians seeking magical help. They had asked him whether they could find the *Petit Albert* in Geneva, which, they explained, 'was a very useful book for obtaining riches'. Lambert told them that the *Petit Albert* was a paltry item compared to the power granted to those who possessed a familiar spirit that he could procure for them. One of his dupes was Bartholomeo Bernardi from Lucca in Tuscany. He had inquired of Lambert, 'if in this country there weren't people who were given to magic, that is to say finding spirits, as in Italy'. More to the point, he wondered 'if there weren't in this town books which were forbidden by the Holy Office, and through which one could obtain great advantages'. Lambert intimated that they had, indeed, come to the right place. Rather than purchase a copy of the *Petit Albert*, Lambert convinced him to buy a box containing what he said was a spirit, as well as an invocation in Italian to control it.[59] Bernardi soon realized he had been defrauded and despite the risk went to the authorities. The Italians were ordered to leave the city and Lambert was banished for life.

One of those making a living from selling grimoires in the famed market in the Place du Molard was Louise Chartier, wife of a printer named Odet Jacques. In 1716 the authorities confiscated two manuscripts entitled, '*Sanctum Regnum seu Pneumatologia Salomonis*, with some other loose leaves from the same book, which explain the nature of the Devil, his figure, his different names, his power, the number of his officers'. Chartier confessed that she had paid a Savoyard to make copies. Several decades later, copies of the *Clavicula Salomonis* were being produced by a group of conspirators made up of an innkeeper named Charles Empeyta, a bookseller Pierre Lombard, a school master Jacques Dueros, and Jacques Minot, an artist. Judging from the experience of a young man who was staying at Empeyta's hotel with his aunt, the innkeeper acted as the inveigling agent for Lombard. Empeyta persuaded the young man that Lombard possessed a manuscript that would make his fortune. For the price of two gold Louis, and a commission for Empeyta's service on top, he received his *Clavicule*, which consisted of eighty-eight pages written in red and black ink by Ducros, who had copied it from an 'original' he had previously sold. At the end of the manuscript was a picture of the Devil in red crayon drawn by Minot. The outfit had also sold copies of the same to people from Italy, Lyon, and Languedoc.[60]

By this time the *Grand grimoire* had joined the *Petit Albert* as a publishing sensation. In the 1770s we find the 64-year-old printer and straw merchant Moyse Morié offering copies of the *Grand grimoire* for extortionate sums. References in the trial records regarding its blue paper cover confirm its identity as a member of the *Bibliothèque bleue*. Morié, who had long had a reputation in the region for selling books of sorcery, offered a copy to a marcasite crystal merchant named Vincent Carret for the huge sum of 300 livres. After negotiation he accepted the still substantial payment of 16 livres, 11 gold sequins, some silver, and an IOU for 5 gold Louis to be cashed six months hence. The reason for paying such a large sum was the promise of treasure of course. Morié assured him that his fortune would be made once he made a pact with a spirit. Carret soon regretted his decision after a friend opened the book and declared that it contained nothing more than a lot of 'twaddle'.[61]

Delving further into the court records reveals that the authorities were keen to find out where the *Grand grimoire* sold by Morié had been printed. A bookseller was called to give testimony on the subject. 'Having examined the print and characters of the said book,' he concluded, 'I have found nothing which makes me believe that this book might have been printed in Geneva, and I think I can state to the contrary, that it is impossible to determine in what place the said book was printed.'[62] Fortunately Carret's copy was kept by the authorities and survives today in the dossier on the case. An inspection confirms that, although bearing the bogus date of 1603, it was a copy of the French edition published around 1750. It had also been used, presumably by Carret, to make a pact with the Devil. On one blank page a crude image of the Devil has been drawn in red ink or blood with the command that the book seal a deal with the prince and emperor Lucifer. A similar pact appears at the end, next to the image and character of Lucifugé Rofocale.

The second coming of St Cyprian

One of those who made his way to Geneva and found himself in court for his troubles was a Spaniard named Moyse-Joseph Agilar, a failed priest and healer from Segorbe, Valencia.[63] His energies were mostly directed at trying to find hoards of gold ingots and pistoles hidden in the Spanish mountains. He teamed up with two French treasure seekers, a leather worker named Jean de la Guarrigue from Quercy and Antoine Riccard from near Toulouse. According to the two Frenchmen, Agilar had convinced them of their quest by relating how a Jesuit priest had informed him that in Geneva he could find books of magic and the 'characters' of the 'Prince of Devils', which would drive away the minor demons that guarded treasures. The three men arrived in the capital of Calvinism via Lyon in 1672. Agilar set about searching first for a copy of the *Virtutes Herbarum* by Albertus Magnus, in other words the *Grand Albert*, from which he wanted to learn the magical properties of herbs and stones. Then they tried to obtain from a shopkeeper books that would call up the Devil to aid them in their treasure quest. Shortly after, someone informed on them and they were arrested. They claimed at first that their travels were nothing more than a simple desire 'to see the world and foreign countries'. Over a century later another Spanish priest, Juan Soler, was directly involved in similar treasure endeavours that led to Geneva. Soler boasted to his treasure-seeking companions that he had procured, on the advice of the Devil, a book of conjurations from Geneva. He said he had bought it during a record-breaking 48-hour round trip from the Catalonian town of Girona. The same treasure-hunting group subsequently turned to a Frenchman to lead them.[64]

As we have seen, until its disbandment in 1820, the Spanish Inquisition expended much effort rooting out grimoires, and numerous copies were confiscated during the two hundred or so cases of treasure seeking the Inquisition investigated between 1700 and 1820.[65] The Spanish *Index* listed the addition, in 1817, of a manuscript called the 'Book of conjurations for obtaining treasures'. It joined another manuscript described as containing 'rules, conjurations and exorcisms to discover and to extract occult treasures'.[66] It is understandable that Agilar felt it safer to take the arduous journey north rather than try and obtain one at home. Across the border in Portugal the secular authorities were also active in censoring publishers, with new regulations being instituted in 1768 to ban books that promoted 'superstition'.[67] Yet, despite the attentions of Church and state, grimoires continued to circulate throughout the Iberian Peninsula. A major reason for this was the porous boundary between France and Spain, in particular the Basque region straddling the western Pyrenees. In 1785 an Inquisitor ordered that the sentence against a 'superstitious' treasure seeker be read in the church of Mercadal, east of Santander, to warn people of the iniquity of the offence, which he thought was more rife in the Bishopric than elsewhere 'because of the close proximity with France'.[68] The French influence permeated to further parts of the country. The Zaragoza tribunal dealt with a healer who said she learnt her knowledge from the book of a French doctor. It also heard another case in which the defendant related that a Frenchwoman had told him that treasure could be found by releasing a black hen at the spot were the treasure was hidden and then offering it to the Devil. Frenchmen were also implicated in several cases of treasure hunting heard by the Inquisition during the century.[69]

In the eighteenth century Bayonne in particular had a reputation amongst Spaniards as a centre of magical practice second only to Geneva. This was in part because it was the nearest large French town to the western Spanish border, and therefore the most likely place to be able to obtain the *Petit Albert* and *Grand grimoire*. It was also due to the town having a well-known *marranos* and Jewish population. *Marranos* were Spanish and Portuguese converted Jews ('New Christians') who fled the attentions of the Spanish Inquisition and who were, following a French royal edict of 1555, allowed to settle in the territory of the Bordeaux Parliament, which stretched to the Spanish border. By the early eighteenth century the Jewish faith was being openly practised in the town, predominantly by new arrivals, despite the heavy restrictions on them instituted by the Bayonne authorities. Meanwhile back in Spain the Inquisition launched another major wave of suppression against converted Jews during the 1720s, leading to further movements of *marranos* across the border.[70] A case heard by the Zaragoza tribunal demonstrates the attraction of Bayonne for Spanish seekers of magical knowledge. In 1740 a shoemaker named Andrés Jaso visited the town and consulted a Jewish magician in order to learn how to conjure up familiars or demons that would aid his personal enrichment. He naturally returned disappointed, and subsequently went to Geneva on the same quest.[71]

By the mid-eighteenth century the *Petit Albert* was already influential amongst cunning-folk in southwestern France. In 1742 a copy was confiscated along with a book of exorcisms and various medical texts from a 'so-called surgeon' named Jean Labadie, and a copy was found on a 'pretended' Béarnaise magician in 1783.[72] When, in the 1760s, the authorities of Dax arrested the magician and itinerant house painter Dominique Lalanne they found a manuscript of *Les véritables clavicules de Salomon*. He was also accused of having obtained a copy of Del Rio's *Disquisitionum Magicarum*. The authorities, ignorant of the nature of the book, evidently thought it suspicious.[73] But it would seem that the usual grimoires had a rival in the region—the *Agrippa Noir* or Black Agrippa. In his unpublished memoirs, written in 1744, Mathieu du Bourg Caunègre, a townsman of Magescq, referred to an 'Agrippa le Noir with all the figures', when discussing with a friend what he should consult to make a spirit appear.[74] The Pyrenean geographer François Flamichon, writing during the 1780s, related a legend of Moorish treasure hidden in a cave near the village of Esquiule. Villagers had failed to find it and so called in a Jewish conjurer from Saint-Esprit, a Jewish suburb of Bayonne, who said he could get his hands on an 'Agrippa le Noir'. He charged them a considerable sum for his services and absconded with their hard-earned money, leaving his dupes to wait in vain for his return.[75] We know such a grimoire really existed in the region for we find a copy of *Agrippa le Noir* among the books and manuscripts confiscated from Dominique Lalanne. From the prosecution of an itinerant magician and doctor named Gracien Detcheverry we also know that it circulated beyond the French-speaking community.

Born in the Basque region around 1700 Gracien Detcheverry, unlike most of his kind, was a formally trained and licensed surgeon.[76] He plied his trade and mixed in dubious company both sides of the Pyrenees. It was during a visit to the home of a Spaniard in the town of Saint-Jean-de-Luz in 1733 that he caught sight of a manuscript in Spanish entitled 'Agripa Negra'. He bought it for the considerable sum of seventy-five livres, and with it his career as a conjurer began in earnest. Armed with his grimoire he professed to be able to find treasure and open the doors of prisons, amongst other magical feats. He was arrested in Bayonne for his nefarious activities and found guilty. Detcheverry's 'Agripa Negra' was burned publicly in the Place Notre-Dame, and he was sentenced to the galleys for the rest of his life. The court, however, ordered that a translation of the grimoire be made so that they could better judge its contents, and this copy survives in the archives. It is nineteen pages long and is primarily dedicated to treasure hunting. It consists of a compilation of conjurations and receipts from several grimoires. More to the point it is not a straight copy of anything in print at the time. Several of its conjurations, such as one for the 'Rois d'Orient', are clearly from the *Grimoire du Pape Honorius*, as is a conjuration for the spirit 'Nembrot'.[77] This does not mean that all *Agrippa le Noirs* were the same or similar to Detcheverry's, but it represents a distinct regional tradition that crossed linguistic and political frontiers.

Further south in Spain the old Moorish influence lingered, with Arabic magic texts being much sought after. In 1730 the Inquisition tried an old illiterate man from Carlet, near Valencia, who owned a book in Arabic that instructed that two slaves had to be present when searching for treasure. These he bought and then brought to the treasure site where he sacrificed a kid goat. When nothing happened he cut the arms of one of the slaves so that they bled on the spot. In Majorca several decades later a treasure hunter was found with a little book written in Moorish language that contained magical 'triangles'.[78]

During the nineteenth century a new and influential addition to the canon of popular grimoires was born—the *Libro de San Cipriano* (*The Book of St Ciprian*). The usual bogus claims were made as to its authorship. Some editions claimed that a German monk named Jonas Sufurino, the librarian of the monastery of Brooken, discovered or wrote it in the year 1000. Popular legend had it that the original manuscript was safely locked away in the university or cathedral library in the Galician capital Santiago.[79] Although modern editions claimed an initial publication date of 1510, there is, in fact, no mention in Spanish sources of a grimoire with such a title until 1802, when the Inquisition prosecuted a priest for possessing a manuscript called the *Libro de San Cipriano*, which he used to find buried treasure.[80] The papal *Index*, however, had long included 'prayers ascribed to S. Cipriano' against evil spirits, incantations, witchcraft, and any other adversity.[81] Significantly their use was evidently widespread in southwestern France during the eighteenth century. In 1753 the Bishop of Oloron warned against the 'pretended exorcisms of Saint Cyprien that are to be found in the hands of some in our diocese'. It consisted of a prayer to Christ in which, amongst other things, he is beseeched to protect people from the 'evil eyes of demons and from their hearing, from deceiving tongues, from thunder, from lightening, from storms, from all sort of enemies and evil spirits'.[82] It is easy to imagine that, at the time, Cyprian's name might be added to a manuscript version of the *Grand grimoire* or *Grimoire du Pape Honorius*. In fact extracts from a manuscript *Libro de San Cipriano* published by a Galician historian in 1885 contain a Spanish version of the *Grand grimoire*'s instructions for addressing Lucifugé Rofocale.[83]

In a French trial of 1841 we find an intriguing reference to a book printed in French and Latin entitled *Cyprien Mago ante Conversionem*. Its spurious place and date of publication was 'Salamanca 1460'. It contained various 'magic, cabbalist and diabolical' images, and instructions on how to obtain a treasure of eighteen million with the help of the Devil. It was owned by a gunsmith, Jean Grangé, from near Toulouse, who inherited it from his father. Seduced by the prospect of huge wealth Grangé consulted a local sorcerer, named Lagrange, on how best to use the book, and was advised that to proceed it would be first necessary to procure the Devil's signature. Grangé was hooked and the sorcerer orchestrated an elaborate hoax conjuration of the Devil which involved an accomplice dressed in red trousers and a black lambskin helmet in imitation of his satanic highness. Despite being in a foul mood the Devil signed a piece of parchment and received a fee before exiting.[84]

I have not been able to trace any surviving copies of the *Cyprien Mago ante Conversionem*. It was almost certainly a local *Bibliothèque bleue* publication, and confirms that a Cyprian treasure grimoire had been printed and circulated in southwest France before it had in Spain. Yet it is quite possible that the *Cyprien Mago* was an example of the flow of magical culture from Spain to France with a French printer being inspired by a manuscript *Libro de San Cipriano*.

The publication of Spanish books with the title *Libro de San Cipriano* only began in the late nineteenth century.[85] Two distinct genres emerged.[86] One version of the *Libro de San Cipriano* was essentially a translation of the French *Grand grimoire*. A Spanish edition of the latter, the *Gran Grimoirio*, had apparently appeared in 1820, and this may have led to a further proliferation of manuscript versions under the Cipriano name. In the 1840s, furthermore, one Spanish bookseller, and no doubt others, was also selling the Nîmes edition of the *Dragon rouge*, copies of which may have also been transcribed and circulated under the Cipriano name.[87] The second genre of the *Libro de San Cipriano* was a distinctively Spanish creation rather than a comprehensive borrowing from the French tradition. It was not concerned with diabolic invocations but rather contained exorcisms and prayers for dispelling demons, healing the sick, finding lost items, and providing protection against the evil eye. Some editions of the book even advised that it was intended to help the clergy in aiding their parishioners.

What undoubtedly most attracted readers, though, were the instructions on how to obtain hidden treasures *without* recourse to the Devil. This could be achieved by drawing a magical circle at the spot, entering, and praying to God, the saints, and the angels, while reciting sacred names. The key to the success of this *Libro de San Cipriano* was that it also provided a detailed list of the places in Galicia where treasure could be found.

Why Galicia? The popularity and knowledge of the *Libro de San Cipriano* was particularly strong in the province, and in neighbouring Asturias, where it was popularly known as the *Ciprianillo*. Its cultural influence is evident from its presence in the literary canon of the region. The Galician poet Manuel Curros Enriquez (1851–1908) wrote a poem entitled *O Ciprianillo*, while in one of the novels of his compatriot, the dramatist and novelist Ramón del Valle-Inclán (1866–1936), there is a passage in which an old man tries to find some treasure by reading from a magic book entitled the *Libro de San Cidrian* (an obvious reference to the Cypriano) by candlelight after sunset.[88] The region is rich in prehistoric monuments, Neolithic and Bronze Age dolmens, burial mounds, and Iron Age *castros* (hill forts). Galicia was also a major centre of prehistoric mining with its tin and gold highly prized by the Roman conquerors, and continued to be so into the early modern period. Consequently the area accrued a reputation for ancient buried treasures.[89] It was not ancient peoples, however, that came to be associated with this landscape of treasure but the Moors who had been driven out of Galicia during the eighth century AD. Numerous legends evolved of Moorish gold hidden in the *castros*, many protected by spells and spirits that only the *Ciprianillo* could break. In the early 1930s the Galician writer Vicente Risco collected various oral accounts of the successful conjurations of such Moorish treasure involving the *Ciprianillo*. One legend told how a man consulted his *Ciprianillo*, drew a Solomonic circle on the ground, and thereby hauled out all the bad spirits, 'souls in sorrow', which guarded the treasure. All night long he and his lucky assistants removed bars of gold and silver from the site. In another instance a group read from the *Ciprianillo* for two hours and then the ground began to shake, thunder shook the sky, and a series of devils emerged from a hole in the ground dragging carts full of gold.[90]

It would seem that from the seventeenth century onwards printed and manuscript *gacetas* (gazetteers) listing the locations of such buried treasures were popular in parts of Spain.[91] In 1739, for instance, a priest of Albacete confessed that he had been guilty of treasure hunting after a soldier based in Granada had 'shown him a book in Arabic . . . which indicated several places and spots where the Moors had buried precious objects and treasures'.[92] The *gacetas* seem to have been particularly influential in the old Moorish kingdom of Granada and in the northwestern provinces. Writing in 1750 the Benedictine monk Benito

Jerónimo Feijoo (1676–1764), an arch-critic of popular 'superstition', noted from his own experience that treasure seeking for Moorish gold was rife in Galicia and Asturias. During his childhood in the region he heard stories of prized manuscripts that revealed the location of treasures. Some believed that such tomes did not exist and were merely the products of peasant tales, but Feijoo was persuaded of their reality when one of them was given to him in which directions were provided for locating twenty treasures hidden in the countryside around the city of Oviedo.[93] People puzzled over where these *gacetas* came from. Some believed that such knowledge of Moorish treasure originated from those who had been held captive and ransomed by Barbary pirates in Algiers and Morocco—a profitable line of trade right into the nineteenth century. Others thought such secret knowledge must have derived from documents in the famed Royal Archive of Simancas.[94]

The influence of these *gacetas* certainly remained strong in Asturias and Galicia throughout the nineteenth century, where old manuscript and printed versions continued to circulate. Around 1850 an enterprising Galician publisher produced a cheap, poorly printed hoax *gaceta* entitled the *Millonario de San Ciprian*, which purported to contain a list of the hidden Roman and Moorish treasures secreted in the neighbourhood of the city of Coruña. It had the bogus imprint of 'Amsterdam', mimicking the ruse used by Spanish publishers wishing to avoid the censorious attentions of the Inquisition, and the date 1521. Its purported author was Adolfo Ojarak. The surname spelt backwards is the rude Spanish exclamation 'Carajo!', and the author used the same technique to turn derogatory coarse phrases addressed to its readers into supposed secret words of power.[95]

For Feijoo the worst thing about the 'vain and pernicious' preoccupation with *gacetas* was that it seduced people into resorting to magic. This was brought home to him by perusing a grimoire owned by the same person who gave him the *gaceta*. The man handed both over to Feijoo after becoming disillusioned with his lack of success and fearful over their sinful, 'superstitious' influence.[96] During the early twentieth century one Asturian folklorist recorded an account of a man from the hamlet of Vildas, who, frustrated in his attempt to dig up treasures mentioned in a *gaceta*, resorted to the *Libro de San Cipriano* to invoke a demon to aid him.[97] It is no surprise, then, that in the late nineteenth century an enterprising publisher hit upon the idea of packaging a *gaceta* for Galicia with the *Libro de San Cipriano*, thereby providing both the location of buried treasures and the magical means of capturing them. Some editions also published a list of treasures in Portugal, ensuring the spread of the *Cipriano*'s influence on local traditions, particularly in the Barroso region of northern Portugal, with its strong cultural and linguistic ties with Galicia.[98] As we shall see in a later chapter, it was not long before it was also being sold far and wide across Latin America.

The land of Faust

The late eighteenth century saw the beginnings of *volkskunde*—the study of the life and culture of the 'people' and the precursor of what we know today as 'folklore'. In Germany this interest grew out of the Romantic movement, and while it was not a specifically German phenomenon, the likes of the Grimm brothers were hugely influential in inspiring others around Europe to explore the stories and beliefs of the poor and uneducated.[99] Conveniently forgetting that the judiciary in some central European states had only recently rejected the crime of witchcraft, the interest in what were now seen as the mental relics of an unenlightened medieval age took several forms. There were those learned men and women across Europe who considered it necessary to identify and understand 'vulgar' beliefs and practices the better to stamp them out in the name of either God or rationalism. Others were more compassionate, recognizing the aesthetic and cultural worth in the *märchen* or tales of the peasantry, while acknowledging that such survivals would succumb to the necessary forces of progress.

Grimoires, seen as the remnants of benighted medieval magic, did not conveniently fit into the romantic perception of folklore as oral culture. Yet their continued influence on popular beliefs rendered them of interest to those whose enthusiasm for *volkskunde* was matched by the natural curiosity of the bibliophile.[100] The most well known of these was the celebrated writer Johann Wolfgang von Goethe (1749–1832), best known for his verse drama of the *Faust* legend. He certainly had an interest in Western esotericism, paid serious attention to the spiritualism of Swedenborg, and was fascinated though sceptical of the occult exploits of Cagliostro.[101] There is no evidence that Goethe ever dabbled in the magical arts, though, and so his enthusiasm for collecting grimoires was probably born more of inquisitiveness and bibliomania than any practical interest in their contents. He expressed a book collector's embarrassment over the money he paid out for one grimoire that he had been tracking for a considerable time. It was a handsome manuscript dating to around the middle of the eighteenth century entitled *Bibliae Magicae*, and is noteworthy for being the earliest known German grimoire professing to consist of the *Sixth and Seventh Books of Moses*. Goethe also owned a version of another distinctively German grimoire entitled *Faust's Höllenzwang* (*Faust's Infernal Command*), which, like the *Grand grimoire*, concerned the calling up of the Devil, and was much sought after by treasure seekers.

Different motives led the German philologist and librarian Johann Christoph Adelung (1732–1806) to include a copy of a *Faust's Höllenzwang* in his *History of Human Folly*.[102] This was possibly the first printed version of the grimoire, though disappointingly, as Adelung explained, it had to be stripped of the original manuscript's magical signs and sigils in order to reduce the cost of publication.

What remained were various prayers and adjurations for calling the angels and spirits, which were included at the end of a volume that extensively trashed the reputations of John Dee, Nostradamus, and Paracelsus. Adelung published it for the same reasons that Reginald Scot published charms and conjurations—to expose the folly of believing in them. Just as with Scot, it probably proved a counter-productive exercise in the long run. At the end of the eighteenth century by no means all bibliophiles were averse to the lure of the occult. A university-educated town councillor in Darmstadt called Karl Wunderlich (1769–1841) used his extensive collection for alchemical and magical purposes. Amongst the 1,700 volumes in his study were copies of the *Sixth and Seventh Books of Moses*, the *Höllenzwang*, and other books of conjuration attributed to Dr Faust.

The attribution of many of the eighteenth-century grimoires to Faust is perfectly understandable considering the huge popularity of chapbook accounts of his life. The town most associated with him, Wittenberg, had also long had a reputation as a centre of magic. When Fynnes Moryson visited the town in 1591 he noted that 'they shew a house wherein Doctor Faustus a famous conjurer dwelt . . . and had a tree all blasted and burnt in the adjoining, where hee practised his Magick Art.'[103] Some early Lutheran Reformers expressed their chagrin that the popular association of Faust with the town overshadowed its place as the heart of Lutheranism. The town's reputation continued into the nineteenth century. According to one legend recorded in the town of Chemnitz, Saxony, in the 1840s, the original *Sixth and Seventh Books of Moses* were kept at Wittenberg.[104]

The Faust grimoires by no means completely dominated eighteenth-century literary magic. As well as Moses, of course, there were other prominent authors such as a Renaissance mage named Dr Habermann and another named Rabbi Rabellina. Both were bogus it would seem. The secretary of the Dresden Royal Library, and later its chief, Friedrich Adolf Ebert, recalled that in 1817 he and his colleagues received numerous urgent requests for a work by Rabellina called *Die goldne Tabella Rabellina*, which was described by inquirers as containing an image of a raven with a ring in its beak and various occult characters. The image of a raven, it should be noted, was a common element in German grimoires, and one genre of grimoire was entitled *The Black Raven*. Ebert's curiosity was provoked and he searched in vain for a copy amongst the library's books and manuscripts; neither could he find any clues to the identity of Rabellina. His interest waned but was roused again when one of the inquirers subsequently wrote to say that he had found a copy owned by a Dresden resident and offered to show it to Ebert. Ebert later published a description of it for the benefit of his 'brother librarians, who may have been wearied with similar inquiries'. It was a printed edition, published sometime after 1750, consisting of forty-eight badly written and poorly produced pages. It was entitled *Trinum perfectum magiæ albæ et nigræ*, and professed to consist of magical wisdom from the *Sixth and Seventh Books of Moses*. It contained many characters and seals, which had been produced by hand rather than woodcut. Ebert considered it to be 'from beginning to end the merest nonsense'.[105]

The *Trinum perfectum* provided instructions on how to command spirits, and one suspects that some of those writing to the Dresden Library had treasure on their minds. It was, after all, this activity that fuelled the production of the manuscripts collected by the likes of Goethe and Wunderlich. Until the middle of the century treasure seeking remained a capital crime in some German Catholic states, and a mandate against it was issued in the Prince-Bishopric of Bamberg as late as 1776. Prosecutions occurred periodically throughout the century, and numerous grimoires were confiscated in the process.[106] In 1773, in the south-western town of Günzburg, for instance, the ringleader of a group of treasure seekers was punished by having to kneel in the marketplace with his magical manuscripts.[107] Among them was the much sought after St Christopher Prayer for compelling the spirits and demons that guarded treasure. In southern Germany during the mid-eighteenth century Protestant and Catholic theologians alike condemned its use.[108] It consisted of a long-winded plea to the saint, which, in some versions, beseeched him to send a spirit in human form with 99,000 ducats of currency. It was described by the English scholar of German magical literature, Eliza Butler, as 'an interminable, hysterical and maddeningly repetitive series of prayers and conjurations which could I think only have emanated from a German brain'.[109] (Needless to say, Butler, a Cambridge professor of German, had a deeply prejudiced view of German culture. A few years after the Second World War she wrote several books on the history of magic, which were underpinned by her belief that in Germany's literary and magical traditions she could identify traces of the psyche that bred Nazism.)

By the end of the eighteenth century treasure hunting was creating a considerable market for German grimoires not only in the German states but also in Austria and parts of neighbouring Switzerland. In a series of trials in the Vorarlberg, the westernmost Alpine state in Austria, we find would-be treasure seekers going to considerable effort and expense to find copies.[110] Amongst the most prized in this part of the Catholic Alps were grimoires attributed to the Jesuits, such as one handed over to the Austrian Church authorities in 1823 entitled *Der wahrhafte Jesuiten allerhöchste Höllenzwang* (*The Truthful Jesuit's Very Highest Infernal Command*).[111] The Jesuits were expelled from Austria in 1773 following a papal decree, and it is likely that the concept of the Jesuit grimoire, containing the hidden knowledge of a forbidden society, developed there afterwards. Another distinctive grimoire tradition in this part of the Alps concerned a magical prayer book said to have been written by the thirteenth-century mystic and prophetess St Gertrude of Helfta. The prayers in the *Gertrudenbüchlein*, like those of St Cyprian and St Christopher elsewhere, were thought to be hugely useful in dealing with the spirits and devils that guarded treasure. Pious Gertrude prayer books had been circulating in the German language during the seventeenth century, but it was probably only in the following century that her association with treasure hunting developed in Alpine folklore.[112]

The extent to which grimoires circulated in popular as well as learned culture is indicated by the case of the itinerant glass-painter Joseph Reuther. During the 1770s he was hired to seek out magic manuscripts on his travels through the towns and villages of Bavaria. As Reuther could not read Latin, the language in which parts of some of the grimoires were written, he went into partnership with a weaver named Christopher Reger, of Lauingen, who could. Reger made German translations to sell on, though he admitted that he could not understand everything he read in the manuscripts gathered by Reuther and so omitted such passages in the copies he made.[113] One of their treasure-seeking acquaintances, a tailor, owned a magical manuscript in Latin that he passed on to his landlady, who then applied to Reger.

Around 1775 someone, somewhere, printed a 32-page German work entitled *D. Fausts Original Geister Commando*, apparently written by Dr Habermann, and dated Rome 1510. Professing to be based on a Solomonic tract, the *Sixth and Seventh Books of Moses*, and Tabella Rabellina, it contained a depiction of a raven perched on a book, magical sigils, and lists of the secret holy names of God and the spirits, including Mephistopheles. This very rare book, now in the British Library, was poorly printed, suggesting it might have been an early attempt at reaching a popular market. It was evidently one of several printed versions judging from Ebert's account of the similar Rabellina *Trinum perfectum*. Other *volksbucher* containing magical receipts, though not spirit conjurations, proved far more successful around the time. One was a chapbook entitled *Die Egyptische Geheimnisse* (*Egyptian Secrets*), which was attributed to Albertus Magnus. It contained what were purported to be gypsy (i.e. Egyptian) charms like those contained in French grimoires and the *Médecin des pauvres*, for a range of human and livestock ailments, as well as other simple household spells to protect against thieves, evil spirits, and wicked people. Even more popular was a similar compilation of 'gypsy' magic called the *Romanusbüchlein*, the first known edition of which appeared in Silesia in 1788, though Venice was given as the place of publication.[114]

The influence of the *Bibliothèque bleue* grimoires beyond the French border has already been noted. As national boundaries changed during the upheaval of the Napoleonic wars, so concerns over the circulation of illicit French publications fluctuated. The Prussian authorities in the Rhineland territories annexed in 1815, for instance, were very wary of French political and religious influence, and consequently kept a close eye on the flow of books. When, in 1834, a peddler

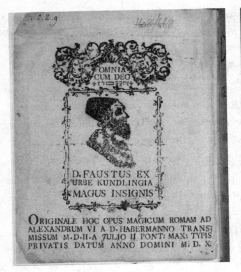

FIG. 8 *D. Faust's original geister commando* (*c.*1775)—frontispiece and title page.

from near Trier applied for a passport to go to Lyon, officials expressed concern that he might bring back pernicious publications.[115] They may not have been thinking of grimoires but Lyon certainly had a reputation in German states as a centre of occult publishing second only to Rome. This was in part due to the legendary Beringos Fratres. Some of the German Faust grimoires circulating in the eighteenth century stated they were copied from works published in Lyon, such as one held in Dresden Library entitled *D. Johannis Fausti Magia celeberrima*, dated 1511, and another entitled *Doct. Joh. Fausten's Miracul, Kunst und Wunderbuch*.[116] At the time, the Prussian authorities also had a burgeoning German market to police. In 1824 an edition of *Albertus Magnus's Egyptian Secrets* was confiscated from one trader.[117] By 1850 a fourth German edition of the *Dragon rouge* had apparently been published in Ilmenau in the centre of Germany.[118] Ironically, the biggest boost to the democratization of German grimoires did not come from abroad or from illicit publishers, though, but from scholarly exercises in historical inquiry.

Between 1821 and 1826 the Protestant pastor Georg Conrad Horst (1769–1832) produced a six-volume compilation of magical works printed by the Mainz publisher Florian Kupferberg. Considering the long history of Protestant clerical condemnation of grimoires, it is somewhat surprising that a pastor would be responsible for the first major grimoire publishing exercise since the seventeenth century. Horst certainly had an abiding interest in the history of witchcraft and magic, and in 1818 had written a widely read encyclopaedic history of the subject,

Daemonomagie oder Geschichte des Glaubens und Zauberei. Horst, who unlike some of his brethren, looked detachedly upon witchcraft as a historical phenomenon, was one of the first witchcraft historians to delve into the archives and it was presumably his research in this area that led him to seek out 'medieval' magic manuals that represented the mindset of the age. But the most far-reaching influence on the spread of German grimoires was the publishing venture of the Stuttgart antiquarian bookseller Johann Scheible. Very little is known about him despite considerable archival research.[119] He seems to have set up his first publishing house in 1831 and over the next few years it went through various partnerships. There is nothing to suggest he had any occult interests. A catalogue of 1836 contains no magic works. So it remains a complete mystery as to why, between 1845 and 1849, he included some forty grimoires in a twelve-volume collection of old 'miraculous and curious' German literature, *Das Kloster*.[120] Unlike the *Bibliothèque bleue*, *Das Kloster* was a purely antiquarian exercise and certainly not affordable for or produced for a popular readership. Scheible went to considerable effort to gather manuscripts from libraries and private owners of varying social levels and occult interests. Amongst those manuscripts he included were a copy of the St Christopher Prayer, several grimoires attributed to Habermann, Faust, and Solomon, and *Das Buch Jezira* and *Trinum Magiae* by Rabellina. Of all the magic books that Scheible put into print for the first time, the most influential was the *Sixth and Seventh Books of Moses*. Some German scholars have pointed to an advert that appeared in the literary periodical *Allgemeiner Litterarischer Anzeiger* in 1797 offering magic books for sale, including the *Sixth and Seventh Books of Moses*, as proof of a late-eighteenth-century first edition. It would seem, however, that Scheible was the first to print a full version.[121] This may seem a pedantic point, but it is a significant detail considering that Scheible's edition would be copied by others and go on to have a global cultural impact comparable to the *Petit Albert*.

Black books in the North

There is no doubting the effect that German manuscript grimoires had on the magical tradition of its northern neighbours. The influence was strongest in Denmark where we find references to the '*Faustbog*' and the '*Romolus-bog*', the latter presumably a version of the *Romanusbüchlein*.[122] Legends circulated in Sweden and Norway regarding those who possessed the *Sixth and Seventh Books of Moses*.[123] In 1802 the Danish authorities arrested an itinerant cunning-man and treasure hunter named Jens Clemmensen and confiscated a magic book in German bearing the title 'Julius Ciprianus den XII & D.J. Faustus Dreyfaices Höllen Schwang'. The book survives today in the Danish Royal Library.[124] Considering the close trading links between the Baltic neighbours it is no surprise that German grimoires circulated freely enough in Scandinavia. Military relationships also provided another conduit. Both the Danish and Swedish monarchs relied heavily on German mercenaries during the seventeenth and eighteenth centuries. Indeed, Germans trained the Danish Norwegian army during the eighteenth century, and German was the language of military command there until the 1770s. As we shall see, though, *svarteboken* or *svartkonstboken*, 'black books' or 'black work books', as grimoires are known in Danish and Swedish, accrued their own distinctive traditions and content.

It has been estimated that over a hundred black books survive in Norwegian libraries and museums alone, most dating to the late eighteenth and nineteenth centuries.[125] This figure is by no means representative of the number that must have been produced, and so for Scandinavia as a whole it is not unlikely that several thousand manuscripts circulated during the period. In the 1820s one poor Danish cottager, an autodidact, made a living transcribing and selling upwards of a hundred copies of one manuscript black book in his possession.[126] Despite sharing the same name the content of the Scandinavian black books are surprisingly diverse, a consequence perhaps of the limited print tradition during the eighteenth century. Some were simple charm books and herbals rather than grimoires, providing practical medical advice, some of it illicit. Several Norwegian black books, for instance, contained herbal recipes to procure abortions using savin, a non-native juniper.[127] Most included spells for the usual desires. Treasure hunting was, of course, as popular as elsewhere in Europe.[128] Some black books also provided instructions on how to make a pact with the Devil, such as the following from an example dating to around 1790–1820:

> When you want to release the angels from Hell, you should in the morning when you rise say this:
>
> I renounce you, God the Father that has made me. I renounce you, the Holy Spirit that has blessed me. I will never worship or serve you after this day, and I completely swear to Lucifer, ruler of the dark abyss. And I swear to his rule, and he shall serve me and do what I ask of him. In exchange I will give you my own blood as insurance and a pledge. This insures me to him with body and soul for all eternity, if he does what I ask, order, or command of him. And thereupon I sign my own hand and with my own blood. This to be certain and true in every possible way.'[129]

The influence of such literature on young men was of particular concern to Danish and Swedish authorities during the eighteenth century. A series of trials were held in Denmark in the 1720s involving soldiers who had made such written pacts with the Devil. Several of the men were publicly executed as a warning of the heinousness of this ultimate act of blasphemy. Over the next decade or so

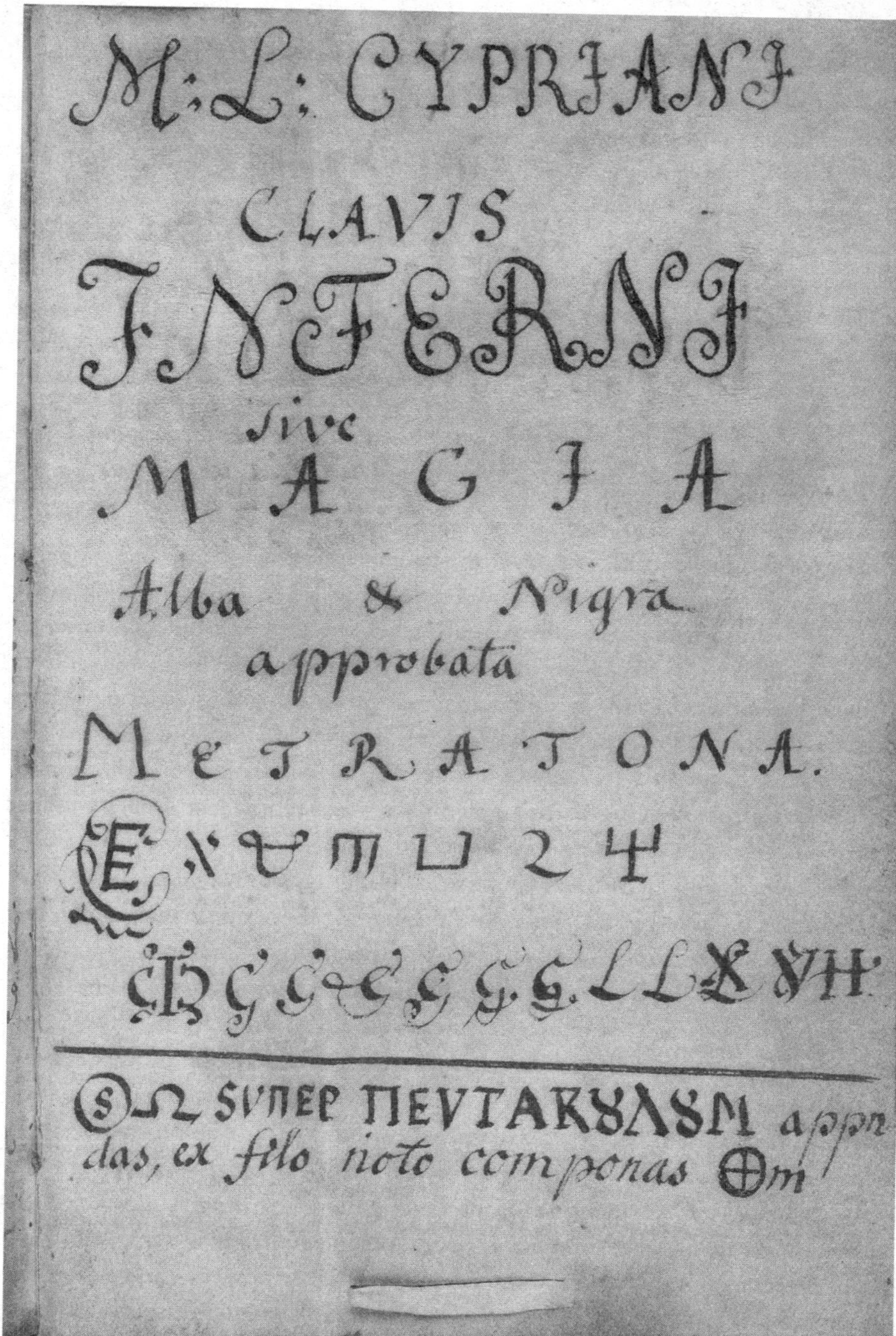

FIG. 9 Title page from a late eighteenth-century Latin *Cyprianus* entitled the 'key of hell or white and black magic'.

Danish theologians and jurists spilt much ink debating the religious and legal position of pact making. Likewise in Sweden at least twenty-nine people were tried for the same crime between 1680 and 1789.[130]

In Denmark and Norway, the latter remaining a Danish territory during the eighteenth century, many black books were attributed to the authorship of St Cyprian, though by the nineteenth century there was confusion about his identity. In Holsten, Denmark, Cyprianus was believed to be an evil Dane kicked out of Hell, while a Norwegian black book described him as a 'tender and decent' student.[131] Why the Lutheran Danes adopted him as their grimoire author supreme is less obvious than his hold in Catholic Spain, where churches as well as prayers were dedicated to the real rather than legendary saint. Germany was the most likely influence. We find a grimoire entitled 'Cyprianus Höllenzwänge' circulating in Germany at the time, and Scheible printed a text entitled 'Cyprian's Invocation of Angels, with his Conjuration for the Spirits guarding Hidden Treasures'.[132] Jens Clemmensen's treasure-conjuring manual was probably a version of this manuscript. Whatever the path of influence, the pre-eminence of the title in Danish magical tradition was certainly sealed by the publication in the 1770s of the first printed Scandinavian black book—more of which a little later.

Because there was no chapbook grimoire revolution in Scandinavia, ownership during the eighteenth and early nineteenth centuries was restricted largely to the educated middling sort, namely civil servants, teachers, clergy, and soldiers. The latter had a particularly strong influence on the circulation of grimoires in Scandinavian society. One black book owner was a Norwegian military officer and farmer named Ulrich Christian Heide (d. 1785).[133] He was in many ways a typical 'enlightenment' man. He spoke several languages and donated some 457 of his books in English, French, and Danish, including the writings of Voltaire, to a military school. His *svartebok* was not among them. Was his interest in his black books that of the detached antiquarian? Or did it contain occult secrets in which Heide had an earnestly professional interest? One can understand why a finely produced Cyprianus of Danish origin, written around the same time as Heide's black book, was owned by a succession of Norwegian officers during the early nineteenth century.[134] It contained magic to improve one's shot and to curry favour with superiors.

As has already been mentioned, the other great attraction of black books for soldiers was the information some of them contained regarding the Devil's pact. Soldiers made up nearly a half of those prosecuted in eighteenth-century Sweden for attempting to make a pact with Satan. As well as money they understandably asked for protection from bullets and a guaranteed lifespan. Military interest was further enhanced by the legendary diabolic activities of the French general the Duke of Luxembourg, who, as we have seen, was caught up in the Affair of the

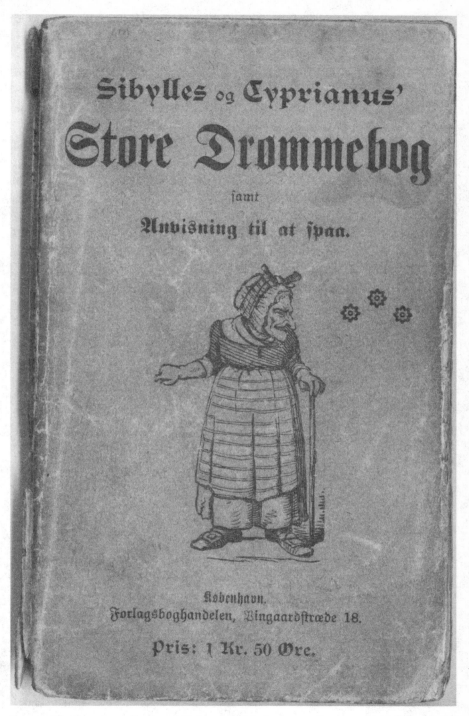

Sibylles og Cyprianus'

Store Drømmebog

samt

Anvisning til at spaa.

København.
Forlagsboghandelen, Vingaardstræde 18.

Pris: 1 Kr. 50 Øre.

FIG. 10 *Prophetesses and Cyprianus' Big Dream Book*. A nineteenth-century Danish divination manual.

Poisons. The magician Lesage claimed Luxembourg had requested his magical aid in military matters amongst other things, while Marie Bosse stated, under torture, that Luxembourg desired to call up the Devil. Luxembourg was known to have a weakness for fortune-tellers and admitted under interrogation to having consulted Lesage on a couple of occasions. He said that Lesage had offered to sell him a copy of the *Enchiridion Leonis papæ*, but he declined.[135] There was no mention in the police archives that he had ever attempted a Devil's pact.

Rumours of his occult dabblings were quickly used for propagandist purposes, and in 1680 the first of numerous editions of a German chapbook appeared, which gave an account of how the duke had sold himself to the Devil while in the Bastille in 1659.[136] The myth was further promoted in a couple of English publications following his successes against the English King William in Flanders during the early 1690s. In one an English soldier reflects, 'the Devil and Luxemburg did bewitch us: And that damn'd Magician may brag of this, as one of his bravest Feats.'[137] More to the point, Danish editions of the German Luxembourg chapbook also appeared during the second half of the eighteenth century.[138] There is no doubt that the story was influential in Scandinavia. An account of Luxembourg's pact, presumably a German edition, was found amongst the possessions of a Swedish diabolist in 1776. His name also found its way into several Norwegian black books. A treasure-digging spell from around 1800 mentions 'Doctor Factus' (Faustus) and 'Luxenborg' as the Devil's servants, and a black book Devil's contract from around 1780 refers to 'Lukemborgs'.[139]

Scandinavian manuscript grimoires were commonly given a foreign origin. We have seen this was standard practice elsewhere, but in Scandinavia little reference was made to such legendary centres of grimoire production as Rome, Salamanca, Toledo, and Lyon. The owner of one *svartebok*, a Norwegian schoolteacher named Arne Larsen, wrote in it that he had purchased it in Amsterdam on the 15 September 1816 and paid three Dutch stivers for it, the equivalent of a few pence at the time. Another example stated that it had been written by one Bishop Johannes Sell 'from Oxford | in England | year 1682'. This is undoubtedly the Bishop of Oxford John Fell (1625–86), who in 1681 had published a translation of St Cyprian's *Of the Unity of the Church*.[140] It is obvious, then, why Fell was picked on to be a black book author, but he was nevertheless an unusual choice. A couple of manuscript versions of a Danish Cyprianus claimed to be copied from one supposedly printed in Stavanger, Norway, in 1699. For Danes, Norway, like Finland, had a reputation as a land of magicians due to legends surrounding the Saami of the northern territories.[141]

By far the most widespread belief was that the black books came from Wittenberg, where folklore had it that the Scandinavian clergy trained in a school for the black arts. Only once they had been awarded their black books could ministers return to their parishes and command and exorcize the Devil. According to a Norwegian legend, though, some ministers left Wittenberg empty-handed, as there were more students than available black books.[142] Numerous black books adhered to this Wittenberg derivation, such as one manuscript entitled 'Cyprianiugs Kunstboeg', which explained that it was found in the 'Vittenbergs Accademie in 1722'. In another we find an inscription that it was 'a copy of the actual Black book, written at the university of Wittenberg year 1529 and thereafter found at Copenhagen Castle in the year 1591'. In both cases, and in others, we also find the motif that the manuscript was found in a marble chest.[143] This Wittenberg tradition was obviously influenced in part by the Faust legend. People in Scandinavia certainly tried to emulate him. A Devil's pact written by a shoemaker of Odense, Denmark, in 1634 began, 'I give myself to Satan to be his own with body and soul. Just as Dr. Faustus became Satan's own, may I do the same.' A Danish soldier named Johan Pistorius, prosecuted in 1718, said he was inspired to make a pact with the Devil after reading a book on Doctor Faustus.[144] But in Lutheran Scandinavia the notion of ministers training at a School of Black Arts in Wittenberg suggests a blending in popular tradition of the town's dual reputation as both the home of Faust and the home of Martin Luther and the Reformation. Indeed, a Danish Church Ordinance of 1627 requiring all prospective Lutheran ministers to obtain a university degree meant that some Norwegian clergymen did attend the University of Wittenberg, as well as that in Copenhagen and the north German town of Rostock.[145]

The advent of print grimoires did little to undermine the Wittenberg tradition. The first one printed in Scandinavia, *Sybrianus P.P.P.*, was produced in Denmark in 1771, around the same time as they were starting to be published in Germany. It was penned by an impoverished writer named Sören Rosenlund, who, under the nom de plume 'Junior Philopatreias' had written works on a variety of mundane topics. We can assume that Rosenlund's decision to publish the *Sybrianus* was motivated purely by money rather than an Enlightenment exercise in highlighting the folly of grimoires. The content was made up of a mix of his own inventions along with recipes and conjurations culled from manuscripts. It is likely that he made use of those housed in the Danish Royal Library, and it is presumably from these that he borrowed the various runic symbols that made the *Sybrianus P.P.P.* distinctive. There is no doubting the significant impact the *Sybrianus P.P.P.* had on the Danish manuscript tradition. Numerous handwritten black books from the late eighteenth and nineteenth centuries share the same title, the various runic formulae it contained, and the distinctive and curious descending kalemaris charm, which worked in the same way as abracadabra, was commonly employed:[146]

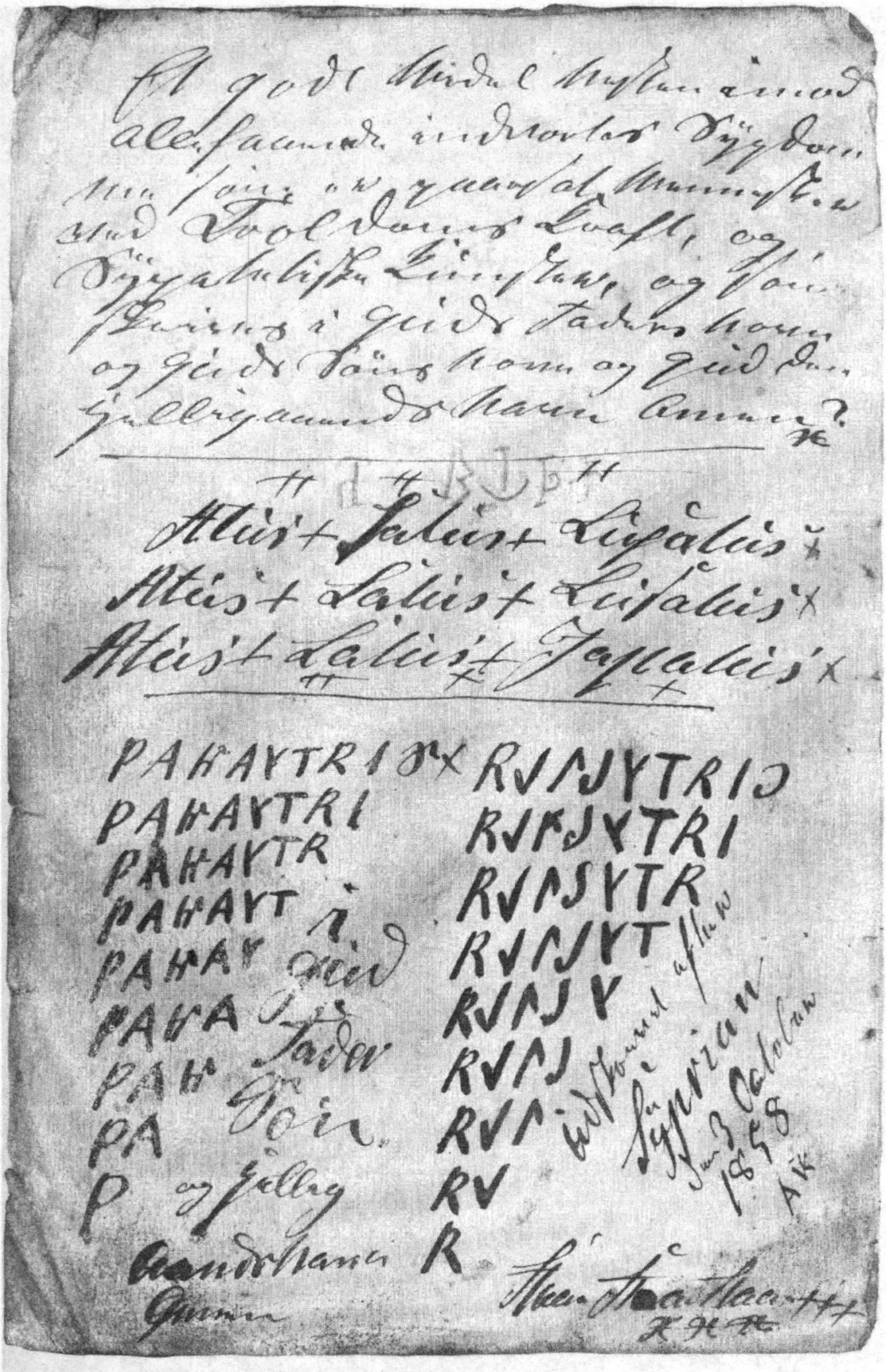

Side af Anders Ulfkjærs Cyprianus.

FIG. 11 Page from the Danish cunning-man Anders Ulfkjær's *Cyprianus*.

KALEMARIS
KALEMARI
KALEMAR
KALEMA
KALEM
KALE
KAL
KA
K

Around 1890 another enterprising Dane named Henrik Kokborg, an apothecary, photographer, and small-time book publisher on the Danish mainland produced a cheap grimoire under the title *En lille Udtog af Syprianus* (*A Little Piece of Syprianus*).[147] As the use of the 'S' in Syprianus suggests, some of its contents shared similarities with Rosenlund's production, but otherwise much of it was probably garnered from several manuscript black books that Kokborg was known to have possessed. Kokborg had a reputation for practising magic and various legends tell how he bewitched people and called up the Devil. He certainly knew that there was money to be made from such beliefs. As well as a Celestial Letter, he published a couple of broadside charms to help the bewitched, and his *Syprianus* contained more spells against witchcraft than Rosenlund's and other manuscript black books.[148]

It was only during the second half of the nineteenth century that similar cheap grimoires were printed in Sweden. One of the first, published in Stockholm in 1877, was entitled *Svartkonstboken*, and had a stylized image of the Devil on the front. It cost 25 öre, the price of a few postage stamps at the time. It began with an account entitled 'How I got the Black Art Book', which ignores the black book legends mentioned earlier. The narrator tells a story of how he became acquainted with a strange old man with gypsy blood in his veins. He was a '*trollkarlen*'—a 'witch-man' or cunning-man who said he gained some of his powers from his black book. He said that when he first read it sparks emanated from it, he was sick for days afterwards and subsequently began to behave strangely. One dark and foul night the narrator visited the strange man in his hut in the woods, hoping to get a glimpse of his mysterious book. The cunning-man led him into a small room, lifted up a log, and in a hole beneath lifted out an old, yellowing book, which he gave to the narrator. It contained passages in Latin and so the narrator concluded that the monks must have had some hand in its content. The narrator in presenting its magical contents to the reader said he reproduced it for the sake of curiosity rather than as a valuable manual of magical aid.

The importance of print is a surprising recurring motif in the Scandinavian black book tradition. The act of transcription and the rituals associated with the creation of magic manuscripts, the use of parchment and consecrated inks for example, meant that, in general, print was seen as inherently less magical. It would seem that in Scandinavia, though, print was a seal of authority and occult legitimacy. We see this in the statements in several Cyprianus grimoires that they were copies of one printed in Stavanger in 1699, and the claim in the 'Cyprianiugs Kunstboeg' that it derived from a copy found in 1722 and subsequently printed. A Danish cunning-man prosecuted during the mid-nineteenth century made the point of telling the court that he had obtained his knowledge from a 'Sympathie Book' 'published by Cyprianus and printed in red letters'.[149] In Finland, which had long been a Swedish territory until it was incorporated into the Russian empire during the early nineteenth century, the tradition of 'Black Bibles' used by *tietäjäs* (cunning-folk) was evidently shaped by Swedish print culture. As recorded in late-nineteenth- and early-twentieth-century Finnish folklore, the Black Bibles were thought to consist of white or red print on black pages. One Finnish folklorist, commenting on the reputation of a *tietäjäs* named Old Aapa who was known to possess a Black Bible, noted that some 'claimed that while Aapa certainly had some kind of book, it was just an old Swedish medical handbook'.[150] The Black Bible with its red print on black pages had clear diabolic associations, which were in turn coloured by resentment regarding Swedish cultural influence. A similar demonizing of ruling elites has been identified in Estonian folklore regarding German landlords.[151]

English reserve?

As elsewhere, there was a ready market for grimoires in Britain. Eighteenth- and early-nineteenth-century cunning-folk treasured copies of Reginald Scot's *Discoverie* and Robert Turner's edition of Agrippa's *Fourth Book of Occult Philosophy*. Manuscript versions and extracts circulated in popular culture, and evidence of their use can be found in the counter-witchcraft charms sold by Welsh and English cunning-folk.[152] The birth of new evangelical, mystical, and prophetic movements, such as the Swedenborgians, also sustained a favourable environment for the continued interest in Neoplatonic magic in certain social circles, mostly among inquisitive young men from artisan or middling-sort backgrounds. Yet a chapbook grimoire revolution never happened. This is remarkable considering that, in the period, English and Scottish publishers produced huge numbers of chapbooks on astrology and divination. Apart from love spells there was very little practical magic in these chapbooks, and none of the healing charms and spirit

FRONTISPIECE.

FIG. 12 A magician at work. From the *Conjurors Magazine* (1792–3).

conjurations found in the Continental examples.[153] Scot's *Discoverie* and the *Fourth Book* could easily have been plundered, and copies of the *Petit Albert* were being sold by London booksellers and could have been pirated, but they remained largely untouched.[154] The only work comparable to the Continental chapbooks was *Witchcraft Detected and Prevented: or The School of the Black Art Newly Opened*, which was printed in Peterhead, Scotland, and went through at least three editions in the 1820s. It borrowed heavily from Scot's *Discoverie* and also included extracts from an edition of the secrets of Albertus Magnus. There is no evidence to suggest that it disseminated widely enough to have made an impact on popular tradition.

England's contribution to the diffusion of ritual magic and conjuration lay not in the chapbook genre, but in the production of several expensive, hefty compilations of early modern Neoplatonic wisdom. The first off the presses was the work of one of the most influential occultists in modern British history—the astrologer and Freemason Ebenezer Sibly (1751–c.1799). Sibly, the son of a mechanic, had practised as an astrologer in Bristol, and by the time he moved to London around 1788 he had already written his huge four-part work of occult philosophy, *A New and Complete Illustration of the Celestial Science of Astrology*. Sibly was no spirit conjurer, though, and condemned such attempts as wicked black magic. The blessed angelic host, who were so crucial to the working of celestial influence on Earth, were not at the beck and call of mere mortals. Nevertheless, the numerous editions of the *Complete Illustration* provided a treasure house of information on magical procedure, including a description of the infernal spirits and their powers taken from the 1665 edition of Scot's *Discoverie*.[155] The significance of this will be revealed in the next chapter. The *Complete Illustration* also excited others to explore beyond the boundaries of magic acceptable to Sibly, including provincial cunning-folk who evidently treasured the book.[156]

Sibly moved to London at a time when, as the historian E. P. Thompson put it, the capital was experiencing an 'explosion of anti-rationalism'.[157] There was a heady mix of political radicalism inspired by the French Revolution, spiritual interest provoked by the angelic communications and mystical writings of Emanuel Swedenborg (1688–1772), a surge in millenarian prophecy, and magical experimentation. A short-lived periodical entitled the *Conjuror's Magazine, or, Magical and Physiognomical Mirror*, was produced in London between 1792 and 1793. The capital's big booksellers, such as James Lackington, acted as important repositories of magic. Lackington's 'Temple of the Muses' in Finsbury Square was a London wonder. Above the entrance were the words 'Cheapest Bookseller in the World'.[158] The shop of the occult book dealer John Denley contained one of the best collections of magic books and manuscripts in the country. Before becoming a Swedenborgian preacher, Ebenezer Sibly's brother, Manoah, had also been a more modest London dealer in occult works. Thanks to the *Complete Illustration of the Celestial Science* Ebenezer also became a magnet for others wishing to learn more of the occult sciences. One such disciple who removed to London to consult from the master was a Lincolnshire cunning-man and self-publicist named John Parkins.[159]

During his sojourn in the capital, and shortly after Sibly's death, Parkins also said he received instruction from another self-proclaimed adept of the occult sciences named Francis Barrett.[160] Barrett, described in one newspaper report as 'a miniature-painter, and an amateur of chemistry', was better known in his lifetime for his failed ballooning exploits than his knowledge of magic.[161] Three times in the year 1802 he drummed up a large paying crowd to see him attempt a balloon assent, and three times he failed embarrassingly. Regarding his attempt at Greenwich, one reporter complained, 'at no public exhibition do we ever recollect such a complete want of management as at Mr. Barrett's Balloon,' while at Swansea the platform collapsed as he began to address the crowd, damaging his balloon, and causing injury to a number of spectators. He departed to the sound of hootings and howlings from the crowd. Reporting on this third fiasco *The Morning Chronicle* stated, 'we hope it will be the last. In short, he does not seem to posses a sufficient knowledge of chemistry.'[162] Decades later, long after his ballooning disasters had faded from popular memory, he achieved a degree of notoriety as the author of the first major English discourse on spirit conjuration since the seventeenth century. *The Magus: or Celestial Intelligencer*, published by Lackington in 1801, ventured where Sibly refused to go. It was, however, still little more than a compilation of material quite skilfully culled from a range of books borrowed from John Denley. It relied heavily on the seventeenth-century English editions of Agrippa's *Three Books of Occult Philosophy*, the *Fourth Book of Occult Philosophy*, and the *Heptameron*.[163] Barrett considered his work a contribution to the magical renaissance in the country: 'At this time,' he said, 'the abstruse sciences of Nature begin to be more investigated than for a century past, during which space they have been almost totally neglected.'[164]

At the time of its publication it proved no more successful than his ballooning activities. Its distinctive, original colour plates of the heads of several principal spirits rendered it expensive to produce. A review in *The Critical Review* began, 'In vain do we boast of the progress of philosophy;—for, behold! In the beginning of the nineteenth century appears a work which ought not to have surpassed the fifteenth.' It went on to comment, 'It would be loss of time to criticise with gravity so weak and ignorant a book.'[165] A couple of decades later it was fetching high prices in the antiquarian book trade, and its impact on the country's popular magic was very limited compared to Sibly's opus. A rare example of its use was recorded in 1857 in a report on a visit to a Liverpool fortune-teller. The investigating journalist noted that in the diviner's study there was a large oval crystal

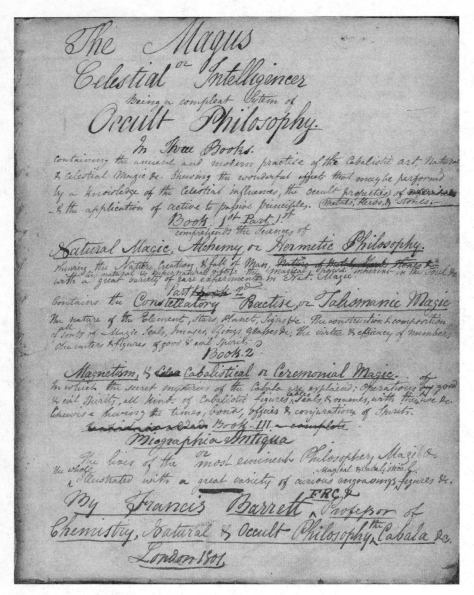

FIG. 13 Manuscript title page of Francis Barrett's *The Magus* (1801).

lying on a copy of *The Magus*, a book which the fortune-teller 'professed to value highly'. It seemed to serve, however, more as a prop than a well-thumbed spring of magical knowledge.[166] In the long term, though, *The Magus* would become a major influence on the middle-class occult revival of the late nineteenth and twentieth centuries.

What of his pupil John Parkins? If anyone was to write a populist grimoire at the time he was the most likely candidate. He was a sophisticated exploiter of print, producing puffs advertising his magical powers, talismans, and handwritten copies of his own grimoire, *The Grand Oracle of Heaven, or, The Art of Divine Magic*.[167] Such was the reputation he generated through his herbal and fortune-telling publications, and his advertisements in the regional press, that his death was even recorded in the respected periodical *The Gentleman's Magazine*. In 1830 it noted the demise, at the age of fifty-nine, of 'Mr. Parkins, commonly called "Dr. Parkins," a celebrated astrologer and fortune teller'.[168] Yet he never moved into the chapbook grimoire market, even though he worked with chapbook publishers. His *Universal Fortune-Teller* (1810), for example, was produced by the London bookseller and publisher Thomas Tegg, one-time owner of the Eccentric Book Warehouse in West Smithfield. Tegg produced an eclectic mix of high-minded improving literature, gothic tales, and chapbook adventures. He also produced a range of guides on stage magic and legerdemain.[169] Would Tegg have added a popular grimoire to his stock if Parkins had presented one to him? Probably not. British chapbook publishers evidently practised a degree of self-censorship, particularly during the period of Revolutionary and Napoleonic France, during which the British government kept a close eye on the printers. Fortune-telling and a bit of love magic were all that was considered acceptable. Any magical content darker than that was out of bounds, even if it was prefaced with disingenuous provisos that such information was published as an illustration of the superstitions of the past. An equation can be drawn with pornography. As with grimoires this was a forte of illicit French publishing, but it was kept relatively suppressed by both the authorities and political self-censorship amongst British Radical populist publishers.[170]

With *The Magus* being too expensive and difficult to obtain, and with Parkins declining to go into the print grimoire business, the only other affordable source of instruction on spirit invocation and talismans was to be found in the works of Robert Cross Smith (1795–1832). He was another Bristolian astrologer who made his way to London, and soon found himself at the heart of a mutually supportive group of astrologers and occultists during the 1820s. His first foray into occult publishing was *The Philosophical Merlin* published by John Denley in 1822. It purported to be a translation of a magical manuscript owned by Napoleon, but was in fact a mish-mash of material culled from Barrett's *The Magus*. It was a flop and most of the stock was remaindered.[171] Smith then took over the editorship of a weekly periodical called *The Straggling Astrologer*, which contained a diverse selection of articles, excerpts, and advice on astrology and magic. It folded after only twenty-two issues, but in 1825 it was repackaged as a book entitled *The Astrologer of the Nineteenth Century*, claiming bogusly to be in its seventh edition. It contained numerous talismans and spirit invocations, including incantations for raising the spirit of a suicide. For this it was advised that:

> the exorcist, being prepared with the pentacles of Solomon, the two seals of the earth, and other necessaries, he must bind upon the top of his wand, a bundle of St. John's wort (*milies perforatum*), with the head of an owl; and, having repaired to the spot where the corpse of the self-murderer lies, at the solemn hour of midnight, precisely at twelve o-clock, he must draw the circle, and having entered it, solemnly repeat the following words[172]

Smith claimed some of these conjurations and talismans were culled from ancient manuscripts in the possession of the Mercurii, a secret magic society of which he was a member—perhaps the only one. However, one was also attributed to George Graham, a friend of Smith's, who was a disaster-prone occult balloonist in the Barrett mould. Most of the extra material not culled from Sibly or Barrett probably derived from Denley's collection. *The Astrologer of the Nineteenth Century* unfortunately suffered a similar fate as *The Philosophical Merlin*. Its publisher, Walter Charleton Wright, went temporarily bankrupt, as did the next owner. No further editions appeared.[173] Smith's occult publishing career certainly seemed ill-starred until he finally made money by entering the almanac market under the nom de plume Raphael.

Caution on behalf of the chapbook publishers and over-ambition on the part of occultists seems to have ensured that there was no grimoire revolution in Britain, and consequently British print culture had a limited influence on the magical traditions of its colonies around the world. Only Sibly had some impact in India where there was a venerable and influential astrological culture receptive to his English language opus.[174] Apart from an intriguing early nineteenth-century American interlude, Britain's international influence would only emerge in the second half of the century when a new breed of middle-class ritual magicians began to form occult organizations and launch the next big exercise in magical publishing.

ACROSS THE OCEANS

We saw in an earlier chapter how grimoires soon found their way to the Americas amongst the possessions of the early colonists. The flow was a mere trickle though, and their cultural influence very limited. With the expansion of Atlantic trade during the eighteenth century, and the increasing number of emigrants crossing the ocean, the influence of grimoires overseas was bound to increase, but not everywhere and not with the same impact. The power of the Inquisition largely prevented the substantial infiltration of European grimoires into the Spanish colonies until the twentieth century, whereas the *Bibliothèque bleue* led to French grimoires having a huge influence on the diverse medical and magical traditions generated in the Caribbean. Let us turn first, though, to how the grimoire slowly but surely inveigled its way into the heart of the cultural and spiritual world of North America's British and German settlers, inspiring new beliefs and uniquely American controversies.

By the late seventeenth century there is evidence that American cunning-folk were using works of occult philosophy and practical magic, as well as English books on palmistry and astrology.[1] In 1695 Robert Roman of Chester County, Pennsylvania, was prosecuted and fined £5 and costs for practising 'geomancy according to Hidon and divining by a stick'. 'Hidon' is obviously a misspelling of Heydon, for we find this author's geomantic text *The Temple of Wisdom* amongst the three books confiscated from Roman. The other two were more overtly magical—'Scot's Discovery of Witchcraft, and Cornelius Agrippa's, teaching Necromancy', the latter presumably a copy of the *Fourth Book of Occult Philosophy*.[2] Moving further up the social scale, works on astrology, those of the London astrologer-physicians Nicholas Culpeper and William Salmon in particular, were evidently not uncommon in the libraries of the prosperous elite of the early eighteenth century. We have already heard of the impressive library of John Winthrop Jr. That of Edmund Berkeley, a member of the Virginia Council, contained a copy of Richard Saunders' palmistry manual, *Physiognomy and Chiromancy* (London, 1653). This was the same sort of book—maybe the very book— that landed Dorcas Hoar in so much trouble during the Salem trials.[3] The Governor of New England, William Burnet, who died in 1728, owned a copy of Turner's 1665 edition of *The Fourth Book of Occult Philosophy*.[4]

The British by no means held a monopoly on Colonial American occult literature during the early eighteenth century. The various German Protestant mystical colonies in Pennsylvania were also foci for the accumulation of esoteric and magic books. Millenarian Pietists, Mennonites, and Moravian groups from the Low Countries, Germany, and Switzerland were drawn to the English colony thanks to the religious tolerance instituted by the state's Quaker founder William Penn. But religious peace and harmony had their limits, and once settled in Pennsylvania schisms amongst pious Protestant immigrants led to further spin-off sects following variant doctrines and new self-proclaimed prophets. While the influence of Kabbalah and Rosicrucianism were evident in the teachings and practices of a number of these religious communities, one group of German colonists in particular was renowned for its occult interests.[5]

Germantown, founded in 1683, was a modestly thriving Pennsylvanian settlement by the time the followers of Johann Zimmerman, a Pietist mathematician, astronomer, and adherent of the mystic Jakob Boehme, arrived there. Zimmerman, who at one time taught at the University of Heidelberg, believed that the apocalypse and second coming of Christ would occur in 1694. He believed the wilderness of America an appropriately biblical location to await Armageddon and the new millennium: he died shortly before setting sail from Rotterdam. His followers, a brotherhood of learned Pietist men who had vowed to practise celibacy, chose Johannes Kelpius, a young Transylvanian theologian to lead them. The group arrived in 1694 and settled in huts along the Wissahickon Creek near Germantown awaiting the new millennium. As soon as it became clear that Christ was not going to return as predicted the thought of celibacy proved too much for some. After the death of Kelpius in 1708 most remaining members drifted away. In the meantime, those followers of Zimmerman who remained true to their initial guiding principles, and were inspired by their mystical philosophy and intellectual curiosity, immersed themselves in the occult possibilities of alchemy, Kabbalah, and astrology during their hermit existence.

One of those original members who stayed on and continued his hermit's existence was Johann Gottfried Sehlee (Seelig) (d. 1745), who apparently drew up horoscopes when requested, and who in his will bequeathed to a friend, '1 scale, with gold and silver weights', which indicate alchemical activity, along with '5 bibles, 14 books, 10 of Jacob Boehmen's books, and 120 Latin, Dutch and Greek books'.[6] His name would later become confused with that of a German publisher on Judaism Gottfried Selig (1722–95), who produced a German language version of the Jewish mystical text *Sefer Shimush Tehilim* concerning the magical powers of the Psalms. In the early twentieth century this would reappear in a popular format as Godfrey Selig's *The Secrets of the Psalms*.

Christopher Witt, an English physician, clockmaker, botanist, and occultist, was another well-known figure who joined Kelpius in 1704 and remained in Germantown to the end of his life. A letter recounting a visit to Witt written in 1743 described his study as 'furnished with books containing different kinds of learning; as Philosophy, Natural Magic, Divinity, nay, even Mystical Divinity'. He lent out some of his books and evidently tried to enthuse others in magic. One botanical acquaintance wrote, 'when we are on the topic of astrology, magic and mystical divinity, I am apt to be a little troublesome by inquiring into the foundation and reasonableness of these notions.'[7] One of Witt's friends, Christopher Lehman, who had arrived in Germantown from Germany in 1730–1, shared not only Witt's botanical interests but also his occult philosophy, and amongst his surviving papers there is a geomantic manuscript.[8] The activities of this small group left Germantown with a long-lasting reputation for magic.

Germantown's only rival in terms of occult standing was Ephrata, which is now in Lancaster County. Its founder was Conrad Beissel (1690–1768), a Pietist baker who had arrived in Germantown in 1720 expecting to find Kelpius's movement alive and well. Disillusioned with the various sects he found instead, he set forth into the Pennsylvanian wilderness and formed his own monastic-like community for men and women who came to be known as German Seventh Day Baptists. One of their main activities was the creation of impressive illuminated manuscripts. With the installation of a printing press in 1745 the Ephrata community also became a major centre of Gothic type German language publication, and producer of the occasional mystical and magical publication.[9]

The private libraries of wealthy colonialists and Protestant mystics were not the only repositories of European occultism. That admirable eighteenth-century urban institution, the subscription library, also provided access to magical knowledge for those who had a few shillings to spare annually and the time to peruse their holdings. The very first such institution, the Library Company of Philadelphia, founded in 1731 by Benjamin Franklin, had, by the early nineteenth century accumulated a 1651 edition of Scot's *Discoverie*, the 1651 translation of Agrippa's *Three Books of Occult Philosophy*, the 1658 edition of Porta's *Natural Magic*, and a 1650 Latin edition as well. It also had copies of the new generation of

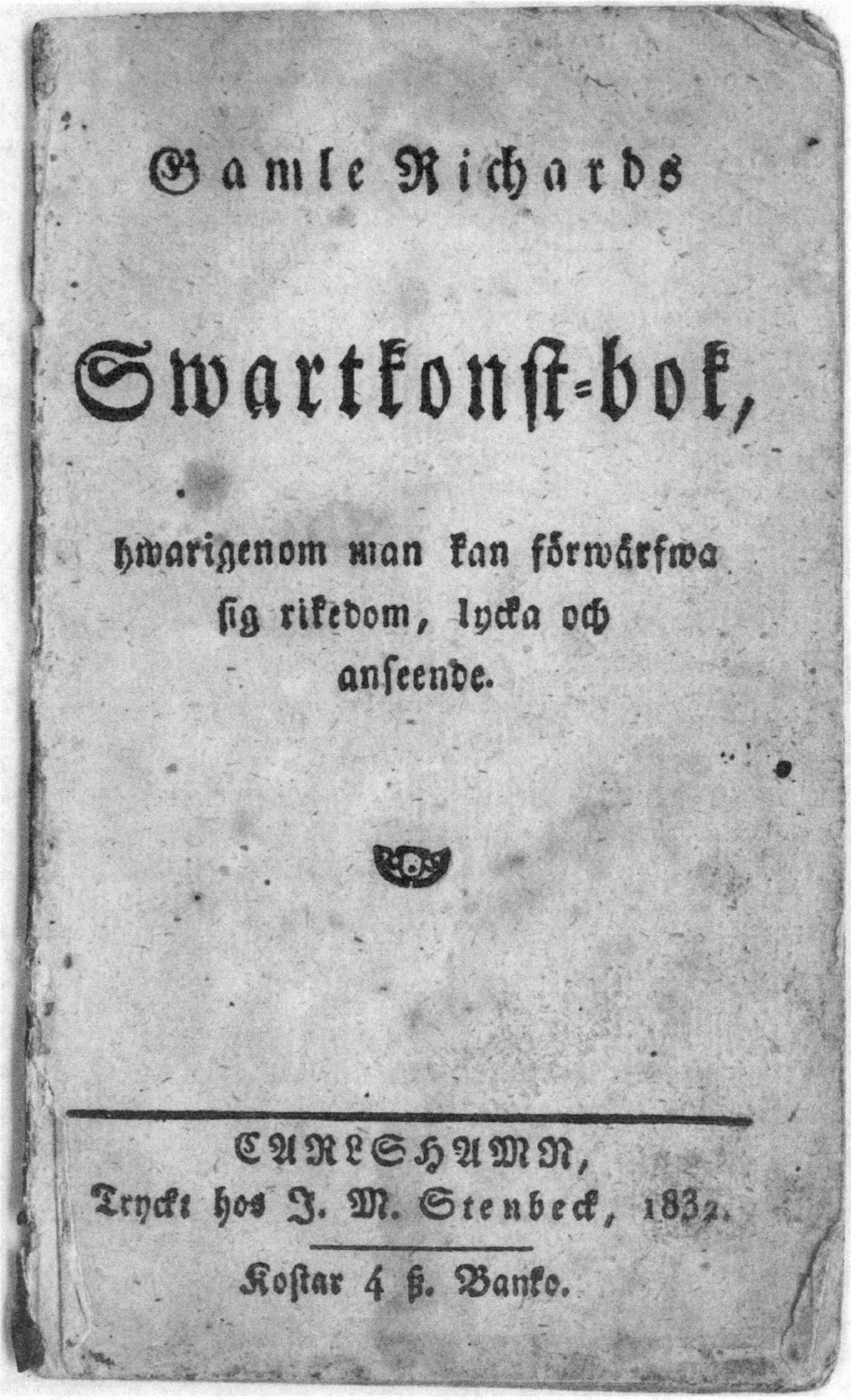

Gamle Richards

Swartkonst-bok,

hwarigenom man kan förwärfwa
sig rikedom, lycka och
anseende.

CARLSHAMN,
Tryckt hos J. M. Stenbeck, 1832.

Kostar 4 ß. Banko.

FIG. **14** Title page of *Gamle Richards Swartkonst-bok* (Karlshamn, 1832).

magical disquisitions, namely a 1784 edition of Sibly's *New Illustration of the Celestial Science of Astrology*, Raphael's *Sanctuary of the Astral Art*, and Barrett's *The Magus*.[10] This must have constituted the largest public resource on practical magic in the country at the time. Subscription libraries spread along the eastern seaboard during the second half of the century and some of them held at least one or two of the key works. The New York Society Library, to which some of John Winthrop's books were donated, possessed a 1584 edition of Scot's *Discoverie*.[11] During the mid-nineteenth century grimoires also moved west with the gold prospectors. In 1854 the San Francisco Mercantile Library housed a copy of Agrippa's *Three Books* and an edition of the *Arbatel of Magic*, presumably extracted from Turner's edition of the *Fourth Book of Occult Philosophy* or a rare eighteenth-century edition.[12] While admission to these libraries, whether private or public, was restricted to a very small percentage of the population, they confirm that America had its own palaces of occult enlightenment. It is not unlikely, furthermore, that these repositories generated manuscript grimoires produced by copyists who did have access.

So far, our history of American magic has concerned the books that immigrants took with them. It was only during the late seventeenth century that printing presses were permitted in English territories. Around the same time the French had banned all publishing in New France. Tellingly, the first publication produced by the first printing office in Pennsylvania was an astrological almanac released in 1685, and others followed. The success of the *American Almanack*, compiled by Daniel and Titan Leeds, which ran during the early eighteenth century, shows there was considerable demand for such occult aid. Titan Leeds was the butt of Benjamin Franklin's satirical wit when, in 1732, Franklin launched his own mock astrological guide entitled *Poor Richard's Almanack*. Franklin was one of the most influential men in eighteenth-century America, a scientist, statesman, and later a national hero for his role in ensuring the success of American Independence. *Poor Richard's* purported author was an astrologer and 'friend' of Titan Leeds named Richard Saunders. Over the next few years *Poor Richard's Almanack* regularly speculated on Leeds' death, to his understandable chagrin. The mock formula was as big a success as the earnest astrological almanac, selling up to 10,000 copies annually during the quarter century of its existence.[13] Some no doubt bought it under a misapprehension as to its contents. Years later, Franklin's spoof would be the first American 'occult' publication to make a significant impression back across the Atlantic. One French edition of Poor Richard's collected advice was translated under the title *le Chemin de la fortune, suivie de la veritable Poule Noire, ou la Connaissance des trésors*, and in Sweden as *Gamle Richards Swartkonst-bok*.[14] In each case the popular fascination with grimoires was used to lure people into reading a determinedly rationalist message.

Until the late eighteenth century run-of-the-mill chapbooks were imported from Britain in large numbers. They were reproduced locally only when imports did not match demand, and this was due more to the economic restrictions of a chronic shortage of rags for paper than the hindrance of the censors.[15] We get some sense of the influence of and concerns regarding such literature from the writings of Revd Ebenezer Turell of Medford, Massachusetts. He had maintained a sceptical stance during a local case involving some girls who maliciously claimed to be tormented by witches, and evidently considered popular literature, and the 'devil's playthings' it contained, to be responsible in part for the continuance of such pernicious beliefs. He wrote in 1720, 'Young people would do wisely now to lay aside all their foolish books, their trifling ballads, and all romantick accounts of dreams and trances, senseless palmistry and groundless astrology'.[16]

It was not until after the War of Independence that American publishers began to pump out the wide range of chapbooks available on the Continent. Amongst them, inevitably, were versions of the run-of-the-mill cheap fortune-telling and dream books that had proved so popular in England, such as *The New Book of Knowledge* published in Boston in the 1760s, and *The Universal Interpreter of Dreams and Visions* (1795).[17] The popularity of such literature was boosted further by the huge growth of legal and illicit lotteries—the urban treasure trove of the nineteenth century. In 1826 one critic of these lotteries described how whole streets were being converted into lottery shops, with 'boys standing at every corner to thrust printed schemes and advertisements of lucky lottery offices into the hands of the passers by.'[18] The most popular of the schemes was the policy system based on the selection of three numbers. By mid-century American dream books included three-number combinations in relation to different visions. One edition, for example, attached the numbers 2, 7, and 41 to dreams about ants.[19]

Several versions of the enduringly popular Dr Faust chapbook were printed in Pennsylvania, Massachusetts, and Connecticut during the 1790s. As elsewhere, they may have excited some young men to seek out the means of conjuring up the Devil. The story was no doubt already well known to both English and German settlers in the colonial period.[20] But otherwise, during the nineteenth century, the seeker of practical magic in America remained dependent primarily on seventeenth-century English printed editions and German manuscripts. Until the publication of John George Hohman's *Der lang verborgene Freund* in 1820, which will be discussed in a later chapter, all that was produced other than astrological almanacs and simple fortune-telling tracts were the decorative, German language house-blessings and celestial letters or *Himmelsbrief* printed in Ephrata and elsewhere in Pennsylvania.[21] As in northern Europe, copies of these blessings and apocryphal correspondence were commonly hung on walls or kept on the person to protect against illness during childbirth, fire, and evil.

So far I have been exploring the presence and possession of grimoires as part of a wider emigration of occultism across the North Atlantic, but to what extent were they actually used and for what? There is certainly little evidence that any of the educated elite with their large libraries actually practised spirit conjurations and the like; their occult interests were mostly philosophical, astrological, or alchemical. By the early nineteenth century, however, the Germantown mystics were characterized as practical magicians in reminiscence and folklore. A history of Pennsylvania written in 1829 suggested that although Witt's medical practice flourished, the 'superstition of his neighbours, probably rendered his profession of necromancy the more lucrative.' He acted as a cunning-man, detecting the whereabouts of stolen goods, identifying thieves, and combating witchcraft.[22] He was also said to have trained up others in the practical occult arts including his successor in the cunning-trade Dr Frailey, a Germantown resident whose one-story house was decorated with German poetry painted in oil colours.[23] As to the reality, Witt, Lehman, and other leading Germantown residents like John Seelig certainly cast nativities and followed astrological principles—Witt evidently on a commercial basis. He provided a certificate, an example of which survives, to at least one student confirming his successful training in the 'Arts & Mysteries of Chemistry, Physick, & Astral Sciences'.[24] As to the use of practical magic garnered from grimoires, the main evidence is the corpus of *anhängsel* or *zauber-zettel*, amulets and talismans, created by the occult adepts of the Pennsylvanian German Pietists for the benefit of their communities. These magical lamens, containing astrological and angelic signs like those espoused by Paracelsus, were usually drawn on parchment and paper and were widely worn among German settlers to ward off evil spirits, witchcraft, gunshot, and ill health. Some were engraved or stamped in brass, silver, and even gold. A nineteenth-century historian of the Germantown mystics possessed one such brass, a *wunder-sigel*, which was warmed with a flame and impressed on the skin of humans and animals at the spot where their malady was manifest while a charm was spoken. This branding technique was also used to prevent cattle from straying or being stolen—something you do not see in Hollywood westerns.[25]

Pirate treasure

As in Europe, the search for treasure provides us with the most references regarding the use of grimoires in the eighteenth century. America may not have been dotted with the ruined monasteries, castles, stone circles, dolmens, and hill forts that attracted treasure legends across Europe, but this did not prevent settlers from creating a new geography of treasure—one based on buried pirate booty supposedly secreted by the notorious William Kidd and Jean Lafitte, lost Spanish gold mines, and ancient Indian treasure.[26] The West may have had its gold rush in the mid-nineteenth century but, long before, the countryside of the northeastern Atlantic seaboard was dotted with the explorations of those seeking hidden riches. In 1729 Benjamin Franklin co-wrote a newspaper essay highlighting the 'problem', bemoaning the great number of labouring people who were bringing their families to the brink of ruin in search of 'imaginary treasures'. The physical signs of their activities were apparent around and about Philadelphia. 'You can hardly walk half a mile out of Town on any side, without observing several Pits dug with that Design,' Franklin moaned. He took a particular swipe at the role of astrologers, 'with whom the Country swarms at this Time', in promoting such fruitless endeavour. The article contained a mock letter from one such devotee of the celestial art who boasts of having 'read over Scot, Albertus Magnus, and Cornelius Agrippa above 300 times'. A hundred years later the town's residents could still point out the various spots were holes had been dug.[27] It is possible that the popular preoccupation with treasure hunting during the eighteenth and early nineteenth centuries was fertilized by German immigrants. Although England had long had a tradition of treasure hunting, which had caused particular concern to the authorities in the mid-sixteenth century, by the eighteenth century it was by no means as strong as it was in parts of Germany, where as we have seen numerous prosecutions took place during the eighteenth century.

The author of a 1767 comic opera—indeed the first American opera—wrote in the preface that it was partly written with the aim 'to put a stop (if possible) to the foolish and pernicious practice of searching after supposed hidden treasure'.[28] The plot of the *Disappointment* concerns four Pennsylvanian gentlemen who test the credulity and cupidity of four tradesmen by concocting a story of Blackbeard's hidden booty, the location of which is revealed in a map sent by the English sister-in-law of one of the pranksters. One of the gentlemen, Rattletrap, pretends to be a conjuror, no doubt modelled on the Germantown magi, who offers to use his magical knowledge to ward off the spirits of Blackbeard's crew, which guard the treasure. Amongst his accoutrements are a hazel staff, magnet, telescope, an ancient quilted nightcap, and a 'brass bound magic book'. 'This book my wonders contain', he boasts, 'Twou'd deceive the devil himself, And puzzle a conjuror's brain.' He learns some arcane words from reading the canto of Hudibras and Sydrophel, which together with his mathematical knowledge 'qualify him for a modern conjuror'.[29] At the site where the treasure is said to be hidden Rattletrap draws a large circle in the ground with his wand and plants twelve pieces of wire around it each with a paper cut into the shape of a star. Then the pseudo-conjurations begin, 'Diapaculum interravo, tenebrossitas stravaganza!'[30] In a side plot a female character also pretends that a 'Dutch almanac' is a grimoire, explaining, 'you must know when I was about fifteen years of age, I lived at Germantown with my uncle, a high German Doctor, who could tell fortunes, find stolen goods, discover hidden treasure, lay spirits, and raise the devil. And his whole art is contained in this little book.'[31]

The *Disappointment* is generally thought to have been written by Colonel Thomas Forrest (1747–1825), a Philadelphian congressman who in his roustabout youth pulled off a very similar prank to that recounted in the opera. He gulled a German printer into believing that he possessed the dying testimony of a pirate named Hendricks, who was hanged at Tyburn, in which he revealed where he had buried his pot of money. The tailor called in an adept of the black art named Ambruster, who said he could conjure up Hendricks to give up his booty. Ambruster's method required no grimoire though, as he merely shuffled and read out cards on which were inscribed the names of the New Testament saints.[32]

As elsewhere, conjurations were not necessarily required to retrieve buried treasure. Divining rods, which had a pseudo-scientific reputation, were used to locate precious metals for example. But as treasure was often thought to be guarded by the spirits of pirate prisoners and slaves, deliberately killed so their ghosts were bound to protect their masters' booty, none but the most rational treasure hunter dismissed the importance of supernatural aid.[33] American treasure seekers seem to have relied mostly on the Bible and the psalms rather than magical conjurations, though there are examples of magic circles being employed. While this is understandable, considering the Bible was the only widely available occult repository during the eighteenth century, English grimoires with explicit treasure-seeking advice, namely Scot's *Discoverie* and the *Fourth Book of Occult Philosophy*, were present in America. Furthermore, although there is no mention of the St Christopher Prayer in American sources, it is quite possible that ethnic German settlers brought copies with them. In the late nineteenth century, American editions of the *Sixth and Seventh Books of Moses* were used.[34] Digging deeper into the history of grimoires in American treasure hunting brings us to the most contentious and current debate regarding magic in America—the occult activities of the founder of the Mormons.

Mormons and magic books

Joseph Smith (1805–44) was brought up on a poor farm near the town of Palmyra in New York State. During the 1820s he and his family were involved in a series of expeditions looking for ancient treasure and Spanish silver mines in and around the area, and further afield in Pennsylvania. Smith Snr and Jnr were useful people to have along as they were reputed for their divinatory skills, particularly the use of seer- or peep-stones in which they could see visions of hidden treasures and much else besides. It is clear that the Smiths, like other treasure seekers at the time, also employed magic circles and talismans in order to deal with guardian spirits. Smith Jnr also claimed to have received divine communications. From 1823 onwards he was subject to a series of visitations from an angel named Moroni, son of the prophet Mormon, who, according to Smith, had been a soldier and historian during the reign of an ancient American civilization that collapsed around 400 AD. Moroni told Smith that he was the guardian of two golden plates containing a chronicle of its thousand-year existence. The Lord God Jesus Christ had ordered Mormon to compile it and Moroni completed it. Moroni told Smith he had buried this 'Golden Bible' in a stone box in a hill not far from Palmyra after a great defining battle between the Nephites and Lamanites. These were two Israelite tribes who arrived in the promised land of America around 600 BC. In September 1827 Moroni let it be known that Smith was to be permitted to dig up the golden plates in order to translate the hidden history they contained. The Book of Mormon was born.[35]

During the early years of the Mormon movement critics used rumours and testimonies of Smith's treasure-hunting and magical activities to denounce and ridicule his nascent Church. As the movement eventually grew in numbers and influence after its move to Utah, the focus on its activities shifted away from magic and treasure to the controversial practice of polygamy. During the 1970s and early 1980s, however, Mormon and non-Mormon scholars began an earnest reappraisal of the occult activities of Smith and his early followers. In 1985 wider public awareness of Smith's treasure seeking was reignited. Mark Hofmann, a well-known dealer in early Mormon archives, claimed he had discovered the written testimony of an early Mormon regarding Smith's experience of digging for Moroni's golden plates. Known as the 'White Salamander Letter', it related how Smith had encountered a salamander in the stone-lined pit containing the plates, which transformed itself into a guardian spirit that initially denied him the treasure. When suspicion was aroused about the authenticity of the letter and other Mormon artefacts Hofmann had sold to the Church, he tried to cover his tracks by setting two bombs for people he had dealt with, killing two. He is now serving a life sentence.

Of all the books and articles that appeared in the 1970s and 1980s it was a study by the Mormon historian Michael Quinn, *Early Mormonism and the Magic World View*, that caused the most controversy. Quinn synthesized a huge amount of primary and secondary sources to trace the origins of and influences on Joseph Smith's magical practices, and how they fed into early Mormonism. A revised edition was published in 1998 in which Quinn bolstered his claims with extensive endnote references, and prefaced it with a self-reflexive account of how the critical reception of the original book had impacted on his professional and personal life. As a Mormon, Quinn came under sustained attack for his work, losing his professorship at Brigham Young University. Quinn argued that the content of the *Book of Mormon*, whether written by Smith or divinely translated by him, was influenced by the literary tradition of early modern and eighteenth-century hermeticism, Kabbalah, and mysticism.[36] Others had already made these connections but Quinn went further than anyone in trying to trace the exact sources of Smith's magical possessions.

Quinn analysed three surviving magical parchments, and a dagger inscribed with the occult Seal of Mars, all of which the Smith family had evidently cherished.[37] One of the Smith charms, described as the 'Holiness to the Lord', concerned the communication with good angels. Another, 'Saint Peter bind them', served a protective function, and the third, 'Jehovah, Jehovah, Jehovah', was also a protective amulet.[38] Quinn rightly suggested that several of the symbols they contained were taken variously from Scot's *Discoverie* (1584), the 'discourse' attached to the 1665 edition of *Discoverie*, or extracts reprinted in Sibly's *New and Complete Illustration of the Occult Sciences*.[39] The 'Saint Peter bind them' and 'Holiness to the Lord' parchments, for example, contained the symbol of the angel Nalgah, which was only depicted in the 1665 edition of Scot's *Discoverie* and Sibly's opus. The 'Holiness to the Lord' charm also contained a magical seal found in all editions of Scot's *Discoverie*. Quinn also believed that a silver talisman or lamen with the seal of Jupiter possessed by Joseph Smith had been copied from one in Barrett's *The Magus*.[40] He further suggested, less convincingly, that a symbol of the Moon consisting of two back-to-back crescents presented in the *Magus* was also the source for Smith's prophecy to another prominent Mormon, Alpheus Cutler, that 'two crescent moons with their backs together' would appear to him when the time had come to reorganize the church.[41]

Quinn's reconstruction of the popular magical beliefs of the social milieu in which the Smiths and their followers lived is convincing, and is supported by the work of other historians of eighteenth-century American religious cultures. Furthermore, as we have seen, it mirrors the continuance of similar magic traditions in the European countries from where the Smiths and their followers emigrated. While there is no evidence that the Smiths owned copies of Scot, Sibly, or Barrett, there is little doubt that the Smith parchments were used for overtly magical protective purposes, and were derived primarily from Scot and Sibly. Yet Quinn's conviction, that the Smiths were practitioners of traditional magic was outrageous, even heretical, to the hierarchy of the Church of the Latter Day Saints.

Numerous attacks were launched against Quinn's thesis, but I shall focus on that of the Mormon scholar William J. Hamblin published in 2000. In this lengthy, scholarly, and meticulous rebuttal, Quinn's book was described as 'unmitigated nonsense', and Hamblin further advised that it 'should not be taken seriously as history'.[42] Part of Hamblin's critique rests on the availability and nature of occult literature in late-eighteenth-century America. Hamblin makes some pertinent criticisms. Quinn certainly conflated cheap and easily available fortune-telling tracts and astrological works with grimoires and other scarce works of intellectual magic. In doing so he gave the impression that magical literature circulated widely in Philadelphia and New York State at the time. Yet by this period American astrological almanacs, as in England, had very little magical or 'occult' content.[43] I am also inclined to agree with Hamblin that it is highly unlikely that the Smiths owned a copy of or had access to Barrett's *The Magus*.[44] True, as we saw earlier, there were copies available in American libraries at the time, but a few years after its publication it had already become a rarity in England let alone America, and second-hand copies were expensive. When a copy of *The Magus* owned by the English-born American theatre impresario William Burton was auctioned in 1860 it was described as 'extremely rare'.[45] A copy sold in England the year before was advertised as 'very scarce' and cost £1 8s.[46] For this reason there is little evidence of English cunning-folk possessing or using *The Magus* let alone American ones.

When it comes to the sources for what Quinn asserted were Smith's ritual knife for making a magic circle, Hamblin overplays the scarcity of Scot's *Discovery* as a possible source. For Hamblin it 'is the least likely that Joseph would have obtained'.[47] In fact it is the most likely. The 1651 and 1665 editions were frequently being sold at auction in England during the late eighteenth century for a price usually between 5 and 8s. In 1772 the bookseller Benjamin White even offered a copy of the 1651 edition for a very reasonable 2s. 6d.[48] Compare these prices with the first edition of Sibly's *New and Complete Illustration*, which was being sold for between £1 9s. and £1 15s. during the early 1790s—more than four or five times the average price of the much older Scot editions.[49] It is hardly beyond the realms of possibility that some of these editions went overseas and into the hands of humble Americans on the eastern seaboard. As to Sibly's *New and Complete Illustration*, which Hamblin describes as so rare that he was unable to consult an edition, numerous reprints in the early nineteenth century would have made it realistically purchasable.[50] It was certainly quite widely used by English cunning-folk. Furthermore, Hamblin's belief that Scot's *Discoverie* was not used as a book of magic—'it is not a book designed to help someone learn how to be a magician'—is also contradicted by the English evidence.[51] It has been shown that the *Discoverie* was a key source of magic charms during the nineteenth century, with the character of Nalgah and the magical seal in Smith's 'Holiness to the Lord' charm being used in charms concocted by English and Welsh cunning-folk.[52]

6. Thefe are the feven *good Angels,* or *Dæmons.*

Iubaniadace a mighty Prince in the Dominion of Thrones, he cometh unto fuch as follow national affairs, and are carryed forth unto warr and conqueft; he beareth alwayes a flaming Sword , and is girded about, having a helmet upon his head, and appearing ftill before the party in the Air: he muft be folli- cited and invocated with Chaftity , Vows, Fumes, and Prayers: and this his is Character to be worn as a Lamin.

Pah-li-Pah one of the Powers, accompanying fuch as are Virgins, and de- voted to Religion, and a Hermits life: he teacheth all the names and powers of Angels, and gives holy Charms againft the affaults of *Evil Dæmons :* he muft be addreft unto by Prayer, refignation, and fafting , with a celeftial Song out of the Canto's of *Nagar :* this is his Character.

Nal-gah appearing to thofe that are devoted to the knowledge of Magick ; teaching them how to exercife Infernal Witchcraft without danger , and in de- fpight to the Devils: he muft be fought by hours , minutes , conftellations, privacy and blood, &c. He hath a bow bent in his hand, and a Crown of Gold upon his head: this is his Character.

Maynom one of the Powers who hath the ability of fubfervient adminiftra- tion ; that is, at one time to be prefent with many ; he refembleth a Ew with Lamb , typifying his nature in that appearance.

Gaonim an Angel, caufing his Pupil to go invifible, and transporting him at his pleafure in a moment, to the outmoft parts of the earth.

Yalamu the Inftructer in Manual operations, by whom *Bezaliah* , and *Aholi- bah* were divinely infpired for the ftructure of the Tabernacle.

Kama-umi who is the Inftructer in Cabaliftical Magick, and reveals the fe- crets of numbers , the names of Angels, and the vertue of *Boim.*

7. Thefe are the feven *bad Angels* or *Dæmons.*

As the power and capacity of the *good,* proceeds from the ftrength of God, in the quality of heaven ; fo is the force of the *evil Genii,* in the hellifh quality correfpondent : for it is to be noted , that thefe *evil Angels* did before their fall, enjoy the fame places and degrees that now the *good* or *holy Angels* do : fo that as their power is to inftruct men in Government, Abftinence, Philofophy, Magick, and Mechanick Arts, for a good intent, and for the glory of God : The power of the *evil* ones is the very fame to inform and inftigate unto the fame attainments, as farr as they may be inftrumental for the Devil, or the Kingdom of Darknefs therein.

8. Their names are 1. **Panaicarp,** like a Crocodile with two heads. 2. **Bara- tron** appearing like a Conjurer in a Prieftly habit. 3. **Sondennah** like a Hunts-man. 4. **Grezjnodal** accompanying his Pupil like a Spaniel-Dog. 5. **Wallifargon** the grand Inticer to theeving and robbery, till he hath brought his followers to deftruction. 6. **Morborgran** who can put on various likeneffes, efpecially appearing as a Serving-man. 7. **Barman** who moft com- monly poffeffeth the foul of thofe that are joyned unto him.

9. Thefe

FIG. 15 Reginald Scot, *The Discoverie of Witchcraft* (London, 1665).

Quinn's thesis does not stand or fall on the basis that Smith owned copies of Scot and Sibly, since extracts from all three were to be found in the manuscript grimoires and charms kept by some English cunning-folk, and in those sold by the London occult bookseller John Denley. It is quite likely that some of these found their way to America where they were copied once again.

It is not surprising that the Mormon faith was, in part, born out of the magical milieu of the period. Whether Protestant or Catholic, German or British, magic was a central aspect of most people's conception of Christianity in colonial America. Colonization itself was inspired not only by commerce but also by supernatural inspiration. Confronted by the challenges of their new world, European emigrants, insecure as to their future, understandably placed reliance on the magic of their homeland cultures. The search for treasure was part of a wider quest for security. Cunning-folk, and diviners like the Smiths, were, therefore, valued members of their communities, and more so if they were perceived to have physical and linguistic access to literary as well as oral sources of occult power.

New France

During the early nineteenth century a group of Pennsylvanian German farmers, Mennonites and Amish, trekked north and settled in Ontario, mostly in what is now Waterloo County. They brought with them their distinctive magical remedies and folk medicine, and the *Sixth and Seventh Books of Moses* can be found in legends recorded in their communities at the end of the century.[53] But it was the French grimoire tradition and not the German that had the most substantial influence on Canadian popular magic.

The history of French emigration to Canada contrasts strikingly with that of Germans and the British to North America.[54] The Catholic French were reluctant emigrants, and the Huguenots were barred from settling in French territories. By the end of the seventeenth century New France covered a huge swathe of the eastern half of America and Canada, but it was only in the latter that emigration was significant enough to generate a lasting French cultural presence. Quebec was founded in 1608, and two other permanent settlements, Trois-Rivières and Montreal, had developed into small towns within a few decades. Yet although at least 27,000 French came to Canada in the period from 1608 until its surrender to the British in 1763, some two-thirds returned to their homes, predominantly in Normandy, Poitou, and the Paris basin. By that time, French Canada or Quebec had a population of around 70,000, made up primarily of those born in the territory descended from seventeenth-century pioneers, along with disbanded soldiers, refugees from Acadia (mostly consisting of the former French territory of Nova Scotia), and petty criminals exiled there during a period of penal transportation between 1721 and 1749. Following British rule French emigration reduced to a tiny trickle. In the 1851 census only 359 people in Quebec had been born in France.[55]

In June 1682 a Montreal innkeeper Anne Lamarque was tried for practising magic principally on the basis of her possession of a mysterious book. Anne was born in the diocese of Bordeaux and was married to another emigrant named Charles Testard, who was from Rouen. Their hostelry was evidently popular, but the downside was that gossip soon spread amongst her customers regarding a book that she was seen holding. Numerous witnesses came forward to testify that they had seen her with a 'book of magic or sorcery'. One described it as a 'huge book four or five inches square and the thickness of a finger or thereabouts, handwritten, in a bold hand and in both French and Latin, and some Greek words'. Serious doubt was cast on the evil nature of this book, however, when one witness, a lodger whose curiosity had been aroused by the gossip, testified that he had asked her if it was true that she had a book of magic in Latin and Greek. She replied that it was no such thing, it was merely 'a book of herbs or medicines'.[56]

We find little further evidence regarding grimoires in Canada until the nineteenth century, though as Lamarque's case shows, rumours about them circulated. It is likely that some copies of the *Petit Albert* found their way there in the packs of settlers and soldiers before the British takeover. Copies could also have been brought over and traded by seamen. In the early twentieth century a Quebec man told a folklorist how an uncle had come by a copy of the *Petit Albert* from some French sailors and had lent it to his family. His father threw it into the fire.[57] Despite the potential demand, however, in 1861 it was estimated that no more than twenty-five to thirty copies could be found in the province.[58] If this was so, then the *Petit Albert's* cultural influence far outweighed its actual presence in Quebec society. It was central to Canada's early literary heritage. Just as the first American opera was concerned with treasure hunts and magic books, so the first French-Canadian novel, *L'Influence d'un livre*, similarly centred on alchemy, treasure, and the *Petit Albert*—the '*livre*' in the title.[59]

Written in 1837 by Philippe Aubert de Gaspé, the son of a Quebec lawyer, this gothic story primarily concerned a poor Canadian alchemist called Charles Amand, who in the 1820s could be found in his cabin on the south bank of the St Laurent River poring over his *Petit Albert* day and night in his quest to create precious metals. A footnote in the text referring to one of his failed ritual conjurations to achieve this goal notes that Amand's *Petit Albert* was not one of the run-of-the-mill copies of the grimoire. His 'true' copy was tellingly obtained from a Frenchman.[60] The story also concerns the search for hidden treasure and the desire to obtain the Hand of Glory, the recipe for which was the most notorious aspect of the *Petit Albert*. One reviewer criticized the way that the novel portrayed his countryman as being so 'superstitious' as to practise magical rituals, and thought it would have been appropriate to set it further back in time before education had enlightened the people.[61]

In 1861 a book was published in Quebec with the enticing title *Le Véritable Petit-Albert ou secret pour acquérir un trésor*. But this was not the first Canadian grimoire. It was an attack on such works by a Quebec typographer and social commentator named Joseph-Norbert Duquet. The first half of the book provided an account of the history and content of the corpus of chapbook grimoires available in France at the time. To demonstrate their pernicious influence he also provided some accounts of the recent prosecution of cunning-folk in the mother country. He then went on to relate various cases of treasure seeking in Quebec. The second half of the book consisted of a discussion on the social and economic structure of the province along with 'improving' advice and rational recipes for the labouring classes of Quebec to whom the book was dedicated. His concern was that Canada should defend itself from the corrupting forces at play in Europe and America, amongst them the influence of the *Petit Albert* and other populist occult works. These had 'spread strongly in America; but fortunately in Canada, we can say with rightful pride, we are far from the sale of thousands of copies of this cheating book to the inhabitants of our rural areas.' Duquet was a staunch supporter of the social and moral importance of the Church in Québécois society, and he praised its role in suppressing the *Petit Albert*, as well as commending the French-Canadian libraries that refused to stock it.[62]

For Duquet the most obvious sign of the *Petit Albert*'s influence in Quebec was the continued practice of magical treasure hunting in the province. In 1843, for example, a group tried to conjurer up a treasure guarded by ghosts buried in or around Chateau Mctavish near Montreal, which was built in the late eighteenth century by a hugely wealthy Scottish fur trader and businessman. As to those who engaged in such activities, Duquet wrote:

> Tell him that you have the *Petit-Albert*, or some other book of marvellous secrets, and then you can be certain of pulling at the heartstrings of all his desires. You will see his face bloom with happiness, his eyes light up, mouth open, and his chest heave, a sigh escapes followed by this request: 'Ah! Monsieur, if you would be so good as to provide me with the *Petit-Albert*, or the *Dragon rouge* or else the *Grimoire*, you would make me happy a thousand times'.[63]

Duquet's book was a massive hit in Quebec publishing terms. It sold 3,000 copies in a matter of weeks, at a time when successful novels sold only a thousand copies or so.[64] While his aim was to destroy the belief in grimoires surely the only reason for the book's success was that many people bought it under the mistaken assumption that it was an edition of the actual *Petit Albert*.

The influence of French grimoires is more difficult to assess in Louisiana, the only area of North America that maintained a substantial French language culture after the demise of New France. The word 'Cajun' is a corruption of 'Acadian', referring to those French settlers who were forced out of Nova Scotia by the British in the mid-eighteenth century and who subsequently settled in Louisiana. Today Cajuns are generally presented as synonymous with French Louisiana, yet they were not a large population and had little direct contact with France compared with those settlers in Quebec. Furthermore, any consideration of French influence on magical cultures in the region needs to consider the input of Creoles, French-speaking Native American Indians and, most significantly, slaves and ex-slaves. Eighteenth-century advertisements regarding runaway slaves, mostly from Louisiana and St Domingue but also from across the eastern seaboard, confirm that French was quite widely spoken amongst the black population, and by the early nineteenth century French-speaking slaves and former slaves were a major influence on French language and culture in the southern states.[65]

One rare nineteenth-century reference to the *Petit Albert* in Louisiana is in George W. Cable's classic novel of *Voodoo*, racism, and murder in New Orleans, *The Grandissimes*, published in 1880 but set in 1803. It contains a scene in which a Paris-educated 'free man of color', Honoré Grandissime, visits a German-American New Orleans apothecary to obtain a love powder. 'M'sieu',' he asks, *'vous êtes astrologue—magicien'*. 'God forbid!', replies the apothecary.

> 'You godd one 'P'tit Albert.'
> He dropped his forefinger upon an iron-clasped book on the table, whose title much use had effaced.
> 'That is the Bible. I do not know what the Tee Albare is!'

This literary reference is hardly concrete evidence of the grimoire's use at the time, but the scenario is perfectly reasonable. If the *Petit Albert* was a significant element in the magical cultures of French Louisiana it was most likely due to Caribbean rather than Acadian influence. As one recent major study of Creole French culture affirms, throughout the Creole world the '*Petit Albert, Grand Albert,* and to a lesser extent, *Dragon rouge* are major and constant references.'[66] How did this come about?

Creolization

Colonization, slavery, and immigrant labour in the Caribbean and the Americas generated a fascinating and diverse fusion of beliefs and practices regarding religion, magic, and medicine, derived from European, African, Asian, indigenous

Carib, and Amerindian cultures. In the British colonies the *Orisha* religion developed in Trinidad and Tobago, and in Jamaica we find the collection of magical practices known as *Obeah*. In Guyana there is *Comfa*, and on the French islands of Martinique and Guadeloupe the magical practices known as *Quimbois*. Amongst former Spanish colonies we find *Santería* in Cuba and *Espiritismo* in Puerto Rico. *Candomblé* developed in Brazil. Most well known outside the region is, of course, the Haitian spirit religion *Voodoo*.[67] The African influence in these religious traditions depended on the tribes from which different slaving countries took their terrible cargo. The African elements in *Comfa* can be identified as Bantu, while the word *Obeah* derives from the Ashanti. Elsewhere Yoruba beliefs were a major influence in *Santería* and *Voodoo*. The latter, also termed *vaudou, vodou,* and *vodoun* at different periods and in different cultural contexts, means 'spirit', and derives, along with other deities in its pantheon, from a group of West African languages spoken particularly in the kingdoms of the Yoruba and Fon.[68] Turning to the European influences, Catholicism and its demonology dominates not surprisingly. After all, up until the mid-nineteenth century, it was the only permitted religion across much of the region. But the Church's conception of Catholic worship was far from uniformly understood and adhered to in European popular cultures. White migrants brought with them their own folk conceptions of the magical efficacy of religious practices, which had affinities with other non-European cultures. Saints, African deities, and indigenous spirits could rub along together, while charms and talismans were adapted to incorporate the magical potency of local flora and fauna. Just one example of this is the tradition of *mandinga* pouches in Brazil. As a series of eighteenth-century Inquisition trials reveal, these protective pouches were a fusion of the African Islamic tradition of the *alherces* containing passages from the Koran, the European tradition of wearing printed or written prayers mingled with occult symbols, and indigenous amulets. One of those confiscated by the Inquisition, and used to instil bravery consisted of a prayer to Jesus and St Cyprian and a piece of altar stone. Others contained a dead man's bone.[69]

Scholarly interpretations of the processes by which these new religious and magical traditions grew out of the established religions of Europe, Africa, and to a lesser extent India, have changed over the past fifty years or so. The concept of 'acculturation' was widely applied until recently. In historical and anthropological contexts the acculturation process has been understood generally in terms of dominant cultures, usually European or American, deliberately supplanting or suppressing what were seen as inferior or less 'advanced' cultures, by means of force, religion, education, and media. This concept, however, does not entirely square with religious developments in the Caribbean. What European authorities attempted in terms of promoting and enforcing Christianity, and suppressing

African beliefs and practices, by outlawing *Obeah* for example, was certainly acculturation. But they did not fully succeed. Aspects of Christian liturgy, primarily Catholic, were key ingredients in the syncretism or blending of religious traditions that took place because of, and to a certain extent in defiance of, colonial rule. The term creolization—*creole* referring to persons born in the region who have non-native ancestry—encapsulates better this complex creative process, which was beyond authoritarian control. The creolization of religion and magic may have been forged out of cultural repression and violence, but its development was one of continuing cultural negotiation, fusion, and adaptation.

The European literary esoteric tradition, as well as the oral, played a major part in this creolization of Caribbean beliefs. The Bible was, of course, hugely influential, but for a more recent introduction we can look to the growth of Kardecism. In the mid-nineteenth century a French schoolteacher and author of pedagogical texts, Hippolyte Léon Rivail, developed a spiritualist doctrine distinct from the American spiritualism born in 1848. For Rivail contact with the spirits of the dead convinced him of the reality of reincarnation, opening up a new philosophical and moral doctrine for life and the afterlife. It was during a seance that spirits informed him that his name in a former life was Allan Kardec, and it was this he adopted when writing his most important works, *The Book of the Spirits* (1857), *The Book of Mediums* (1861), and *The Gospel According to Spiritism* (1864).[70] Within a few years they had been translated into Spanish and quickly became hugely influential in Latin America—more so than in Europe. They were adopted initially by the liberal middle classes who were disillusioned by the conservative political grip of the Church. By the twentieth century *The Gospel According to Spiritism* was apparently achieving better sales than the Bible in Puerto Rico, despite being banned.[71] Kardecism also flourished in Brazil with the first Spiritist society being created in the late 1860s in the face of hostility from the Catholic Church. Over the decades, Brazilian Spiritism developed into a form distinct from Kardec's initial teachings. It became a religion rather than a philosophical–ethical system, feeding into other Afro-Brazilian religious systems, such as *Umbanda*, which are based on the healing abilities of mediums working through spirit communications.[72]

The reception and absorption of European grimoires in South and Central America was rather more complex. Seen as potent sources of physical as well as spiritual empowerment, grimoires were viewed by some indigenous peoples as the pernicious tools of foreign colonizers. The Quiché Indians of Guatemala, for instance, came to believe that some sorcerers (*ajitz*) who caused harm learned their powers from books of magic, described to one anthropologist as 'books of the Jews'.[73] For some indigenous Indians in southwest Colombia *magia*, which they define as deriving from books of conjurations that allow one to pact with the Devil, are considered to be an instrument of social control. The whites had brought *magia* with them, and as one Indian complained, 'They use it to take our land.'[74] These perceptions were not only born of suspicions regarding Christian magic but were also an aspect of wider concerns about how books were being used as a means of enslavement. We see this expressed in a magic tradition found amongst the largely indigenous Quichua population of the town of Salasaca, Ecuador. In the provincial capital of Ambato lies the seat of a 'witch-saint', Saint Gonzalo, patron of the main church, who is believed to kill people through a book in which victims' names are written. The main focus of this belief was not the large statue of San Gonzalo, which depicts him with a sword plunged into his back and blood trickling down his face, but a small copy of the statue in private ownership. It is the *blancos* (whites) who own the latter, and who are the guardians of a large 'witch book'. People pay them to include the names of their enemies, who the saint will then curse, or conversely to have their names removed. This is no legend, but a real money-making activity for the guardians, who have on at least one occasion been charged with adding names to the book to extort money.

The anthropologist who studied this tradition, and was surprised and suspicious to find his own name in the book during a visit, suggests it is not just the book and the power of writing that has shaped this belief and practice.[75] It is the implicit association Salasacas make between it and their experience of record keeping by the predominantly white Church and secular administration. The witch book is no mock grimoire with occult signs and pictures of the Devil; it is a functional large notebook consisting of lined paper, not unlike those used for Civil Registry and Church record keeping. In other words, the archival function of books, which serve as a means of social control in an administrative sense, can also be used to subjugate through magical means—an echo of the early modern witch trials and the belief in the Devil's book.

In much of the Caribbean the pattern of colonial experience was different to that of parts of Central and South America. Islands shuffled between Spanish, French, and British rule, with each colonial power imprinting their linguistic and cultural influence to varying degrees. The remnant indigenous populations had to negotiate not only with European hegemony but also with the cultures of African and later Asian arrivals, and vice versa. The grimoire was not necessarily seen wholly as the white man's legacy. In Martinique, Creole legends developed regarding the *Livre Caraibe*, which was thought to contain all the magical secrets of the Caribs written in Latin. People also told of notorious black magic books with 'Holy Bible' on the cover supposedly distributed by a St Lucian evangelist around 1900.[76] When the Haitian writer and communist activist Jacques Roumain was incarcerated in Port-au-Prince prison during the late 1920s, the country being under American occupation at the time, he requested a copy of William

Seabrook's recently published populist account of Haitian magic and *Voodoo, The Magic Island*, which was simultaneously published in French. His guard refused suspecting that he might use such a book to escape through magical means. His suspicions were understandable. Seabrook's book provided translated excerpts from a Creole grimoire found on the body of the rebel commander Benoit Batraville, who was shot dead by American marines in 1920. It included instructions on how to call up the dead, a prayer against bullets, a charm to protect against torture, and a spell to ensure one's release from prison.[77]

The French connection: sacrifice and science

In 1885 a newspaper correspondent to the *Philadelphia Press* described the accoutrements of the 'West Indian Obeah Man'. They included a 'cabalistic book (albeit he can seldom read), full of strange characters, crude figures, and roughly traced diagrams and devices, which he pretends to consult in the exercise of his calling'.[78] One such manuscript was found on a magic worker named Adolphe Lacroix, executed in St Lucia in 1876 for the murder and mutilation of a disabled boy.[79] A few years later a folklorist astutely remarked that 'The book of magic, with its diagrams, sufficiently indicates that "Obeah" sorcery in the West Indies has been affected by European influences.'[80] The British may have been the most dominant colonial power at the time, but it was the grimoires of their French rivals that seeped deeply into the psyche of the Caribbean.

Although, as we have seen, grimoires were present in early colonial America, it was in the former French colonies that they first became a concrete, visible, attainable, and pervasive reality for people of whatever economic or ethnic background. To be more precise, it was the French *Bibliothèque bleue* grimoires that first gave the Caribbean its literary magic tradition. In Martinique, for instance, *La Poule noire*, and the *Grand* and *Petit Albert* were all frequently mentioned in popular discourse on magic, and considered evil by those that did not use them. *Le Dragon rouge* was perhaps the most evil of all, it being thought that the Devil could be summoned by standing under a fromager tree (*Ceiba pentendra*) with a copy. A perusal of the libraries of Martinique cunning-men or *quimboiseurs*, and those in the Antilles, reveals that the *Albert* titles and *Le Dragon rouge* were common enough. A Guadeloupe sorcerer prosecuted in 1953 owned, amongst a range of more recent French works on exorcism and occultism, *Le Dragon rouge* and the *Grand* and *Petit Albert*.[81] However, *La Poule Noire, Clavicule of Solomon, Grimoire du Pape Honorius*, and the *Enchiridion du Pape Léon* were more talked about than circulated on the island.[82] It was the *Petit Albert* that had the most demonstrable influence on magical practices.

In the British Windward Islands during the early twentieth century there was some suspicion that the French-speaking portion of the population practised the more sinister aspects of *Obeah*. Robert Stephen Earl, a British Commissioner and medical officer in the Virgin Islands at the time, observed that blood was more important amongst *patois* speakers in the Leeward Islands, particularly in Dominica, which although it had been ceded to Britain in 1763 retained a strong French influence. In the Virgin Islands police had arrested one man with numerous *Obeah* accoutrements who was returning from Santa Domingo (Dominican Republic). The same police force was also suspicious of a man who had recently arrived from Martinique with a cock, which they suspected he subsequently sacrificed in order to find treasure.[83] There was a strong Anglo-Saxon perception that there was something about the French that exacerbated the sinister aspects of Caribbean 'superstition'. One of America's early leading sociologists, Ulysses G. Weatherly, wrote in 1923 that the French, in comparison with the English, were

> more congenial to the simpler nature of the African. They had less of race prejudice; they crossed more willingly with the blacks . . . . They also had more gaiety, a keener artistic and dramatic sense, and less rigorous attitudes. Once in full contact with French national culture, the Negro was likely to readily absorb its type and long retain its influence.

No surprise then, according to Weatherly's view, that fragments of the 'great magic books of the Middle Ages' passed into *Obeah* and 'the dim ghost of Albertus Magnus flits in and out'.[84] One of his colleagues, the respected early-twentieth-century historian of the Caribbean, Frank Wesley Pitman, put a different emphasis on the 'failure' of French policy. He postulated that the French authorities' policy of education and the promotion of the assimilation of European culture backfired. 'Catholicism was fetishized by French Negroes,' he explained, 'and the almost complete reversion of Haytians to barbarism in the nineteenth century is a sad commentary on the futility of the work of the French.' The British, who had been less dedicated in their educational provision, had, he thought, been more successful in eradicating 'the atrocious tendencies of fetishism'.[85]

British visitors to the country back in the 1820s and 1830s had already made snide observations about the inability of the French-trained Catholic clergy to suppress 'superstition' and 'heathenism'.[86] While the British authorities explained this with smug reference to their better administration, later the finger also pointed to the pernicious influence of French grimoires. They may have had a point. It is possible the Martiniquan mentioned earlier was following the ritual of the *Poule noire* contained in the *Dragon rouge*. Pitman suggested that the strength of *Voodoo* in Haiti was perhaps due to the fact that the 'sacrificial prescriptions for child-murder, receipts for hidden treasure, and prayer formulas were early committed to print in a sort of manual for obeahmen published at Nantes in patois and atrocious Latin.' He meant the *Petit Albert*.[87]

Animal sacrifice, usually a chicken, was certainly a part of *Obeah*, *Comfa*, and *Voodoo* rituals, used as offerings to the spirits along with food and libations to ensure good harvests and the like. The killing of a chicken and the sprinkling of its blood was a common foundation ritual to ensure the protection of new dwellings. Such magic was an integral part of the religious worship in the West African regions from which most of their slave ancestors were taken, and similar foundation rituals requiring the burial of an animal were also widely practised in Europe. As we have seen, the sacrifice of a chicken was also a key element in diabolic pacts in France. In other words, such animal sacrifice was just another area of common tradition in the multicultural mix that was Creole magic. There was a widespread belief amongst Europeans that human sacrifice and even cannibalism were also practised by adherents of *Voodoo* in Haiti, and by magical practitioners in other French-speaking colonies. Haiti's pre-eminent and enduring reputation for obscene and horrific *Voodoo* rituals was cemented by the popularity of the sensational accounts provided in Sir Spenser St John's *Hayti, or the Black Republic* (1884). St John was a well-travelled journalist who in 1863 took up a post as *chargé d'affaires* in Haiti, later becoming consul-general.[88] His stridently critical account of the country was reviled by Haitians but widely read in Europe and America. When it came to a second edition in 1889 he added further details, stating he had 'underrated' the 'fearful manifestations' of *Voodoo*. His accounts of terrible *Voodoo* rituals, seen as a hangover from the barbarous practices of African ancestors, were taken as fact and became the key source on the subject for several decades. Their apparent veracity was reinforced by St John's account of a trial he had attended in 1864 concerning apparent sacrifice and cannibalism in the village of Bizoton, near the capital Port-au-Prince. Eight people were found guilty of murdering a twelve-year-old girl named Claircine and then eating her flesh for magical purposes.

Even before the second edition of *Hayti, or the Black Republic* appeared, the American folklorist William W. Newell was waging a scholarly campaign to dispel the malodorous myth of child sacrifice that clung to the country.[89] He dismissed St John's accounts as unsubstantiated hearsay, highlighting the pernicious influence of local and international newspapers in peddling sensational false accounts, such as the report that human flesh was on sale in Haitian markets.[90] As to the 1864 case, just like those in early modern Europe who confessed to participating in the Sabbat, the defendants had been tortured into confessing their supposed heinous activities. St John reported that one young defendant pleaded in court, 'Yes, I did confess what you assert, but remember how cruelly I was beaten before I said a word.' But to St John, who was no stranger to enacting brutal suppression on disturbers of the peace, torture seemed justified. He believed that the defendants had initially refused to speak due to believing that their *Voodoo* spirits would protect them, and so 'it required the frequent application of the club to drive this belief out of their heads.'[91] Newell consulted B. F. Whidden, the first minister of the United States to Haiti in the 1860s, who had also been present at the trial. Whidden believed the prosecution was unfair and that the stories of *Voodoo* sacrifice and cannibalism circulating at the time were mere rumour sometimes maliciously spread. There was no more cannibalism in Haiti than in Jamaica, he concluded.

Newell had his own theory as to the origin of the lurid legends of *Voodoo* sacrifice and cannibalism circulating in Haiti. They originated in old beliefs and superstitions regarding the diabolical activities of a medieval sect brought to the island by French immigrants. This theory was built around the mistaken idea that the word *Voodoo* derived from the term 'vaudois', a name given to the followers of the medieval Waldensian heresy in Alpine France, which around the mid-fifteenth century became synonymous with satanic witchcraft. *Vauderie* became another term for 'sabbat'. Where Newell was right, however, was in underlining that there was a significant French influence on the nature of sacrifice in Creole religions. It was left to others to identify grimoires as the source of inspiration, and another case of apparent ritual murder in 1904 seemed to confirm it.

Rupert Mapp, a twelve year old was lured to the island of St Lucia from his home in Bridgetown, Barbados, on the pretence that he would be employed as an errand boy.[92] Mapp spoke only English and must have had little inkling of the plans being hatched for him during his brief time in French-speaking St Lucia. The man who brought him over was a licensed butcher and magical practitioner named Edmond Montoute who had spent some time on Haiti, apparently evading imprisonment for forgery. Montoute took the boy to the house of an old friend St Luce Leon, a prosperous small farmer. There, on the night of 29 September, and with the help of another man Edgar St Hill, Mapp was strangled, his heart was ripped out and his hands cut off at the wrist. The body was buried and Leon was set to work pounding salt, presumably to preserve the hands and heart. Montoute said he would send him some other stuff to sprinkle over them.

When Montoute was arrested shortly after, police found in his house a bloody rag, two serpents' skins, five pieces of bone, some sulphur in rock and powdered form, and a phial containing a dark liquid. More to the point, in Montoute's pocket they found a mysterious manuscript in French. When it was produced during his first appearance before a magistrate, Montoute said it did not 'contain anything of any consequence. It is an old manuscript book of prescriptions which I carried with me when I went to St. Luce's house as I was treating him for an old disease.' Edgar St Hill's testimony suggests it was something more than a mere collection of medical receipts, and was, in fact, the key to the murder. Shortly before they slaughtered the boy, Edgar said that Leon 'asked Montoute whether he had read the book again.' Montoute replied, 'since I read it this morning I do not require to read again.'

The exact purpose of the murder was never fully clarified during the trial. It was assumed by the authorities to be some awful *Obeah* ritual. Edgar St Hill provided conflicting statements. Initially he confessed that Montoute had asked him to go to Barbados to get two boys that they would sacrifice to the Devil in order to obtain money from a bank. He later said, however, that he had gone to Leon's on the night of the murder to help in the cure of Leon's hernia. This was somehow to be achieved by Montoute hypnotizing St Hill. On awaking from his trance his two friends pointed to Mapp's mutilated body lying on the floor and accused him of having committed the atrocity while under hypnosis. St Hill's mention of a diabolic plan to enrich themselves by getting money from a bank, coupled with the mysterious book owned by Montoute and the severing and preserving of Mapp's hands, suggested another alternative: they were seeking to create Hands of Glory to render them invisible and so enter the bank unseen. Their inspiration? The *Petit Albert* of course. Montoute's manuscript was apparently identified as being a copy of the grimoire during the trial. All three men were executed. Recent anthropological studies confirm that stories of human sacrifice continue to circulate in the Caribbean. One study of folk religion on Montserrat suggested that if the reports of goats sacrificed on rocks and the ritual murder of a young girl were to be believed, then such actions 'seem to be influenced by European, Medieval Cabalistic books'.[93]

Thousands of miles away in the Indian Ocean the colonial history was quite different to that in the Caribbean in the sense that there were no native populations. Nevertheless, grimoires took a similar hold on the Creole psyche. The Mascarene Islands of Mauritius, Rodriguez, and Réunion were uninhabited until a permanent presence was established in the early seventeenth century, consisting mostly of runaway slaves brought there by Dutch and Portuguese traders. It was the French, though, who stamped their cultural identity on the islands and developed their economies, taking permanent control over Réunion in the 1640s and Mauritius and Rodriguez in the early eighteenth century. African slaves were brought to Mauritius and Réunion in significant numbers, followed later by Chinese and the more culturally influential Indian immigrants as the East Indies trade route developed. Although the islands were seceded to the British during the Napoleonic Wars, Réunion was returned to the French in 1815.

The history of grimoires highlights the strong French influence on the two islands that remained under British colonial rule. We can see this in English reports from Mauritius during the late nineteenth and early twentieth centuries expressing concern over the influence of the *Petit Albert*. In 1879 the British judiciary on the island dealt with a horrific case of murder that reminds one of the St Lucia murder twenty-five years later. It concerned a sorcerer named Virgile Picot, who abducted and mutilated a six-year-old girl apparently to obtain human flesh for a magical ritual. Picot was thought to be deep in 'Petit Albert'. This did not mean he possessed a copy of the grimoire. For the authorities the name expressed more than a book; it was *the* magical tradition. A correspondent reported from the island in 1884 that its 'professors' were 'generally negroes with a sprinkling of Indians among them, and, although they practise on the lines laid down in "Petit Albert," not one in 20 ever saw the book or could read it if laid before them. The precepts it contains are handed down by word of mouth.' He went on to talk of the 'believers' in and 'priests and priestesses of "Petit Albert"' amongst both the poor and wealthy Creole population. In 1928 the British Bishop of Mauritius wrote in the *Church Times*, in similar vein, complaining of the hold sorcery had over the island: 'witchcraft or Petit Albert is practised by many thousands of persons . . . Petit Albert is nothing less than the cult of the Devil.' [94]

By the twentieth century it is fair to say that the *Petit Albert* had achieved legendary status across the archipelagos, even if most inhabitants of the islands have never seen let alone read it. On Rodriguez Island, for example, it has been observed that 'everybody knows *titalbèr*, without knowing exactly what it is.'[95] Judging from the corpus of twentieth-century anthropological studies it is in Réunion, the only one of the islands to remain a French colony, that the *Grand* and *Petit Albert* have had the most enduring influence on magical and medical traditions.[96] One renowned Réunion healer during the 1980s was the son of poor farmers who, as a young man, learned his calling from frequenting various Indian cults active in the town of Saint-Pierre and reading French esoteric works such as the *Grand Albert*. He combined these foreign traditions with his knowledge of the healing properties of local plants and animals.[97]

There has been considerable debate amongst anthropologists of folk medical traditions in the Caribbean, the Americas, and the Mascarene Islands about the origins of the beliefs and practices recorded in the twentieth century. One area of contention concerns the humoral conception of human illness. Ancient Greek physicians believed that health was governed by the balance of four substances, yellow bile, black bile, blood, and phlegm. Illnesses were caused by the imbalance of these substances, which led to excessive heat/cold, moistness/dryness in the body. Cures required the ingestion of foods, liquids, or herbs that had hot/cold, wet/dry properties that counteracted the identified imbalance, or methods like bleeding that reduced humoral excesses. It was the writings of the ancient Greek physician Galen that sealed the orthodoxy of this theory in European medicine right into the eighteenth century. It is still with us in popular notions, such as that being in the 'cold' can cause a cold. Similar concepts have been identified in the various popular medical traditions of the Caribbean and Central and South America. Although some have argued that they derive from similar indigenous medical notions, there is evidence pointing to a European rather than native origin.[98] We need to be aware, though, that humoral theory is not uniformly central to medical beliefs across the region, and other therapeutic principles, such as those based on spirits, coexist with humoral causation.[99] Where the European influence was strongest it presumably spread slowly but surely over the centuries via hospitals, pharmacies, and missionaries. Galenic medicine was still being taught in some Central and South American universities until the early nineteenth century, long after it had been banished from the curricula of European universities.

It was popular access to literature that had the most effect. Manuscript *recetarios*, or household medical receipt books, which borrowed from more august tomes first printed in the early modern period, certainly circulated in Mexico during the eighteenth and nineteenth centuries.[100] The role of grimoires in this process has been little considered, though it has been suggested that humoral theory introduced to Haitian folk medicine by the early French colonialists was revived and perpetuated through the widespread circulation of the *Grand* and *Petit Albert* during the nineteenth century.[101] Much of the *Grand Albert* and the medical content of the *Petit Albert*, such as the 'curious secrets touching the effects of nature', were clearly based on humoral theory. The strong grimoire influence on folk medicine is certainly confirmed by changing conceptions of medical-magical power. A study of Carib settlements in Dominica suggested that by 1945 the indigenous healers, who cured by going on soul flights to intercede with the spirits on behalf of clients, had largely died out. The role of these healers had been usurped by *divineurs* whose power was based on skills learned from literature, with the *Albert* books being the main source of spells and healing recipes.[102] Across the Caribbean such book magic was defined as 'science'. As one old *Obeah* practitioner from Santa Domingo and the Windward Islands told a folklorist in the early 1970s, the way to invoke the dead to help you was to go to a cemetery around midnight with 'a Black Arts book' and make 'necromaney, making science'.[103] A practitioner on Montserrat who described himself as a 'scientist' explained, 'I have read a lot of books written by occult scientists; we draw symbols and words from the ancient Egyptians which would cast away or protect from the evil influence.'[104] Working with 'science' was dangerous for all but the adept. Those who merely dabbled with the likes of the *Petit Albert* or the *Grimoire du Pape Honorius* risked madness and suicidal impulses. Only the *gadedzafe* healers of the Antilles could read them because they already possessed 'the power' and the natural gift to access their contents without harm.[105]

Islam

If French grimoires acted as multicultural glue, and were easily adopted by a wide variety of religious and magical traditions, why did they not become influential in French Africa? The answer lies in the influence of Islamic popular religion. As we have seen, magic, divination, prophecy, and astrology had an equivalent influence on medieval Arabic literary culture as they did in Christian Europe, and continued to do so into the modern period. Writing in the early twentieth century Reginald Campbell Thompson, an expert on ancient Semitic magic, noted from personal experience, that 'from Morocco to Mesopotamia, books of magic are by no means rare, and manuscripts in Arabic, Hebrew, Gershuni, and Syriac can frequently be bought.'[106] A recently uncovered eighteenth-century Iranian magic manuscript is an excellent example of the sort of manuals carried across the region by wandering fortune-tellers and healers. It consists of a mix of Arabic Koranic talismans and Persian spells. One talisman depicted, for instance, carries the following advice: 'He, who eats the roasted testicle of a black cat, can never be satisfied by intercourse, [and] who copies this talisman and binds it to his right hand, the enemies of him will be cast down.'[107]

The Islamic folk magic tradition continues to thrive in modern print culture as well. By way of illustration Campbell Thompson mentioned that in the Sudan he was offered a poorly printed astrological work with rough, worn-out woodcuts. In modern Cairo manuals on how to prepare amulets and talismans, and how to deal with *jinn* or demons are 'available in the streets everywhere'.[108] The *Shams al-ma'arif (Illumination of Knowledge)* written in the thirteenth century by Al-Būnī, which is one of the most enduringly influential Arabic works on talismans, magic squares, and protective prayers, was being printed in India during the 1880s and in Cairo around 1900, and continues to influence more recent Islamic magic books in northern and western Africa.[109]

To put this Islamic influence in a colonial context we can turn to the experience of the Mende tribe of Sierra Leone. As in much of West Africa, the first literary cultures that impacted significantly on the Mende world view were those transmitted by Arabic traders, migrants, and missionaries. This was long before the Christian European influence permeated through the repatriation attempts of the anti-slavery Sierra Leone Company in the 1790s, and the region's subsequent adoption as a British colony. It was the Koran, rather than the Bible or European esoteric traditions, that consequently became most deeply engrained in Mende conceptions of literary magic.[110] Mandingo and Fula *marabouts*, Islamic holy men and healers, became a major part of the Mende's magical outlook. A similar situation existed in other parts of colonial West Africa. Pagan rulers in nineteenth-century Ivory Coast and Ghana relied considerably on the services of

Islamic *marabouts* to help maintain their aura of spiritual power. Just like many European cunning-folk, the *marabouts* made considerable play of their books, and used them to construct Arabic charms consisting of passages from the Koran, or magic squares and symbols from manuscripts and printed works of medieval origin. These were considered holy texts, which, when written on slips of paper and kept as amulets, had protective functions against the supernatural.[111]

So, the venerable Islamic tradition of literary magic that infused through trade and cultural contact, acted as a buffer against the European grimoires made available through colonial rule. While colonial French Africa was largely Islamic, significant areas of British West Africa and the Caribbean were either Christian-ized or beyond the influence of Islamic religious tradition. Though there is evidence of Islamic written charms, *alherces*, being brought over to the Caribbean and Latin America during the early modern period and eighteenth century, by either Muslim slaves or Spaniards, it was the Christian religious monopoly there that sealed the dominance of the European magic books.[112] In the absence of cheap British grimoires, entrepreneurial American publishers would step into the magical breach.

Chapter Five

Rediscovering Ancient Magic

I n the nineteenth century archaeological revelations about the world of ancient
Egypt reinvigorated old conceptions of the country's place in the history of the
occult and inspired new magical traditions. But it is important to acknowledge
that ancient Egyptian culture was not as remote to the people of early modern
Europe as one might think. In learned medical practice pieces of Egyptian
mummies were prized for their potent blend of resins, gums, oils, and decayed
bodily fluids.[1] The Medici popes and prosperous merchants of early sixteenth-
century Italy generated an enthusiasm for Egyptian monumental architecture and
antiquities as part of a renewed respect for the military achievements of their pagan
ancestors, giving pride of place to the obelisks that had been brought back in the
heyday of the Empire.[2] In intellectual circles hieroglyphs fascinated the Renaissance
occult philosophers and alchemists. As with the Jewish Kabbalah, hieroglyphs
represented both the key to and substance of ancient wisdom, and their meaning
could only be revealed through divine communication or by intuitive inspiration.
For some they represented a universal code, the first language created by God.
Travellers and antiquarians examined them at first hand on the monuments
of Rome or in Egypt itself. Interest was further heightened by the publication of
Pyramidographia (1646), the first scholarly study of the Giza complex, written
by John Greaves. During the mid-seventeenth century the number of curious
European visitors to Egypt was sufficient for a French goldsmith named Louis
Bertier to run a successful cabinet of curiosities in Cairo. At a time when people
were being prosecuted and executed for witchcraft and conjuration across Europe,
Egypt maintained a reputation as the heartland of magic, the home of Moses the

magician and Hermes Trismegistus. Greaves could not help remarking that 'the Arabians and moors use much witchcraft in Cairo'.[3]

Hieroglyphs had been depicted in print as early as 1505 with the publication of the *Hieroglyphica*, a manuscript detailing the allegorical symbolism of the hieroglyphs. Like the *Corpus Hermeticum* it was discovered in the early fifteenth century, and it was attributed to an ancient Egyptian priest-magician named Horapollo.[4] While occult philosophers and Renaissance magicians held hieroglyphics to be an occult key, other scientists and philosophers saw them in a more mundane light. The philosopher Francis Bacon, writing in 1605, dismissed their mystical interpretation and determined that the hieroglyphs were far from being the sacred code of a higher philosophical civilization. They were, he wrote dismissively, the primitive means of recording the thoughts of a less advanced stage of human society.[5] Still, how could Bacon know? No one could translate them, though some thought they had cracked the secrets they contained. The most notable was the Jesuit mathematician, cryptographer, and scientific showman Athanaseus Kircher (1601–80). He wrote a series of publications on the subject, including the monumental *Oedipus Aegyptiacus* (1654), in which he proudly set out not only the meaning of the hieroglyphs but the origin of Egyptian civilization. He believed that the hieroglyphs were the invention of Hermes Trismegistus. While recognizing the simple phonetic and figurative representative basis of hieroglyphs, and correctly observing analogies with other ancient writing, Kircher was led almost entirely down the wrong path due to his adherence to the notion that they encapsulated a secret symbolic meaning, that they were the language of divine communication.

The mystical interpretation of the hieroglyphs and their link with Hermeticism was reinvigorated during the second half of the eighteenth century by the flourishing interest in Freemasonry. Up until this point, Freemasonry was mostly inspired by the symbolism and mythology of Solomon's temple, the Kabbalah, and the Knights Templar. The increasing antiquarian interest in Egypt now entered the mix.[6] One manifestation of this appeared in the 1770s when the French Freemason Antoine Court de Gebelin claimed that Tarot card images constituted a symbolic essence of the Book of Thoth, thus encapsulating the wisdom of ancient Egypt. Then there was Count Cagliostro. On a visit to London in 1777 he founded his own branch of Egyptian Freemasonry. While riffling through the barrows of a bookseller in Leicester Square, so the dubious story goes, Cagliostro came across a manuscript treatise on the Egyptian origins of Freemasonry written by one George Cofton, a man of whom nothing concrete is known whether he existed at all. Through the aid of a translator the manuscript revealed to Cagliostro that Freemasonry was founded by an Egyptian high priest called the Great Copt in the time of the pyramid builders. The essence of this

Egyptian Freemasonry was the goal of human reunification with the divine. Cagliostro now set out to spread the message amongst his fellow Freemasons across Europe, preaching that the Great Copt had personally charged him with restoring the purity of Freemasonry from the devil worshippers and rationalists who had corrupted it. He took to wearing a black silk robe with red embroidered hieroglyphs while acting out his esoteric rituals.[7] A few years later, independent of Cagliostro's Masonic revelation, the Freemason Ignaz Edler von Born, a major figure of the Austrian Enlightenment, provided an alternative vision of the importance of Egyptian religious culture to Freemasonry. Interpreted through the prism of early modern Hermeticism, von Born saw the Egyptian priesthood as the servants of science serving the welfare of the people, rather than as magicians keeping them in dread thrall or a permanent state of spiritual readiness.[8]

It was only with the discovery in 1799 of the Rosetta Stone, a black granite slab inscribed with a Ptolemaic decree written in Demotic Egyptian, Greek, and hieroglyphs, that translation was made possible. The Stone was found by a French soldier working in the Egyptian town of Rosetta (Rashid) and was swiftly appropriated by a general based in Alexandria. When Napoleon heard of its discovery he ordered that it be removed to the recently created *Institut National* in Cairo and that copies of the inscriptions be made and distributed to the scholarly community. With the surrender of the French to the British in 1801 the Rosetta Stone, along with numerous other major antiquities, was packed off to London and took pride of place in the British Museum. Thanks to Napoleon, though, scholars were able to work on the inscriptions without having to travel to Britain, and within two decades several had groped their way to partial understandings of the hieroglyphs. But, perhaps fittingly, it was a French philologist, Jean François Champollion (1790–1832), who, with his detailed knowledge of Coptic, Demotic, and Greek, fully cracked the code in the 1820s. What his work revealed was not a mystical language but a sophisticated means of recording the mundane legal, fiscal, and administrative workings of a sophisticated society—and the magical practices that underpinned its conception of life and the afterlife.

The discoveries made by the archaeologists who joined Napoleon's expeditionary force to Egypt between 1798 and 1801, and the beautifully illustrated publications on Egyptian antiquities they produced, fired the imagination of European urban society. The exhibits of the British Museum and the Louvre became the most enduringly popular part of their collections. A dedicated Egyptian Museum was founded in Berlin in 1850. Pyramids, temples, and sphinxes influenced garden design and architecture. Egyptian features could be seen in the streets of the European capitals. Londoners marvelled at the temple facade of the Egyptian Hall, built in Piccadilly in 1812, and which hosted numerous popular exhibitions of curiosities from across the world. A report in the *New York Herald* in

1881 observed that 'it would be absurd for the people of any great city to hope to be happy without an Egyptian obelisk.'[9] Mummies proved hugely popular with public unravellings being put on by scientific showmen. They joined shrouded ghosts as familiar supernatural beings in plays, stage magic, and fiction.[10]

The old use of 'Egyptian' to mean 'gypsy', which had been used in English vagrancy laws for centuries, fell out of usage. The gypsies' reputation for magic was based partly on the notion that they originated from the magical land of Egypt, and that some of the old magic of the priests and pharaohs was in their blood. We have already seen that the German charm chapbook *Die Egyptische Geheimnisse* (*Egyptian Secrets*) proved popular in eighteenth-century Germany. Around the same time several cheap fortune-telling guides in Britain also played on the tradition. The *New and true Egyptian fortune-teller* was, for example, attributed to 'Ptolomy, King of the Gypsies'. Thanks to 'Egyptomania', however, by the 1820s 'Egyptian' came to mean 'Egyptian' in such popular literature. Romany gypsies retained a reputation for magic nevertheless, and with ethnographic research relocating their origins to India rather than the Near East new traditions emerged regarding their mystic Hindu powers.[11]

Having Egyptian as distinct from gypsy associations became an increasingly common claim of fortune-tellers, occultists, and the producers of practical occult guides. The most popular of the latter was the dream divination manual *Napoleon Bonaparte's Book of Fate*, which as the title suggests, was said to have been used by the French Emperor. Most versions of this claimed that it was a German translation of an ancient Egyptian manuscript found in an Egyptian royal tomb in 1801 by one M. Sonnini—a reference probably to the French traveller and historian Charles S. Sonnini, whose book *Travels in Upper and Lower Egypt* was published in 1800.[12] The first edition of the French grimoire *La poule noire*, printed in 1820, also reflected the occult zeitgeist. It described how the magical instructions it contained derived from a French soldier in Egypt who was rescued from an Arab attack by an old Turk who hid him inside a pyramid. The old man instructed him in the secrets of ancient magic from manuscripts that survived the burning of Ptolemy's library. The same story was repeated in another *Bibliothèque bleue* grimoire that appeared a few years later entitled *The Old Man of the Pyramids*.

The new vogue for Egyptian association went down particularly well in America where the old European traditions regarding gypsies had less relevance. Charles Roback, a notorious mid-nineteenth-century American quack and cunning-man, claimed he visited Cairo and the pyramids, then followed the Nile to its source. 'I made myself familiar with all that could be elicited from the modern Egyptians, respecting the incantations and prodigies performed by the priests of ancient Egypt,' he boasted. In a village near ancient Thebes he said he collected several astrological papyrus rolls written in cuneiform that served him well in his future career.[13] A survey of late-nineteenth-century American fortune-telling advertisements revealed that many diviners claimed to have Egyptian ancestry. 'The Great Egyptian Prophetess, Sentinella Guzhdo', who circulated leaflets in New Jersey, claimed her parents were born near Cairo and that she was 'a lineal descendant of Zindello, king of one of the most ancient tribes of Egypt'. Her ability to 'remove spells, and cure diseases' was due to charms carefully preserved by her tribe.[14]

It was only from the late 1820s onwards that the magic books of the Egyptians were decoded for the first time. The most important find occurred shortly before 1828 when Egyptians digging for grave goods near Thebes found a cache of magical papyri rolls written in Greek, Demotic, and Coptic. It is worth noting at this point that from the late medieval period onwards, Egyptian treasure hunters had used Arabic grimoires in order to conjure up treasures and deal with the djinns and other spirits that guarded them. The most widely used text was *The Book of Buried Pearls*, dated to the fifteenth century, which, like the *Libro de San Cipriano* in Spain and Portugal, combined geographical details of sites where treasures lay buried with the magical means of obtaining them. Cheap Arabic and French versions were published in Cairo in 1907 on the instructions of Gaston Maspero, Director of Antiquities in Egypt. Maspero and the editor of the publication, the archaeologist Ahmed Bey Kamal, believed the *Book of Buried Pearls* had caused more destruction to ancient monuments than war and the ravages of time. They hoped that making such 'secret' knowledge more widely available would help dispel the book's aura and undermine its pernicious influence. It was probably a vain hope. Writing in the 1930s a former British Chief Inspector of Antiquities for Middle Egypt noted that the book continued to be much studied by treasure seekers. To give a taste of the advice it contained, here are instructions for finding treasure near the pyramid of Cheops:

> Make a fumigation with tar, styrax, and wool from a black sheep, and a door giving access to a dyke enclosing four feddans will be opened to you. Make then your fumigation and jump across the dyke, then dig into the enclosed area, and you will find, at one cubit's depth or a little more, some nuggets of gold. Take all you desire, continuing the fumigation until you have finished.

As a footnote, in the 1920s the search for the 'lost' or legendary oasis and city of Zerzura, supposedly situated in the Egyptian portion of the Libyan Desert, was given fresh impetus by the discovery of a reference to it in the *Book of Buried Pearls*.[15]

The sensational finds at Thebes, which would come to be known as the Theban magical library, were swiftly sold to Giovanni Anastasi, the Swedish consul in Alexandria.[16] This interesting character has a rather obscure background with various conflicting accounts of his origins. One suggestion is that he was Armenian by birth, and arrived in Egypt around 1797 with his father, a trader who supplied the French troops. What is certain is that Anastasi became a wealthy merchant and prospered in the antiquities trade. He broke up the Theban magical library selling parts of it to museums in Leiden and Stockholm, as well as to the British Museum. Other significant discoveries appeared over the next few decades, but nothing matching the Theban library in scope and quantity. It is likely that some of these later magical papyri, such as several rolls purchased from Anastasi by the Louvre, were probably part of the cache found in 1828 but it is impossible to prove conclusively.

Now the slow process of translation began. In 1830 the Dutch scholar Caspar Jacob Christiaan Reuvens published excerpts of the Leiden rolls, and a few years later a German translation of these appeared. Over in Britain, in 1853, one of the papyri held by the British Museum was translated into English with a commentary by Charles Wycliffe Goodwin. It was the Viennese papyri expert Carl Wessely (1860–1931) who did most to make knowledge of the Graeco-Egyptian grimoires accessible. In the late 1880s he produced transcriptions of the Paris and London rolls, while an edition of the British Museum's magical papyri was published independently by Frederick George Kenyon.

Meanwhile cuneiform, the earliest form of writing used by Middle Eastern civilizations such as the Assyrians, Babylonians, and Akkadians, was also being deciphered, though with much less fanfare and public interest. German and British scholars were at the forefront of cracking the meaning of the cuneiform pictographs, but it was a Frenchman, François Lenormant (1837–83), the son of a well-respected archaeologist who had accompanied Champollion on an expedition to Egypt, who brought translations of this earliest written magic to the wider public.[17] Lenormant made his reputation working on the archaeology of southern Italy but he was also an authority on Near Eastern civilizations, though his reputation suffered from accusations of forgery. It was his work *La Magie chez les Chaldéennes* (1874) that added a new dimension to Western understanding of ancient written magic. The book was based around what were known as the Evil Spirit Texts, Assyrian–Babylonian cuneiform tablets containing spells and exorcisms to ward off devils, ghosts, and other malign influences such as plague. A few years later English and German editions appeared, both of which went on to be republished numerous times and can still be found in the Mind, Body, and Spirit sections of major bookshops.

Despite all the academic interest in ancient civilizations—a professorial chair in Egyptology was created at Berlin University as early as 1846—the scholarly community was not exactly consumed by curiosity regarding the secrets of the magical papyri.[18] In fact the history of magic was not considered worthy of much serious attention at all. When, in 1875, Maspero produced an edition of a Demotic magical papyrus he felt it necessary to excuse the publication of these 'magical formulae without much interest for science'. He was trying to deflect such criticism as that uttered by the scholar who complained that the magical papyri 'deprived antiquity of the noble splendour of classicism'.[19] In his review of Kenyon's *Greek Papyri in the British Museum* (1893), the Cambridge lecturer J. Rendel Harris observed regarding the magic rolls, 'To most people these are very void of attraction. The recipes for raising spirits or for seeing one's own double, side by side with plans for detecting thieves and for the expulsion of vermin, are in themselves stupid enough.' He went on to argue though, that 'we ought not neglect them simply because we find them made up largely of Coptic, Hebrew and Syriac Abracadabra.' Magic, he concluded, was too near religion to be neglected by scholars.[20]

This message may not have attracted widespread sympathy amongst archaeologists and biblical scholars, but new academic disciplines that embraced it were developing. Anthropology and the History of Religions were gaining respect. By the end of the century professorial chairs in the History of Religion were created in universities across Europe and in America, and dedicated journals appeared in German and French. As an overview of the subject written in 1926 commented, 'It was the sign of a new spirit, a thrust towards objectivity, an effort to escape the hampering hand of apologetics.'[21] At the heart of both disciplines in their early years was the comparison of religious beliefs from across the globe in the search for similarities that could reveal the cultural and mental evolution of humankind. Thanks to the archaeologists and cryptologists, the genesis of ancient religions and their relationship to magic could be pushed back beyond ancient Greece. Another interested group who had a particular interest in this, and in tracing the possible survival of ancient magic into the present, were those participants in what is known as the Occult Revival of the second half of the nineteenth century.

Another magical renaissance

As we have already seen, despite the so-called Enlightenment the practice of magic never disappeared in Europe, manifesting itself in the activities of treasure seekers and cunning-folk, and in the rarefied esoteric religious and Freemasonry movements of the eighteenth century. During the early nineteenth century new pseudo-sciences such as mesmerism renewed intellectual interest in universal hidden forces. It was spiritualism, though, that truly galvanized public interest in the occult and provided a magnetic focal point for the swirl of disparate esoteric groups and ideas circulating in educated society.

From the simple 'yes'/'no' table-rapping sessions with the souls of the dead in the late 1840s and 1850s, spiritualism developed in surprising directions, from the quest to capture images of the spirit world using that new-fangled device, the camera, to the later formation of its own organized religion. Spiritualism had its mystical, esoteric angles as well, and Egyptology entered the mix, with the adoption of Egyptian iconography by clairvoyants and in the reformulation of the old conceptions of a universal spiritual truth. The journalist and poet Gerald Massey (1828–1907) is worthy of note in this respect. A working-class lad from Hertfordshire, Massey was a Christian Socialist who found in spiritualism and ancient Egypt the key to understanding modern man.[22] He wrote a series of books on the origins and legacy of Egyptian civilization in which he came up with some extraordinary claims. He was convinced, for example, that the five books of Moses were Egyptian astronomical allegories. Adopting the comparative approach of early anthropology he believed he had found linguistic and cultural traces linking the British Celts with ancient Egypt and Africa. During the 1870s and 1880s he conducted several lecture tours in North America and Canada explaining his spiritualist and cultural theories to audiences already primed by similar home-grown ideas, such as those of the Congressman Ignatius Donnelly. In a best-selling book published in 1882 he posited that ancient Egypt and the Americas were both part of the world of pre-Flood or antediluvian Atlantis, as proven by the existence of pyramids and obelisks in both regions.[23]

The Theosophical Society, founded in 1875, was the most influential occult movement to form out of the spiritualist social ether. At one time or another most occultists of the era either joined the Society or engaged with the writings of its charismatic co-founder, the well-travelled Russian émigré Helena Petrovna Blavatsky (1831–91). In her early career as a seeker of secret universal wisdom Blavatsky had been much influenced by Rosicrucianism and Kabbalah, but by the time the Theosophical Society was founded the focus of her spiritual tenets had shifted eastwards to India and Tibet. It was there, she claimed, resided the mahatmas or ancient holy men, adepts in the mysteries of the world, with whom she maintained a direct psychic contact. It was they who dictated to her the founding text of Theosophy, *Isis Unveiled*.[24]

But what of the role of magic in this occult revival? Over and over again when reading through the voluminous and often turgid library of occult expositions produced during the second half of the nineteenth century, one finds one name recurring over and over again: Éliphas Lévi. This was the Hebrew pseudonym of the son of a poor Parisian shoemaker named Alphonse Louis Constant (1810–75).[25] Lévi trained to be a Catholic priest but left the seminary shortly before his ordination, explaining later in life that he could not take his vows 'before the altar of a cold and egotistical cult'. He never lost his Catholic faith however, just his respect for the Church. Following his mother's suicide, Lévi, now scraping a living from teaching, found his way into the mystical, political, and prophetic milieu of backstreet Paris. He became a voracious reader of old and new occult works, and a visitor to the *Bibliothèque de l'Arsenal*. The first of his books on magic, *Dogme et ritual de la haute magie* (1856), reveals a familiar set of influences. Kabbalah and the Tarot underpin his conception of magic, though mixed with these we find the more recent theories of mesmerism and animal magnetism, with Lévi describing how the aim of the magician was to control the astral fluidic forces that he believed infused the Universe. He loathed black magic, the conjuration of devils and the spirits of the dead, describing its practice and its manuals as 'an epidemic of unreason'.[26] It was a view echoed by the generation of magicians he influenced.

Lévi said he had studied numerous grimoires over many years and had come to the conclusion that the only useful ones were all in manuscript and required deciphering using the codes formulated by Trithemius; 'the importance of others consists wholly in the hieroglyphs and symbols which adorn them.'[27] The *Clavicule of Solomon* was evidently one of the few legitimate grimoires in his estimation, for in 1860 he made an annotated manuscript copy of one version, perhaps from a text in the *Bibliothèque de l'Arsenal*.[28] He knew well the *Bibliothèque bleue* grimoires, dismissing them as 'catch-penny mystifications and impostures of dishonest publishers'. In a discussion on love philtres he declined to provide any examples from the *Petit Albert*, a book he described as common in the countryside, remarking that its spells were 'either foolish or criminal'. Of the *Grand grimoire* and its instructions for calling up the dead, he wrote, 'No doubt anyone who is mad enough and wicked enough to abandon himself to such operations is predisposed to all chimeras and all phantoms. Hence the recipe in the *Grand Grimoire* is most efficacious, but we advise none of our readers to have recourse to it.'[29] As a conscientious Catholic he had further reason to denounce grimoires such as the *Grimoire du Pape Honorius* for they besmirched the pious reputations of the saints and popes. Only the Devil could profit from such pernicious mischief making.[30] The only good he could find in the *Bibliothèque bleue* genre were the Paracelsian lamens and receipts that the compiler of the *Petit Albert* had included. Lévi had great respect for old Theophrastus Bombatus von Hohenheim. He once fell asleep over a copy of one of his works and experienced a vision of meeting with him in his alchemical laboratory. On waking he rationalized the experience, but this dream encounter with Paracelsus nevertheless left a strong and lasting impression on him.[31]

Lévi hoped his writings on magic would combat and expose black magic and diabolic grimoires, those 'unhappy aberrations of the human mind'.[32] As evidence of their pernicious contents, he referred to the experiments on the occult power of symbols by the mesmerist Jean Du Potet de Sennevoy (1796–1891). These involved exposing people to a series of lines and symbols, including circles, stars, and serpent shapes, drawn on the floor in chalk and charcoal. Lévi described them as being analogous, 'if not absolutely identical, with pretended diabolical signatures found in old editions of the Grand Grimoire'.[33] The idea was that certain combinations of signs and lines exuded a magnetic influence over people, and could even induce a profound sense of fear and cause the mind to conjure up frightening visions.[34] For Lévi the evil hold that malign grimoires could have over the weak or unstable was brought home to him by his encounter with a young priest who inquired of a bookseller where the master of magic lived. An appointment was arranged and the priest said he desired to obtain the *Grimoire of Honorius* and would pay as much as one hundred francs for it. When Lévi queried whether he intended to practise forbidden black magic, the priest merely smiled sarcastically. It transpired later that the priest was Jean-Louis Verger, a troublesome and mentally unstable young man who, in 1857, murdered the archbishop of Paris during service.[35]

Lévi made two well-received visits to England in 1854 and 1856, where his main contact was with the novelist, politician, and student of the occult Edward Bulwer-Lytton (1803–73), whom later magic groups would falsely claim as a high profile member.[36] By 1860 Lévi's works had proven so influential that he was receiving admiring visitors from abroad. One of them was the writer, magazine editor, and mason Kenneth Mackenzie. His place in the history of modern occultism is partly due to an account he published of his visit to Lévi's home, but primarily because of his early membership of the Societas Rosicruciana in Anglia, which was founded in 1865 by its Supreme Magus, the Freemason Robert Wentworth Little.[37] Other members were a London coroner named William Wynn Westcott, who we shall meet again a little later, and Frederick Hockley (1808–85). The latter was a last link with the turn-of-the-century London occult network that circled around John Denley's bookshop. Hockley was at one time employed by Denley, transcribing and compiling expensive and cheap grimoires for sale, and his own collection of magical manuscripts was much coveted.[38]

Another foreign traveller passing through the London occult scene around this time was the African-American spiritualist Beverly Randolph (1825–75).[39] Born in the New York slums and brought up in an almshouse where his mother died, he signed up as a cabin boy to escape life on the streets. Despite the challenges of his miserable youth he managed to teach himself to read and write. He set himself up as a barber in Utica and began to make a name for himself as an antislavery orator and as a clairvoyant physician and spiritualist, adopting the title of 'Dr'. Randolph visited England in 1855 and 1857, circulating amongst the feverish spiritualist community but also, according to his own account, meeting Bulwer-Lytton and the Rosicrucian writer Hargrave Jennings. There is no reason to doubt this. Bulwer-Lytton's fiction was certainly the inspiration for Randolph's own attempts at writing Rosicrucian novels. There is also little doubt that his interest in sex magic was stimulated by Jennings curious works on phallic-Buddhist Rosicrucianism.[40]

Randolph's life-long fascination with scrying and magic mirrors was also due to his experiences in Paris and London. At the time, experimenting with contacting the spirit world through crystal balls and magic mirrors was a major preoccupation of mesmerists, spiritualists, and occultists. In the English occult scene instructions on how to prepare and use magic mirrors were available in Barrett's *The Magus*. Frederick Hockley had posed thousands of questions to the angels via his crystal, and around the same time Richard James Morrison, better known as the author of *Zadkiel's Almanac*, was also busy with his ball. In 1863 he took the bold step of suing an admiral who had written a letter to the *Daily Telegraph* accusing him of fraudulent pretences in his scrying sessions. Meanwhile in Paris, Randolph had letters of introduction to meet Du Potet and another prominent spiritualist and dabbler in magic mirrors Louis-Alphonse Cahagnet. Fanciful stories have circulated about Randolph being initiated by Lévi, but there is absolutely no evidence for it.[41] It was the influence of Du Potet's and Cahagnet's experiments with narcotics to induce trance states that led Randolph to become an enthusiastic user of hashish, and at one time he was probably the biggest importer of the drug into the United States.[42]

Back in America, Randolph renounced spiritualism and entered the mystical phase of his life. He set up the first Rosicrucian order in the USA, the Fraternitas Rosae Crucis, espousing, teaching, and writing about magic mirrors, free love, and the use of sex to reach magical enlightenment. For Randolph the ritualized use of the orgasm could provide a gateway to the universal mystery of life, giving a new meaning to the magic wand. He set sail once more for Africa and the Near East in the early 1860s in order to complete his mystical enlightenment, though details of his journey there are suspiciously sketchy, as were those of a previous visit to the region in the 1850s. Whatever the facts, it was certainly important to be known to have made a pilgrimage to the pyramids, the home of Rosicrucianism. 'During my travels through Africa, Egypt, Turkey, Arabia, Syria, and my intercourse with the Voudeaux of New Orleans and Long Island, I became thoroughly convinced of the existence of two kinds of magic,' he wrote. 'One good and beneficent, ruled and governed by the Adonim, the other foul, malevolent, revengeful, lustful, and malignant.'[43]

Randolph's significance in the story of grimoires lies in the interest he generated in ritual magic in America and the demand he might have created for books of magic. Randolph certainly made money importing and selling magic mirrors and it is not unlikely that he was involved in selling books other than his own.

This was certainly the case with an occult group founded in the USA a few years after Randolph's death that was influenced by the sex magic and mirror rituals he taught. The Hermetic Brotherhood of Luxor was a mail order organization founded in 1884 by Peter Davidson (1837–1915), a Scottish violinmaker.[44] Davidson claimed the Brotherhood originated in Egypt long before the time of Hermes Trismegistus, and stressed to initiates that it was a Western order as distinct from the Eastern esotericism of the Theosophists. While living in the Highlands of Scotland Davidson had maintained a regular correspondence with the London occult scene, including members of the Societas Rosicruciana in Anglia and Hargrave Jennings. It was this experience of postal fraternity that gave him the idea that a mail order Order was feasible. After arriving in America in 1886 to set up a utopian community, he successfully continued to orchestrate the running of the Brotherhood's predominantly British and French members. The utopian community never materialized though, and Davidson scraped a living as a herbal doctor and supplier of magic mirrors, crystals, and books from his home in Loudsville, Georgia. In a letter dated 1886 a prospective member of the Brotherhood enquired of Davidson about purchasing a copy of Barrett's *Magus*. Davidson replied that it was selling for £1.5s. 6d. He also said, 'I can get you Agrippa's 4 Books if you wish. I have not them in stock just now; they are rather difficult to be had now as they are getting very scarce.'[45]

The Brotherhood's initial representative in England was the Revd William Alexander Ayton, the vicar of Chacombe, Northamptonshire, who when not carrying out his pastoral duties pursued his interest in Freemasonry and Theosophy.[46] His consuming passion was alchemical experimentation, and he whiled away many hours in his laboratory hidden away in his cellar under the rectory. Ayton provides a neat link to the two men who more than anyone during the Occult Revival opened up the secrets of the grimoires for an English readership who could not access the German editions of Horst and Scheible. Ayton conducted the marriage ceremony of the first of the two, Samuel Liddell Mathers (1854–1918).

It was while living with his widowed mother in the seaside town of Bournemouth that Mathers, the son of a Hackney merchant's clerk, befriended a neighbour and Freemason named Frederick Holland.[47] His exploration of esotericism began, and in 1882 the pair were admitted to the Societas Rosicruciana in Anglia. As his social circle widened the Hackney boy began to craft a new persona for himself. His love of all things military nearly matched his fascination with the occult. He joined a volunteer regiment and enthusiastically participated in crowd control duties. More surprising was his adoption of the Scottish title Count MacGregor of Glenstrae, bogusly claiming that Louis XV had bestowed it on an ancestor after the Jacobite rebellion. After his mother's death in 1885 Mathers moved to London and it was there that he began to publish the first of his books on occultism and magic. In 1888 he produced the *Qabbalah Unveiled*, a translation of a seventeenth-century Latin treatise, and a book on the Tarot. The following year he sealed his place in the history of grimoires by putting together the first English print edition of the *Key* or *Clavicule of Solomon*.

As has already been noted in an earlier chapter, there were myriad versions of manuscript grimoires bearing the title of the *Clavicule of Solomon*. Mathers was well aware of this, mentioning that he had seen grimoires ascribed to Solomon which were 'full of evil magic, and I cannot caution the practical student too strongly against them.' So he pored over and transcribed passages from a number of mostly seventeenth-century manuscripts in French, Hebrew, Latin, and English in the British Library, filtering out the contaminating elements of diabolic magic and constructing what he considered a pure version of the *Clavicule*. This would encapsulate the wisdom of the ancients and serve as a companion to Lévi's theoretical construction of practical magic.

In 1890 Mathers was employed as curator of the then private Horniman Museum, though today it is a fascinating public museum of cultural and natural history. He obtained the position thanks to the influence of the occultist Annie Horniman, the daughter of the museum's founder and benefactor. When, four years later, Mathers and his French-born wife moved to Paris, Annie continued to pay them an allowance, but when this ceased he eked out a living selling Turkish Railway shares to supplement his income from writing. During his time in Paris he consulted the grimoire collection of René de Voyer d'Argenson in the *Bibliothèque de l'Arsenal* and was particularly struck by one entitled the *Book of the Sacred Magic of Abra-Melin*, which was written in a French hand of the late seventeenth or early eighteenth century. It was quite possibly one of those confiscated by the Paris police in their campaign against the magicians. Mathers explained in the preface to his 1898 edition of the manuscript that he had been informed of its existence many years earlier. He believed Bulwer-Lytton and Lévi knew of it, but it was the poet Paul Bois who urged him to immerse himself in its wisdom.[48]

Like numerous other manuscript grimoires of the seventeenth and eighteenth centuries it provided its own founding myth, telling how it was a translation from the Hebrew script of a mage and celebrated Kaballist called Abra-Melin. According to the manuscript he was born in 1362 and had written down the secrets of his magical knowledge in 1458 as a means of passing on the wisdom to his son. During his life he had travelled far and wide in search of knowledge, performing at the courts of European nobles, including that of the English King Henry VI, eventually settled in Würzburg. He was, then, an archetype of the Jewish Renaissance mage. Mathers was ready to believe in this story and thus seal the importance of the *Sacred Magic of Abra-Melin* as a profound work on the ascetic,

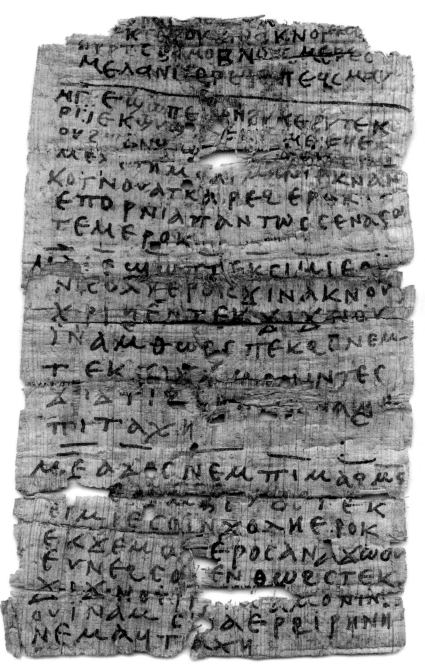

1. Coptic papyrus magical handbook, containing recipes for sexual problems.
Duke University Library

2. The magician Zoroaster conjuring up two demons. From a copy of *Le Livre du Trésor* by Brunetto Latini (1425)

3. King Solomon reading the Torah (*c.*1280).

4. Moses and Aaron at Pharaoh's court (*c.*1300).

5. Conjuring demons to bring treasure. *Cotton MS Tiberius* (fourteenth century)

6. Preaching before Pope Honorius III. Giotto (*c.*1295).

Alfredo Dagli Orti/San Francesco Assisi/The Art Archive

7. Elizabethan grimoire that borrows from the *Key of Solomon*, and which purports to contain the magic of Roger Bacon

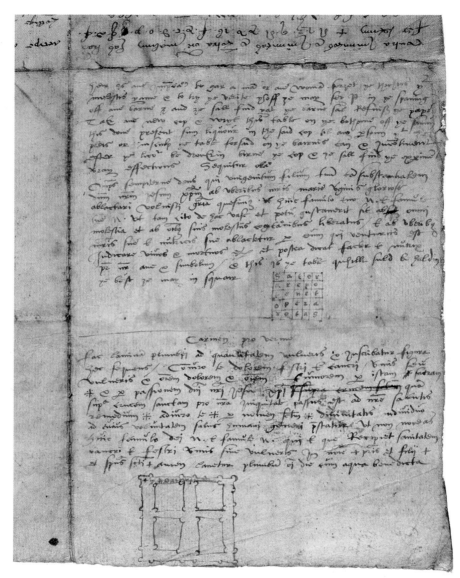

8. Manuscript of Bartie Patersoune, a Scottish cunning-man executed in 1607

National Archives of Scotland (JC26/5)

9. The Danish cunning-man Anders Ulfkjær, and his wife Mariane. Ulfkjær owned and used a manuscript *Cyprianus*.

Reprinted from H.P. Hansen, *Kloge Folk* (Copenhagen, 1961), vol. 2, plate 1

10. The defendants in the murder of Nelson D. Rehmeyer and images from the *Sixth and Seventh Books of Moses*

Charleston Daily Mail, courtesy of the West Virginia State Archives

11. Pulp grimoires for sale

Henry Gamache, *Mystery of the Long Lost 8th, 9th and 10th Books of Moses* (New York, 1948)

12. Book display in the Hindu Mysterious Store, Harlem, photographed in 1943
Weegee (Arthur Fellig)/International Centre of Photography/Getty Images

13. The Hindu Mysterious Store in Harlem photographed in 1943

Weegee (Arthur Fellig)/International Centre of Photography/Getty Images

14. Putumayo herbalist's stall, Colombia

Courtesy of Professor Michael Taussig

15. Johann Kruse, the German campaigner against magical practitioners and grimoires
PA Photos

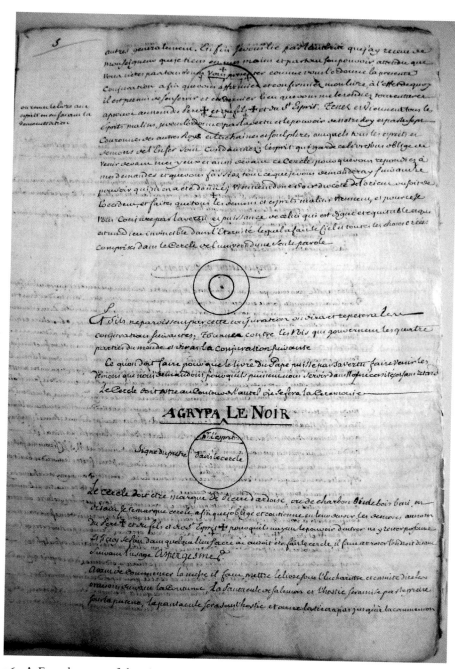

16. A French copy of the *Agrippa Noir* belonging to the Basque conjurer Gracien Detcheverry. The original was publicly burned in Bayonne in 1750

Archives Communales de Bayonne

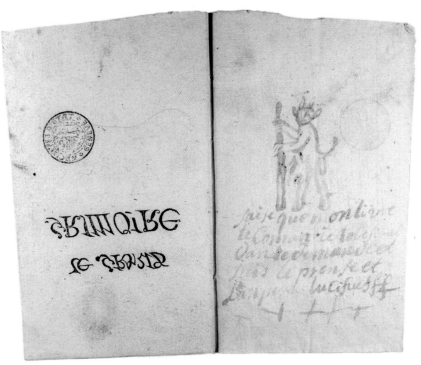

17. A Devil's pact written in a copy of the *Grand grimoire* sold by the eighteenth-century Genevan grimoire dealer Moyse Morié

Archives d'Etat de Genève

spiritual basis of ancient Kaballistic magic largely free of the contamination and meddling that had marred many of the versions of the *Clavicule of Solomon*.[49] Neither of Mathers' published grimoires made much money or circulated much beyond the small circle of practising occultists in London and Paris. They were produced in limited print runs and within a couple of decades they were running at a high price in the second-hand book market.

Arthur Edward Waite (1857–1942) was a more successful and widely appreci-ated author.[50] Born in New York, the illegitimate son of a merchant marine who drowned a year after his birth, Waite was taken to England by his mother, an educated middle-class English woman, where he was brought up in north London. His only formal education was two terms at St Charles's College in the London suburb of Bayswater, which makes his later literary career all the more impressive. Unlike most of the influential male occultists of the late Victorian period his path to esotericism did not begin with Freemasonry. It was his Catholicism and fascination with ritual that briefly led him to consider joining the priesthood, and which subsequently, in the early 1880s, drew him to the work of Blavatsky and through her to Lévi, whose works he would later translate and comment on critically for an English audience. His other love, poetry, was hardly bringing in a living wage for his wife and young daughter so he turned to churning out occult studies of varying quality. He did not even put his name to the hackwork *Handbook of Cartomancy*. In contrast, his *Devil Worship in France* (1896), an exposé of supposed Satanists, was praised in the academic journal *The American Anthropologist* as an 'invaluable' work for serious students of occultism and mysticism.[51] His most unusual publishing venture was the translation of various alchemical writings, including those of Paracelsus, which was financed by the aristocratic alchemist Fitzherbert Edward Stafford-Jerningham (1833–1913), who frittered away his family fortune in the deluded attempt to make gold.[52] Looking back on this 'Hermetic adventure' Waite pondered, 'it can only be regarded as a remarkable bibliographic fact that such texts were issued, and on so great a scale, in the last decade of the nineteenth century.'[53]

Waite's most successful venture was a Tarot pack published in 1910, but the publication of most interest to us is his *Book of Black Magic and of Pacts* (1898).[54] This was the first major history and exposition of the whole genre of grimoires, providing bibliographies and extracts from the range of works I have discussed so far, such as the *Arbatel*, the *Clavicules of Solomon*, *Fourth Book of Occult Philosophy*, the *Grand grimoire*, *Book of Honorius*, and the *Poule noire*. Waite's motivation—apart from money—was the same as the likes of Reginald Scot and Georg Conrad Horst in that he set before readers a cornucopia of practical magic for the explicit purpose of undermining it. Despite his occult interests Waite was no practical magician, and his view on the subject is summoned up in his comment that 'the distinction between White and Black Magic is the distinction between the idle and the evil word.' Waite was well aware, of course, that its contents would be of huge interest to practical occultists and pointedly stated that he intended to provide them with 'the fullest evidence of the futility of Ceremonial Magic as it is found in books'. The conjurations and spells they contained were 'ridiculous', 'absurd', 'iniquitous' even—if 'it could be supposed that they were to be seriously understood.'[55] No surprise then, that Waite made some withering comments regarding Mathers' publications. Without naming him directly, he referred to the editor of the *Key of Solomon* as 'an expositor of the more arid and unprofitable side of Kabalistic doctrine'. He went on to demolish Mathers' view that the *Sacred Magic of Abra-Melin* was copied from a Hebrew text or that it even originated any earlier than the seventeenth century. I have to agree with him.[56]

With its 170 woodblock engravings of lamens, talismans, signs, and seals, its numerous transcriptions of conjurations, exorcisms, and prayers, the *Book of Black Magic and of Pacts* constituted the richest, most comprehensive grimoire ever produced in one printed volume. Waite stripped the great grimoires of their philosophical and mystical content and provided a condensed manual of practical ritual magic. Only 500 copies were printed initially, selling for the considerable sum of £2 2s. Although Waite obviously hoped to make money from the book, it was certainly not an exercise in popular publishing, though a new edition for the cheaper price of 15s. appeared in 1910 under the title *The Book of Ceremonial Magic*.

Considering their antipathy towards each other and their respective views on magic, it may seem strange that Mathers and Waite were fellow members of the Hermetic Order of the Golden Dawn, which was the first nineteenth-century occult organization explicitly dedicated to the practice of ritual magic.[57] Founded in 1888, it had direct links with the Societas Rosicruciana in Anglia and most of its members had been immersed in the Theosophy movement. Following the creation of the initial Isis-Urania Temple of the Golden Dawn in London, regional branches were set up: the Osiris Temple in Weston-super-Mare, the Horus Temple in Bradford, and the Amen-Ra Temple in Edinburgh. Their magic was obviously not that of the cunning-folk who continued to provide magical solutions for the misfortunes of the general populace of Britain at the time. The Golden Dawn's magical philosophy was essentially another reformulation of early modern Hermeticism, Rosicrucianism, and Kabbalah, particularly as viewed through the lens of Lévi's work. Added to this was a hierarchical structure borrowed from Freemasonry and a ritual basis influenced by the old and new Egyptology. The Golden Dawn never consisted of more than a few hundred members at its peak, nearly all from the middle classes, but it was notable for welcoming women and attracting members of the artistic community such as the actress Florence Farr and the Irish poet and mystic W. B. Yeats.

Mathers was largely responsible for creating the Golden Dawn's rituals, with some initial input from his fellow founding member William Wynn Westcott, who continued to be active in the Societas Rosicruciana in Anglia, becoming its 'Supreme Magus' in the 1890s. There was, of course, a foundation text with the usual dubious history. In one version of its discovery this cipher manuscript was found in a London bookshop just like Cagliastro happened upon his Egyptian Masonic revelation. The alternative story is that it was owned by Frederick Hockley. When he died in 1885 it was passed on with other papers to the clergyman A. F. A. Woodford, another founder of the Golden Dawn. He, in turn, handed it to Westcott who, recognizing the cipher as one described by Trithemius, set about decoding it. It turned out to consist of five otherwise unknown rituals of a Rosicrucian Freemasonic nature. It also contained the address of one Anna Sprengel, a Rosicrucian adept in Nuremberg whose order had a direct line of descent from the medieval brotherhood. Westcott wrote to her and received her authorization to set up a Temple of the Golden Dawn. As can be imagined, this account has been called into doubt. In fact, in 1900, Mathers wrote a letter to Florence Farr stating that Westcott had forged both the cipher manuscript and the correspondence with the mysterious Anna Sprengel.[58]

As the rituals of the Golden Dawn developed, incorporating elements of John Dee's system of magic, and to a lesser extent Mathers' grimoire publications, Egyptian pagan influences also seeped in.[59] This is not surprising considering that Mathers once described himself as 'a student of Occultism, Archaeology, and Egyptology'.[60] By the 1890s the rolls of the Theban Magical Library and other papyri had been published, and Lenormant's work on Chaldean magic texts was widely known. Mathers referred to it in his introduction to the *Sacred Magic of Abra-Melin*. So it is not surprising that along with the old Renaissance notions of ancient Egypt that permeated Hermeticism and Rosicrucianism, the nineteenth-century archaeological discoveries of actual Egyptian magic also influenced the practices and rituals of the Golden Dawn. In 1896 Florence Farr produced a short book entitled *Egyptian Magic* for which she consulted Goodwin's work on the Graeco-Egyptian magical papyri, and mentioned in a letter that she had met with an 'Egyptian Adept in the British Museum' which had opened up 'possibilities'. Mathers also taught one of the invocations translated in Goodwin's article to other members of the Order.[61]

The numerous popular publications by Ernest Alfred Wallis Budge (1857–1934) were the most significant influence in exciting practical interest in Egyptian magic.[62] Budge, who was possibly the 'Egyptian Adept' mentioned by Florence Farr—though there is no evidence he was an occultist—began studying ancient languages while a youthful employee at W. H. Smith's, and encouraged by the keeper of oriental antiquities at the British Museum went on to study Semitic languages at Cambridge. On graduating he joined the Department of Oriental Antiquities at the British Museum where he remained the rest of his working life. He paid numerous short visits to Egypt, purchasing antiquities from local dealers and a limited number through excavation. He was particularly successful, though not always scrupulous, at collecting papyri and inscribed clay tablets from across the Near and Middle East. Over his lifetime he wrote over a hundred monographs, the most well known of which were *Egyptian Magic* (1899) and the *Book of the Dead* (1901). The latter, which developed from a facsimile of the *Papyrus of Ani* published by the British Museum in 1890, was a funerary text consisting of a series of prayers and rituals to guide the dead into the afterlife. Elements of it were incorporated into the Golden Dawn's tenets. Its wider public reach was furthered by reference to it in early-twentieth-century fantasy fiction, such as in Sax Rohmer's *Brood of the Witch-Queen* (1918) and in the casebooks of Algernon Blackwood's occult detective *John Silence* (1908). Budge's work is no longer treated seriously by Egyptologists, though, as he wrote quickly and often without appropriate scholarly caution or rigour. Numerous mistakes in translation and interpretation littered his work. Nevertheless, with the expiry of the copyright on his books, they are still probably the most widely disseminated and used works on the subject today.

Much of the contents of the magical papyri were concerned with spells, exorcisms, and conjurations for the usual practical ends, to heal the possessed, protect against evil, provoke love, and cure the sick. The magic of Lévi and the Golden Dawn, like the Renaissance occult philosophers they revered, was concerned with the much more lofty desire for spiritual enlightenment. So to make use of the magical papyri it was necessary to incorporate them into a ritual religious framework that transformed them from the practical into the mystical. This was essentially a reversal of the process by which cunning-folk took the rituals, symbols, and words of high magic and reformulated them into elements of popular magic. It was this mutability of the contents of grimoires that ensured their enduring relevance across different continents and eras.

In 1903 a long-brewing schism occurred in the Golden Dawn, brought about primarily by Mathers' arrogance and erratic and dictatorial behaviour. Waite, by now earning a living as a manager for the malted milk drink company Horlicks, took over effective control of the London Temple, nudging the group's occult philosophy and ceremonies away from ancient paganism and towards Christian mysticism. One source of contention had been Mathers' support for a new and rapidly rising member named Aleister Crowley, whose interest in magic had been piqued by reading Waite's *Book of Black Magic*.[63] Crowley would go on to become the most notorious magician of the twentieth century. A cruel, egotistical sex magician who believed he was the reincarnation of Cagliostro and Lévi, he was dubbed the 'wickedest man in the world' by the tabloid press, but died quietly and alone in a Hastings boarding house in 1947 with less than a pound to his name. The story of his rise and fall is a fascinating one, but his presence in the pages of this book is due to an act of treachery. In 1904 relations between Crowley and his patron had turned sour with Crowley suspecting that Mathers was using black magic against him. In turn he consecrated talismans to protect himself. As an act of revenge, he published under his own name a British Library manuscript, the 'Lemegeton; Clavicula Salomonis or the Little Key of Solomon', which consisted of a list of spirits and their characters, that Mathers had transcribed.[64] A few years later Crowley also published the rituals of the Golden Dawn in an occult journal he had founded, despite Mathers' legal attempts to stop him. The 'secrets' of the Golden Dawn were now out in the open, allowing later historians to piece together the various old and new occult sources from which Mathers and Westcott had stitched together the Order's ritual magic.

Writing for the people

Much of this chapter has been concerned with the world of, at the most, a few thousand occultists across Europe and America. It could be argued that they constitute a mere footnote in the story of grimoires. But while histories of the Occult Revival focus almost exclusively on the esoteric philosophies, personal relations, and internal tensions of the occultists, certain products of the Revival reached far beyond the parlours of Paris and London and away from the esoteric byways of the intellectual fringes of nineteenth-century Western society. One of Peter Davidson's guides to the healing power of herbs and their mystical properties, *Man Know Thyself* (1878), was, for instance, used by folk healers in Trinidad. *Behold the Sign: Ancient Symbolism*, a small book published by the Ancient Mystical Order Rosæ Crucis (AMORC), founded in the USA in 1915, was adopted by some *Obeah*-men in Guyana. It contained hieroglyphs and symbols, such as a five-pointed star 'held to be a talisman against witchcraft'.[65] In early-twentieth-century Germany esoteric publishers pumped out cheap editions of the *Sixth and Seventh Books of Moses* that found their way into the hands of many rural cunning-folk. It was in France though, the home of the cheap print grimoire, that the occultists were most attuned to a wider audience and the mundane magical needs of the people. The most successful at tapping into this was Julien-Ernest Houssay (1844–1912).

Abbé Julio, as Houssay was better known, was forced to leave the priesthood after alienating himself from his superiors and being accused of fraud.[66] Freeing himself from the ties of the Roman Catholic establishment he devoted his energies

INVOCATION
POUR DEMANDER L'INTERCESSION
DE L'ABBÉ JULIO
dans toutes les maladies physiques et morales

*(Cette prière doit se réciter avant de se servir
des livres et pentacles de l'Abbé Julio)*

---

† Bienheureux Abbé Julio, zélé et fidèle ser-
viteur de Jésus-Christ, vous qui avez tant guéri
et soulagé tous ceux qui venaient vous en prier ;
vous qui avez promis d'accorder votre puissante
intercession à ceux qui vous imploreraient avec
confiance, secourez-nous.

† Bienheureux Abbé Julio, priez Dieu, nous
vous en supplions, pour qu'il nous accorde notre
demande, nous vous le demandons avec confiance.

Recevez, ô Dieu infiniment bon, les suppliques
que nous vous adressons par l'entremise de
l'Abbé Julio, nous vous implorons par votre
Fils Unique qui vit et règne avec le Saint-Esprit
en l'unité d'un seul Dieu. Ainsi soit-il.

FIG. 16 A prayer to recite before reading the books or using the pentacles of Abbé Julio. A single sheet sold separately from his books.

to various popular Catholic publishing enterprises. His immersion in the occult side of religion seems to have been inspired by his relationship with a well-known faith healer named Jean Sempé. It was partly on the basis of the latter's reputation that Abbé Julio founded his own. He was also profoundly influenced by his discovery of a seventeenth-century book of blessings in which he found all the 'curious exorcisms, ignored by the modern Church', which he subsequently incorporated into his various publications.[67] Although Houssay was apparently never a member of any occult group, there is no doubt he was influenced by the activities and writings of the second generation of French fin-de-siècle occultists who followed in Lévi's footsteps.

As we saw earlier, Mathers was living in Paris during the 1890s and was attracting considerable attention with his series of public ritual dramas called the Rites of Isis, starring his wife, Mina, in Egyptian dress. But the main focus of Parisian magical activity was Gérard Encausse (1865–1916), better known as Papus.[68] Born in Spain to a Spanish mother and a French father, he was brought up in Paris where, while studying for a qualification in medicine, he began to immerse himself in the literature of alchemy, Kabbalah, and Hermeticism housed in the National Library. The works of Lévi were no doubt his first occult port of call. In January 1886, he wrote an admiring letter to the old master not realizing he had been dead for more than a decade.[69] A year later he presented a paper at a conference on French Occultism which generated mixed reviews, with one requesting that he give up public speaking.[70] He signed up for the Theosophical Society, though he left not long after, put off by its Eastern mysticism. Instead he founded the Christian mystic Martinist order and an Independent Esoteric Study Group. He also joined the Cabalistic Order of the Rosy Cross, set up by his friend, fellow Lèvite, and shining light in the Parisian occult scene, Stanislaus de Guaita. Both Papus and de Guaita were at the centre of lurid claims in the mid-1890s that France was under threat by an outbreak of Satanism inspired by Freemasons and occultists with Encausse being denounced as 'the demon Papus'. The accusations were spread through a series of articles written by Léo Taxil, a scurrilous anti-clerical writer who converted to Catholicism and who, to prove his new-found dedication to the Church, launched a campaign against Freemasonry. A. E. Waite investigated the whole affair in his book *Devil Worship in France*.[71]

Papus was a prolific author on occultism and alternative medicine, but the book that had a significant influence on the wider world of popular magic was his *Traité méthodique de magie pratique*, first published in 1898. It was heavily influenced by Lévi but contained so much information on practical magic that parts of it resembled a grimoire, and it was probably used as such by some French cunning-folk. Numerous talismans, characters, and prayers were provided, along with advice on such familiar grimoire topics as how to render oneself invisible and deal with witchcraft, all offered without the scathing critical tone of Waite's *Book of Black Magic and of Pacts*.

Abbé Julio, who was more rooted in the provincial religious culture of healing and magic than the urbanite Papus, innovated by stripping out the esoteric and philosophical content of such nineteenth-century occult works and providing practical help under the auspices of Catholic piety. So, in 1896, four years after Jean Sempé's death, Abbé Julio published a book of the healer's miraculous prayers entitled *Prieres Merveilleuses pour la guerison de toutes les Malades Phisiques et Morales* (*Marvellous prayers for healing all physical and moral illnesses*). Other works soon followed on the back of this success. *Les véritables pentacles et priers* contained a series of talismans to be employed against evil spirits, witchcraft, and ill health, while *Le livre des grand exorcismes et benedictions* provided exactly what it says, a series of exorcisms and blessings—but for the laity rather than the clergy. The Julio oeuvre would not have been out of place amongst the old *Bibliothèque bleue* grimoires. As we saw in the previous chapter, the Catholic Church in France was quite successful in demonizing the *Petit Albert* and its ilk. So for those fearful of the old popular grimoires the 'Catholic' works of Abbé Julio provided protection from misfortune, evil spirits, and ill health but under the label of 'religion' rather than 'magic'. In this sense they echoed the reception and popularity of exorcism manuals during the early modern period. No wonder, then, that like the *Petit Albert*, they were quickly assimilated into the cultures of popular magic both at home and abroad. Abbé Julio's books were adopted by *quimboiseurs* in Martinique and the *gadedzafe* healers of the French Antilles.[72] One man interviewed in the 1980s recalled a Guadeloupe sorcerer who 'used books like the books of spells of Abbé Julio'. The Julio spell book was described as 'terrible' in the sense that it was dangerous to use, for if one read it at the wrong time and without properly understanding the words the angels would come and destroy you.[73]

The greatest popularizer of grimoires to emerge from the Occult Revival was, however, to be found across the Atlantic. Through the publishing activities of the American book pirate William Lauron DeLaurence, the occultist of the High Seas, the works of Waite and Mathers, and that of many others, travelled far beyond the claustrophobic occult circles of France and Britain. They would find an unimagined readership amongst African-Americans and the folk healers and magical practitioners of the Caribbean and West Africa. So it is to America we must now return to find out how this came about.

GRIMOIRES USA

The production of grimoires was an entrepreneurial enterprise that thrived wherever the influence of secular and ecclesiastical censors was restricted by geographical, educational, or political factors. The opening up of America created just such an environment, and hucksters, quacks, astrologers, fortune-tellers, and occult practitioners of all shades thrived. It is in America that grimoire authorship becomes a history of real if slippery personalities, whose success was tied to the immigrant experience and the unique opportunities and social mobility that opened up for those who were not enslaved or hindered by racial prejudice. A door-to-door salesman from Ohio named William Delaurence would emerge from this entrepreneurial world to become a transatlantic sensation—as we shall see later.

The newspaper was a crucial facilitator in the development of the huge free market for occult services, both nationally and internationally. One late-nineteenth-century folklorist, Henry Carrington Bolton, attempted to trace the advancement of American society and consequent decline of 'superstition' through studying the advertising pages of the press. Writing in 1895 he observed:

> These advertisements used to be far more numerous in the daily papers of our Eastern cities than at present, and their decrease in number probably denotes increase in intelligence; on the other hand, San Francisco news-papers are especially rich in these curiosities of literature, a fact indicating that superstition goes hand-in-hand with the adventurous spirit of the rough characters who first settle in newly-opened lands.[1]

With hindsight we know that Harrington was way off the mark. It was the cities of the eastern half of the country that would, in the next few decades, become the generators of numerous occult organizations and magical publications, with far-reaching consequences. One reason for this was the development of African-American consumerism.

The first surviving occult book possibly written by, and perhaps for an African-American readership, was *The Complete Fortune Teller and Dream Book* by 'Chloe Russel, a Woman of Colour, in the State of Massachusetts', published in 1824. Russel's introductory account of her harrowing life tells that she was born three hundred miles southwest of Sierra Leone around 1745 and enslaved at the age of 9. She and her brother were bound with ropes by white men, whipped, and dragged miles through the bush and bundled unto a ship bound for Virginia. Cruelly treated by her master she determined to kill herself but her father appeared to her in a dream to persuade her not to. Her prophetic powers developed through such dreams and word of her abilities spread. People began to consult her about lost property and she accrued the name the 'Black Interpreter'. It was her success at divining the whereabouts of a treasure for a plantation owner that led him to buy her freedom. There was a Chloe Russel in Massachusetts at the time and it is quite possible that she was the real author. As to its divinatory content, it was a run-of-the mill chapbook with much of its advice on palmistry, the signification of moles, and rituals for obtaining husbands, culled from other such publications. It was only towards the end of the century that there developed an identifiable African-American market for cheap fortune-telling booklets, such as *Aunt Sally's Policy Player's Dream Book*.[2] As its title suggests it was aimed primarily at petty gamblers, like most such publications at the time.

There was nothing distinctively African-American about the divinatory methods explained in these books, and nothing of practical magic. Yet African-Americans in the southern states had a well-defined and widely practised magical tradition waiting to be tapped commercially—hoodoo. The use of the term was first recorded in the 1880s, and although it is sometimes used as a synonym for *Voodoo* they were two distinct traditions. Hoodoo lacked the organized aspects and religious framework of Haitian *Voodoo*, which in the USA was largely restricted to New Orleans and was in terminal decline by the late nineteenth century.[3] Hoodoo doctors, also known as 'conjure doctors' and 'root-workers', practised a mix of herbal medicine, charms, magic, and prayers, and it was the Bible rather than the pantheon of Yoruba divinities that underpinned their efficacy. The first cheap grimoire to exploit the hoodoo tradition was *The Life and Works of Marie Laveau*, published in the early twentieth century. It sold on the basis of the legendary exploits of a New Orleans *Voodoo* priestess of that name. Detailed research has shown that Marie Laveau was a real person, but her portrayal in fiction and folklore as an inspirational *Voodoo* leader of New Orleans' African-American community is far from the mark. Her practice was hoodoo not *Voodoo*.[4] This was at least reflected in the contents of a copy of *The Life and Works* advertised for sale by a New Orleans drugstore owner. Reports of his prosecution in 1927 describe a mail order catalogue he issued that itemized some 250 charms, as well as *The Life and Works*, which contained 'instructions for the use of charms to win husbands, cause bad luck to befall a neighbor, and prevent others from working evil'.[5] *The Life and Works* does not seem to have circulated widely beyond Louisiana and neighbouring states. This is not surprising really for in the north there was already a long-established grimoire industry born out of the pow wow magical tradition of the ethnic Germans of Pennsylvania.

'Pow wow' obviously does not sound Germanic. It is thought to be a corruption of an Algonquin Native American word, and was recorded in early-seventeenth-century English publications on New England to describe the native medicine men who were said to conjure up the Devil and practise 'exorcismes and necromanticke charmes'.[6] By the nineteenth century it had, by an intriguing process of cultural osmosis, come to define the magical healing tradition of the Pennsylvanian Germans, which was otherwise known in local dialect as *brauche* or *braucherei*.[7] As one might expect from the descendants of the Pietist communities of the eighteenth century, pow wow doctors and their clients viewed healing as a Christian gift bestowed on a select few. Andrew C. Lenhart, a well-known practitioner in York, Pennsylvania, during the early twentieth century, explained, 'Some men have power. I have it. Power is given some men as a talent, just as Jesus gave power to his apostles.' As a prominent unlicensed healer Lenhart was well known to the state board of medical licensure, but he was never arrested for practising medicine illegally.[8] While pow wow doctors were important figures, the fundamental Protestant belief in a personal relationship with God also generated a strong self-help culture of medicine and protection in Pennsylvanian Germans. Books of simple Christian charms and prayers consequently proved popular. One in particular came to dominate the market—the *Long Lost Friend*. 'Anybody could use the book,' explained one woman. 'You had to have a little faith, you know, you would have to believe in God.'[9]

Friends reunited

The first American-printed charm book produced for the ethnic German market was *Der Freund in der Noth; oder, Geheime Sympathetische Wissenschaft*. This was a small twenty-four page collection of medical receipts and magical charms to stop thieves, charm guns, and the like. It traded on the success of a non-occult 'book of useful information' for the benefit of farmers called *Der Freund in der Noth*, which was published in Germantown in 1793. The preface to the magical *Der Freund* provided a typically hoary tale of a mythical foreign book filled with hidden knowledge:

> The following secret remedies were taken from an old Spanish manu-script, which was found at an old hermit's who for over a hundred years had lived in a cave in the dark valleys of the Graubünden land, perform-ing in the same region many wondrous works, among others totally expelling from said regions the monstrous dragon with four young, which dwelt upon those fearsome mountains in Unterwalden.[10]

The charm book that rose to greatest cultural prominence in the region was another 'friend'—*Der lang verborgene Freund*, first published in Reading, Pennsyl-vania, in 1820. It generously contained 'true and Christian instructions for everyone', and its altruistic author and publisher was John George Hohman. Along with his wife and son, Hohman, a Roman Catholic unlike most of his fellow German emigrants, sailed from Hamburg in 1802 and arrived in Philadelphia in October that year. Like many such immigrants they began their new life as indentured servants to pay for their passage. The Hohmans settled in Alsace Township, Berks County, and John soon began to earn extra income by publishing and peddling German broadside ballads. In 1811 he published the first known *Himmelsbrief* or *Celestial Letter* in America, claiming it was a copy of one he brought with him from Europe. He later expanded his publishing business, producing a series of occult, religious, and medical tracts for the ethnic German population, including a version of that European chapbook classic, the Wandering Jew, a book of New Testament apocrypha, and a collection of hymns.[11] It would seem that Hohman also practised as a healer, publishing twelve testimonials from satisfied patients. Among them was an account of his successful cure, in 1817, of a wheal in the eye that afflicted the son of Benjamin Stoudt, a Lutheran school-master, and also his treatment of Landlin Gottwald, of Reading, who suffered from a painful arm. It was, though, the enduring influence of *Der lang verborgene Freund* that has led the leading expert on Pennsylvanian folk culture to describe Hohman as one of 'the most influential and yet most elusive figures in Pennsylvania German history'.[12]

Demand led to several German language editions appearing over the next couple of decades, which were joined in 1842 with the first American printing of *Egyptische Geheimnisse*. Hohman's place in wider American history was sealed when English versions began to appear.[13] It would seem that the first awkward English translation of 1846, *The Long Secreted Friend*, was one of Hohman's very last publishing enterprises. It is now extremely rare, with a copy recently being offered for sale for $5,000. There was a more fluent, anonymous translation,

THE
LONG LOST FRIEND.

A COLLECTION

OF

MYSTERIOUS & INVALUABLE

ARTS & REMEDIES,

FOR

MAN AS WELL AS ANIMALS,

WITH MANY PROOFS

Of their virtue and efficacy in healing diseases, &c., the greater
part of which was never published until they
appeared in print for the first time in
the U. S. in the year 1820.

BY JOHN GEORGE HOHMAN.

HARRISBURG, PA.—1856.
T. F. Scheffer, Printer.

FIG. 17 Title page of John George Hohman's *The Long Lost Friend*.

published in Harrisburg, Pennsylvania, in 1856, presumably after Hohman's death, which sealed its fortune and the Hohman legend. Another independently translated version, *The Long Hidden Friend*, which contained some small variation in content, was published in Carlisle, Pennsylvania, in 1863.[14] Both English editions spawned further reprints, but it was the Harrisburg edition that became ubiquitous through numerous pulp editions produced during the early twentieth century under the title *John George Hohman's Pow-Wows*.

Hohman was refreshingly outspoken, tackling potential critics head on. He said he would have

> preferred writing no preface whatever to this little book, were it not indispensably necessary, in order to meet the erroneous views some men entertain in regard to works of this character. The majority, undoubtedly, approve of the publication and sale of such books, yet some are always found who will persist in denouncing them as something wrong.[15]

He went on to point out that he sold his books 'publicly, and not secretly, as other mystical works are sold', and drew on his European experience when expressing his appreciating that 'useful' and 'morally right' books were 'not prohibited in the United States, as is the case in other countries where kings and despots hold tyrannical sway'.[16] For Hohman, God would not have revealed 'sympathetic words' if he had not meant them to be used for the good of the people. He was dismissive of the vain conceits of the medical profession, stating 'whatever cannot be cured by sympathetic words, can much less be cured by any doctor's craft or cunning.'[17]

As to the nature of Hohman's 'sympathetic words', many of them were simple healing charms for natural ailments in the tradition of those contained in French *Bibliothèque bleue* grimoires and *Medicin des Pauvres*. In fact, much of Hohman's corpus was taken directly from the *Romanusbüchlein*, which as we saw in Chapter 4 had first appeared in Germany in the 1780s. Hohman could have brought a copy with him, though no doubt some already circulated in America. Some of the charms were short adjurations, such as a remedy for the colic:

> I warn ye, ye colic fiends! There is one sitting in judgement, who speaketh: just or unjust. Therefore beware, ye come colic fiends![18]

Others belonged to the European genre of apocryphal biblical charms. A previous owner of my own 1856 edition of *Long Lost Friend* pencilled the words 'very good' next to this charm 'For the Scurvy and Sore Throat':

> Speak the following, and it will certainly help you: Job went through the land, holding his staff close in the hand, when God the Lord did meet

him, and said to him: Job, what art thou grieved at? Job said: Oh God, why should I not be sad? My throat and my mouth are rotting away. Then said the Lord to Job: In yonder valley there is a well, which will cure thee, (*name*), and thy mouth, and thy throat, in the name of God the Father, the Son and the Holy Ghost. Amen.

This must be spoken three times in the morning, and three times in the evening; and where it reads 'which will cure,' you must blow three times in the child's mouth.[19]

The book ventured into grimoire territory with several spells against thieving and witchcraft. It also contained instructions for conjurations, such as that 'To make a Wand for searching for Iron, Ore, or Water'. A twig of one year's growth broken from a tree on the first night of Christmas was to be struck against the ground while the operator said: 'Archangel Gabriel, I conjure thee in the name of God, the Almighty, to tell me, is there any water [iron, ore] here or not? Do tell me!'[20]

People purchased the *Long Lost Friend* not only for its contents but also for its inherent protective power. Indeed, Hohman was commercially savvy to make this explicit, stating prior to the preface: 'Whoever carries this book with him, is safe from all his enemies, visible or invisible; and whoever has this book with him cannot die without the holy corpse of Jesus Christ nor drowned in any water, nor burn up in any fire, nor can any unjust sentence be passed upon him. So help me.' In 1928 an African-American named Charles D. Lewis explained that he had carried the book with him for sixteen years and consequently no accident had befallen him all that time. He had an adventurous and dangerous life working as a fireman on steamships. During the First World War the White Star liner on which he worked was requisitioned by the British Admiralty while sailing near Suez. Soon after losing his trusty copy he suffered an accident. He purchased another, and avowed that he never employed its contents to play the pow wow doctor.[21]

By the early twentieth century numerous further editions of the *Long Lost Friend*, some under the title *Pow-Wows*, had ensured that it was firmly cemented in the medical tradition of ethnic Germans. The extent of its influence in Pennsylvania was revealed during an investigation by the Berks County Medical Society into the practices of pow wow doctors in the region. In 1904 it was reported that the Society had found that it was 'almost exclusively used by the witch-doctors in preparing their charms and in giving advice'.[22] Their concerns about its use were periodically born out over the next few decades. In 1951 a Mennonite couple from Ephrata were reported to the police after they refused to have their seriously injured child treated by 'scientific' medicine. The couple had been ejected from the Mennonite Church 'for faith healing beliefs stemming from a book by John

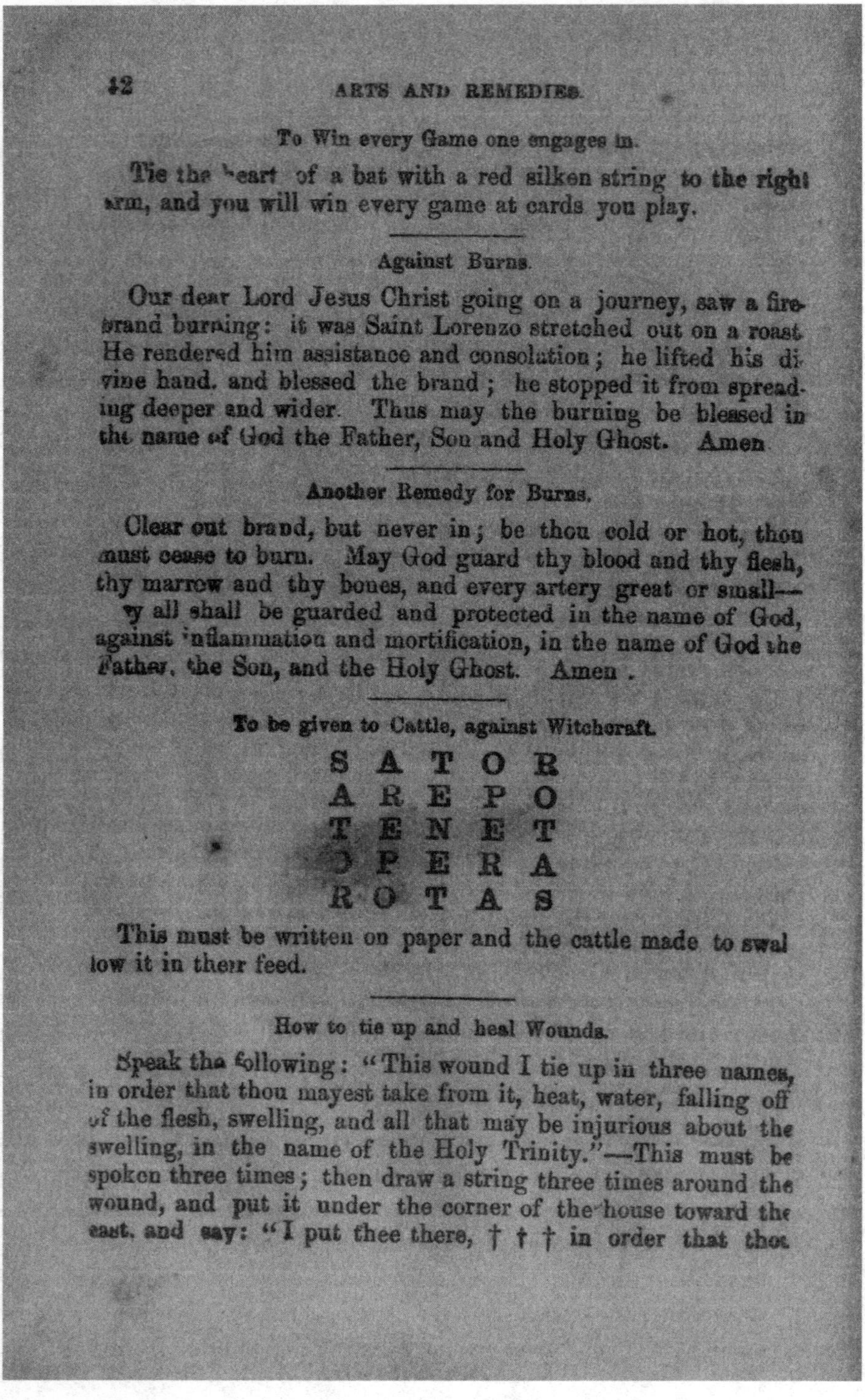

To Win every Game one engages in.

Tie the heart of a bat with a red silken string to the right arm, and you will win every game at cards you play.

Against Burns.

Our dear Lord Jesus Christ going on a journey, saw a firebrand burning: it was Saint Lorenzo stretched out on a roast. He rendered him assistance and consolation; he lifted his divine hand, and blessed the brand; he stopped it from spreading deeper and wider. Thus may the burning be blessed in the name of God the Father, Son and Holy Ghost. Amen.

Another Remedy for Burns.

Clear out brand, but never in; be thou cold or hot, thou must cease to burn. May God guard thy blood and thy flesh, thy marrow and thy bones, and every artery great or small—y all shall be guarded and protected in the name of God, against inflammation and mortification, in the name of God the Father, the Son, and the Holy Ghost. Amen.

To be given to Cattle, against Witchcraft.

```
S A T O R
A R E P O
T E N E T
O P E R A
R O T A S
```

This must be written on paper and the cattle made to swallow it in their feed.

How to tie up and heal Wounds.

Speak the following: "This wound I tie up in three names, in order that thou mayest take from it, heat, water, falling off of the flesh, swelling, and all that may be injurious about the swelling, in the name of the Holy Trinity."—This must be spoken three times; then draw a string three times around the wound, and put it under the corner of the house toward the east, and say: "I put thee there, † † † in order that thou

FIG. 18 Charms in John George Hohman's *The Long Lost Friend.*

G. Hohman, "The Long Lost Friend"'. The father told the state troopers who took the boy to hospital, 'If the Lord wants to heal the boy, He will heal him.'[23]

In a letter written to the press in 1904 a Lutheran Minister suggested that its influence extended beyond Pennsylvania, 'possibly the larger portion of the country east of the Mississippi, and possibly even beyond.'[24] Folklorists have revealed that its influence extended to the 'Cajun in Louisiana, the hill man in the Ozarks, and other groups'.[25] In the 1930s an anthropologist researching African–American culture in a Mississippi cotton town interviewed the most reputed 'conjure-doctor' in the area, who also received letters from white and black clients from Louisiana and as far as Oklahoma. Unlike some of his local competitors the 'doctor' did not claim religious inspiration or innate healing powers, but relied totally on his herb and magic books.[26] He was a man of little education, but like many a cunning-man in centuries past, he set great store by his display of book knowledge, being the proud owner of a six-foot shelf of large encyclopedias. His magical prowess depended on a copy of *Pow-Wows* and a copy of *Albertus Magnus, or Egyptian Secrets*, which was also published in cheap paperback form during the 1930s. When someone once offered to buy his *Pow-Wows*, 'he at first refused for fear the white purchaser would use it in the service of the Devil, instead of for God and Christ.' Several decades later the owner of a Chicago candle shop, a place where the accoutrements of folk magic and medicine could be bought, recommended that along with the Bible the only two medical books that were required to stay healthy were the *Farmer's Almanac* and Hohman's *Pow-Wows*.[27]

Roback the wizard

The Long Secreted Friend may have been the first English language grimoire to be published in the USA, but the first to boldly declare its contents as providing 'magical' wisdom appeared a few years later. In the 1840s another north European followed in Hohman's footsteps and boarded a ship at Hamburg with a prodigious occult career in America waiting. He was the astrologer, quack doctor, and purported seventh son Charles W. Roback, the self-styled 'President of the Astrological College of Sweden, and Founder of the Society of the Magi in London, Paris, and St. Petersburg'. These impressive-sounding institutions were the inventions of an inveterate liar.

Roback was born Carl Johan Nilsson in the village of Fallebo, Småland, in southern Sweden, on 22 November 1811.[28] He first worked as a farm hand, but in his late twenties he moved to the nearest town in the area Döderhultsvik, now part of Oskarshamn, where he ran a general store selling coffee, sugar, soap, and other staples. By this time he had changed his surname to the more impressive-sounding Fallenius and married a woman named Greta Cajsa. In 1843, however, he abandoned his family and set sail for America. The fact that he had been caught out perpetrating a series of petty frauds, including signing a promissory note using a false name, just might have had something do with his desertion.

Roback's humble and inglorious life before arriving in America is in stark contrast with his own autobiographical account, which tells a far more noble and extraordinary story. The Robacks were a family renowned from Viking times, he claimed, and his ancestral home was a castle near Falsters, surrounded by rocks and 'tall spectral firs'. His childhood was one of great privilege and reverence. Five of his brothers were 'courted, caressed, and helped forward by powerful friends in their careers'. It was around the age of ten that one of them, Frithiof, disclosed to Charles his occult heritage as they talked in a vast apartment in the castle hung with axes and spears: 'He informed me that our race had been renowned for their prophetic gifts, and their skill and attainments in Magic, Astrology, and other occult lore, for more than four hundred years.'[29] Frithiof revealed to Charles that these hereditary powers were rendered more potent in him by being the seventh son of a seventh son. At the age of fourteen Charles applied himself to the study of 'every species of Magic' and then for many years he travelled across Europe, Asia, and Africa perfecting his knowledge of the magical sciences. 'It would occupy too much space, and might seem like egotism,' he said modestly, 'to recount the honors that were paid to me at the various capitals of Europe.' Naturally bored with his celebrity and the adulation he received, and 'longing for a less artificial state of society than that in which I had lately moved, I now determined to visit that land of the frank and the free—the United States.'[30]

The only passage of his autobiography that has any truth in it is his account of his vaunted success in the land of the frank and the free. He landed in America on the 14 June 1844 and over the next nine years resided in Baltimore, Philadelphia, New York, and Boston. This itinerary is partly confirmed by Roback's most ardent critic, Thomas Hague, a disgruntled Philadelphian astrologist who styled himself the 'United States Astrologer'. He claimed to be the first American to write or publish a line on the subject of astrology. He had certainly been publishing a range of astrological almanacs since 1838, including the long-running monthly *United States' Horoscope*.[31] But Hague was no stranger to puffery and untruths. In the November 1851 edition he boldly stated that 'Even the incumbent of the highest office in the United States, as well as their cabinets and senators, has honoured it by a perusal: and why? Truly it is, they have adopted the Astrologer's system, in his search of truth.'[32] Hague denounced Roback as a vile impostor and a corrupting social influence. On a personal level, he was incensed to find that Roback on first coming before the people as an Astrologer, paid several heavy sums of money for judgements on nativities, which had been given by me,—and I have in my possession two purporting to have been written by him, which are almost verbatim copies of those obtained of me, a beautiful commentary upon his Astrological abilities!!![33]

In 1851 Hague decided to pour 'heavy metal' on his rival in the form of a coruscating pamphlet, *Exposition of C. W. Roback*, which included letters on the matter addressed to William F. Johnston, Governor of Pennsylvania, and Charles Gilpin, Mayor of Philadelphia.[34] According to Hague, Roback's first occupation in America was running a grog shop in Baltimore, where he passed himself of as William Williams, alias Billy the Swede or Dutch Bill. Around 1847 he was obliged to decamp and pitched up in Philadelphia where he spent some months in the city hospital. Once back on the streets Roback made a brief living charging the curious two cents a peek to see a small alligator he kept in a tin box, which he claimed was a crocodile he had caught during his travels in Africa. He raised enough money to rent an office on South Eight Street, setting himself up as a cunning-man, curing the sick, detecting stolen goods, offering to cast out Devils, and practising 'Geotic Magic'. He now discovered the power of the burgeoning American press and began to pepper the local newspapers with puffs. One such advertisement published in 1850 consisted of a testimonial from a Jane Carney, said to live three miles below Wilmington. She recounted how, frustrated by her lover's timidity in proposing marriage, she had consulted Roback. He successfully used his magic to induce the man to get betrothed, and performed the further service of recovering the sum of $10 stolen from her by a servant.[35]

Hague tells of Roback's next bold move into the quack medicine business in Philadelphia. Noticing the popularity of a local brand of German Bitters produced by Dr C. M. Jackson, Roback got together with a local German druggist to produce his own version of the panacea—Hufeland's Bitters, named after the renowned German physician Christoph Wilhelm Hufeland (1762–1836), who had been the admired doctor of Goethe and the King of Prussia. Hufeland's name was well known across Europe, due in part to the popularity of his book *The Art of Prolonging Life*, which was published in several languages. The great doctor's reputation would certainly have been known to many German settlers in Pennsylvania during the mid-nineteenth century, and in 1829 a translation of his *Treatise on the Scrofulous Disease* had been published in Philadelphia. Rather disingenuously, Hague does not mention that Jackson also played on the same association, calling his product Dr Hoofland's German Bitters. Roback went one audacious step further in his publicity campaign though. He employed an associate to pass himself of as the grandson of the great Hufeland newly arrived from

Berlin. This impostor would prescribe Roback's bitters and then refer his patients to the conjuror.

For reasons unknown, but presumably related to legal heat generated by Hague's exposé, in 1852 we find that Roback had removed to No. 6 White Street, New York. Once again, with his irrepressible entrepreneurial flair, he began to build his occult business through a series of advertisements in the local press. One example took the form of a 'Lecture on Astrology and Magic' in which he stated, 'Things which appear incredible to the skeptic and are scoffed at by the shallow smatterers in science, are admitted by the candid and the reflecting when the evidence is of a character so overwhelming and positive that to question it is to doubt all history'.[36] Another puff, which boasted of his many prophetic successes in Europe and the United States, also asserted that he could cure diseases considered incurable by the rest of the medical profession. For those who came to his office he offered to 'make no charge, except for the conjurations he shall make use of'. He also advertised his 'power for the restoration of stolen or lost property, which he has used for the advantage of thousands in this City and elsewhere'.[37] Another advertisement eulogized 'Roback the Oracle' in verse, concluding with the boast that he had 'assisted thousands of the world's weary wanderers with profitable advice, bringing them out of the shadows of despondency'.[38] One of his most sophisticated puffs, devised during a sojourn in Boston in 1853, was disguised as a news item. It described how a band of around 200 Swedish immigrants had just arrived in Boston, and remarked that 'while passing the residence of Prof W. C. Roback, the noted Astrologer, in High-street, the Swedes honoured the Professor with three hearty cheers...as a testimonial of respect to their countryman.'[39]

Such was Roback's success at exploiting the burgeoning American newspapers that his rise to national notoriety was swift. A book on *The Philosophy of Human Nature*, published in 1851, mentioned him in passing as a quack and conjuror noteworthy for his skill at playing on public stupidity.[40] The following year Charles Wyllys Elliott reprinted one of Roback's advertisements in his book on the supernatural to show that the 'mystical profession is not exploded'. 'Can it be possible', he mocked, 'that there is any prospect of their endowing a professorship in Yale College?'[41] By 1860 Roback was the most well-known occultist in America. He received his own entry, 'Roback the Wizard', in Lambert Wilmer's coruscating attack on the role of the newspapers in promoting bunkum and exploiting credulity, published in 1859.[42] Another book published in the same year entitled *Humbug*, which sought to expose popular impositions, also singled him out. 'Who does not remember "Prof. Roback," "the seventh son of a seventh son," who sent you those "Astrological Almanacks," and who is a swindling humbug of the most barefaced character.'[43] It is possible that it was such national press coverage of Roback's notoriety that provoked the Pennsylvania General Assembly to introduce a statute against fortune-telling in 1861.

The laws against magic and divination were patchy. In the 1840s the Massachusetts Penal Code included the prohibition of 'Any person who, by palmistry, cards or otherwise, for gain, tells or pretends to tell fortunes, or predicts or pretends to predict future events, or who practises as a profession, trade or occupation the discovering, or pretending to discover to others, for gain, where things lost or stolen are to be found.'[44] However, at the same period, no such law had been instituted in Pennsylvania—as Roback was apparently aware. According to Hague, a sympathetic city alderman had reassured Roback that there was no state statute that applied specifically to his magical and divinatory services. The lack of one was highlighted during Roback's prosecution for fraudulent pretences before the Philadelphia quarter sessions in February 1850. Mary Meehan, perhaps having read the testimonial of Jane Carney, had paid Roback $3 on the under-standing that he would, by his conjurations, force a thief to return some clothes that had been stolen from her. The jury found him guilty but Judge King cast doubt on the law of false pretences being appropriate in such a case. 'In England', he observed, 'there was a special statute in relation to cheating by these means [1824 Vagrancy Act], and he thought that it would be well for our Legislature to make an enactment on the subject.'[45] According to Hague, he had been sued several times for false pretences, but had the charges dropped through bribery and by paying off witnesses and buying false ones.[46] It was not until a decade later that the Pennsylvania General Assembly instituted an 'Act for the Suppression of Fortune Telling', which went far beyond the British Vagrancy Act which inspired it.[47] It was directed against:

> any person who shall pretend, for gain or lucre, to predict future events, by cards, tokens, the inspection of the head or hands of any person, or by any one's age, or by consulting the movement of the heavenly bodies; or who shall, for gain or lucre, pretend to effect any purpose by spells, charms, necromancy or incantation.

It also covered those

> Who shall pretend, for lucre or gain, to enable any one to get or to recover stolen property, or to tell where lost articles or animals are, or to stop bad luck, or to give good luck, or to put bad luck on any person or animals, or to stop or injure the business of any person, or to injure the health of any person, or to shorten the life of any person, or to give success in business, enterprise, speculation, lottery, lottery numbers or games of chance, or win the affections of any person, or to give success in

business, enterprise, speculation, lottery, lottery numbers or games of chance, or win the affections of any person whatever for marriage or seduction, or to make one person marry another, or to induce any person to alter or make a will in favor or against any one, or to tell the place where treasure, property, money or valuables are hid, or to tell the places where to dig or to search for gold, metals, hidden treasure.

This was an unusually detailed statute in that it pretty much covered every aspect of magical practice, presumably with the intention of leaving as few legal ambiguities as possible.

It was while in Boston that Roback branched out into the publishing world, first producing *Roback's Astrological Almanac*, and *Dr C. W. Roback's Family Pictorial Almanac*. In 1854 he published his magnum opus, the rather handsome, gilt-edged *Mysteries of Astrology, and the Wonders of Magic*, dedicated magnanimously 'To the People of the United States, a Nation neither Skeptical nor Credulous', and in which he boasted he had 'given audience to more than two hundred thousand applicants for magical information'.[48] It was not a roaring success and its contents did not live up to the anticipated occult treasures the title suggested. Regarding its astrological worth, the astrologer Luke Broughton (1828–98), a linen weaver's son from Leeds, England, claimed that Roback paid a newspaper reporter to compile the astrology sections of the book. He denounced Roback as 'a perfect fraud and an impostor, who knew no more of astrology than he did about flying'.[49] Broughton, who came from a family well known in Leeds for their astrological skills, arrived in America in the 1850s and settled in Philadelphia. He claimed he was soon 'acquainted with nearly every man in the United States who had any knowledge of the subject'. At the time, he recalled, 'there was not an American, either man or woman, in the whole United States who could even erect a horoscope,' and the few astrologers who could were French, English, and German immigrants.[50] Amongst them he presumably included Hague, who, as the 1850 census shows, was also born in England. Of the six astrologers recorded in the 1880 American census three were English and one was German.

As to the magical content of the *Mysteries of Astrology*, it contained neither spells nor instructions on conjuration. Yet some people no doubt purchased it presuming that it did. In 1863, for instance, the Mormon William Clayton wrote to a New York City bookseller requesting two copies of *Mysteries of Astrology*, and 'the finest and best article of Parchment that can be obtained'. While he later said he required the parchment to draw up deeds, the fact that a few months later he desired to obtain a 'Secret Talisman' suggests that he wanted to consult Roback's book for advice on magical protection. If so, he was destined to be disappointed.[51] The book was a flop. As well as lacking practical occult information, with its thick,

FONTISPIECE.

FIG. 19 Purported portrait of Charles W. Roback looking suspiciously like a seventeenth-century astrologer.

gilt-edged pages it was also too expensive to be a mass success. In 1857 a Philadelphia bookseller was selling it for $2.50,[52] which was nearly as much as a week's wage for an agricultural worker and a third of an artisan's weekly salary.[53]

In 1855 we find Roback advertising his astrological services from his new base in Cincinnati, Ohio, where he lived out the rest of his life.[54] By 1860 he seems to have stopped promoting his astrological and magical powers and prospered by selling his own brand of quack medicines, cashing in on the vogue for blood purifiers and bitters. He continued to maintain sporadic contact with his family back in Småland until his death in Cincinnati on the 8 May 1867. In his will he set aside $6,000 in restitution of lawful claims made against him by Swedish creditors. He also left a thousand dollars in gold to his brother-in-law, $300 to his nephew, and the rest of his estate to his son Carl Wilhelm.[55] His dubious life and flourishing career in America did not go unnoticed in his homeland. Two pamphlets were published shortly before and after his death recording the progress of the Fallebo *gök* (peasant), the 'humbug' who found an ideal outlet for his huckstering in the land of opportunity.[56] He was portrayed as the anti-Lind; in other words, a Swede who gave a bad name to his homeland in contrast to the soprano Jenny Lind, the internationally popular ambassador of Swedish culture who toured America in 1850. The visit was a great financial success for herself and her promoter P. T. Barnum, and Roback, of course, could not help make capital out of his fellow countrywoman, boasting that he had 'foretold the success of Jenny Lind, and actually named in advance the sum she would realise in the United States'.[57]

Roback traded on his foreignness, advertising himself at one time as the 'great Swedish Soothsayer and Necromancer', and in the *Mysteries of Astrology* he played on his Viking heritage.[58] He also laid claim to the exclusive possession of the medical secrets of his homeland, marketing quack medicines such as his Scandinavian Vegetable Blood Pills and Purifier, which he said consisted of 'twenty-three different species of mountain herbs of his native land'.[59] Yet, unlike Hohman, he did not write specifically for an ethnic immigrant audience. His magical and astrological knowledge was not based on the Scandinavian black book tradition, and he did not even refer to the possession of such a grimoire in his advertisements. Large-scale Scandinavian emigration to the United States only began in the late 1860s, and so in Roback's day the Swedish settler communities could not provide the strong ethnic market that sustained Hohman's occult enterprises. Roback was hugely successful at appealing to all Americans through the canny exploitation of newspapers. What he failed to grasp was the appeal of the older chapbook tradition and the demand for practical magic.

The honour of producing the first American Scandinavian black book goes to the publisher John Anderson (1836–1910), who arrived from Norway at the age of 9 and went on to set up a Norwegian language press in Chicago. The city was the main destination for many Norwegian emigrants, with around a third of the estimated 150,000 Norwegian Americans settled there by the end of the century. Anderson was concerned about the decline of the Norwegian language in America, observing that to preserve it 'we will have to supply our bookshelves with some of our fatherland's literature.'[60] Up until Anderson's venture in the 1870s nearly all the Norwegian literature printed in America had been religious in nature, so Anderson set about producing books of folklore, poems, novels, histories—and magic. A former employee recalled in his memoir that in 1899 'Svarteboken, dealing with witchcraft' were amongst the firm's best sellers.[61] One of them was probably a cheap book entitled Oldtidens Sortebog (Ancient black book), published in Chicago in 1892.[62] Only one known copy survives today. It is an almost exact reproduction of a charm book of the same name published in Denmark, the main difference between the two being the cover. The Copenhagen edition depicts the Devil sitting on a crescent moon while the Chicago version displays its American status by having a picture of a bald eagle. It contained a familiar mix of magical charms for ailments, catching thieves, warding off enemies, and provoking love. A 'key' to the secret of the charms, signed 'Cyprianus', was provided at the back of the book, which reveals that the formulas provided had to be read in reverse. The most unusual aspect of Oldtidens Sortebog is the story it tells of its origin. In the introduction, purportedly written by a monk, Cyprianus is revealed to be a beautiful, fourteenth-century Mexican nun! Incarcerated in a dungeon by a debauched cleric, Cyprianus makes pages from shreds of her clothes and writes down her accumulated wisdom in her own blood to preserve them for posterity. This book of secrets later finds its way into the possession of a Danish knight and magician who buries it in a golden box. It lays hidden for ages until a peasant stumbles across it while ploughing and becomes rich from the power it gives him.

No doubt Anderson had dual motives in publishing svarteboken. They were evidently a profitable business proposition. Although some Norwegian immigrants brought black books with them, demand for familiar medical charms must have been considerable, particularly amongst rural dwellers. For those Norwegian settlers who founded Coon Prairie, Wisconsin, for instance, there was not a trained doctor within 150 miles. Others desired the means to call up the Devil. In the early twentieth century a Norwegian-American farmer from Dawson, Minnesota, wrote a letter to the Oslo University Library requesting: 'Do you have the Black Book that can release Satan and bind him again? If you have it in clear Norwegian, let me know the price.'[63] Yet at the same time as Anderson was commercially exploiting popular magical belief, he was also fulfilling his aim of ensuring that Norwegian-Americans had access to the literary and cultural heritage of their homeland.

Hex doctors and murderers

There was no clear-cut distinction between a pow wow doctor and a hex or witch doctor in Pennsylvanian German folklore, but there were those who did much more than cure ailments with herbs, prayer, and charms from the *Long Lost Friend*. Hex doctors were known for not only curing the bewitched but also for preventing witchcraft and dealing with witches. For such a task Hohman's book was useful but not as potent and rich in talismanic aid as the *Sixth and Seventh Books of Moses*. Considering that the magic book market of the mid-nineteenth century primarily catered to Pennsylvania Germans, it is no surprise that the first American edition of the Moses Books appeared in German in the 1860s. English editions, clearly based on an example given in Scheible's *Das Kloster*, were printed in New York and Elizabethville, Pennsylvania, in 1880.[64] The preface of the New York edition shared the forthrightness of Hohman's defence of the value of cheap occult literature, and was honest regarding its usage. 'Let us not, therefore, underrate this branch of popular literature,' it stated, observing that 'the issue of a cheap edition will be more serviceable than the formerly expensive productions on sorcery, which were only circulated in abstract forms and sold at extortionate rates.'

While the *Long Lost Friend* was considered a pious work *The Sixth and Seventh Books of Moses* had a more sinister reputation amongst Pennsylvania Germans. In 1929 the hex doctor Andrew C. Lenhart told a journalist that he had read both the *Long Lost Friend* and the *Sixth and Seventh Books of Moses*, but 'once was enough' regarding the latter. A friend had asked Lenhart to obtain a copy from Harrisonburg. He read only a few pages before becoming afraid, and recalled:

> I was sitting in my home at night. Suddenly a voice in the hallway called me. I went there. I said, 'Who is it?' There was no answer. I started to read again. The voice called me once more. It was spooky. I went to the hallway again, but there was no answer. I again started to read. Suddenly in the silence of the room I heard awful voices which sounded as if a flock of geese were quacking. It was terrible. I closed the book and the noises ceased.[65]

For hex doctors, though, possession of the *Sixth and Seventh Books of Moses* was essential to building a reputation. In 1900, for instance, Mr and Mrs Frederick Garl of Reading hired a hex doctor to rid the family of the witchcraft they believed had killed eleven of their infants in succession. He provided a charm to protect the twelfth baby, which he said was from a copy of the *Seventh Book of Moses* written in pen and red ink.[66] In February 1906, a few days before his fight with the Chicago boxer Kid Hermann, the Mexican-American Aurelio Herrera received a letter from a woman, who described herself as a 'student of the occult science', which contained a charm to help him win. 'I have a receipt taken from the seventh book of Moses', she wrote, 'which I have prepared and feel confident that if concealed upon your person during the battle you will be victorious.' The charm consisted of a bit of cardboard decorated with horseshoes, symbols, and writing in German script. 'Should you win', concluded the entrepreneurial occultist, 'you will be glad to reward me. The amount I leave entirely to your good judgement.' When Kid Hermann was told about the charm, he quipped, 'If Aurelio wins next Friday night he'll have to have one of those German charms in each glove.'[67] The fight ended in a draw after twenty rounds.

The *Sixth and Seventh Books of Moses* was more generally associated with bewitching rather than countering witchcraft. During a divorce hearing in Pittsburgh in July 1919 Mrs Sarah Bickel testified that her husband 'took the *Seventh Book of Moses* and tried to put spells on me and he said would put spirits in the house after me.'[68] Its malign reputation was enhanced by a widely reported murder case in June 1916.

Peter Leas, a 41-year-old blacksmith of Reading, Pennsylvania, ambushed a friend named Abraham Fick, a farmhand, stunned him with the handle of an axe and then chopped off his head. Leas was evidently psychotic, his wife and children having fled two weeks previously after he had threatened her with a knife. Leas gave himself up to the police shortly after the murder; 'A Handbook for Bible Readers and Christian Workers' and a memorandum book containing numerous scriptural passages were found in his pockets. In his confession Leas said that he had visited a charcoal burner several miles from his house who had consulted *The Seventh Book of Moses* and declared that Fick intended to murder Leas. So Leas decided he had better act first. The suggestion by some of the press was that Leas's insanity had been provoked by his own reading of the *Seventh Book of Moses*.[69]

Some of the Moses books' baleful associations were transferred to the *Long Lost Friend* following another 'hex murder' that gripped the American press. In late November 1928 the bound, beaten, and burned body of Nelson D. Rehmeyer was found at his isolated farmhouse in York County. John Curry, aged 14, Wilbert Hess, aged 18, and a petty pow wow man named John Blymyer were soon arrested on suspicion of murder. The Hess family, who were Rehmeyer's neighbours, had been experiencing a series of misfortunes on their farm. Wilbert had succumbed to a series of illnesses which had only been cured after his parents had him powwowed. Witchcraft was suspected. Blymyer, along with his sidekick Curry, was called in to offer his advice and identify the witch. Blymyer, who suffered from hallucinations, believed he was also hexed, saying he had been told as much by the pow wow doctor Andrew C. Lenhart. He had also consulted Rehmeyer on several occasions.

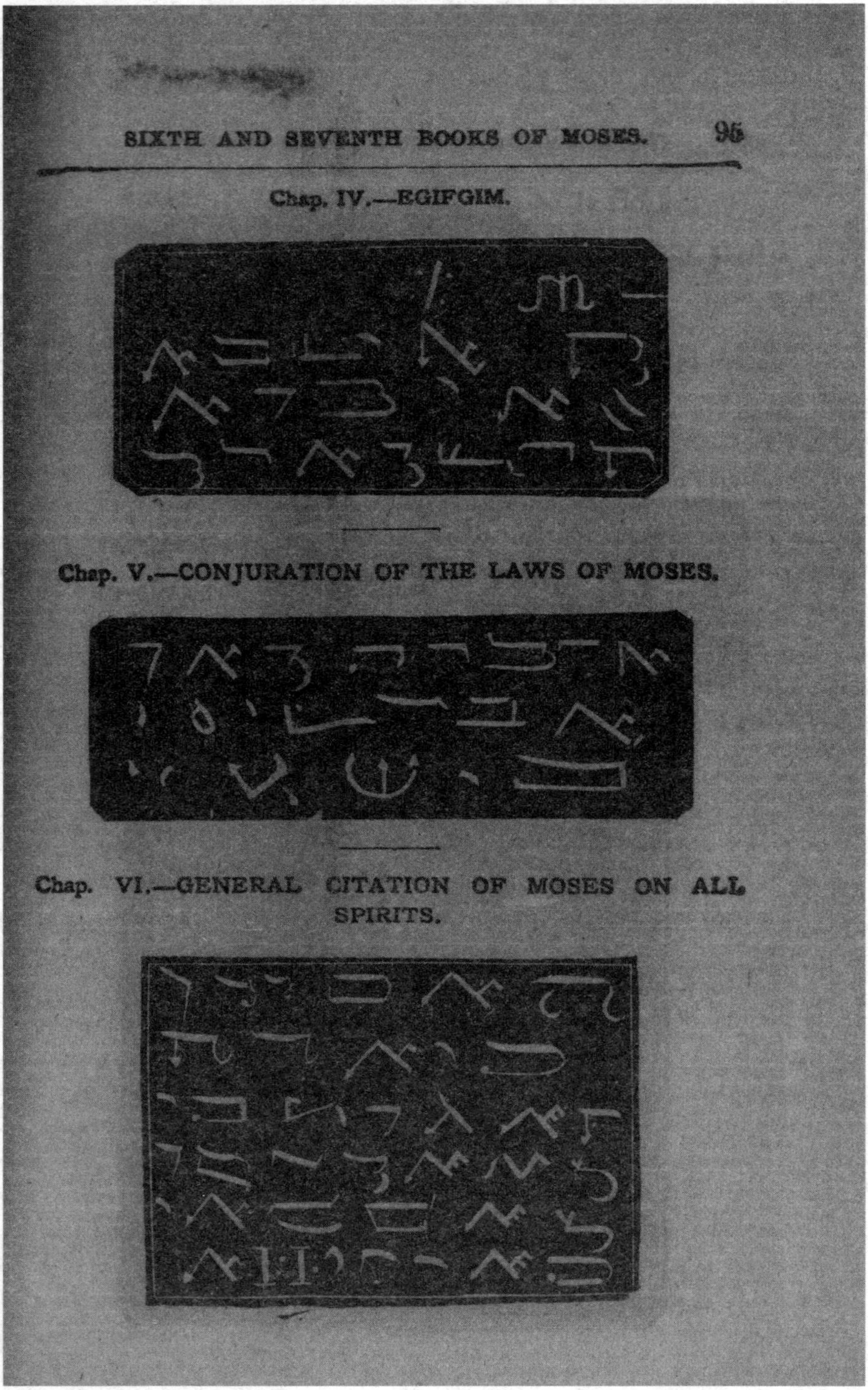
SIXTH AND SEVENTH BOOKS OF MOSES. 95
Chap. IV.—EGIFGIM.
Chap. V.—CONJURATION OF THE LAWS OF MOSES.
Chap. VI.—GENERAL CITATION OF MOSES ON ALL SPIRITS.

FIG. 20 Talismans from an early twentieth-century pulp edition of the *Sixth and Seventh Books of Moses*.

Rehmeyer was considered a peculiar fellow in the area. This was partly because he was separated from his family, and partly because he was an active and vocal socialist: it was also because he was thought to dabble in *braucherei*. Blymyer and others knew he possessed the *Long Lost Friend*, and it was Blymyer who pointed the finger at Rehmeyer as the cause of all their problems. Blymyer believed that he could break the hex upon them by cutting a lock of Rehmeyer's hair and burying it, and confiscating and burning his *Long Lost Friend*. It is not clear from the trial reports whether Blymyer believed that Rehmeyer used the *Long Lost Friend* to hex people or whether he thought that the protective powers of the book made him immune to counter witchcraft. The latter seems the most likely considering its content and generally benign reputation. Blymyer knew the book well enough, for when police searched his room in York they found notes and charms transcribed from the *Long Lost Friend* and the *Sixth and Seventh Books of Moses*.

On the evening of 27 November Blymyer, Curry, and Wilbert set off for Rehmeyer's farmhouse to fulfil Blymyer's plan. They brought with them a long length of rope to bind him. There is no evidence to suggest they had murder on their minds, but in the struggle to pacify Rehmeyer, they kicked him and hit him over the head with a piece of wood and a chair. As soon as they realized he was dead they doused the corpse and set it alight. They fled not realizing that the fire soon extinguished itself, leaving the murder scene intact. Blymyer and Curry were convicted of first degree murder and sentenced to life imprisonment. Blymyer's life term in the Eastern State Penitentiary was commuted in 1953. He took up a job as a night watchman and died a lonely recluse in 1972. Curry served ten years of his sentence and was then granted a special dispensation to join the army. After receiving training as a cartographer he participated in the drafting of the Normandy invasion maps. He returned to York County and became respected for his work on behalf of the York Art Association. He died in 1963. Hess served a ten-year sentence for second degree murder and lived out his life in welcome obscurity.[70]

As the news broke and the trials proceeded, the press went into overdrive with headlines screaming, 'York's Voodoo Cult', 'Scores of Deaths are Laid at Door of Pow-Wow Cult', and 'York County Held in Grip of Black Art Practices'.[71] Over the next few years the Pennsylvania authorities were highly sensitive to the influence of hex doctors and their books. Only a couple of months after the trial, state troopers arrested an Allentown hex doctor named Charles T. Belles after the body of a young woman named Verna Delp was found in a field near Catasauqua, Pennsylvania. The District Attorney became convinced that her death was linked with *hexerei*. What newspapers described variously as 'three mystical scrolls of witchcraft' or 'cryptic missives' were found on the body.[72] Furthermore Delp, the adopted daughter of a prosperous farmer named August Derhammer, had, on the recommendation of her father, visited the hex doctor on several occasions for an undisclosed illness. The District Attorney expressed his frustration at the wall of silence from the local community, who were reluctant to talk of the hex doctor and his activities.[73] In January 1932 suspicions of *hexerei* were also raised when the lacerated body of a young Mennonite church worker, Norman Bechtel, was found in Germantown. He had been stabbed some twenty times with a stiletto knife. One newspaper reported that 'weird symbols' had been carved into his forehead. Another called it 'a crime of mysticism', another a Pennsylvania 'hex murder'. A few days later, however, investigators shifted their attention to the idea that he was a victim of a serial killer at large nicknamed '3X'. Two years later the Department of Public Instruction launched a campaign against hex doctors after a young farmhand named Albert Shinsky, of Shenandoah, shot dead a 63-year-old woman believing she had bewitched him.[74]

The press portrayal of the *Long Lost Friend* as a black arts or 'witch book' left an enduring stain on its reputation. When, in the early 1950s, a folklorist mentioned it to a Dutch Pennsylvania farmer he was told, 'To hell with that ... I wouldn't have one in the house, and the old folks would've been better off if they hadn't.' Twenty years later, an acquaintance of another folklorist tried to buy a copy from a bookstore in Norristown, but was asked to leave. The most recent detailed study of pow wow practices in the state turned up no examples of its use amongst current practitioners, though its influence continues through the charms and remedies that have been handed down.[75]

Chicago: city of magic and mysticism

Chicago may have an image as a grim, grey industrial city but in the early twentieth century it was also a hotbed of mystical, magical, and prophetic activity. Rural Pennsylvania may have been the centre of pow wow and New Orleans the home of hoodoo, but Chicago was the undoubted centre of organized occultism and grimoire publication. It was the archetypal American cultural melting pot, with a large portion of its population being foreign born, mostly from Germany, Poland, Austria, Russia, Sweden, Norway, and Ireland.[76] This national diversity was reflected in the police department. The city's chief of police, Herman Schuettler, worked conscientiously towards having every nationality represented in the force. When, in 1908, the first Persian policeman was recruited, the press joked that 'a Chinese patrolman is all that is lacking now'.[77] The city's population swelled further during the great wave of African-American migration from the south to the cities of the industrial north during the 1910s. Racial tensions soon ran high in the city with considerable violence being directed against African-American communities, including the bombing of homes.

With its diverse immigrant population seeking social and economic stability and a sense of community, Chicago proved fertile ground for mystical and magical groups. The prophet Cyrus Teed (1839–1908) evidently found it a more conducive environment than his previous troubled residences in Syracuse and New York, even if, according to Upton Sinclair, 'the street urchins of the pork-packing metropolis threw stones at him'.[78] Teed claimed that in 1869 he had received a divine revelation from God in the form of a beautiful woman, who gave him knowledge of the secrets of the Universe. He subsequently took the name Koresh and preached variously that the Earth was hollow, and that he would return immortal after his death.[79] He once announced that he could make gold at will. The newspapers had great fun reporting on the pronouncements, fantastical schemes, and legal scrapes of what one newspaper dubbed the 'Chicago Messiah'.[80]

More influentially, Chicago was also a spiritual home of African-American mystical organizations. At the Chicago World's Fair in 1893 a group of African-American masons launched their own branch of the white Masonic Ancient Arabic Order of the Nobles of the Mystic Shrine. It is significant that they inserted 'Egyptian' between 'Ancient' and 'Arabic'. The Black Shriners, as they were more commonly known, never became a major African-American fraternal society.[81] One reason may have been that as well as its charitable activities more of its members were serious about the mystical aspects of their order, contrasting with the millions who joined the White Shriners, whose meetings were fondly mocked by Laurel and Hardy in their 1933 classic *Sons of the Desert*. The Fez-wearing Ancient Arabic Order of the Nobles of the Mystic Shrine, co-founded by the actor Billy Florence in 1871, stated that their guiding principle was founded on a secret Koranic work obtained in Mecca, which revealed a hidden Islamic tradition. While this story was generally taken lightly by its white members, the Black Shriners took their own version of their Arabic mystical origins more seriously as an empowering tradition.[82] In the 1920s this, along with the Christian revivalism brought to Chicago by southern African-American migrants, growing Black Nationalism, and a flourishing occult publishing industry, helped foster the Moorish Science Temple. This was founded by the Chicago prophet Noble Drew Ali, a self-proclaimed 'Angel of Allah', and a major influence on the development of the Nation of Islam, which in its early years during the 1930s was labelled by an ignorant Detroit police force as the 'Voodoo Cult'.[83]

According to the unreliable hagiographic history that surrounds his life, Timothy Drew was born in North Carolina in 1886 to ex-slaves living among Cherokee Indians. He joined a band of travelling magicians in his early teens, fell in with some gypsies for a while, and at the age of 16 found himself in Egypt. Here he met the high priest of an ancient mystical religion and underwent an initiation in the pyramid of Cheops. On returning to America the re-styled prophet Noble Drew Ali preached that African-Americans were the descendants of an Asiatic nation descended from the Canaanites and Moabites, which in ancient times stretched from South America, to Africa and Atlantis. The descendants of this nation were the founders of the Islamic Moorish empire. Like the Black Shriners, then, the followers of the Moorish Temple reinforced the notion that Black Americans may have come from Africa but their origins lay in the great civilizations of Arabia, Egypt, and the East. They were the rightful heirs to the ancient mystical magical traditions that had fascinated Europeans for so long.

Ali set up the Canaanite Temple in Newark in 1913 to spread this empowering message amongst the African-American population, though in 1925 schisms led him and his followers to regroup in Chicago, which he believed would become the second Mecca. His followers were easily recognizable in the city's streets as they were required to wear red fezzes at all times. It was not long before internecine strife began to fracture the Chicago movement. One cause of conflict was that several leading members were apparently making considerable money selling herbs, magical charms, and cult literature to followers.[84] The prophet died in mysterious circumstances in 1929 shortly after being released by the police, who had interrogated him, perhaps brutally, following the murder of a leading Temple follower. The revelatory foundation text of Moorish Science, *The Holy Koran of the Moorish Science Temple*, was originally self-published by Drew Ali. Despite its title it actually had little to do with Islamic teaching, and was largely inspired by two early-twentieth-century mystical works, the authors of which spuriously claimed their revelations to be based on secret texts discovered in Tibetan monasteries.[85] One of them, Levi Dowling's *The Aquarian Gospel of Jesus Christ* (1907), purported to reveal the story of how Jesus wandered across Africa and Asia accumulating and spreading secret wisdom as he went.[86] The other text, *Infinite Wisdom* (1923), claimed to be distilled from the mystical knowledge preserved in Tibetan manuscripts containing the writings of the second millennium BC Pharaoh Amenhotep IV.

The reputation of Africa as the repository of ancient magical wisdom also rested on the portrayal of Moses as an African. In the 1930s an octogenarian African-American resident of Yamacraw, Georgia, explained how the biblical stories of Moses showed that Africa was a land of magical power since the beginning of history. As a consequence the descendants of Africans from biblical times had a gift for doing 'unnatural things'.[87] Advertisements in the African-American newspaper the *Chicago Defender* in the 1920s show how gypsies and Hindu swamis were being challenged by Africans in the magical image stakes. Some advertisements included photographs of the practitioners in African-style robes. One professor intimated he had 'just had some very wonderful African Temple Powder sent from Africa to help his many friends'. Another 'Master of Science' described himself as a 'Mohammedan native of Africa', who would astonish clients 'with the marvels of African Science, Powerful Root Herbs and Incense'.[88]

Interest in ancient magical wisdom was also being fuelled by a burgeoning occult press. In 1918, in a piercing attack on religion and spiritual quacks in the USA, the socialist author Upton Sinclair described how the shelves groaned with mystical magazines with titles like 'Azoth; Master Mind; Aletheian; Words of Power; Astrological Bulletin; Unity; Uplift... also shelves of imposing-looking volumes containing the lore and magic of a score of races and two score of centuries—together with the very newest manifestations of Yankee hustle and graft.'[89] The advertising columns of the newspapers also indicate there was a vibrant trade in new and second-hand books at the time. In 1912 the Southern Astrological School, Fruithurst, Alabama, advertised a full line of occult books for sale, while in the Oakland Tribune in 1923 advertisements appeared for a circulating 'Hermetic Library' of 'occult and mystical books' at 138 Grand Avenue.[90]

For the reasons described above, Chicago became an important centre of occult publication. At the makeshift end of the city's publishing industry there was Feliks Markiewicz, aka Professor S. Lanard, alias K. W. Sikonowski. In 1912 we find him selling a version of the Seventh Book of Moses and other 'secrets' via his Great Supply Book Company. His customers must have been bitterly disappointed, though, for Markiewicz's version of the Seventh Book apparently consisted of no more than mundane recipes on how to cure colds and remove warts. His boasted 'secrets' were no better. One costing $3 concerning how to bewitch cows read as follows:

> If you want to revenge yourself on a neighbour by making his cow dry, steal into the barn of your enemy before dawn in the morning and milk the cow yourself and take the milk home. Get him to leave his home afternoons on some pretext, and during his absence repeat the performance.

The spell for increasing milk yields was equally disappointing: 'First get a good milch cow; if she is only a moderate milker, feed her some bran mixed with oats and corn, and she will immediately give more milk.' Markiewicz evidently found a niche conning Polish immigrants in this way. He advertised that for $2.50 one of his publications would enable them to speak, read, and write English in seventy-two hours. It turned out to be a basic Polish-English dictionary with an instruction that the purchaser memorize all its contents in three days. It was presumably one of his many dissatisfied customers that reported him to the Post Office authorities.[91]

In 1900 the little known Egyptian Publishing Company of Chicago produced the first version of the *Sixth and Seventh Book of Moses* to be printed in a couple of decades. But it was an edition published in 1910 by another Chicago enterprise, Delaurence, Scott and Company, the producer of numerous esoteric and magical publications, which proved particularly influential in spreading its influence amongst the African-American population. In contrast to the malign reputation of the Moses Books amongst Pennsylvania Germans, they were treated with reverence in African-American hoodoo and mystical movements. While this was predominantly due to the huge importance of Moses in African-American faith and religious identity, the fact that it was produced by Delaurence may have also given the edition an extra degree of spiritual aura. The Delaurence influence is evident from some of the African-American cults and sects that flourished in the northern cities. Rabbi Wentworth Arthur Matthews (1892–1972), founder of the New York Black Israelites, was the leader of one such organization. It was one of numerous Black Jewish sects that believed they were descended from the ancient Hebrews. Matthews told his followers that he was born in Lagos, Nigeria, whereas in fact he was brought up on the Caribbean island of St Kitts. It was perhaps here that he first came into contact with Delaurence books. Raised a Methodist he became a Pentecostalist minister in Harlem and during the 1920s, at a time when Jewish families were moving out of the area, he began to integrate Judaic ritual and celebration into his church's worship. An examination of his papers reveals how he also wove grimoire magic into his communication with the Divine. Matthews was no doubt familiar with Delaurence's esoteric religious publications on the immanence of God and the like. It was, however, the apparently Hebraic symbols and seals that attracted him to the *Sixth and Seventh Books of Moses*, and which shaped what he called his 'cabalistic science'. From amulets found in Matthews personal papers we can see how he borrowed from those in the *Sixth and Seventh Books of Moses* to invoke the presence and power of God.[92]

The same Delaurence edition also seeped deep into the thoughts and practices of rural African-Americans as well. In the 1930s, the folklorist Harry Middleton Hyatt travelled up and down the eastern half of the country interviewing over 1,600 African-Americans about their magical beliefs. He found the *Sixth and Seventh Books* was already an integral aspect of hoodoo conjuration, used in conjunction with the Bible. As one hoodoo practitioner from Washington DC explained, 'you kin take and look in de Sixth and Seventh Book of Moses and find out whut to read, and den you go in yo' Bible and read it from yo' Bible.' The practitioner said that he was particularly familiar with the fourth psalm 'in order to accomplish things that you desire'.[93] It runs as follows:

If you have been unlucky hitherto, in spite of every effort, then you should pray this Psalm three times before the rising of the sun, with humility and devotion, while at the same time you should impress upon your mind its ruling holy name, and each time the appropriate prayer, trusting in the help of the mighty Lord, without whose will not the least creature can perish. Proceed in peace to execute your contemplated undertaking, and all things will result to your entire satisfaction.

The holy name is called: Jiheje (He is and will be), and is composed of the four final letters of the words Teppillati, verse 2; Selah, verse 5; Jehovah, verse 6; and Toschiweni, verse 9. The prayer is as follows:

> May it please Thee, oh, Jiheje, to prosper my ways, steps and doings. Grant that my desire may be amply fulfilled, and let my wishes be satisfied even this day, for the sake of Thy great, mighty and praiseworthy name. Amen!—Selah!—[94]

Hyatt asked, 'Is this Psalm in the Bible or in the Book of Moses?' The reply was, 'Both—but de meanings in de Book of Moses—Sixth and Seventh Books of Moses.' During the 1930s cheap paperback editions of the *Sixth and Seventh Books* were produced in their thousands, but Delaurence's name remained indelibly associated with it—besides much else magical. When Hyatt asked another Washington DC interviewee who used the *Sixth and Seventh Books* where to obtain the necessary 'dove's blood' ink and parchment to write magic prayers, the reply was, 'Ah know one in Chicago.' When asked the name, the reply was a hesitant, 'Ah don't lak tuh call dese names. Ah don't know whethah ah'd be doin' right den.' Reassured by Hyatt, he then said, 'Well, de Lawrence.'[95]

Delaurence

William Lauron Delaurence was born in Cleveland, Ohio, in 1868.[96] His father was French-Canadian and his mother Pennsylvania Dutch. Around the age of 17 he worked as a flagman on the Pennsylvania Railroad, warning those working on the tracks of oncoming trains, before taking up the same role at the Euclid Avenue Crossing, Cleveland. In his early twenties he started to sell books on psychology and hypnotism door-to-door, first in Cleveland and then further afield. Around the age of 24 or 25 he saw a hypnotist on stage at the opera house in Parkersburg, West Virginia, and began to study the subject and devise his own modest show. In the late 1890s 'Professor' Delaurence commenced offering lessons in hypnotism in

Pittsburgh before setting up a school of hypnotism in Chicago around 1900. So began the career of America's most influential occultist.

While on the road Delaurence had put together his own manuscript on hypnotism and submitted it to Fred Drake of the Donahue Company in Chicago. Donahue's main business was publishing children's literature such as *Black Beauty* so it is not surprising that the company was not interested in Delaurence's manuscript. When Drake left to join the Henneberry Company he was able to contract Delaurence's manuscript and it was published in 1901. The book sold well but when Delaurence paid a visit to Henneberry to collect his royalty payment he was told that the costs of production had been set against his royalties and that, in fact, he owed the publisher $15. Delaurence hired a lawyer and apparently successfully sued Henneberry for $350. Drake left shortly after to found his own publishing house, producing a couple of books on the tricks of card sharpers before finding success with an enduring series of do-it-yourself manuals on engineering, electrics, sign-writing, and other such trades.

The sales success of *Hypnotism: A Complete System*, coupled with his bitter initial experience of the publishing world, inspired Delaurence to set up his own company, Delaurence, Scott and Company. It is likely that Scott never existed. When Delaurence was questioned in 1919 about his mysterious partner he was certainly evasive on the matter.[97] The first of Delaurence's publications was a revised edition of *Hypnotism*, followed in 1905 by *The Sacred Book of Death*, which purported to be a book of Hindu spiritism, though it is largely plagiarized from Allan Kardec's *Spirits' Book*. By this time Delaurence, who had dropped the title of 'Professor' and adopted the more modest 'Doctor', had become a self-styled adept of Eastern mysticism, presenting himself as a Hindu swami. A trade directory at the time lists him as the president of 'The Delaurence Institute of Hypnotism, Hindu Magic, and East Indian Occultism'.[98] He also advertised his prowess as a palmist in the press, boasting of his international reputation and offering to help in 'business, love, marriage, domestic troubles and all affairs of life'.[99] As to Delaurence's success with the *Sixth and Seventh Books of Moses*, he obtained the printer's plates from Fred Drake, and later recalled, 'I bought the book because there were many people selling it at that time for $5.00 a copy and I supposed it would be a good seller.' He thought Drake's plates were a translation from the German, but was not sure.[100] This was one of a series of magic books compiled and plagiarized from a variety of published sources. One of his other successes was *The Great Book of Magical Art, Hindu Magic and East Indian Occultism*, which initially sold for $12. As he advertised, it was 'handsomely bound with a durable expensive binding, with lettering, oriental and occult symbols stamped in a beautiful bright metal known as oriental gold'. There was nothing Hindu or Indian about its contents though. It was, in fact, a chopped-up version of Barrett's *The Magus* with added photographic scenes of India and other extraneous engravings. Wherever Barrett wrote 'we' Delaurence merely replaced it with 'I'.[101] It was an outrageous act of piracy and one he would go on to repeat with numerous other English occult works of the period. In his reprints of the *Lesser* and *Greater Key of Solomon*, and the *Sacred Magic of Abre-Melin* he did at least mention Mathers' authorship in passing. Regarding the latter book, though, more space was given to the sales pitch that Delaurence had paid $75 for a copy in London while he was selling his American edition for a mere $5.50. He asserted that the cost of publishing and advertising what he described as his 'superior in every way' edition amounted to $9,000. None of the profits found their way to Mathers' estate of course.[102]

A hitherto unknown aspect of Delaurence's career was his brief stint as leader of a magic and miscegenation cult known as the Order of the Black Rose, which apparently worshipped at the feet of a perfumed, wooden cigar-store Indian. The cult sought to elevate African-Americans and consisted of two orders. Novices were initiated into the Order of the White Willow, which apparently consisted mostly, perhaps exclusively, of white women. Before being admitted each woman was weighed in the nude. The ideas seemed to be that only women with good figures could progress. Delaurence would come to regret offending an initiate named Augusta Murie, who he said was 'too fat to be an angel' and suggested that she take medicine to slim down. The Order of the Black Rose, the cult elite, naturally consisted of Delaurence and a select group of African-American men.

While it is likely that the Black Shriners influenced Delaurence's mystical racial ideas, his cult aspirations were probably inspired by the Mazdaznans, a Chicago sect that also claimed a mystical Eastern heritage. The movement was founded by Otoman Zar-Adusht Hanish and was a modern formulation of Zoroastrian Sun worship, which married Eastern mysticism with the vogue for dietary fads.[103] Hanish claimed to be of Persian descent, though others stated he was German, Polish, or Russian. One report in 1908 suggested he was from Ireland and was known as Hennessy during an early sojourn in New York.[104] As one of his admirers, Professor Ardesher Sorabji Wadia, recalled, 'I know very little about the life of Dr Hanish for the simple reason that he himself kept it a sealed book.'[105] What a surprise.

By the time of Delaurence's arrival in Chicago, Hanish's Sun cult had drawn many adherents from the city's wealthy white population, particularly the female portion. In 1906 one newspaper estimated that he had 10,000 Mazdaznan members in the city alone.[106] This is highly unlikely though, as his followers desired social exclusivity and probably never numbered more than a few hundred in Chicago. Considering his high society clientele, and rumours regarding the sexual and ritual activities of his members, Hanish periodically found himself targeted by the police and press. In 1908 he was at the centre of a court cases involving a wealthy disciple named Ellen Shaw, who desired to give her fortune to the Mazdaznan church, believing she was to become the mother of a new Messiah. Three years later the press reported that the Juvenile Protective Association was investigating claims that the Sun Temple was luring wealthy young boys.[107]

Hanish initially set up the Sun-Worshiper Publishing Co. and then the Mazdaznan Publishing Company to spread word of his mystical insights. This included his 1902 work *Inner Studies: A Course of Twelve Lessons*, which included such topics as 'The Secrets of Lovers Unveiled' and 'Magnetic Attraction and Electric Mating'. It was his mail order marketing of this and other works, particularly to wealthy women, which attracted the attention of the Chicago authorities. He was charged in 1912 and 1913 for circulating obscene literature.[108] These concerned his descriptions of the naked form. Books of his sayings and precepts, such as the *Green Book* and *The Royal Goat*, were produced in evidence, copies of which I have been unable to locate. They may have been the product of journalistic imagination—or Hanish's. Then again, they may have been in manuscript or small private print runs. During the 1908 prosecution case it was stated that some of his publications were only issued to the 'royal family' of the cult. One newspaper reported that 'these books are guarded almost with the life of a worshipper. There are very few in existence and only the very select are allowed to see them.'[109]

In November 1912 the Chicago police raided Delaurence's 'palatial headquarters' at 3340 Michigan Avenue after receiving a complaint from the defector Mrs Augusta Murie. Investigations were launched by the Post Office and the Department of Justice, and consequently Delaurence and several white women and black men were arrested for suspected mail fraud and offences under the Mann Act (White Slave Traffic Act).[110] Shortly before this police raid, members had been agitated by the plight of Jack Johnson, the world heavyweight champion boxer who was in gaol awaiting trial under the Mann Act for taking a white woman, Lucille Cameron, from Minneapolis to Chicago for 'immoral purposes'. The whole of Chicago was galvanized by the affair. When the news first broke in October angry crowds gathered in the streets and his appearance led to cries of 'Lynch Him'. The bigoted Chicago clubwomen started a national campaign to support the prosecution.[111] In this racially charged atmosphere members of the Order of the Black Rose argued that their followers should employ their occult arts to ensure Johnson's release. Delaurence disagreed, however, believing that such a task was beyond the society's jurisdiction. Shortly after this meeting, Delaurence and eighteen of his followers also found themselves in gaol.

In the end, the authorities did not pursue a prosecution under the Mann Act, and the trial was concerned only with fraud. An African-American attorney defended Delaurence and his followers. Murie testified that she only joined the cult in order to learn the art of hypnotism and became disillusioned when she claimed to have discovered that Delaurence had hidden dictographs in the lecture rooms to record his disciples' conversations. The personal information he gathered this way was then used to give the impression he could read their minds when under the hypnotic state. Delaurence was fined $200 and his followers released.[112] It would seem that Delaurence disbanded the cult after this, though a reference to it cropped up in 1923 during a curious federal investigation into the claims of Helen La Maie, wife of the film director and theatre manager Elsier La Maie, that her husband had tried to sell her to a mysterious, wealthy black gambler named Lou Harris for $500,000. Helen told the authorities that her husband wanted her to become queen of the Order of the Black Rose, and that this would require that she take a black lover in order to further the Order's aim of equalizing the rights of 'Caucasians and Ethiopians'.[113]

This was not the end of Delaurence's trouble with the law. Press advertisements for his books and his Institute were circulating in Nigeria. In 1911 Michael D. Williams, an African pharmacy student at the Colonial Hospital, Lagos, came across a Delaurence advertisement in a West African newspaper. Impressed by Dr Delaurence's vaunted powers and potent occult publications, he purchased a copy of the *Book of Magical Art* and the *Book of Death*. In 1914 Williams decided he wanted to learn directly from the Master and set sail for the USA. He made his way to Chicago, where he stayed at the African-American YMCA on Wabash Avenue, which had only been completed a year earlier but had already become an important centre for migrants. Delaurence gave him employment and received a money order from his brother back in Lagos to pay for his teaching. Williams was evidently by no means the first to make his way there. According to Delaurence a great many men had done so before. 'I never created a desire in any of these men to take up the study,' he said. As to Williams, he 'seemed to be well educated—and told me he wanted to be well up in occultism, and it is a well-known fact that on the gold coast of Africa that is practically the religion, and he said he wanted to perfect himself on that.'[114] Relations soon turned sour, however. Delaurence described him as 'an aggressive, quarrelsome educated proposition'. They had several altercations over Williams' apparent habit of peering up the skirts of Delaurence's female employees when they climbed the stepladder in the stockroom. On one such occasion Delaurence struck Williams who then went and lodged a complaint with the police. Williams claimed Delaurence tried to hypnotize him against his will and had beaten him over the head with a chair. He returned to the premises with two plain-clothes detectives and Delaurence made out a cheque for $150 to settle their accounts. Delaurence later accused him of going to the Chicago press and inducing 'reporters there to write up certain copy about me, how I treated Negroes and everything of that sort'.[115]

Delaurence's last brush with the wrong side of the law was in April 1919 when he was tried by the Post Office for 'conducting a scheme for obtaining money through the mail by means of false pretenses, representations and promises'. By this time Delaurence, who described himself in his puffs as 'the greatest teacher, author and publisher of Occult and Magical Works the world has ever known', had given up the troublesome business of occult instruction. He had created a very successful mail order and retail business, selling not only grimoires but also all the equipment and 'talismanic and symbolic jewellery' required by students of the occult and those wishing to better their lives. There were invocation candles for calling up spirits, 'receiving of oracles, adjurations, and casting out of evil spirits' ($2 a dozen); the Venus, Woman's Love talisman with special silken bag ($1.25); red coral rings and necklaces to ward off evil spirits and melancholy; and the 'seven sacred magical art talismans, on genuine virgin parchment'. There was also a range of Hong Kong and East Indian remedies, some of which, like the 'Lion Stomach Tonic', he bought in from the Chicago Pharmacy Company.

By his own account he had recently taken in gross receipts of around $40,000 a year and owned around $100,000 in plates, stock, and merchandise. He estimated that around 20 per cent of business was overseas, mostly from Africa it would seem, since he complained that his profits were slim on such orders due to the cost of first-class post. He also sold a lot of books locally through Chicago and New York book dealers and stores including well-known names such as Charles Scribner and Son and Sears, Roebuck and Company. He also supplied the Western News Company which operated railway newsstands.[116] One of his most regular clients was the less well-known Oriental Esoteric Library in Washington DC. This had been founded in 1905 by the retired chemist and occultist Henry Stokes to promote the dissemination of occult literature. It was initially part of an esoteric cult known as the Order of the Initiates of Tibet, though following a bust-up and consequent court case Stokes, who had ploughed some $35,000 into building up the library, assumed full control.[117]

Delaurence was planning on opening a store and was negotiating a five-year lease at $3,000 a year when he was ordered to appear at the Post Office Department. While he was building up his retail business a Chicago Post Office inspector named Dana Angier had been collecting damning material against Delaurence. One piece of evidence produced in court was Delaurence's response to a letter Angier wrote to him under an assumed name, Gabriel Martin, in July 1915. Angier was aware of the Michael Williams affair and was evidently posing as another African student of the occult.

> Dear Sir:
> Having been in this country now a year and wishing to complete my training, I am writing you for books on occultism and magic, having known of you before.

THE UNMISTAKABLE MARK OF
GOOD TASTE

The articles listed and described in this Catalogue, show the unmistakable marks of good taste, and are for those who want only the best. Wherever this Catalogue goes there are men and women whose cultivated tastes admit of no insincerity or pretense, whose trained minds judge Book, Bible, Jewelry, Diamond, and Merchandise values fairly.

Every customer on our Big Mailing List demands the best, and it is for them that this Catalogue, which costs thousands and thousands of dollars, was published. A High Grade Catalogue like this one makes little or no appeal to cheap vanity, pretense or sentiment, to crude or untrained buyers, to bargain hunters or pretenders. It was published exclusively for those who are able to appreciate Values.

Every customer realizes the worth of our Rule of Honesty that governs all transactions. A rule that has been directly responsible for our world-wide success. This rule briefly means: List and sell at the lowest possible price, the best Occult and Spiritual Books, Bibles, Solid Gold Jewelry, Diamonds, and Merchandise to be had.

FIG. 21 One of many puffs in the *De Laurence's Catalog* (Chicago, 1940).

In reply he received some testimonials, a blank order slip, and an offer to send his forthcoming catalogue for the price of ten cents. A correspondence ensued with Angier receiving numerous further advertisements for Delaurence books and products. He sent off $2.50 for a two-inch gazing crystal and ten cents for the catalogue and requested:

> Now, sirs, I want you to tell me about your great book 'Albertus Magnus.' Are these secrets genuine and such as I would be able to perform as I would like to do wonderful things. I will have money soon so I will be able to buy this book if it is genuine.[118]

Although Delaurence or one of his staff did not elaborate on the genuineness of Albertus, Angier purchased a copy for $3.35 for his dossier. When it was produced during the trial the acting solicitor for the Post Office took a particular interest in its contents, and several passages were read out, such as the following: 'When a horse is stubborn while being shod. Speak into his ear: Caspar raise thee, Melchior bind, and Balthasar entangle thee.' When he was informed that the book was 'sold by hundreds of different stores throughout the country', he remarked, 'We ought to get the names of some of those.'[119] Delaurence claimed in his advertisements for the book that it was a revised and enlarged edition under his editorship, but during the trial he admitted that he had done no such thing. 'I attached my name there for the reason that I believe that when my name is on the book it helps create a sale,' he said.[120]

The trial also exposed his limited knowledge of the grimoires he sold. Regarding Albertus Magnus, he was asked, 'You put him down as a very great man, and enlightened in his writings, do you believe in them?' 'I am not familiar enough with his writings to say whether I would or not.' When asked, 'who was Albertus Magnus?', Delaurence replied, 'He was a character we find in the Bible. I can't give the details, he is, I have heard of him spoken of many times.'[121] When questioned as to his key references on occult matters the following exchange occurred:

> 'Well, there is another book called "Transcendental Magic." '
> 'Who wrote that?'
> 'Levi.'
> 'Is he a doctor of medicine?'
> 'I don't know as he is a doctor, I don't think he is.'
> 'What is his education along those lines?'
> 'He is an author on natural magic.'
> 'What are his qualifications as an expert?'
> 'I could not tell you. . . . '
>
> 'Any other authorities that you know about that would give any knowledge on these things?'

'Well, there is a Waite, who recently died, he is the author of several
books in London. . . .'
'What is Waite's reputation?'
'Waite is held by the English press to be one of the greatest writers in
the world upon magic.'
'By the English press, what do you mean by the English press?'
'Well, the same as the press in this country.'

A. E. Waite was actually alive and well at the time and outlived Delaurence by
several years. He was hardly a darling of the English press though. While Delaurence
knew little of Waite the man he was certainly very familiar with some of his work.
He had the cheek to pirate the *Pictorial Key to the Tarot* (1910), written and illustrated
by Waite and Pamela Colman Smith, under the title *The Illustrated Key to the Tarot*,
and brazenly identified himself as the author.[122] He also reprinted the *Book of Black
Magic and of Pacts* and Waite's edited digest of Lévi's writings, *The Mysteries of Magic*,
claiming mendaciously that the production of the English original was of poor
quality compared to his American edition printed 'on the finest plate paper'.[123]

Yet over the seventy typescript pages of his cross-examination it becomes clear
that Delaurence was not a completely cynical con artist exploiting beliefs he
despised. He accepted that some of his products had no power, that he had no
medical qualifications, that his virgin parchment was often not exactly virgin. But
he discussed his personal beliefs and experiences of the occult with an honesty that
intrigued and impressed his examiners. When asked whether he believed in the
power of his parchment talismans he replied: 'I believe in them. I have one of
them, my boy has one. I know one man who I don't think would part with the
talisman he has got for ten thousand dollars.' He experienced premonitory dreams
and visions, said he had seen a vision in a crystal ball of men carrying a crystal in a
box, and four weeks later he was burgled.[124] He had also received many visitations
from astral beings, such as those of Hindu adepts, and departed spirits, including
numerous communications with his dead brother regarding his wife, and more
sensationally Paracelsus.[125]

Although it would seem that Delaurence gave up the idea of opening a retail
store in light of the close attentions of the Post Office Department, his mail order
business continued to prosper. We get a glimpse of his continuing success in
November 1931, when his new premises at 179 North Michigan Avenue were
robbed once again as the day's receipts were being counted. The thieves bound
Delaurence, his wife, and a stenographer with wire, and made off with $2,500 of
jewellery. Tellingly, of the $500 of cash taken $300, was in foreign currency.[126]

Delaurence died in 1936 but for many in the Caribbean and West Africa he
became more than a mere mortal. We saw in Chapter 5 how French grimoires

influenced the generation of new magical–medical religious cultures forged through colonization and slavery. In contrast the influence of Delaurence overseas was not a consequence of authoritarianism and population movements. It was symptomatic of the rise of American cultural imperialism rather than colonial imposition. Before the Coca–Cola Export Corporation was set up in 1930 to mastermind what would become the global dominance of the beverage, Delaurence had already successfully masterminded an American cultural export revolution. But it is important to remember that Delaurence was not pushing an iconic American product, or even promoting American values. He was successfully exploiting American commercial techniques to repackage and promote the wisdom and mysticism of the East and not the superiority of the West.

Delaurence overseas

Until Delaurence the impact of European grimoires in colonial Africa seems to have been negligible. The *Bibliothèque bleue* did not have the same impact in France's North African territories as in the Caribbean and Indian Ocean. There was no cheap occult publication industry in Britain to export to its colonies. Delaurence filled the gap in the English-speaking African market. Nowhere were his publications more influential than in Nigeria. As is evident from the Michael Williams affair, his catalogues and his reputation was already circulating there before the First World War. There was a strong educated interest in foreign occult traditions, the Kabala and freemasonry in particular. A branch of AMORC was established there in 1925, and Western occult literature and charms were advertised in the Nigerian press and were available in the streets of Lagos and other towns.[127] The circulation of Nigerian magazines and newspapers also led to the Westernization and Delaurencification of medical traditions in the neighbouring former German colony of Cameroon. Work among the Wimbum tribe has shown that *The Sixth and Seventh Books of Moses* has altered their beliefs about the source and workings of 'bad' or magical medicine.[128]

Delaurence's works influenced the development of several popular religious movements in Nigeria, such as *Mami Wata* worship. This was centred on a water spirit, the image of which was taken from a German chromolith of a snake charmer printed around 1885 and copied and reprinted many times in England and India. The popularity of the image in central and West Africa generated a demand for Indian prints of other gods, goddesses, and spirits, which became incorporated into the *Mami Wata* pantheon displayed in shrines. These also led to an interest in both Hindu and Western ritual magic, to which many Africans attributed the financial success of Indian immigrants and Europeans. Delaurence's role in this is evident from an interview in the early 1980s with a *Mami Wata* priest of the Igbo ethnic group in Nigeria. Chukwu Emeka Ifeabunike, alias 'Dr Candido of India', who claimed to have studied Hindu occultism in Bombay and New Delhi, practised magical healing, counter witchcraft, and fortune-telling. His shrine was full of images and statues of Hindu gods and spirits, a small coffin, candles, pots, incense sticks, and other accoutrements of his trade. Amongst his most prized possessions were two books from the Delaurence company, the *Great Book of Magic* and *The Sixth and Seventh Books of Moses*. He kept one of these outside the entrance to his shrine opened at a page in which magical signs were clearly depicted. The door to a ritual bathing area was carved with images based on illustrations from Delaurence books. Dr Candido, like many Delaurence adherents, was unaware that he had long since died, praising him 'as a very knowledgeable man', and saying that 'one day he hoped to go to America and visit him.'[129] During the 1980s, anthropologists studying the Ibibio tribe of southeastern Nigeria found that people were also ordering charms from the Delaurence Company at considerable personal expense.[130]

The influence of Delaurence is less obvious but still evident in the influential Church of the Lord (Aladura) movement founded in 1930 by the Nigerian Yoruba prophet Josiah Olunowo Oshitelu. This former Anglican schoolteacher experienced a series of visions and divine communications, which he wrote down in six large journals in his own arcane script, written from right to left as in Arabic and Hebrew. They also contained a series of sacred seals and signs. Magic and traditional cures were prohibited by the Church, as followers need only place their faith in God and seek his aid through fasting, prayer, and the power of the psalms. Yet studies of the Church written in the 1960s noted that members consulted Western occult literature, and suggest that the *Sixth and Seventh Books of Moses* in particular, had some influence on Oshitelu's ideas and the construction of his sacred script and seals. Although Oshitelu never admitted as such, he did mention in one of his publications, *The Book of Prayer with Uses and Power of Psalms*, that 'Some will say this is Moses' Book therefore it is bad.'[131]

Ghana was the other great centre of Delaurence. In the late 1950s anthropologists found copies of the *Sixth and Seventh Books of Moses* circulating in the country. While it is not impossible that German editions found their way there from the neighbouring, pre-First World War German colony of Togoland, the source of the English language editions was almost certainly Delaurence. Some of his publications such as *The Aquarian Gospel, Sixth and Seventh Books of Moses*, and *The Book of Magical Arts, Hindu Magic and Indian Occultism* have been found in the bookstalls of Ghana's towns and cities.[132] In the 1950s a patient at an Asante shrine confided, 'I have ordered the Sixth and Seventh Books of Moses, because with it you can work wonders and without it you can't go to England.'[133] Howard

French, an African affairs journalist for the international press remembered the awe surrounding the *Sixth and Seventh Books of Moses* during his school days in rural Ghana during the late 1940s. Some older boys indulged in fasts and ritual washing and were caught murmuring incantations from the Moses Book, which was thought to have been imported from India, but was almost certainly bought mail order from Chicago despite the fact that the Post Office had prohibited its import. A cousin told him that it contained talismans 'which could be ordered and used to attract girls, or to play better at football'. But if the instructions were not strictly followed it could induce madness, and merely glancing at some of its contents without saying the correct incantations would make one go blind. 'My dread of the Sixth and Seventh Books of Moses was as nothing compared to what I felt when I was told that there was another book that was even more advanced in occultism, called The Eighth and Ninth Books of Moses,' French recalled.[134]

Just as we have seen how in Europe and America grimoires assumed greater potency for having supposedly originated from other countries, so in western Africa overseas objects also accrued magical power. While Americans looked to Asia and Africa for new commercial sources of occult influence, Africans looked to the West. An anthropologist researching the medical beliefs of the Wimbum of Cameroon in the early 1990s found that the tribal elders cherished their collections of Toby jugs from colonial days more than their ritual masks and elephant tusks, while knives and bugles offered as gifts by German colonialists prior to the First World War were thought to have mystical qualities.[135] In the 1950s a Swiss theologian, Hans Debrunner, was disgusted to find that some literate Ghanaians defrauded their fellows by selling magical charms marketed as being from overseas. One of his respondents observed: 'some people, I hear, protect themselves against witchcraft by ordering some Indian and American rings and talismans. Ministers of the Church and even some teachers do it, with the idea that the European-made protectives are neater and more portable.'[136] Some were local knick-knacks given a foreign origin while others were, indeed, obtained from American occult catalogues.

For some outside commentators this injection of Western literary occultism had spread a pernicious mental virus that inhibited the development of West African culture. Hans Debrunner believed the *Sixth and Seventh Books of Moses* had led 'to a sort of psychological slavery' for those who owned it. A psychiatric study of Ghanaians conducted in the 1950s seemed to confirm Debrunner's fears, concluding that the expressed intention to make magic with the *Sixth and Seventh Books of Moses* heralded the onset of schizophrenia. The government's ban on its sale was thought to be in response to 'its frequent use by incipient schizophrenics in cemeteries at night'. For Debrunner, Western grimoires were 'definitely worse than the traditional ways of protection', and he hoped that the pernicious influence of such imported literature would be broken as 'good books' became more accessible through the public library system.[137] Amongst the 'good books' was the Bible of course, but for many the *Sixth and Seventh Books of Moses* were biblical, and attempts to suppress them was just another example of the white man's intention to withhold secret wisdom.

Delaurence was and is respected in West Africa but in the Caribbean he achieved mythical status. The name of Delaurence was legendary in Nevis, being associated with the supernatural figure of a diabolic white-suited man on a white horse that betokened death. In Grenada one man, evidently conflating Delaurence with Father Christmas, described him as a magician 'in Chicago near the North Pole and lives with a large number of pigmy servants'. In the Windward Islands the *De Laurence Catalogue* is considered to be a black arts book in its own right, used by those who call upon the Devil. The Chicago address of the Delaurence Company is consequently a jealously guarded secret.[138] While Delaurence had an impact in former and current French colonies where the *Petit Albert* already had a firm hold,[139] it was in the British colonies that Delaurence had the most profound influence.

In Trinidad, which the Spanish surrendered to the British in 1797, an anthropological study conducted in the 1940s in the settlement of Toco, in the northeast of the Island, revealed how Delaurence had already become central to its magical religious culture. Among village elders 'great interest was expressed in the books of de Laurence'. One man observed that 'the work that de Laurence does is a correct Baptist work. They are taught in the spirit.'[140] The content of his publications were absorbed into both Orisha worship and the rituals of the Spiritual Baptist churches, which went on to flourish after the colonial prohibition of their services was repealed in 1951. The *Sixth and Seventh Books of Moses* were almost certainly the inspiration for the various 'spiritual' symbols used in some Spiritualist Baptist ritual worship, just as they were in some west African religious movements.[141] Small groups of men would club together to share the costs of buying his publications such as the *Greater Key of Solomon*, the *Lesser Key*, and *Albertus Magnus*, as well as the roots, divining rods, and crystal balls offered in the Delaurence catalogue. The island's authorities banned Delaurence publications before and after independence in 1962, but copies remained easy to obtain, though they fetched high prices. Recent studies of religious life in Trinidad and Tobago confirm the lasting influence of Delaurence. Today the *Keys of Solomon, Sixth and Seventh Books of Moses*, and *Aquarian Gospel* are consulted by most Orisha priests, and continue to be quite widely read by members of the various Spiritualist Baptist churches. They are treated as being equally important as the Bible. It has recently been reported that *The Great Book of Secret Hindu Ceremonial and Talismanic Magic* is currently the most widely distributed grimoire in the country.[142]

FIG. 22 Delaurence advertisement in *The Daily Gleaner*, 30 August 1939.

Nowhere in the Caribbean did Delaurence have a more profound social influence than in Jamaica. His works and products played a significant role in the practice of *Obeah*, while the *Sixth and Seventh Books of Moses* formed part of the canon of mystical biblical texts influencing Rastafarianism. 'If you weren't reading de Laurence in those days, you weren't considered to be doing anything great,' recalled one Jamaican talking about the Rastafarian movement in the 1930s.[143] The sociologist and prize-winning novelist Erna Brodber recalled that during her childhood in the mid-twentieth century Delaurence was a 'mighty powerful force in our rural peasant lives'. In her youth she puzzled over 'whether De Laurence was a man, a set of books or both'. As elsewhere in the Caribbean, he was no mere human but a mystical, magical force.[144] Even in the 1980s his name was a potent force, with one businessman telling Brodber that the amazing successes of a recently instituted anti-crime squad were due to the fact that they were trained 'upon De Laurence'.[145]

In 1931 Norman Washington Manley, the lawyer and future Prime Minister of Jamaica, conducted the defence of an 'East Indian' named James Douthal who stood accused of practising *Obeah*. Indians, mostly Hindus, made up the largest ethnic minority in Jamaica, many thousands having settled there and elsewhere in the Caribbean as indentured labourers, encouraged to emigrate by plantation owners following the full abolition of slavery in 1838. Douthal was the victim of a sting by the Jamaican police, who regularly employed such methods to trap practitioners of *Obeah*. An undercover policeman asked Douthal to do something against an enemy who was threatening his livelihood. For £4 4s. Douthal agreed to make his enemy go mad. He tried to achieve this by lighting three candles and burning a black powder and a piece of paper on which he had written something in red ink. The resulting ashes were to be sprinkled around the gate of the enemy's house. On his arrest, police confiscated books of 'a religious, quasi-religious or mystical nature' and 'several letters to and from large publishing companies abroad showing that the accused bought books from them, and was himself a student on the subject of the carrying of talismans and the burning of incense'.[146]

What such imported mystical works might have been is indicated by a trial three years later. In January 1934 a young man of Cold Spring named Leonard Weakley was sentenced to six months' imprisonment for practising *Obeah*. Two witnesses stated they had consulted Weakley regarding the theft of a cow at Montego Bay. They were suspected of the crime and wanted Weakley to use his magic to ensure they evaded the law. When the police searched Weakley's house they found, *The Sixth & Seventh Book of Moses; The Albertus Magnus or the White and Black Arts for Men and Beasts; The Great Book of Black Magic; The Book of Magical Art*; and the *Hindoo Magic and Indian Occultism*. Weakley had obviously been ordering from the Delaurence catalogue. Asked by the judge how he came to be in possession of such books, Weakley lamely replied that they were not his but they were given to him as security for a loan.[147] When, a month later, Ivanhoe Baker was charged with practising *Obeah*, and books of astrology, personal magnetism, and the *Sixth and Seventh Books of Moses* were found in his house, he similarly said that the books were already in the property when he moved in.[148]

The law against *Obeah* in colonial Jamaica was directed at 'any person who, to effect any fraudulent or unlawful, or for gain, or for the purpose of frightening any person, uses or pretends to use any occult means'. More to the point, it also included a section against any person that 'shall compose, print, sell, or distribute any pamphlet or printed matter calculated to promote the superstition of obeah'. The punishment was up to £30, or in default, up to six months' imprisonment.[149] It was presumably the numerous court cases brought during the 1930s that led the British colonial authorities to instigate further legislation to stem the Delaurence influence. Under the Undesirable Publications Law of 1940 it became an offence 'either to import, to publish, to sell, to distribute, to reproduce or without lawful excuse to be in possession of ... All publications of deLaurence Scott and Company of Chicago in the United States of America relating to divination, magic, occultism, supernatural arts or other esoteric subjects.' *The Book of Magical Arts*, *The Sixth and Seventh Books of Moses*, *The Book of Black Magic*, *The Secret Magic of Abra-Melin The Mage*, *The Magic Key*, and the *Great Book of Magical Art* were all specifically mentioned in the Act. Most of the other works on the banned list were trade union and communist works. Magic and socialism were deemed on a par as pernicious social influences.

While the government justified the ban as a means of protecting the people from those who exploited 'superstition' for financial gain, the Jamaican opposition to colonial rule saw it as a cynical attempt by the British to limit the influence of unionism and the American black empowerment movement.[150] Yet the ban remained in place following Jamaican Independence in 1962, and the list of prohibited grimoires continued to be published periodically in the Jamaican newspapers by government order.[151] The ban, like all such prohibitions, may have kept Delaurence off the shop shelves and out of the newspapers' advertisements, but it could not stop his publications being read and used. American visitors were one possible source of new illicit copies. An anthropologist in Dominica described being incessantly asked by islanders to smuggle in illegal Delaurence tarot cards.[152] Although until the mid-1960s the USA had very strict visa regulations regarding Jamaicans, some migrants who were allowed to work or live there must have purchased Delaurence works. One of these was Bishop Kohath, a Kingston auctioneer and spiritualist healer, who read a range of Delaurence books during a lengthy stay in the USA in the early 1960s. They were central to the religious principles of the Black Jewish sect he founded once back in Jamaica, the Yahvah Little Flock Assembly, Mystic Centre.[153]

The law was the cause of considerable embarrassment in 1970 when the leader of another of Jamaica's numerous sects, Wilbert Peynado, Bishop of the Church of Our Lord Jesus Christ, Montego Bay, and his wife, were arrested for possessing ganja and a copy of the *Master Key*, which a detective found in a trunk in their bedroom. The case was swiftly dismissed by the magistrate's court. A chemist said the substance recovered was 'not ganja within the meaning of the Dangerous Drugs Law', while the presiding magistrate decided speciously, 'this book is apparently written by L. W. deLaurence but there is nothing in the book to show that it is published by deLaurence, Scott & Company incorporated of Chicago.'[154] When Michael Norman Manley, son of Norman W. Manley, came to power as leader of the left-wing People's National Party in 1972 he lifted the ban on seventy-one publications listed in the Undesirable Publications Act. Considering Manley's socialist politics, and policy of rapprochement with Cuba, it was no surprise that most of the newly sanctioned publications were of a socialist nature, but the continued ban on occult works puzzled some. A lengthy article in the leading Jamaican newspaper *The Gleaner* failed to make sense of Manley's decision. 'There must be some good reason for this', its author thought, 'but it has not been made clear to the country. There is a strong suggestion here that freedom of political reading is to be preferred to other types of reading such as Black Magic or the Occult.'[155]

Remarkably the ban remains in place today. The website of the Jamaican Customs Service informs visitors that the following are prohibited items: 'All publications of deLaurence Scott and Company of Chicago in the United States of America relating to divination, magic, occultism or supernatural arts.'[156] Recent research on Jamaican folk medicine reveals that, despite the ban, Delaurence's influence spreads far beyond the chapels of the various revivalist and evangelical groups that flourish on the island. He, his publications, and the company have coalesced into a powerful spiritual and magical force. Delaurence is 'science'. It is also a specific category of occult illness. As one practitioner explained, there is 'natural evil' associated with duppies (the restless spirits of the dead), and 'flying evil' which is associated with white spirits originating from Delaurence. They can cross water and are therefore not restricted to the island. They can be sent, some people think, from Chicago, the home of Delaurence, and also from England.[157] Delaurence can also cause stones to rain down poltergeist-like on houses, and send flying razor blades to shred the clothes of people who have not paid their fees to a practitioner of *his* science.

PULP MAGIC

Delaurence began his publishing empire at a time when most books of substantial length were bound in hardback. This kept production costs high and, consequently, while some of his titles went through numerous editions, their price was still out of the reach of many. In 1913, for instance, we find a small advertisement in one American newspaper offering new copies of *The Book of Magical Art* for sale at $5, knocked down from $12.[1] This may have been a bargain indeed, but it was hardly affordable out of loose change. As we have seen, cheap, mass-produced grimoires had been produced for several hundred years in Europe in the form of chapbooks and the *Bibliothèque bleue*. But it was only in the 1920s and 1930s that a similar boom occurred in America as part of the influential cultural phenomenon of pulp literature. While Delaurence continued to publish his handsome hardbacks with their gold embossed occult symbols, other small, enterprising occult publishers exploited this new, mass-market book format, which consisted of coarse wood-pulp paper pages and glued rather than stitched bindings.

American printers had always suffered from a shortage of rags, and by 1857 the USA was importing over forty million pounds in weight of linen and cotton rags from across the globe to sustain its publishing industry.[2] By the end of the Civil War paper prices were at an all time high, and as one newspaper warned, 'while such prices prevail, cheap books and newspapers are out of the question.' Across Europe and America the race was on to find a commercially viable alternative. Considerable entrepreneurial effort was expended experimenting with the production of straw, hemp, and grass paper. It was wood, however, which proved the most appropriate raw material and America certainly had that in plentiful supply.

The first wood-pulp paper mills were set up in the 1860s and the shift away from rag pulp began. The quality and durability of the paper was certainly not as good, but as a government census agent reported in 1884, 'it answers the transient purpose for which it is employed.' In other words it enabled a massive expansion in newspapers and pulp magazines. The latter became hugely popular during the early twentieth century, providing between a hundred and two hundred pages of escapist racy, pacy fiction involving detectives, cowboys, romance, and science fiction for as little as a dime. Sold in drugstores, bus and train stations, and newspaper stands, pulp literature was directed at and primarily consumed by the urban working classes.[3] It was the success of such cheap, populist literature that eventually led mainstream publishers in the 1930s to adopt the same production values, heralding the paperback revolution.

Pulp also came to signify not only the quality of paper but also the merit of the contents printed on it—worthless, pappy, throwaway literature fit only for those too intellectually limited to digest more serious fare. They were not the sort of publication that found their way into academic and public libraries. Yet their influence was such that, by the late 1930s, American educationalists were waging war on the genre. One high school teacher writing in 1937 observed that some 90 per cent of older high school students read pulp magazines that required 'no mental effort from the reader'. The 'mere mention of "pulp" magazines used to fill my mind with pious wrath,' she said. Further investigation led her to develop strategies to wean them off such literature, admitting, 'the process is slow—dishearteningly slow.'[4] While westerns, romances, and detectives were the mainstay of the pulp fiction industry, dream books, fortune-tellers, and grimoires provided the ultimate fantasy. Their contents held out the promise that readers could shape their own destiny rather than merely live vicariously through the sensational exploits of fictional characters. The market for magic and divination was huge. In 1943 it was estimated that $200,000,000 or so was being handed over to an estimated 80,000 professional fortune-tellers in the United States.[5] The pulp publishers responded. Tens of thousands of copies of *The Sixth and Seventh Books of Moses, Albertus Magnus's Egyptian Secrets, Pow-Wows: Or, The Long-Lost Friend*, and the *Secrets of the Psalms* poured from the presses, selling for a dollar a piece on the streets. In the back of some editions was the publisher's statement in large type, 'Agents can make big money with these books—apply to your jobber or direct to us.'[6] As well as through mail order many copies were sold by urban druggists in African-American districts and in occult merchandise shops often known as 'spiritual', 'religious', or 'candle' shops.[7] In 1929 an American newspaper article observed,

> It is amusing to find how possessors of such volumes as the Sixth and
> Seventh Book of Moses, 'Egyptian Secrets' by Albertus Magnus, 'The

Long Lost Friend' and similar publications set exaggerated store upon them. They think they have great rarities of priceless value. Carefully guarded, these books are usually kept for the eyes of the select few. Yet they are the cheapest books in the market and are as common as almanacs when you know where to shop for them.[8]

The most successful of these new paperback occult ventures was the Dorene Publishing Company founded in New York in 1937 by Joseph W. Spitalnick, the son of Russian immigrants.[9] Spitalnick, who anglicized his name to Joe Kay, made a modest living as a jazz musician and in the 1930s decided to supplement his income by becoming a small-time publisher, setting up first Dorene and then Empire Publishing a few years later. His first venture in the occult paperback market was a manuscript given to him in 1937 by a man named Mr Young, as payment for a debt. Kay hawked the publication door to door and found a ready market amongst the numerous storefront fortune-tellers and psychics in New York. Other works followed, selling for between 1 and $3.

One of Dorene's earliest successes was *Black Herman: Secrets of Magic-Mystery and Legerdemain*, which capitalized on the fame of Benjamin Rucker, the most successful and well-known African-American magician of the era. The cover depicted Rucker sitting astride the globe, garbed in a gown, an amulet around his neck and a scroll with 'Power' written on it in one hand. A publicity photograph of Rucker in a similar pose, scroll in hand, ran with the caption, 'the world famous magician, master of Legerdemain, holds in his hand the paper containing all of the magic secrets which have been hidden for centuries.' The image was one of a powerful African-American reclaiming the mystical wisdom that had for so long been withheld by the whites.

Rucker was born in Amherst, Virginia, in 1892. In his youth he became fascinated by the card tricks performed by a travelling salesman of quack medicine called Prince Herman, whose name was presumably inspired by editions of a popular paperback book on conjuring tricks entitled *Herman's Book of Black Art Magic Made Easy*, written by the well-known American stage magician Alexander Herrmann (1844–96). Rucker became the Prince's assistant and on his death in 1909 Rucker began his own career taking the name Black Herman, and later adopting the titles of Professor and Bachelor of Divinity. So far there was little to distinguish Black Herman from the swarms of snake oil salesmen with their bogus credentials who plied their trade around the States. It was when he branched out into faith-healing and fortune-telling that his financial success took off. He also became increasingly skilled and ambitious with regard to the tricks he performed to drum up trade. By the early 1920s he was famed throughout the Midwest and living comfortably with his wife and children in Chicago. His career and fame

The Seal.

(Fig. 8.)

The most obedient Angels and Spirits of this Seal of the Seven Planets are the following: Ahaeb, Baneh, Yeschnath, Hoschiah, Betodah, Leykof, Vamdus, Zarenar, Sahon.

This Seal, when laid upon the treasure earth, or when placed within the works of a mine, will reveal all the precious contents of the mine. As the VII. Arcanorum.

END OF THE SIXTH BOOK OF MOSES.

FIG. 23 Seals from an early-twentieth-century pulp edition of the *Sixth and Seventh Books of Moses*.

advanced even further when he moved to New York where his performances at Liberty Hall, the headquarters of Marcus Garvey's Universal Negro Improvement Association, sold out night after night. He loved to play on the fact that he possessed real magical powers derived from his African ancestry. One room in his New York home was decked out with an altar decorated with occult symbols, candles, and a human skull, and African masks hung on the walls. His success was only marred by a short stint in Sing Sing prison for fortune-telling. He died performing onstage at the Old Palace Theater, Louisville, Kentucky, in 1934.[10]

Although Joe Kay first published *Black Herman* four years after Rucker's death (we can dismiss the Dorene claim that it was the fifteenth deluxe edition), it is possible that the magician wrote some of it. Rucker had some publishing experience, having written a cheap how-to guide called *Easy Pocket Tricks That You Can Do*. In the late 1920s he had also funded the publication of *The Spokesman*, a short-lived monthly magazine for New York African-Americans, in which the occasional interesting article punctuated acres of space devoted to promoting himself.[11] Some sections of *Black Herman* read clearly like the sort of puff that quack doctors and stage magicians had long published to promote themselves on their travels, and the preface and foreword are dated 1925, New York. The section recounting the extraordinary 'Life of the Great Black Herman' smacks of familiar self-publicity. Its vaunted boasts of great secrets discovered during fabled global travels follows in the footsteps of occult hucksters like Charles Roback, though Rucker was perhaps influenced more by the legendary journeys of the likes of Noble Drew Ali.

Black Herman's 'Life' claimed he was born in the 'dark jungles of Africa'.[12] He was possessed of 'knowledge of hidden mysteries' from birth, and it was foretold that he would grow up to be the greatest magician that ever lived. At the age of 10 he was taken to America by a missionary. As a young man he travelled to Cairo, 'where all the secrets of the ages are held'. He next moved on to India where he befriended a great Hindu magician. In China he fell in with a secret society of robbers. He feigned his death by using his arcane knowledge of medicine, and his friends had his body sent in a casket to the Zulu king in Africa. People under-standably fled in fear when he appeared to return from the dead when it was opened. After a few weeks of further amazing adventures in Africa he set sail for France, and then moved on to Britain for a short stay before returning to America the wisest magician in the world. He printed brief encomiums from the places he had visited. London said with regret, 'We hated to give him up,' while Paris uttered messianically, 'He is the first and last.' Columbus, Ohio, was much more down to earth in its praise: 'It is more fun to see Herman than it is to see a barrel of monkeys with their tails chopped off.'[13]

The sum total of the wisdom garnered from Herman's extraordinary experi-ences, as revealed in *Secrets of Magic-Mystery*, consisted of no more than simple

FIG. **24** *Black Herman: Secrets of Magic-Mystery and Legerdemain.*

sleight-of-hand tricks, basic horoscopes for each month of the year, and a guide to the signification of dreams. It is only the poorly written final section, entitled 'The Story of Oriental Magic I found in the Orient an Ancient Practice: Called by some the Magic of the Kabbara Herbologist, Mystic', which takes us briefly into the realms of the grimoire. It includes advice on how 'to bring happiness to broken lives' by carrying the Seal of Moses in one's pocket, and the following instructions on how 'To Cross or Hex a Person: Cast a Spell—No Matter Where':

> There are many different ways I gathered to do this, one of the most popular is to put some hemp string in the person's path and then some Oriental Gum—another way is to use some crossing powder, Confusion Dust—another way is to send them some Black Art Powder and Oil.

A remedy to banish the 'source of unhappiness' required the reader to wash all the floors, doors, and beds, everything in fact, with Chinese Wash and then to say the following prayer every day:

> O! Lord, Father, King please help (name here) thy child to banish unhappiness, misery, to remove it at the source. Help me. Father, to overcome these things that hold me down. Thank you, and then to believe all misery banished and it will be banished.

No ceremonial spirit conjuration here, and as the above extracts suggest, some of the spells were basically vehicles for product promotion. A recipe for gaining the love of the opposite sex also required a pint of Chinese Wash, which was a simple cleansing scrubbing liquid containing 'oriental gums', lemon and ginger grass, which accrued a reputation at the time for also cleansing rooms of evil spirits and bad luck.[14] Another spell for 'uncrossing friends' required Van Van Oil, King Solomon Oil, Dragon's Blood, John the Conqueror Root, and Devils Shoe String, all of which were commercial hoodoo products. Dragon's blood, the red resin obtained from two species of *Dracaena* trees found in Africa, had long been used in Western folk medicine and magic, and in nineteenth-century England it was commonly bought from chemists for use in love spells.[15] John the Conqueror, the legendary name for various roots such as jalap and galangal, which were marketed as powerful luck charms, was a distinctive component of the African-American folk magic tradition.[16]

This commercialization of charm production developed out of the flourishing trade in herbs, charms, perfumes, oils, candles, and other ingredients sold by druggists and the numerous 'spiritual', 'religious', or 'candle' stores that sprang up in urban African-American communities. Many such shops were merely retailers, purchasing goods from mail order wholesalers run mostly by whites. Quite a few of these companies were offshoots of toiletry and cosmetics manufacturers already prospering by making beauty products for the African-American community. As a 1920s survey of advertisements in the *Chicago Defender* and the *Negro World*, the leading African-American newspapers with a nation-wide circulation, showed, there was a huge market for skin lighteners and hair-straightening products amongst the newspaper-reading public at the time.[17] One such enterprise was the Valmor toiletry company of Chicago, a subsidiary of which, the King Novelty Curio Company, produced a comprehensive catalogue of charms and spiritual products during the mid-1930s. It included seals from the *Sixth and Seventh Books of Moses*, dream books, and occult texts, along with lingerie, cosmetics, and hoodoo products.[18] These companies also sent salesmen around southern African-American communities, and hired representatives, such as Mattie Sampson of Brownville, Georgia, who sold the products of the Lucky Heart Company and the Curio Products Company. One of her best sellers was the Mystic Mojo Love Sachet.[19]

Big strides had been made in African-American educational provision during the 1920s and 1930s, though several southern States lagged badly behind. In Louisiana, for example, over a fifth of African-Americans had no schooling at all, leading the founder of the Nation of Islam, the mysterious W. P. Fard, to denounce such obscurantism as 'tricknollogy', the deliberate attempt to keep the people enslaved through illiteracy and therefore ignorance.[20] In the northern States and cities, however, literacy rates were high by the 1940s. Consequently the press came to compete with the Church as the most important institutional influence on African-American social and political opinion.[21] Newspapers depend heavily on advertising revenue as well as purchasers, of course, and so the *Chicago Defender* and the *Negro World* also became important facilitators in the commercialization of off-the-shelf magic. They provided both magical practitioners and mail order manufacturers with a cheap means of reaching potential African-American and white clients living far beyond their shops and warehouses.[22] As we saw in the last chapter, in the nineteenth and early twentieth centuries the press had helped generate the huge market in quack medicines and astrology, and now in the early twentieth century the African-American press led a similar boom for hoodoo and conjure products. A trawl of five African-American newspapers over three months in 1925 turned up numerous advertisements for such products as the Sacred Scarab Ring of the Pharoahs, which would shower riches, success, and happiness on the wearer, the Imp-O-Luck Charm to '*make* things come *your* way', and the Mysto Talisman Ring that 'wards off evil spirits, sickness, spells'.

African-American magic also kept pace with other commercial developments. By the 1960s those Hoodoo favourites, graveyard bones, were increasingly being substituted by plastic ones, while the increasing use of smoke detectors in rental properties led to the development of incense aerosol sprays for ritual use.[23]

Charms, grimoires, and dream books were also bought wholesale and sold directly to clients by hoodoo workers, conjure doctors, and spiritualist preachers. In 1940 *The New York Amsterdam-News* estimated that in Harlem alone more than 50,000 people were consulting such people annually, spending nearly $1,000,000.[24] One of the most common reasons was to ensure success in illicit gambling, the hugely popular Numbers Racket in particular. This involved the picking of a three-digit number, the winning combination of which was picked randomly the following day by such means as drawing it from the racehorse results. A whole magical trade developed around this, just as treasure seeking had done in previous centuries. The commercial success of John the Conqueror was due, in part, to its purchase by gamblers. As one conjure doctor pitched: 'Y'know, the women and the numbers, they's both jus' alike. Ain't neither of 'em can hod out long when yuh got Big Johnny workin' fo' yuh.'[25] Gamblers also splashed themselves all over with magic perfumes such as Essence of Van Van (10 per cent oil of lemon grass in alcohol).[26] If this was not enough, psalms for luck, such as those in the *Secrets of the Psalms*, and the fourth and 114th psalm from the *Sixth and Seventh Books*, could be employed. The latter instructed, 'if you desire success in your trade or business, write this Psalm with its appropriate holy name upon clean parchment, and carry it about your person constantly in a small bag prepared especially for this purpose.'[27] These psalms were also sold in the form of medals and written on pieces of parchment in red ink.

On the last page of *Black Herman* was the following statement: 'I am told one can gain a Mastery over Occultism by reading and studying some of the works of Lewis de Claremont, L. W. De Laurcne, Wait, Macgrueger, Duval Spencer and Young, and in this way can help to become an initiate.' The reader is already familiar with the work of Delaurence, Waite, and Macgregor, but what of de Claremont, Young, and Duval Spencer?[28] It is certainly curious that these are the only three names spelt correctly, the others perhaps being unfamiliar to the typesetter. The reason for this may have been because they were one and the same man; someone who, it is likely, also had a hand in writing parts of *Black Herman*. It was a Mr Young who gave Joe Kay his first occult manuscript for publication. Young's name was also given to a brand of Chinese Wash sold by the Oracle Products Company. The earliest occult publications of Lewis de Claremont, who was described in advertisements as 'the famed adept', and was depicted as a Hindu swami, were *The Ancient Book of Formulas* and *Legends of Incense, Herb and Oil Magic*, both of which were published by Oracle. The latter book contained sections on 'How to fix Devil's Shoestring' and other products mentioned in *Black Herman*. It would appear that de Claremont was the nom de plume of Young, who was also the proprietor of the Occult Products Company.[29] In 1940 de Claremont/Young assigned the copyright of his publications over to

Dorene. Amongst them were *The Seven Steps to Power* and *The 7 Keys to Power: The Master's Book of Profound Esoteric Law*, which contained recipes for candle magic, benedictions against enemies, dream magic, and numerology, along with discourses on hypnotism and Hindu magic. They were advertised a few years later as 'Two of the World's Foremost Occult Best Sellers'.[30] According to Ed Kay, the son of Joe Kay, Young was also the one and the same as Henri Gamache, who wrote a series of magic pulps in the 1940s, which were published by Sheldon Publications and marketed by Dorene, among them the *Mystery of the Long Lost 8th, 9th and 10th Books of Moses* (1948) and the *Master Key to Occult Secrets* (1945). Gamache's *Master Book of Candle Burning* had the most enduring influence. One expert on African-American folk magic, who visited many magic shops during the 1970s, found that it was for sale in every single one.[31]

Whether Gamache and de Claremont were one and the same is open to question. The style and content of Gamache's work are significantly different from that of most of de Claremont's booklets, which heaved with product plugs.[32] Gamache's approach consisted of the presentation of conscientiously referenced snippets of spells and magic culled from an eclectic mix of nineteenth- and twentieth-century discourses on ancient Judaism, Christian, and other Middle Eastern religions, and studies of African, Indian, European, and Caribbean folk-lore.[33] Indeed, the subtitle of the *Master Key* was 'A study of the survival of primitive customs in a modern world with sources and origins'. In the Preface he explained how it had taken him three years to accumulate all the material. His reason for going to all this effort? Because 'it presents truthfully the lengths to which humanity will extend itself in an endeavour to gain what its heart desires.' Gamache was not disingenuous enough to claim that his motives were solely educational, yet neither was he ready to acknowledge that the book was intended to be used as a grimoire; yet it was, along with the *Mystery of the Long Lost 8th, 9th and 10th Books of Moses*. Chapter 3 of the latter, entitled '44 Secret Keys to Universal Power', consisted of a series of magical seals and amulets for love, recovering buried treasure, wreaking vengeance, and protection gathered from diverse sources. Gamache turned educational literature into magical literature, performing a sort of alchemy by taking a mish-mash of excerpts from magical traditions across the globe and revealing them as the universal keys to the founding occult wisdom of Moses.

It is revealing of the cultural reach of American pulp magic that as early as 1949 an anthropologist researching the Carib culture in British Honduras, now known as Belize, referred to the influence there and in neighbouring countries of *The Seven Keys to Power*, *The Secrets of the Psalms*, and *The Ten Lost Books of the Prophets*.[34] In Jamaica, and elsewhere in the Caribbean where the Delaurence oeuvre had been banned in 1940, the de Claremont and Gamache books filled the vacuum.[35] During the second half of the 1940s a Kingston mail order company, Spencer's Advertising Service and Commission Agency, regularly advertised the full range of Gamache and de Claremont publications in the *Daily Gleaner*, along with *Secrets of Psalms* and the *Long Lost Friend*, all of which were available from Dorene.[36] A survey of the books sold by Kingston drugstores half a century later found that they consisted almost exclusively of dream books and the works of Gamache and de Claremont.[37] They never achieved the mythic status of Delaurence, but their works were seen as being more accessible. As a Montserrat 'scientist' explained, '*Sixth and Seventh Books of Moses* do not help much. Help only a master or adept. The naïve medium not able to operate that book. They use *Black Herman* or the *Seven Steps to Power* and the *Seven Keys to Power*.'[38]

The Hispanic market

Dorene also turned an eye to the burgeoning Hispanic market, producing a Spanish translation of de Claremont's *Legends of Incense, Herb and Oil Magic* in 1938.[39] The decision to do this may have been triggered by the evident growth of the Puerto Rican population in New York, the area of East Harlem in particular. During the 1920s it had been a predominantly Italian district, the biggest in America, with a large Jewish community as well, but in the 1930s many moved out while increasing numbers of African-Americans and Hispanics, mostly Puerto Ricans, moved in.[40] The sound of Spanish voices became a familiar sound on the streets of northern cities for the first time.

Botánicas were and are key institutions in Puerto Rico's tradition of folk medicine, selling not only herbs but also Catholic sacramentals, incense, candles, oils, statues, and representations of the saints, along with charms and grimoires—in other words, all the ritual paraphernalia required by adherents of *Espiritismo* and *Santería*.[41] As One Puerto Rican *botánica* shop owner in 1960s Chicago reported, most of her business was not concerned with drugstore medicines for natural ailments, but 'supplies to people affected with *brujeria* [witchcraft]'. Another important sideline for her were products such as incense and bath herbs to promote luck, particularly for the numbers.[42] Probably the first High Street *botánica* to be set up in America was that established in East Harlem in 1921 by a Guatemalan named Alberto Rendón. He had worked in a drugstore and noticed how many African Americans and West Indians came to purchase herbal remedies, bath oils, and powders for magical purposes. So he opened the West Indies Botanical Garden, selling his own herbal products, some of which were based on plants sent to him especially from Puerto Rico. As the ethnic balance of the area changed Rendón shifted the focus of his product range from the hoodoo and *Obeah* requirements of his black customers to those of the followers of Central American *Espiritismo*. The store's name was consequently changed to Botánica.[43] Over the next few decades, as Hispanic immigration increased, particularly with the huge exodus from Cuba as a consequence of the Cuban Revolution of 1959, *botánicas* spread across the United States.[44] By 1970 there were at least twenty-five in Chicago, and in the past couple of decades they have become particularly popular in the Southwest of the USA, with several hundred stores in Southern California alone.[45]

The Mexican magical healing tradition of *curandismo* has been practised in the southern USA for much longer, and in the mid-twentieth century folklorists and anthropologists commented on how it had remained largely impervious to European-American influence. It was not completely free of it though. The lure of foreign occult secrets was irresistible to some. In the 1970s a Texan *curandero* practitioner attempted to impress one researcher by showing him 'two books on witchcraft, which he would not let me touch. Since he could not read English, he showed us pictures from the books, commenting on each.' Another *curandero*, eager to impress, read some passages from the Bible and a bilingual edition of Mary Baker Eddy's *Science and Health with Key to the Scriptures*.[46] It is true, though, that the North American grimoire tradition had less impact in Mexico and other Central American countries than it did in the Caribbean. A major reason for this is that Spanish grimoire publishing kept apace.

Between the two World Wars several editions of the *Libro de San Cipriano* were produced by publishers in Barcelona and Madrid, and Portuguese versions in Lisbon.[47] These could be ordered by overseas customers of course, but during the late nineteenth and early twentieth centuries there was a huge migration of Spaniards to the Americas. Between 1900 and 1924 some five million left, heading mainly for Argentina and Cuba, though 3.8 million returned home. Around one-third of the emigrants were Galicians, and another 20 per cent came from neighbouring Leon and Asturias.[48] These were, of course, the northwestern regions where the *Libro de San Cipriano* or *Ciprianillo* tradition was strongest and some emigrants must have brought copies with them. Ethnographers studying the religious cultures of Cuba during the first few decades of the twentieth century found the *Libro San Cipriano* had been adopted by *Santería* practitioners, and was being sold along with editions of the main French grimoires.[49] Judging from a copy found on a wizard imprisoned by the São Paulo authorities in 1904, Portuguese migrants also brought copies with them.[50]

Under Franco's regime occult publications were effectively suppressed in Spain, and it was only from the late 1970s onwards that a new wave of editions poured off the Spanish presses.[51] In the meantime Spanish language grimoire

FIG. 25 *La Magia Suprema Negra* (1916).

production shifted decisively to Latin America.[52] Buenos Aires, the principal post-war publishing centre in the region, and also the home to hundreds of thousands of Galicians, was one source of grimoires. As early as 1916 a limited edition Solomonic work entitled *La Magia Suprema Negra* was produced there, though its stated place of publication was Rome. Its equally spurious author was the legendary tenth-century monk Jonas Sufurino, finder of the *Libro de San Cipriano*.[53] The man who supposedly translated it from the German and edited it was the mysterious Dr Moorne. An early-twentieth-century catalogue of cheap occult publications produced by the Madrid publishers Librería de Pueyo shows that Dr Moorne was cited as the translator of a raft of cheap magic books at the time, few of which now survive, such as *El Libro de Simón el Mago* (2 pesetas), and a joint Spanish edition of the *Enchirideon* and *Grimoire de Pape Honorius* (6 pesetas).[54] It was in South America, though, that his name became most well known, particularly in Argentina. This was not only due to the grimoires he purportedly translated, but also for a long-running, successful set of Tarot cards attributed to him, *El Supremo Arte de Echar Las Cartas*, which were first published around the 1930s and sold far and wide by peddlers.

It is possible that the earliest South American edition of the *Livro de São Cipriano* was produced in neighbouring Brazil. A São Paulo publisher advertised a booklet for sale in 1916 entitled *O Verdadeiro e Último Livro de São Cipriano* (*The True and Last Book of Saint Ciprian*).[55] Dr Moorne's *Magia Natural* was certainly published there in 1928, testifying to the pre-war origins of Brazil's occult publishing industry. It was in the 1960s, though, that the first mass-market editions of the *Livro de São Cipriano* were printed in the country. By the 1990s publishers in Rio and São Paulo had put out at least seventeen different editions.[56] Some continued to reprint the lists of buried treasures to be found in Portugal and Galicia.[57] Treasure was probably not uppermost in the minds of most purchasers of the *Livro de São Cipriano*. Many were and are followers of *Umbanda*, a hetero-dox, protean religion based around a pantheon of spirits including Yoruba deities, and the spirits of native Indians and slaves. It emerged in the 1920s, growing out of *Candomblé*, folk Catholicism, Kardecism, and spiritualism, and spread rapidly from the mid-century onwards in the country's industrial centres.[58] The *Livro de São Cipriano* was added to the mix and became a popular seller for the Rio de Janeiro occult publisher Editora Espiritualista, which, from the 1950s, produced a range of books on magic and spiritualism for those interested in or initiated into *Umbanda*.[59]

It is likely that it was these Latin American editions of the *Libro de San Cipriano*, rather than the earlier Spanish ones, that leached into the indigenous Indian magical traditions in some regions of South America. In the 1970s the anthro-pologist Michael Taussig found itinerant Putumayo Indian magical healers selling a version of the *Libro de San Cipriano*, along with roots, barks, sulphur, and mirrors, in their street stalls in the southern Colombian town of Puerto Tejada. One copy he saw was ascribed to Jonas Surfurino and contained 'The Clavicule of Solomon, Pacts of Exorcism, The Red Dragon and the Infernal Goat, the Black Hen, School of Sorcery, The Great Grimorio and the Pact of Blood'. The Putumayo were thought by the dominant Hispanic population of the region to be adepts in the healing arts and deep in both good and bad magic—a reputation that they understandably exploited commercially.[60] In the 1980s the *Libro de San Cipriano* was similarly found to be a significant component of the famed healing practices of the Bolivian Kallawaya. Since at least the eighteenth century the Kallawaya, who live on the eastern slopes of the Andes near the Peruvian border, have been consulted from far and wide for their herbal and magical knowledge. Some of the tribe continue to make a living as itinerant practitioners, bringing their herbs, stones, and amulets with them. Not only do they consult the contents of the *Libro de San Cipriano*, the book itself is imbued with purifying qualities.[61]

During the second half of the twentieth century Mexico City was probably the most active and influential centre of pulp grimoire production in Latin America.[62] A survey of the cheap books on magic and divination sold by peddlers in two Peruvian towns in 1967 revealed Mexican titles such as *La Magia Negra*, *La Magia Blanca*, and *La Magia Roja*.[63] In 1976 a Mexican publisher produced the first Latin American edition of the *Sixth and Seventh Books of Moses*. It was apparently a translation of one of the US editions and had a print run of 5,000.[64] Copies of these Mexican grimoires became a staple product for *botánicas* and *yerberias* across Central and South America, and in southern US towns with large Hispanic populations like Tucson, Arizona.[65] In the past few years a new generation of Mexican pulp spell books with cheap-looking garish covers have appeared, such as *Brujeriía: hechizos, conjuros y encantamientos* and *Brujeria a la Mexicana*. These also sell well across the border and can be purchased mail order from the likes of Indio Products, one of the biggest mystical supplies companies in the States, founded by Martin Mayer in 1991. Mayer's aunt and uncle had run a hoodoo drugstore in Chicago's South Side during the 1920s.[66]

The cultural influence of Mexican magical commerce in the USA is also evident in the recent growth of the Catholic folk cult of *Santísima Muerte* (Holy Death), which some of the recent Mexican pulp grimoires promote. The image of the spirit of the Holy Death is that of a robed female skeleton. Because of this macabre image she is associated with evil by some, and is seen as the patroness of Mexican drug lords. Yet in Mexican folk religion the *Santa Muerte* has also become an intercessionary patroness, resorted to by 'good' Catholics as well as those seeking to inflict harm.[67] The creators of spiritual products have been quick to adopt the striking image, using it to market prayer cards, Holy Death incense sprays, and the like, supplanting that of the Hindu Swami popular on earlier hoodoo product labels. It is through the *botánicas* that she has also been incorporated by some into the pantheon of *Santería*, which has become increasingly popular amongst Mexicans. A few years ago the Bishop of León called on the Mexican government to suppress a newly created independent church, *La Iglesia Católica Tradicional Mex-Usa*, dedicated to the worship of the *Santa Muerte*. The growth of the cult in Southern California and Arizona has also led to expressions of concern regarding the influence of *yerberías* and *botánicas* and their merchandise.[68]

The war against grimoires in Germany

It was in Germany, though, that the publication of cheap grimoires proved most contentious. Esotericism flourished in early-twentieth-century Germany and Austro-Hungary. As in England, America, and France, there was considerable middle-class interest in spiritualism, ancient religions, mystical belief systems, and ritual magic.[69] Theosophy was particularly popular and gave birth to the spiritualist Anthroposophy movement of Rudolf Steiner. By 1912 there were also thirty-three Mazdaznan branches in Germany, Austro-Hungary, and Switzerland. Leipzig became the cult's second home outside of Chicago. Numerous homegrown groups sprung up. A few years before the First World War the *Ordo Novi Templi*, which claimed an occult inheritance from the Templars, was founded by the Austrian right-wing anti-Semite, Jörg Lanz von Liebenfels. He was a follower of the mystical, Aryan supremacist doctrine of his fellow Austrian, the writer and runologist Guido von List (1848–1919). Their racist philosophy of a supreme Teutonic life force, known as Ariosophy, later fed into Nazi racial ideology. Another society that claimed a Templar heritage was the *Ordo Templi Orientis* (OTO), whose overtly magical philosophy was based, they said, on Eastern mysticism, and Masonic and hermetic secrets. Aleister Crowley set up a branch in England. The writings of Éliphas Lévi were an undoubted influence, as was Beverley Randolph's conception of sex magic—a strong theme in German ritual magic.

   This esoteric boom generated a thriving occult publishing industry. In 1906 the German Theosophical Society set up their own publishing house in Leipzig, which produced not only theosophical works but also astrological periodicals and books.[70] The list of the Berlin publisher Herman Barsdorf Verlag contained a mix of erotic books and texts on ancient magic, including translations of the works of Francois Lenormant. Its most impressive occult publishing venture was the five-volume *Magische Werke* (*Magic Works*) (1921), which included editions of the *Heptameron, Fourth Book of Occult Philosophy*, and the *Arbatel*. The 1922 catalogue of another Berlin publisher, Nirwana-Verlag für Lebensreform, contained 937 books on astrology, religion, spiritualism, magic, and sex, which were advertised in the form of a poem:

> Study the catalogue diligently,
> And quickly choose
> Many books, rare, ideal
> Solid works full of power,
> For every scientific branch,
> Especially for the occultist.[71]

Another leading publisher in the field was Johannes Baum. By the 1930s Baum Verlag had become a major force in occult publishing with a series of titles on modern Rosicrucianism and books such as the *Handbuch Der Astromagie* (1926). One of Baum's most prolific authors was G. W. Surya, the nom de plume of the occultist Demeter Georgievitz-Weitzer (1873–1949), who before the First World War was editor of the popular esoteric magazine *Zentralblatt für Okkultismus*, and who later wrote guides on Rosicrucianism, medicine, and alchemy. Equally prolific was an intriguing character named Franz Sättler (b. 1884), an expert on Arabic dialect and founder of the Adonistic Society, a sex-magic group formed in 1925. Under the pseudonym Dr Musallam, he wrote a series of publications for the Berlin publisher Bartels on astrology, chiromancy, magic, and necromancy, which collectively came to be known as the *Zauberbibel* or *Bible of Magic*.[72]

During the first two decades of the twentieth century Bartels was the main producer of grimoires in Germany, reprinting versions of works culled mainly from Scheible's *Das Kloster*. It published several large compilations of between 500 and 700 pages including the *Romanusbüchlein*, *Der wahrhaftige feurige Drache*, and the *Sixth and Seventh Books of Moses*.[73] Bartels was also responsible for the introduction to a wider audience of *Das Buch Jezira*, described as the 'Big Book of the Moses Books'. The title was borrowed from the *Sefer Jezirah*, but its contents consisted of the eighth, ninth, tenth, eleventh, and twelfth books of Moses. In 1917 it was noted that a Munich bookshop was selling numerous copies of this publication to women, probably wives and mothers seeking protective magical aid for their husbands and sons in the trenches.[74] Bartels also sold cheaper single editions of the *Eighth and Ninth Books of Moses*, as did other publishers such as Max Wendels Verlag in Dresden and Hülsmann Verlag in Leipzig. It was sales of the *Sixth and Seventh Books of Moses*, though, that far outstripped the other grimoires in Germany. During the 1920s and early 1930s at least five publishers were producing editions, most with Philadelphia as the place of publication.[75]

It was presumably one of these editions that police found amongst spiritualist books in the house of Fritz Angerstein, the director of a cement works near

Siegen, Westphalia, who in 1924 murdered eight members of his household with an axe, including his wife. She was a devout Pietist who had apparently miscarried several times. These influences no doubt contributed to the morbid premonitions she experienced, and which played on her husband.[76] Rumour would later have it that Angerstein was inspired by the hope of activating a seal said to be contained in one edition of the *Sixth and Seventh Books of* Moses, which would provide great riches to anyone who killed nine people. The case attracted press attention around the world, and he was beheaded in November 1925. As well as the occult connection, the case was also notable as one of the last in which the authorities took seriously the notion that the violent last moments of the murdered were imprinted on the retina for a short time afterwards. Local police took photographs of the eyes of one of Angerstein's victims after someone in the morgue said they saw the image of Angerstein with a raised axe in the eyes of the corpse.[77]

During the Weimar Republic and the Third Reich there were at least seventeen court cases in Germany involving the belief in witchcraft, some of which involved the 'Moses Books'.[78] A report on one trial in the town of Stade in 1931 commented that spell books were to be found in many houses in the area. When, in 1935, an old couple in the Black Forest complained of being plagued by witches and ghosts, they hired two men from the town of Haslach who tried to rid the house of evil influences by reading invocations from the *Sixth and Seventh Books of Moses*.[79] Most such cases seem to have been prosecuted under the general laws for fraud, but the authorities in Bavaria were particularly well equipped to deal with the occult arts. Article 54 of the Bavarian police code allowed for the imprisonment of those who practised magic, spirit conjuring, and divination for profit. Just after the end of the First World War the military authorities in Bavaria extended this clause to punish those who lectured on such subjects without having any scientific qualifications.[80]

Numerous sensational and dubious claims have been made regarding the influence of occultism on Hitler and the architects of the Third Reich. There certainly were prominent Nazis who had an active interest in various aspects of the occult, most notably Himmler, Rudolf Hess, and *SS-Oberführer* Karl Maria Wiligut, who, influenced by the work of Guido von List, developed his own mystic 'key' to the meaning of runes.[81] From the beginning of the Third Reich, however, the authorities were concerned that occult philosophies could undermine popular confidence in the supremacy and glorious destiny of the Reich. A recent authoritative study has rightly stressed that the Nazis' 'selective affinity for occultism was dwarfed by the enormity of their regime's hostility to the occult movement more generally'.[82]

Predictions and prophecies had long been exploited by rulers for political propaganda purposes, but they had to be strictly controlled; otherwise, they could unsettle and sow fear amongst the populace. The Nazi authorities decided that the balancing act was not worth it. In the autumn of 1933 the police in Berlin, Hanover, and Cologne ordered newspapers to cease accepting advertisements for astrologers. The following year, the Berlin police banned the sale and production of astrological periodicals and almanacs. Booksellers' stocks were confiscated.[83] The next step was to suppress the wider occult community. Individuals were targeted—people like Eugen Grosche, a Berlin bookseller and founder of the *Fraternitas Saturni*, whose private library was seized by the Gestapo.[84] In July 1937 an official decree outlawed Freemasonry, occult societies, and religious sects like the Christian Scientists throughout the country. The extent to which these clampdowns affected provincial publishers is not clear, though the occult publishers Baum Verlag and Regulus Verlag of Görlitz, which published books on astrology and Nostradamus, evidently continued to operate until June 1941 when the authorities rounded up occultists of all shades, closed down all occult publishing houses, and confiscated publications.[85] The trigger for this purge was the propaganda embarrassment of Hess's bizarre flight to Scotland, which Goebbels portrayed as the actions of a man unhinged by his association with astrologers and seers. A line was drawn in the sand, and occultism would no longer be a public issue in Nazi Germany.

During the Third Reich the authorities were concerned not only with forms of mass-market divination but also the esoteric belief systems embraced by the middle classes and urban blue-collar workers. Occult philosophies came to be seen as antagonistic to the shared ideology being forged by the Nazi regime. When, in the autumn of 1937 the SS newspaper *Das Schwarze Korps* printed a series of articles on the danger of *Aberglaube* (superstition), which it typically blamed on Jews and the Catholic Church, the focus was on the evils of spiritualism and astrology.[86] The world of rural folk magic slipped under the radar: this was 'superstition' that had no philosophical or organized framework and therefore posed no threat to Nazi hegemony. Cunning-folk were periodically prosecuted, but no more so than in Weimar or Imperial Germany. The Third Reich was, nevertheless, hardly a propitious time to publish popular grimoires—particularly the *Sixth and Seventh Books of Moses* with its pseudo-Hebraic characters.[87]

Neither did the academic study of 'traditional' magical beliefs seem to attract the same opprobrium as intellectual occultism. Indeed, Himmler's interest in the idea that the witch trials were a Church-inspired crime against the German people led to the formation of the *H-Sonderkommando* unit, a team of around eight researchers employed to find and catalogue early modern witch prosecutions in German-language archives.[88] Regarding contemporary folk beliefs, the Nazis enthusiastically promoted the academic respectability of German *Volkskunde* (folklore), funding research and creating the first professorial chair in the subject in 1933. Nazi support for folklore research came at a price of course. The discipline was partly under the brief of Himmler's SS Office of Ancestral Inheritance, and partly under the supervision and control of Alfred Rosenberg, one of the architects of the Nazis' racial policies and Hitler's supervisor for 'All Intellectual and Worldview Schooling and Education'. Folklore had to have a purpose beyond mere scholarly interest. If folklorists wanted to be sponsored they had to work for the good of the National Socialist message, legitimating Nazi racial theories and promoting the purity and nobility of 'true' Nordic–German traditions, folktales, and rural cultures.[89] Those who did not display sufficient enthusiasm for the Nazi 'project' were swiftly unseated from their chairs. One of those who prospered was Adolf Spamer, a Nazi party member and director of the Regional Research Office for Folklore in the Reich Union Folk-Nation and Homeland. He also happened to be the leading expert on German folk grimoires.

In 1907 the German Union of Folklorist Associations agreed to organize the creation of a Collection of German Formulae for Charms and Incantations. This was inspired, in part, by the collection of German manuscript charms, celestial letters, and magic manuscripts gathered by Albrecht Dieterich, an eminent expert on ancient Egyptian magic who was also fascinated by German folk magic. It was no doubt also inspired by the publication in 1902 of the pioneering assemblage of Nordic manuscript grimoires and charms by the Norwegian clergyman and politician Anton Christian Bang.[90] Spamer was instrumental in getting the Union's project underway, and in 1914 published an *Appeal to Collect German Formulae* to German, Swiss, and Austrian folklore associations. Over the next few decades he personally accumulated a comprehensive collection of published grimoires and manuscripts.[91]

Spamer's ambitious ideas for German folklore research and willingness to cooperate with Rosenberg's bureau meant that by 1936 he had been elevated to Professor of Folklore at Berlin University, and was described by one colleague as 'the Pope of *Volkskunde*'. Yet in 1938 he fell out of favour due, in part, to scholarly differences with another influential folklorist more closely associated with Rosenberg's agenda.[92] Ill health further inhibited his work during the early 1940s. His fortunes improved soon after the war, though, when he became the first academic folklorist to be appointed in Russian-controlled East Germany, becoming Professor of *Volkskunde* at the Technical University of Dresden. His passion for folk magic resurfaced publicly and led to the establishment of the Corpus of German Formulae for Charms and Incantations. In 1949 he gave a lecture on magic books and spells to the German Academy of Sciences, and by the time of his death in 1954 the Corpus collection housed an impressive 22,000 items. Some of the fruits of his research on grimoires were collated in a book tracking the bibliographical history of the *Romanusbüchlein* in which he meticulously traced the origins of nineteen of the charm formulae it contained. A posthumous article on magic books also appeared, which recorded the letters received between 1925 and 1935 by a Dresden publisher of grimoires, revealing the popular demand for instruction on practical magic.[93]

For some, the cleansing of the curse of Nazism also required the rationalizing of German society. The enthusiasm for occultism in the early twentieth century was viewed as a contributor to the *Sonderweg*, or special path that the course of Germany history took in its development into a racist totalitarian state.[94] So, in post-war Germany, middle-class occultism, alternative medicine, and folk magic were seen by some as an obstacle to the forging of a new social and moral enlightenment. There was a raft of court cases involving witch belief and magic in post-war Germany. This has been interpreted by historians as a result of increased witchcraft accusations arising from general economic and social instability, and related to the large number of single women returning to rural communities after the war.[95] From a contemporary perspective it was confirmation of the 'superstitious' darkness that had flourished during the Third Reich. For anti-superstition crusaders the two main pillars upholding the edifice of superstition were the influence of *Hexenbanners* (witch doctors) and the dissemination of occult literature prior to and after the Third Reich.

For several years after the war the German publishing industry was understandably in bad shape. Paper and ink were in short supply and the transport network badly damaged. The two major centres of German publishing, Berlin and Leipzig, had suffered from Allied bombing. Currency reform also led to further short-term hardship and a shortage of money. In Soviet-controlled Germany publishing houses were either nationalized or forced out of business. One consequence of the blow to the old established publishing industry was the expansion of publishing in West German provincial centres such as Stuttgart and Hamburg. Although Allied authorities in western Germany banned the writings of prominent Nazis, censorship was not heavy-handed and only in the French sector were publishers required to submit manuscripts for inspection.[96]

The Third Reich and occupation forces aside, democratic Germany had its own strong tradition of censoring *Schund* (trashy) and *Schmutz* (dirty) publications—in other words pulp literature, which was considered deleterious to Germany's youth and therefore the future of the nation.[97] In 1926 the Weimar government had instituted a law concerned with identifying and blacklisting cheap and easily available books and magazines that glamorized violence and sex or offended public decency. However, due in part to excessive bureaucracy the law largely failed in its aims, with the exception perhaps of pornography. The Nazis were, of course, far more successful in controlling popular literature, ensuring the format was used to spread Arian political aspirations. In post-war

Germany the old worries over corrupted youth returned. The concern was not only with the lingering influence of Nazi indoctrination, but also the growth of American cultural imperialism. The influence of American pulp magazines and detective and western serials had already been a concern in Weimar Germany, but now the floodgates were fully open. This was not just a German fear. At the same time a similar vociferous campaign against the tide of American pulp also rose in Canada, with talk of the country becoming an open sewer for what some saw as its neighbour's cultural filth.[98]

Now the political, anti-capitalist sentiments of the Weimar Republic were replaced by a resurgent influence of religious organizations in politics and society. In 1953 a new statute was passed against publications that endangered the morals of the German youth. Between 1954 and 1956 a series of private initiatives, usually orchestrated by religious organizations, led to the setting up of public collection points where trash literature could be swapped for morally improving juvenile literature. Despite acute awareness of the book-burning predilections of the Nazi authorities, several pyres of offensive publications were publicly burned or buried.[99] Hard-boiled detective novels and pornography were the main preoccupation of the moral crusaders but popular literature that encouraged 'superstition' was also deemed fit for the flames.

The words '*Schund*' and '*Schmutz*' may not have found their way into the 1953 law, but they were at the heart of the criticisms of one of the most vocal campaigners against the *Sixth and Seventh Books of Moses*, the respected Austrian forensic doctor Otto Prokop. In an article written in the early 1960s he thought it pertinent to list the range of 'trashy' lifestyle books of what he called the 'cynical' *Schmutzliteratur* publishers who printed editions of the Moses Books.[100] One of those he mentioned was the Brunswick publishing house Planet-Verlag. This was one of the provincial publishers that had been quick to take advantage of the new realities of post-war Germany, exploiting the undoubted thirst for cheap, escapist popular literature. It specialized in guides for women on how to look young, remain desirable, and achieve the perfect bust.[101] More controversially, since the war, it had been re-publishing the pulp science-fiction tales of Paul Alfred Mueller, who also wrote under the noms de plume Freder van Holk and Lok Myler. Mueller's tales of futuristic, Arian scientific enterprise and colonization of Atlantis were hugely popular in Nazi Germany. It was this uncomfortable association that led Planet-Verlag to discontinue the re-editions in 1953, in anticipation of the imminent censorship law.[102] It was not the peddling of rip-roaring Arian fantasies that landed the publisher in court, however, but rather accusations of fostering pernicious magical beliefs. In 1950, it had printed 9,000 copies of a hardback version of the *Sixth and Seventh Books of Moses*. This was not a version of the Scheible edition with its numerous pseudo-Hebraic sigils and amulets, but was nevertheless controversial due to its advice on making a pact with the Devil. Nine thousand was a sizeable print run for the time and Planet-Verlag was obviously confident it could sell them in large numbers. In other words they were aware of the thirst for practical magic in post-war Germany. Not long after it also brought out an edition of *Das Buch Jezira* to capitalize on their initial success.

In 1954 the German Society for Protection against Superstition, or DEGESA (*Deutsche Gesellschaft Schutz vor Aberglauben*), was founded. As one member put it, the Society was dedicated to combating 'the commercial exploitation of superstition'.[103] It acted as a network for a diverse bunch of campaigners against grimoires and their influence. There was Will Emrich, a former president of the German Animal Protection League, who believed the *Sixth and Seventh Books of Moses* had led to the painful deaths of numerous cats, chickens, moles, and toads by followers of its magical cures.[104] Herbert Schäfer was more concerned with the social consequences. He was a criminologist for the West German federal police, who examined the files of ninety-five court cases involving witchcraft beliefs between 1925 and 1956, and twenty-nine legal actions against magical healers between 1947 and 1955. He found the *Sixth and Seventh Books of Moses* was mentioned in 20 per cent of the cases. Amongst them was that of a *hexenbanner* in southern Germany who, since 1941, had been offering to remove evil from farmers' cattle sheds with the help of his 'Moses books'.[105] The Jesuit priest Philipp Schmidt concentrated on the religious and moral threat posed by grimoires. In 1956 he published a book on the evils of magic past and present in which he exaggeratedly stated that magic books had played their part in nearly all the recent cases of witchcraft and magic heard by the German courts. They accounted for the 'almost uniform methods and practices of the "unwitchers"', he asserted, and they were 'calculated to have a pernicious effect on simple minds and on uncritical, credulous persons'.[106] In 1960 another Catholic author, Dr Herbert Auhofer, published a book on the subject, *Aberglaube und Hexenwahn heute* (*Superstition and the Witch-craze Today*), which was apparently officially praised by the Catholic Church.

All these authors fulsomely applauded one man who had pioneered the campaign, a man whom Aufhofer said had 'preached to deaf ears' for four decades and had been unfairly portrayed as a monomaniac for his earnest endeavour.[107] That man was the retired Hamburg schoolteacher Johann Kruse (1889–1983). As a farmer's son brought up in Brickeln, Schleswig-Holstein, he had heard people being accused of witchcraft and seen the suffering and torment it had caused. Indeed, his own mother was also slandered, leading to much family anxiety. While most critical attention was focused on the popularity of spiritualism, theosophy, and other middle-class esoteric interests, Kruse began to wage a lonely campaign against the old, deeply engrained magical traditions rooted in rural

Das sechste und siebente Buch Moses

das ist Moses magische Geisterkunst, das Geheimnis aller Geheimnisse.

Wortgetreu nach einer alten Handschrift

Mit alten Holzschnitten

FIG. 26 The 1950 Planet-Verlag edition of the *Sixth and Seventh Books of Moses*.

German society.[108] In 1923 he published a book on the subject entitled *Hexen-wahn in der Gegenwart* (*Witch-craze in the Present*). He was infuriated by the complacency of folklorists, educationalists, and the clergy for treating witchcraft beliefs as mere folklore and not a serious social menace. It was in the 1930s that he seriously began to mount a national campaign. Although this fitted quite well with Nazi ideas about the pernicious influence of ecclesiastical 'superstition', Kruse was no ardent participant in the Third Reich, and although not actively opposed to the regime he was nevertheless sufficiently lacking in enthusiasm for it to cause him some personal trouble. Kruse's ire was chiefly directed at the thousands of *hexenbanner* who made large amounts of money by defrauding those who thought they were bewitched, and who caused untold suffering to those accused of witchcraft. In 1950 he founded his own Archive for the Investigation of Contemporary Witchcraft Superstition. The following year he published a book based on his extensive collection of cases entitled *Hexen unter uns?* (*Witches Among Us?*), in which he toned down the anti-clericalism of his earlier work. It was his legal challenge to grimoires a few years later, though, that would make him a figure of international interest.

Planet-Verlag placed numerous adverts in popular magazines and newspapers for what was the first widely available German edition of the grimoire for twenty years. The impact of this advertising campaign was evident at the trial, in 1951, of a *hexenbanner* named Wilhelm Lühr of Ebersdorf. In defending his trade, which concerned the selling of celestial letters, Lühr told the judge that the *Sixth and Seventh Book of Moses* was 'openly allowed in the book-trade, and daily extolled in many newspapers and illustrated magazines'.[109] In 1952 the influence of these advertisements came to Kruse's attention and a new front of his campaign against 'superstition' opened up. The following year he denounced the Planet-Verlag edition, alleging that the title page's claim to be a 'Philadelphia' imprint was fraudulent, and, more importantly, that its magical contents was a public menace that could potentially encourage murder.[110] In 1956 he took the bold step of suing the publisher.

Kruse's star expert witness at the trial was Otto Prokop. In his mid-thirties, the high-flying doctor had become a lecturer at the Forensic Medicine Institute at Bonn University in 1953, and in early 1957 he was appointed the manager of the Institute of Judicial Medicine at Humboldt University in East Berlin. Prokop seems to have first come into contact with Kruse in 1954 via a mutual acquaintance keen to help build on the network of anti-superstition activists fostered by DEGESA.[111] As well as his innovative work in forensic science, Prokop had already proved himself an ardent campaigner against magical and spiritual medicine, lecturing on the subject at university and later in several publications. He denounced alternative medicines such as homeopathy and acupuncture as superstitious, and during his long career he was frequently involved in court cases against spiritualist healers and other practitioners of alternative medicine.[112] He, not surprisingly, shared Kruse's disgust for the magical practices of German folk medicine, and saw the suppression of the *Sixth and Seventh Books* as a positive step towards eradicating 'unscientific', 'irrational' medicine.

Planet-Verlag produced its own star academic to counter the Prokop effect— the well-known professor of folklore at Göttingen University, Will-Erich Peuckert (1895–1969). At the time of the trial Peuckert's reputation was at its peak. Only a year earlier a *Festschrift* had been published to honour his sixtieth birthday, with congratulatory signatures from leading folklorists from across Europe and America. He had not always been in such favour, however.

Like Kruse, Peuckert began his career as a provincial schoolteacher. Brought up in the mountainous region of Silesia on the German–Czech border, his industrious research on the popular traditions and beliefs of the region led him to a career in academia and a post at the University of Breslau. During the 1920s and 1930s he wrote a series of books on early modern occult philosophy and mysticism, such as *Böhme* (1924) and *Die Rosenkreutzer* (1928). His most ambitious book was *Pansophie* (1936), which concerned the development of natural and demonic intellectual magic during the fifteenth and sixteenth centuries. Peuckert was labelled as 'politically unreliable' by the Nazi authorities and was stripped of his post. He retired to the Silesian mountains from where he continued to research and publish. Untainted by Nazi associations he was the first professor to be assigned an academic folklore position in post-war West Germany, and was a leading figure in the soul-searching debate that took place amongst folklorists regarding their discipline's role during the Third Reich, and how it should develop in light of its recent history.[113]

Peuckert had a deep understanding of the historical and cultural significance of grimoires. In 1954 he had published an article on the *Egyptischen Geheimnisse* and shortly after the Planet-Verlag trial the fruits of his research on the *Sixth and Seventh Books of Moses* also appeared.[114] His reputation was such that, like Kruse, the magic-believing public saw him not only as a scholar of the subject but also a skilful worker of counter-witchcraft.[115] He received letters from distraught people asking him to unbewitch them and provide love potions. One farmer from a remote village in the wild Lüneburger Heath, north of Braunschweig, wrote to him that his cows were bewitched and that reading the Bible in the cowshed at midnight had failed to remove the spell upon them. Instead of giving the man a lecture on the fallacy of believing in witchcraft, as Kruse might have done, Peuckert visited the man and seeing that the stalls were filthy, he said, 'Witches hate light and air and cleanliness; clean the place out and they will go.'[116]

His support for Planet-Verlag was based, in part, on the historical perspective that the *Sixth and Seventh Books of Moses* provided a fascinating insight into the origin and reformulation of magical traditions over the centuries. From a folklorist's point of view, furthermore, it had been an important influence on rural German folk magic for over a century—part of a valuable tradition that should be understood and preserved, not condemned and suppressed. The prosecution accused him of romanticizing ignorance and credulity.[117] Peuckert was also, perhaps, motivated by professional pique. How dare an amateur like Kruse and a scientist such as Prokop assume expertise on a subject that was the preserve of historians and folklorists?

Peuckert's enthusiasm for finding value in old magical remedies was most graphically demonstrated by his experiments with hallucinogenic plants, which garnered international attention in the press a few years later. In 1960 the 65-year-old academic published a brief account of how he and a lawyer friend had concocted numerous narcotic potions based on early modern magical remedies and spells. He occasionally tried some of these out on himself, most notably a witches' ointment described in della Porta's *Magia Naturalis*. He and his friend rubbed some of the ointment into their skin and soon entered an hallucinatory alternative world. For more than a day and a night they dreamed of wild aerial rides and participated in orgies with grotesque creatures. For Peuckert it was proof that some of those who said they had been to Sabbats were influenced by their drug-induced alternative realities.[118] As a newspaper report explained, 'Peuckert's research has convinced him that there is a scientific basis for many things associated with witchcraft.'[119] But let us return to the rather more sober environment of the Braunschweig magistrates' court, where, in November 1956 the trial came to a head.

Peuckert's testimony failed to convince the lower court, which agreed with Prokop's contention that the Moses book was harmful and 'a danger to the general public'.[120] The owners of Planet-Verlag were fined 9,000 deutschmarks and required to withdraw the remaining stock and the printing plates. They appealed, and in September the following year the two sides were once again back in court and in even bitterer mood. Kruse and Prokops garnered the support of Philip Schmidt and other members of DEGESA. Peuckert was in acerbic form denouncing Kruse's opinions, his book, and his 'useless' archive. The appeals court rescinded the decision, though legal proceedings rumbled on for another three years with the higher court launching an investigation as to whether the publisher's advertisements regarding the origin and contents of the Moses Books had deceived those lured into buying it. Several purchasers were persuaded to give testimony, such as the farmer and mechanic who recounted how he had seen a magazine advertisement for the *Sixth and Seventh Books of Moses*, in which it was stated that it contained valuable old remedies for curing people and animals. He ordered a copy, but on reading it soon realized he could have saved himself some money, as it was merely a 'catchpenny publication'. He showed it to a local veterinarian who agreed it was worthless, and so his wife burned it.[121]

Finally, in July 1960, the court ruled that the publishers should pay a fine totalling several hundred deutschmarks rather than thousands, but otherwise all other charges arising from the original prosecution were to be dropped. Kruse had lost the battle, but the war against the Moses Book was not over. The trial acted as a spur to others, like Schmidt, Schäfer, and Auhofer, to join Kruse's crusade. Another consequence of the case was the international spotlight it cast on Germany's 'problem'. Even though, as we have seen, the USA was by now the leading global purveyor of cheap magic literature, Germany was portrayed in some quarters as a centre of the market in 'superstition'. In 1957, for instance, a report in the North American press regarding the prosecution of a female *hexenbanner* from Offenburg, stated that, 'German book publishers are making fortunes by printing short pamphlets and long volumes with instructions for those wishing to practise or benefit by sorcery.'[122]

So far we have seen how concerns over the social influence of the *Sixth and Seventh Books of Moses* led to the rather unlikely coalition of those inspired by anti-clericalism, professional medical hegemony, and Catholic authority. Protestant participation in the crusade was personified by the industrious Lutheran minister Kurt Koch (1913–87). While Kruse was battling against the influence of the *Sixth and Seventh Books of Magic* in northern Germany, Koch had been orchestrating a similar campaign against the use of such 'devilish merchandise' in the southern German province of Baden and neighbouring Switzerland. He fought, he said, against the 'flood of magical conjuration which washes the Alps'.[123] Koch, whose theological career began after receiving a revelation from God at the age of 17, trained for the ministry at the University of Tübingen, and specialized in the practice of evangelical Christian psychiatry.[124] From the commencement of his pastoral activities in the 1930s he began to record the instances of magical practices he and fellow ministers encountered in parts of southern Germany, Switzerland, and Austria. Over three decades he claimed to have compiled a file containing thousands of cases of occult disturbance, many of them the result of experiences with magical healing and grimoires. During the 1960s he wrote a series of books in German on the perceived occult crisis, and the success of the English translations, marketed for a popular audience, soon gave him international renown. By the 1970s he was lecturing all over the world on the evils of the occult in the modern world. He saw himself as leading a Protestant counselling crusade, believing psychotherapists were failing both religiously and practically to deal with the mental traumas being caused.

Koch shared the same goal as Kruse. He had participated in the Planet-Verlag trial, and considered *Hexen unter uns?* one of the most informative works on contemporary 'superstition'. However, considering Kruse's anti-clerical stance, it is not surprising that the two campaigners did not share the same interpretation of folk magic. Koch accused Kruse of 'failing to recognize its true background'.[125] For Koch folk magic was not merely pernicious or foolish superstition. Whether white or black, it had 'the devil's very own stamp on it'.[126] He recognized that its continued popularity was because it seemed, in many cases, to have successfully cured the sick and the victims of witchcraft and spirits, but Satan's hooks left lasting moral and psychological damage. For the evangelical Koch all this magical activity had apocalyptic significance: 'an increasing flood of occult movements tries to overrule the Church of Christ. We live in the last phase of the end of the age...Empowered by this fact we can dare to face all the onslaughts of the defeated foe.'[127]

Koch detected three groups of grimoire owners. There were those who were aware of the ungodliness of keeping such books and kept them a close secret, passing their copies on to their eldest sons only on their deathbeds. Those in the second group confessed their awful secret to their families and requested them to burn their magic books. During his ministrations many copies had been handed over to Koch to be destroyed in this way. The most disquieting group consisted of those, including churchmen, who believed that some grimoires were godly religious texts, the devilish charms they contained being camouflaged by the use of Christian words, symbols, and customs. During a large conference of pastors, for instance, Koch strongly protested when a local conjurer was characterized as a decent, godly man. How could he be if he practised charming?[128]

In 1961 Koch warned that such books 'circulate among people like poisonous gases, poisoning their very minds and souls'.[129] The *Sixth and Seventh Books*, in particular, had 'caused untold harm in the world and people who read it invariably suffer in the process'.[130] Those who used it were in thrall to the Devil. In evidence he cited the following case:

> At a youth conference a 17-year-old lad came to an evangelical meeting
> with a New Testament in his left pocket and, bound in similar format, the
> 6th and 7th book of Moses in his right. My assistant at this meeting took
> the 6th and 7th Book of Moses from him. We looked through the magic
> book and found that the lad had bound himself to the devil by putting his
> signature underneath a picture of Lucifer. We then burned the book.[131]

The mere possession of the book was enough to cause misfortune and severe psychological damage. An ethno-psychiatric study conducted in 1950s Ghana had suggested that expressions of the intention to practise magic using the *Sixth and*

Seventh Books of Moses 'frequently herald the onset of schizophrenia'.[132] For Koch the Moses Book was the cause not the symptom of mental illness. 'It is a remarkable observation of pastoral experience', he observed, 'that in all homes and families in which the 6th and 7th Book of Moses is kept, or even used, psychological disturbances of various kinds appear.' 'I have not met one possessor of the 6th and 7th Book of Moses who had no psychological complications,' he concluded. One man who used it to charm people and animals died in terrible pain 'amid the spread of a penetrating odour', even though he had burned his copy. When the man's sister, who was sceptical about magic, used some of the formulae in mockery, 'she sensed a change in her emotional equilibrium, became insane, suffered manic attacks', and ended up in a mental institution.[133] It was even the cause of many cases of hereditary psychological problems. Indeed this is how he explained his own childhood experience of terrible nocturnal visions of diabolic beasts. Kurt's father revealed to him that his great-grandmother had used the *Sixth and Seventh Book of Moses*: 'At one stroke I understood the various coincidences in the experiences of my father and his siblings, and also in my own childhood. My grandmother, about whom there had been many rumours, was thus the demon-oppressed daughter of a spell-caster.'[134]

How successful was the anti-grimoire campaign in Germany? Could Koch break the devilish cycle he so graphically demonstrated? Well, perhaps it had a limited localized influence. An ethnological study of witchcraft in the deep rural region of central Germany known as Franconian Switzerland noted in the early 1970s that 'While almost all of the older peasants know of the book . . . few have seen it. I have met only one person who admitted to having seen—indeed used— the book.' It was suggested that this was due to the success of the Church in restricting its availability.[135] As we have seen elsewhere, however, the perceived scarcity of grimoires does not tally with the reality of their easy availability. Koch and his ilk also had to battle the tidal wave of Western occult interest that surged in the 1970s. Ultimately Koch would be no more successful than King Cnut. During the 1970s and 1980s German publishers continued to pump out editions of the *Sixth and Seventh Books of Moses*.[136] Planet-Verlag reprinted its 1953 edition of *Das Zehnte, Elfte und Zwölfte Buch Moses* in the 1970s along with *Das sechste bis zwölfte Buch Moses*. Pulp won with a knockout.

LOVECRAFT, SATAN, AND SHADOWS

W hile the battle over the *Sixth and Seventh Books of Moses* was being fought in Germany, and as the publications of Gamache and De Claremont spread across the Caribbean, a new genre of grimoire was brewing in the Anglo-Saxon world. The merging of fact and fiction had always been an integral aspect of the grimoire tradition, and in the twentieth century this was given a new twist with the genre of literary fantasy not only being influenced by the magical tradition but also inspiring the creation of new grimoires. They also reached a new audience, attracting the attention of counter-culture movements in the post-war West. As a consequence they became the basis for new, non-Christian religions whose appeal stretched far beyond the rarefied, middle-class esotericism of the Golden Dawn and its offshoots.

Necronomicon

Several Victorian and Edwardian novelists, such as Edward Bulwer-Lytton and Arthur Machen, who translated Casanova's *Memoires*, had a personal, practical interest in magic that fed into their work. Bulwer-Lytton's *Zanoni* (1842), which concerned the adventures of a Rosicrucian mage at the time of the French Revolution, begins with a thinly veiled account of John Denley's occult bookshop in Covent Garden. In *The Column of Dust* (1909) by Evelyn Underhill, a one-time member of the Golden Dawn like Machen, the main character, Constance Tyrrel, a bookseller's assistant, conjures up a spirit by reciting from 'a rare old English translation of the "Grand Grimoire" '.[1] It is somewhat surprising, then, that the authors of the two most intriguing fictional grimoires of the early twentieth century had little practical interest in the magical tradition.

The novelist W. H. Hodgson (1877–1918) created the first of these modern grimoires, namely the fourteenth-century Sigsand manuscript. Written in 'ye olde' English, this was the key inspiration for the occult practices of Hodgson's ghost hunter and private detective, Thomas Carnacki, whose amazing exploits were recounted in a series of short stories written between 1910 and 1914. For Carnacki, 'ninety-nine cases in a hundred turn out to be sheer bosh and fancy,' but the other one per cent brought him face to face with various denizens of the spirit world. Despite his usual rationalist outlook, Carnacki relies heavily on magic for protection. In 'The Gateway of the Monster' Carnacki explains to his friends the nature of his main defence against evil spirits. It was a Solomonic pentacle drawn within a circle on the floor. Garlic was rubbed around the circle while just within it he marked out the 'Second Sign of the Saaamaaa Ritual', joining each with a left-handed crescent, in the valley of which he placed a lighted candle. Five portions of bread wrapped in linen, and five jars of a 'certain water' were placed ceremoniously within the pentacle. This 'defence' was taken from the Sigsand manuscript, and had saved his life—but only just. To strengthen its power he enhanced the ancient magic with the power of new scientific forces by positioning vacuum tubes within the pentagram and passing a current through them.[2] Carnacki cites brief excerpts from the Sigisand manuscript here and there in the stories, and its advice constantly frames his understanding of the spirit world and how to deal with it, but otherwise its contents remain largely a mystery.

Hodgson, the son of a clergyman, had a youthful lust for the sea, and his parents reluctantly agreed to him signing on for the mercantile marines. After being bullied by a second mate, Hodgson became an early adherent of judo and body-building, and when his nautical career came to an end he set up a school of physical culture in Blackburn. It was when his school closed down in 1902 that he turned to a career writing tales of the fantastic. He enlisted in 1914, was decom-missioned after an injury on active service in 1916, and then re-enlisted in 1917. He was killed near Ypres in April 1918.[3] Hodgson was certainly an enthusiastic photographer, which may have led to an interest in spiritual investigation, but otherwise there is nothing in his brief and tragic biography to indicate any deep interest in the occult. But there is no reason to suggest that his interest in grimoires was anything but casual. After all, the author of the most enduring and influential fictional grimoire, the *Necromonicon*, likewise had little initial knowledge of the subject.

The childhood of Howard Phillips Lovecraft (1890–1937), the son of a sales representative from Rochester, New York, was not the happiest either. In 1893 his father went insane while they were staying at a Chicago hotel. He was hospitalized and died five years later. Thereafter, Howard was brought up by his mother and her father. A precocious and voracious reader, Lovecraft's imagination was stoked by the eclectic contents of his grandfather's library, and he developed a dual passion for modern science and old traditions and beliefs, devouring the *Thousand and One Nights*, Grimm's fairy tales, and Greek and medieval mythology. Yet, Lovecraft had no interest in merely regurgitating existing folklore and mythologies in his own fiction; rather he advocated using the corpus to create 'new artificial myths'.[4] He became skilled at inventing traditions, creating a verisimilitude of folklore.

Most of Lovecraft's fiction was published in the pulp fantasy and horror magazine *Weird Tales*. For many years after his death Lovecraft's work was not taken seriously as literature because it was published in such pulp publications, but now 'he has become an icon in popular culture in part *because* his work appeared there.'[5] Grimoires were a favourite motif for the writers of pulp horror and fantasy. In a letter written in 1936 Lovecraft listed some of the 'terrible and mysterious books so darkly mentioned in weird magazine stories'.[6] Among them was Robert E. Howard's *Unaussprechlichen Kulten*. Howard, who is best known for his creation Conan the Barbarian, described the first edition of *Unaussprechlichen Kulten* as appearing in Düsseldorf in 1839—a nice touch echoing, whether knowingly or not, the publication of the Horst and Scheible libraries of the occult. Robert Bloch, who would later pen the bestseller *Psycho*, invented the *De Vermis Mysteriis*, a magic book owned by an alchemist and necromancer named Ludvig Prinn burned at the stake in Brussels during the late fifteenth or early sixteenth century. Prinn, who claimed to have lived for several centuries, said he gained his knowledge from Syrian wizards while captive during the Crusades. Incomplete fragments of *The Book of Eibon*, invented by Clark Ashton Smith, contained magical formulae and accounts of the exploits of the ancient wizard Eibon, and were said to exist in English, French, and Latin translations.[7] The community of horror and fantasy authors freely appropriated these creations at the time. Lovecraft made reference to and had a hand in developing the mythology of all three of the above examples, but it was his own addition to the corpus that went on to have the most enduring influence.

Lovecraft's first reference to the *Necronomicon*—the name was probably inspired by Marcus Manilius's astrological poem *Astronomica*—was in a story called 'The Hound', written in 1922 and published in *Weird Tales* in 1924.[8] The story concerns a couple of grave-digging, relic hunters bent on finding ever more items for their private museum of blasphemous 'universal terror'—a collection which already contained the *Necronomicon*. They travel to Holland to plunder the grave of a medieval mage. In his coffin they find a curious jade amulet with strange inscriptions carved on the base:

> Alien it indeed was to all art and literature which sane and balanced readers know, but we recognised it as the thing hinted of in the forbidden *Necronomicon* of the mad Arab Abdul Alhazred ... All too well did we trace the sinister lineaments described by the old Arab daemonologist; lineaments, he wrote, drawn from some obscure supernatural manifestation of the souls of those who vexed and gnawed at the dead.[9]

The *Necromonicon* popped up again in 'The Festival', written a year later and published in *Weird Tales* in 1925, which was inspired by Lovecraft's recent reading of Margaret Murray's *The Witch-Cult in Western Europe*, the wider influence of which I shall come back to shortly. The narrator is compelled by his ancestors to visit the fictional New England town of Kingsport one snowy Yuletide. In 1692 four of his kinsmen had been hanged for witchcraft just outside the town. His destination is the house of an old, mute gentleman. He is shown into a dark, dank candle-lit room where on a table there lay a pile of 'hoary and mouldy' books. Amongst them were the 'terrible *Saducismus Triumphatus* of Joseph Glanvill, published in 1681, the shocking *Daemonolatreia* of Remigius, printed in 1595 at Lyons, and worst of all the unmentionable *Necronomicon* of the mad Arab Abdul Alhazred, in Olaus Wormius' forbidden Latin translation'.[10] The first two books are real, and the last not.

It is possible that the Sigsand manuscript may have been the seed for Lovecraft's *Necronomicon*. Lovecraft had great respect for Hodgson's work, writing in an essay on 'Supernatural Horror in Literature' that 'Few can equal him in adumbrating the nearness of nameless forces and monstrous besieging entities through casual hints and insignificant details, or in conveying feelings of the spectral and the abnormal.'[11] He was less than thrilled by Hodgson's conception of Carnacki's magical defences, though, stating that 'scenes and events [are] badly marred by an atmosphere of professional "occultism."' Lovecraft was more inclined towards Algernon Blackwood's stories about the investigations of the 'Psychic Doctor' John Silence, which were undoubtedly also an inspiration for Hodgson. Silence despised the word 'occultism' and his powers are those unleashed by the power of thought rather than the ritual, magical trappings employed by Carnacki.

Over the next couple of years the mysterious, notorious *Necronomicon* cropped up tantalizingly here and there in several other short stories. Like Hodgson and the Sigsand manuscript, Lovecraft made appetizingly few references to the *Necronomicon*, and so the exact nature of its contents is never clear to the reader. Was it a source of mystical secrets, a demonological disquisition, or a book of practical magic? In 1927 Lovecraft decided to clarify in his own mind what it was by constructing a brief 'history' of its existence to ensure that there was some consistency in his future references to it. According to this history, a mad Yemeny poet named Abdul Alhazred penned the *Al Azif*, or *Necronomicon* as it came to be known, during the early eighth century AD. His wisdom was accrued through his visits to the ruins of Babylon, the subterranean chambers of Memphis, and a solitary spiritual sojourn in the Arabian Desert. As a twelfth-century biographer recounted, through his experiences Alhazred had discovered the existence of a secret race of beings older than Man, entities whom he began to worship and called Yog-Sothoth and Cthulhu. It was in AD 950 that the *Al Azif* was secretly translated into Greek under the title *Necronomicon*, copies of which were sought and destroyed by the Church. Some escaped their attentions and in 1228 Olaus Wormius translated it into Latin. Though quickly banned by Pope Gregory IX, one edition of it was printed in Germany during the fifteenth century and another, probably in Spain, two centuries later. A Greek edition was printed in Italy between 1500 and 1550. The last copy of the latter was found and burned in Salem in 1692. John Dee made a translation that only survives in fragments. Existing Latin versions are kept in the British Library, the Bibliotheque Nationale, Harvard, the University of Buenos Aires, and Miskatonic University Library, Arkham (one of Lovecraft's creations).

This invented history is a prime example of Lovecraft's 'artificial' myth-making, weaving real people, such as Wormius (actually a seventeenth-century Danish physician), Gregory, and Dee, and real events, such as the Salem witch trials, into a realistic sounding history that mimicked the bogus traditions that clung to real grimoires. What inspired it? Lovecraft's knowledge of occult history was surprisingly limited during the 1920s.[12] His main source of information was the entry on 'magic' in the *Encyclopedia Britannica*. Indeed in 1925 he admitted to an acquaintance that he was 'appallingly ignorant' on such matters. 'Are there any good translations of any mediaeval necromancers with directions for raising spirits, invoking Lucifer, & all that sort of thing?', he asked.[13] Lovecraft had little interest in the vibrant folk traditions of the present and so seems to have been completely unaware of the popularity of the *Sixth and Seventh Books of Moses* amongst America's working classes. There is also no evidence that he knew of the *Picatrix*, which would at first glance seem to be the obvious inspiration for the history of the *Necromonicon*. The Arabic context was evidently inspired primarily by his passion for the *Arabian Nights* and *Vathek*, William Beckford's eighteenth-century Gothic Arabian tale of magic.[14] As we have seen with regard to the Shriners, at the time Lovecraft was writing there was also considerable American fascination with legends of rediscovered ancient Arabic mystical knowledge. In 1936, when his knowledge on the subject had certainly improved, he mused that a mix of scraps of medieval European and Near Eastern rituals and

incantations for summing spirits, 'such as A. E. Waite and "Eliphas Levi" reproduce', would 'constitute something vaguely like what the *Necromonicon* and its
congeners are supposed to be'.[15]

It is possible that Lovecraft's interest in mysterious occult books, and that of
his fellow writers of weird tales, was also influenced by the public interest in and
controversy over the Voynich manuscript.[16] In 1912 the political émigré and
London book dealer Wilfred Michael Voynich came across a highly unusual
illuminated manuscript in a wooden chest in the remote Jesuit castle of Villa
Mondragone in Frascati, Italy: at least that was the version of its discovery that
circulated after his death. In his own lifetime he only divulged that he had found it
in a castle or monastery in southern Europe. Not long after his arrival in England,
after fleeing Siberian exile, Voynich accrued a reputation in the trade for his ability
to uncover unknown and lost books. Part of his success was due to the periodic
tours he made across Europe visiting impoverished religious establishments. One
of the medieval manuscripts he found appeared, at first glance, to be an astrological
herbal not unlike numerous others of the period. However, this one was written
in an unknown cipher and contained numerous naked, bathing female figures.
Even more curiously none of the plants illustrated were obviously identifiable.
Voynich displayed it to English and French scholars before moving to America in
1914. Several years later he had photostatic copies made of some of the pages and
sent them to American and European academics. They soon attracted controversy
and intrigue.

Voynich believed his mysterious book to be of the thirteenth century and
suspected that its author might have been none other than Albertus Magnus or
Roger Bacon. He also reckoned he had found evidence that the manuscript had
been in the ownership of John Dee, who subsequently sold it to Rudolf II. In 1921
the scholar William Newbold announced that he had been able to decipher parts
of the manuscript, and confirmed that its author was indeed Roger Bacon.
Voynich capitalized on this sensational endorsement and put the manuscript up
for sale for $160,000—over two million dollars in today's money. The controversy
surrounding it meant, however, that no library or collector was willing to pay
anything near this price. Doubts about Newbold's claim were widespread, and
in 1929 the pioneering historian Lynn Thorndike, who would go on to complete
a monumental eight-volume history of magic and early science, dismissed
Voynich's 'pet' manuscript as 'an anonymous manuscript of dubious value'.[17] It
remained unsold until a New York book dealer paid out $24,500 for it not long
after the death of Voynich's wife. The dealer hoped to make a killing on this now
notorious manuscript, but ended up donating it to Yale University in 1969. There
was too much suspicion surrounding it. If, as it has been suggested, it was an
historical hoax perpetrated by Edward Kelley to fleece John Dee, then it would

still have considerable historical curiosity value. Others, including myself, suspect, however, that it was a modern hoax perpetrated by or on Voynich.

A few months before he died Lovecraft wrote to a friend, 'If the *Necronomicon* legend continues to grow, people will end up believing in it.'[18] By 1936 someone had, as a prank, advertised that copies were available for $1.49. Lovecraft suspected Robert Bloch. The idea of writing a *Necromonicon* certainly appealed to Lovecraft, and he expressed the wish that he would have 'the time and imagination to assist in such a project'. Yet, at the same time, he felt that no such publication would be as 'terrible and impressive' as that which could be hinted at. It would have to run to more than a thousand pages to simulate what he had already described, and so he thought that he could only feasibly achieve the 'translation' of certain passages of the book. Ultimately though, he opined, 'I am opposed to serious hoaxes, since they really confuse and retard the sincere student of folklore. I feel quite guilty every time I hear of someone's having spent valuable time looking up the *Necronomicon* at public libraries.'[19] Others were less conscientious.

Over the decades several authors have claimed to have discovered manuscript versions, and in the 1980s one magician even claimed to have in his possession a 4,000-year-old grimoire from which the *Necronomicon* derived. People now practise 'Lovecraftian' magic.[20] The most successful of the print editions was the Simon *Necronomicon*, a ninth-century Greek text discovered by monks and brought to America in the 1970s by an Eastern Orthodox bishop named Simon. The first 'translated' edition appeared in a limited, leather-bound edition of 666 copies. Subsequent hardback and paperback reprints went on to sell in their many thousands. The Simon *Necronomicon* is a well-constructed hoax. Its contents have been stitched together from printed sources on Mesopotamian myth and magic, and its supposed discovery by monks is a well-worn motif in grimoire history. But as a piece of magical literature it, and other *Necronomicons*, are no less 'worthy' than their predecessors. Like other famous grimoires explored in this book, it is their falsity that makes them genuine.[21] The concern Lovecraft expressed about the blurring of fact and fiction regarding the *Necronomicon*, and the potential for confusing the earnest student of the occult, was born out with much greater consequence with the founding text of modern witchcraft.

The Book of Shadows

In his short story 'The Grimoire', published in 1936, Montague Summers (1880–1948) created the *Mysterium Arcanum*, or to give its full title, *The Secret Mystery, or the Art of Evoking Evil Spirits with certain other Most Curious and Close Matters*. The story tells of how a book collector of agnostic persuasion, Dr Julian

Hodsoll, purchases the *Mysterium* from an antiquarian book dealer for five guineas. It was published in the early seventeenth century and, like numerous printed grimoires, bore the imprint 'Rome'. Hodsoll's experienced eye recognizes that this place of publication could not be true. As he informs the book dealer, the contents 'sound appetizing enough, but it may only be a hash-up of the Petit Albert and that wretched Pope Honorius.'[22] Hodsoll visits his learned friend Canon Spenlow and shows him his latest acquisition. Spenlow quickly realizes the evil, satanic nature of its contents. He recommends that the *Mysterium* should be burned, but Hodsoll's curiosity gets the better of him. That night, he translates one of its conjurations, 'A most Powerful and Efficacious Evocation', reading it through softly to himself. Shortly after, a strange servant enters the room and asks, 'You wanted me, sir' before being dismissed. Over the next few days several uncanny occurrences are experienced in the Canon's house. Fortunately a friend of Spenlow's, a Dominican friar named Father Raphael, an expert on the Dark Arts, pays a visit and is on hand when the mysterious servant reveals his satanic identity and attacks Hodsoll, who had unwittingly summoned him. Raphael banishes the devil, making 'swift sacred sigils in the air and spoke certain Latin words of might'. The story ends with the cautionary coda that the once agnostic Hodsoll sees the error of his ways and becomes a Carmelite priest.

Now, there is definitely something of Montague Summers in the character of Hodsoll.[23] He was a larger-than-life figure who studied theology at Oxford University and was ordained a Deacon of the Anglican Church in 1908. Shortly after, he was charged and acquitted of pederasty. This, along with rumours regarding his interest in Satanism and the occult, cut short his clerical career. The following year he converted to Catholicism, and although he liked to give the impression that he was a priest—calling himself Reverend, conducting private masses, wearing the Carmelite scapular—there is no evidence he was officially ordained. He made a living by pursuing a writing career based on his interest in witchcraft, demonology, Restoration drama, and Gothic literature. As his erudite, populist books *The History of Witchcraft and Demonology* (1926) and *Witchcraft and Black Magic* (1945) show, unlike the creator of the *Necromonicon*, Summers was widely read in the history and content of grimoires. Where he departed from most other historians of the period was that he truly believed that covens of Devil-worshipping witches, who made pacts with their master, had existed in the past and continued to do so secretly in the present. He consequently thoroughly endorsed the witch trials of the early modern period. Summers believed grimoires were an essential link in the perpetuation and promotion of diabolism, providing the means to call up the Devil, describing them as 'abominable', 'vile', and 'dangerous'. We hear Summers' voice when Hodsoll's wonders, 'Could it be that the mysterious book of the witches had fallen into his hands, that volume which was mentioned in more than one trial of the seventeenth century, but which apparently had never been seen by any who was not a member of that horrid society?'[24] What, then, would he have made of the *Book of Shadows*?

In the 1950s a new religion called Wicca emerged in Britain. Its founder was Gerald Gardner (1884–1964), a manager and civil servant in the colonial Far East who retired to England in the mid-1930s. He had an active interest in spiritualism, Eastern mysticism, folklore, and Freemasonry, and steeped himself in the writings of Charles Leland and Aleister Crowley, and the theories of Margaret Murray (1863–1963). It was the latter who inspired Gardner's belief that many of the tens of thousands of people tried and executed for witchcraft in early modern Europe were not Devil worshippers, as Summers believed, but members of an ancient pagan religion that had survived centuries of Christian persecution. In *The Witch Cult in Western Europe* (1921), and in subsequent publications, Murray, who was a respected Egyptologist, argued that what the medieval Church denounced as witchcraft was, in fact, the beliefs and practices of a prehistoric fertility cult based around the worship of a horned God.[25] She arrived at this conclusion by the highly selective and misleading use of sixteenth- and seventeenth-century confessions concerning witches' Sabbats, most of which were obtained through torture. Murray thought that this remnant ancient pagan religion finally succumbed to the weight of persecution sometime in the eighteenth century.

Gardner remarked that he 'did not think that anyone, with the exception of the Revd Montague Summers, dared hint that there might be anything in witchcraft to-day without being laughed at'.[26] Nevertheless, Gardner claimed that in 1939 he had discovered and been initiated into a coven of secret pagan worshippers in the New Forest, Hampshire. Murray's witch cult had survived! He recalled later that, as a member of the Folklore Society and the Society for Psychical Research, he had wanted to announce this amazing discovery to the learned community. But coven members resisted. They were not afraid of being laughed at though. ' "The Age of Persecution is not over," they told me; "give anyone half a chance and the fires will blaze up again." '[27] He was only permitted to describe their existence in fictional terms, and so in 1949 he produced a novel about the witch cult, *High Magic's Aid*, which was set in the distant past. It was only in 1954 and the appearance of his book *Witchcraft Today* that Gardner went public and Wicca was truly born.

According to Gardner the rituals and wisdom of the ancient witch cult had survived—only just—thanks to their being recorded in a grimoire known as the *Book of Shadows*. Copies were passed down through covens from one generation to the next. The nature of this grimoire began to be revealed by Gardner, who had received his own copy after his initiation, and was subsequently developed with input from one of his first followers Doreen Valiente, who would later provide a thoughtful self-reflexive history of the movement. Although pirated versions of the *Book of Shadows* began to appear in print from the 1960s onwards, Gardner had produced a manuscript version in the late 1940s entitled 'Ye Bok of ye Art Magical'.[28] It had the air of a venerable grimoire, with its leather cover, ornate scripts, and spelling mistakes indicative of repeated copying over the generations.[29] But the contents seemed suspiciously familiar to those who analysed it carefully. Could this grimoire really hold the mysteries of an ancient religion?

If 'Ye Bok', and the later *Book of Shadows* copied and passed on by the original members of Gardner's own initiates, was not copied from the New Forest coven, then what source or sources did he draw upon? A perusal of Gardner's library reveals some texts already well known to the reader. There were, of course, the works of A. E. Waite and other members of the Golden Dawn, as well as a manuscript of the 'Grimoire of Honorius'. We also find copies of Henri Gamache's *Long Lost 8th, 9th and 10th books of Moses* (1948), Gamache's *Terrors of the Evil Eye Exposed* (1946), and de Claremont's *7 Keys to Power* (1940).[30] Gardner had probably purchased these Dorene publications during a visit to his brother in America in the winter of 1947–8. While there he may also have read a short story by Lovecraft's friend Clark Ashton Smith, which was published in *Weird Tales* in 1947. This tale of wizardry referred to a magical knife known as the 'arthame', and in Gardner's grimoire we find a ritual knife called 'athame'. Smith did not invent the word, but it is possible that Gardner may have been inspired by his use of it.[31]

Gardner acknowledged that in writing *High Magic's Aid* he borrowed heavily from rituals contained in Mathers' homogenous version of the *Greater Key of Solomon*. He told acquaintances that he resorted to copying its examples of 'Jewish Ritual Magic' partly as a matter of expediency, and also to respect the wishes of his coven members that he should not publish the 'real' rituals of their prehistoric religion.[32] In defence of the notion that the *Book of Shadows* was not completely Gardner's invention, one Wiccan historian has made the good point that as Mathers' *Key of Solomon* was printed in 1888 it could have seeped into English folk magic and been adopted by the New Forest coven prior to Gardner's supposed initiation.[33] As this Wiccan author notes, and as has been demonstrated in this book, printed grimoires infused remarkably quickly into oral magical traditions. But the evidence overwhelmingly suggests that 'Ye Bok' and the *Book of Shadows* were purely Gardner's work, drawn primarily from the *Key of Solomon*, Aleister Crowley's books, which were in turn reliant on Golden Dawn texts, and Charles Leland's *Aradia*.[34]

Gardner was a show-off and not averse to embroidering the truth. He styled himself a 'Dr' though he never wrote a PhD.[35] It is hardly a shocking revelation that he invented the existence of the New Forest coven and therefore fabricated the history of the *Book of Shadows*, though it has taken considerable meticulous research to convince some of his adherents. Yet in creating the *Book of Shadows* Gardner was merely following the long tradition of grimoire formulation, making false attributions, providing false histories, and compiling spells and rituals from unacknowledged sources. In this sense the *Book of Shadows* has both a venerable history and legitimacy in magical tradition. Furthermore, he produced the first 'pagan' grimoire in more than a millennium—even if its contents were based on Judaic and Christian magic. As well as numerous versions of the *Book of Shadows*, Wicca has inspired a profusion of other neo-pagan ritual and spell books, and their production shows no sign of diminishing. These days most pagan witches are aware of Gardner's fabrications and accept that their religion is not part of a continuous tradition.

For many, the *Book of Shadows* is not a Bible, a founding religious text from which one should not deviate. It is, instead, adapted, and personalized according to practitioners' interests, creativity, and needs. As a consequence, the manuscript tradition continues as an important aspect of modern magical practice.[36] Like the scrapbook grimoires of some cunning-folk, *Books of Shadows* are part manual, part diary, and part guide to spiritual or physical well being. Furthermore, book knowledge more generally is central to the creation and spread of neo-paganism in all its various forms: it is born of a literary rather than an oral heritage. As a study of American paganism in the 1980s observed, 'a common feature in the life stories of American witches is that the concepts of the belief system are first contacted on the library shelf.' Around the same time a study of British Wiccans noted that, before their initiation, Wiccans were typically avaricious readers of fantasy and science fiction. They then progressed to reading about magic, tarot, astrology, and the supernatural, and after several years in the 'craft' their libraries on related subjects extended above a hundred volumes.[37] The enthusiasm for reading around the subject of witchcraft has also led to scholarly historical and anthropological books acting as source material and being incorporated into the conceptual and ritual basis of neo-pagan practice.[38]

Satan's Bible?

The *Satanic Bible* completes our triptych of iconic modern grimoires, and was in part a reaction to the *Book of Shadows*. Its author was the showman and entertaining liar Anton Szandor LaVey. Howard Stanton Levey, as his birth certificate records his name, was born in April 1930, the son of a Chicago salesman. The family moved to San Francisco shortly after his birth and nothing of particular profundity seems to have happened in his life until he dropped out of high school and self-consciously immersed himself in the romantically seedy environment of pool halls and gambling dens. He eked out a living playing the organ in nightclubs while instructing himself in the history and practice of the occult arts. His reading seems to have consisted mostly of populist works on witchcraft by the likes of W. B. Seabrook and Montague Summers, along with A. E. Waite's books on magic.[39] LeVey began to shape his occult persona, influenced by the fictional character of Stanton Carlisle in William Lindsay Gresham's 1946 noir pulp novel *Nightmare Alley*, which was turned into a film starring Tyrone Power. Gresham was fascinated with freak shows, stage magic, and spiritualism, writing several non-fiction books on the subject.[40] His interests fed directly into the depiction of the rise and fall of Stan Carlisle, a carny con-artist clairvoyant who sets up his own spiritualist movement to fleece the well-to-do. Anyone who has read the book can see its influence on LaVey's fabricated biography of his misanthropic adventures in the world of carnival life and strip joints.[41] Like many self-proclaimed masters of the occult before him, LaVey claimed gypsy ancestry—this time from a Transylvanian-born grandmother. She fuelled his imagination with accounts of the magical beliefs of her homeland. Another more recent occult tradition he tapped into in his fictitious biography concerned the rumours regarding Third Reich occultism. He claimed to have visited Germany with an uncle in 1945 during which he saw secret Nazi horror films that contained depictions of occult rituals.[42]

During the early 1960s LaVey set himself up as an expert on the Black Arts in San Francisco, giving lectures on a diverse array of subjects from the Black Mass to ghosts and werewolves. He became something of a local celebrity and his Magical Circle soirees attracted the likes of the filmmaker and writer Kenneth Anger. It was in 1966 that LaVey underwent the physical transformation that turned him into a national media figure. He shaved his head and donned a black clerical collar, which along with his carefully arched eyebrows and goatee beard, gave him a theatrical satanic appearance—one befitting the self-styled High Priest of his newly formed Church of Satan.

For the Church to be taken seriously rather than a mere publicity stunt, LaVey now had to devise some sort of founding text that would describe and define his philosophy and belief system. Two years later, LaVey and his wife had only come up with a short mimeograph 'introduction to Satanism', an assortment of brief polemical essays and a handout to new members on conducting ritual magic.[43] Considering his love of publicity, the idea of producing a paperback book for the mass market was surprisingly not LaVey's. It was written at the suggestion of Peter Mayer, an editor at Avon Books—a major publisher of pulp fiction and comics, and, later, Simon's *Necronomicon*.[44] In 1967 Ira Levin's novel *Rosemary's Baby*, about a young pregnant woman living in a sinister New York apartment who believes she is going to give birth to the son of Satan, had become a sensational bestseller. Mayer, having seen some of the press reports about the Church of Satan contacted the LaVeys and suggested they write a 'Satanic Bible' to capitalize on the success of Levin's novel and the film adaptation that came out a year later. Whether pressured by publishing deadlines, or lacking ideas on how to go about writing a sufficiently thick book of the Church's philosophy, the *Satanic Bible*, which came out in January 1970, consisted of the corpus of mimeographs they had already produced, bulked out with a mish-mash of other texts, including a plagiarized extract from an obscure social Darwinist political tract published in 1896, and an adapted version of Crowley's version of the 'Enochian Keys' of John Dee.

Considering its patchwork construction, the *Satanic Bible* has a surprising coherence. It soon becomes quite clear, though, that despite the Church's name, LaVey's own playful appearance, and the media hoo-hah, the *Satanic Bible* does not advocate Devil worship at all, let alone sacrifice. Satan is a symbol of revolt against Christian hypocrisy and societal authority. Satanism is about the worship of the self, of the identity and potency of the individual. Theatrical magical rituals are employed to release and enhance these processes. The *Satanic Bible* is essentially a rejection of the supernatural. The only thing new about its philosophy was, LaVey stated frankly, 'the formal organisation of a religion based on the universal traits of man'.[45] 'Why call it Satanism? Why not call it something like "Humanism"?', he questioned. The answer: 'Humanism is not a religion. It is simply a way of life with no ceremony or dogma. Satanism has both ceremony and dogma.'[46] As Michael Aquino, an early member of the Church and one of its historians commented, if it was not for its existential appeal to the authority of Satan the *Satanic Bible* could be seen as 'merely a social tract by Anton LaVey...just one more 1960s'-counterculture-cynic atop a soap-box.'[47]

You do not sell an estimated 700,000 or more books, as the *Satanic Bible* is thought to have done since 1970, inspire translations into Czech, Swedish, and German, and generate illegal editions in Mexico and Russia, without having conjured up a winning recipe.[48] Over the years there have never been more than a few thousand practising Satanists in the USA and Europe, and some of these belong to other Satanist groups, such as the Temple of Set. So, who has been buying the *Satanic Bible* in such large numbers and why?[49] It obviously appealed to rebellious teenagers. A 1992 survey of adolescent Satanism in America observed how some high school students conspicuously carried the *Satanic Bible* around, aping Christian fundamentalist teenagers who made show of their pocket Bibles.[50] A respondent in another survey wrote: 'My step-father used to be a Christian preacher. After being told my choices in clothing, music, art, poetry, etc. were Satanic, I decided to buy the *Satanic Bible* to see if it was as bad as he made it out to be.'[51]

People have also been lured into buying it, expecting it to be something that it is not—an espousal of ritual satanic worship. Media reporting enhanced its reputation as a modern day Devil's book. Just as in early-twentieth-century Pennsylvania the press and local authorities saw the influence of the *Sixth and Seventh Books of Moses* behind every strange murder, so in the 1970s and 1980s media scares linked teenage suicides with the ownership of the *Satanic Bible* and listening to heavy metal music.[52] As early as 1971 an article in the Church of Satan's bulletin *The Cloven Hoof* complained that on various occasions the *Satanic Bible* had reportedly been found 'at or near the scene of some crime against society', and the finger of blame had been pointed at the Church of Satan, even though the vast majority of owners of the book were not actually members.[53]

It has been suggested that the *Satanic Bible*, with its list of infernal names and its invocations in a mystical language, indicate that the contents of the *Sixth and Seventh Books of Moses* influenced LaVey.[54]

But the presentation of the two works differs markedly. There is a complete lack of occult signs, seals, and tables in the *Satanic Bible*; yet these were essential ingredients of the Moses Book. Still, the one occult symbol depicted in the *Satanic Bible*, which also appeared on the cover—the Sigil of Baphomet—was crucial to its commercial success. The symbol consists of a goat-headed Satan framed within a pentacle, surrounded by two concentric circles containing five Hebraic figures, which, as LaVey explained, constituted a Kabbalistic spelling of 'Leviathan'.[55] On the front cover the symbol is coloured purple against a simple black background. The effect is striking and bound to attract the curious, and sensation seekers and those intrigued by the prospects of Devil worship.

The Church of Satan recently conducted its own research into the origin of the symbol and found its first depiction in Stanislas de Guaita's *La clef de la magie noire* (1897). However, it was a reprint of the image in white against a black background for the hardback cover of a popular *Pictorial History of Magic and the Supernatural*, published in 1964, which inspired LaVey. While the *Satanic Bible* was being written, LaVey had a new version of the symbol created with minor changes. This became the logo for the Church of Satan and was successfully registered as a trademark in 1983.[56] The key significance of the Sigil of Baphomet, from a publishing point of view, is that in the popular imagination it conjures up expectations of Devil worship, black magic, and sacrifice: it creates 'a sense of mystery that can only be dispelled by purchasing and reading the book.'[57] So, many of its readers must have experienced the same sensations of aroused expectations and disappointment as, say, the Danish purchasers of *Gamle Richards Swartkonst-bok* or Feliks Markiewicz's vaunted *Seventh Book of Moses*.

There are elements of the grimoire format in the *Satanic Bible*, and the media and Christian critics have portrayed it as a book of evil black magic à la the *Sixth*

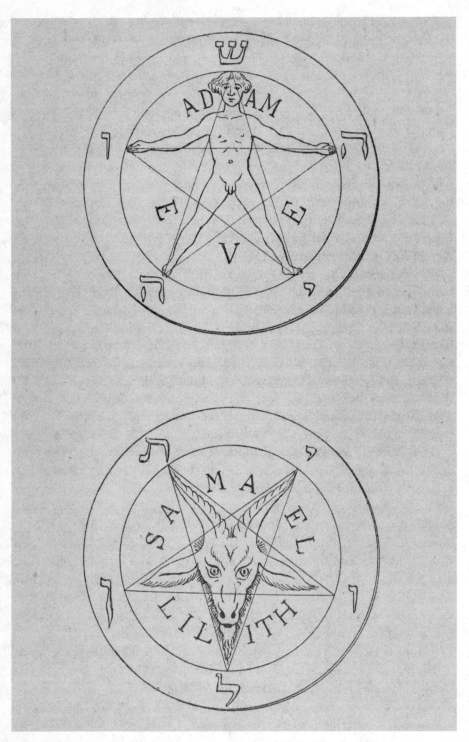

Fig. 27 Sigil of Baphomet from Stanislas de Guaita's *La Clef de la Magie Noire* (1897).

and Seventh Books of Moses, but LaVey was openly dismissive of the whole genre. As he wrote in the preface:

> This book was written because, with very few exceptions, every tract and paper, every 'secret' grimoire, all the 'great works' on the subject of magic, are nothing more than sanctimonious fraud—guilt-ridden ramblings and esoteric gibberish by chroniclers of magical lore unable or unwilling to present an objective view of the subject.[58]

In an article in an early edition of *The Cloven Hoof*, LaVey expanded on this statement, recalling how at the age of 12 he had started to read *Albertus Magnus* and the *Sixth and Seventh Books of Moses*, both of which, he remarked, could be obtained 'in paper before they were called paperbacks'.[59] Even at this tender age he claimed he 'grew disenchanted' with their contents. 'It occurred to me there must be "deeper stuff," so I delved.' However, he found the deeper stuff also constituted an 'ersatz hunk of baloney'.[60] LaVey dismissed the magical writings of Crowley as the work of 'a poseur par excellence', and was withering in his comments on Wiccans.[61] He nevertheless borrowed and prospered from the renewed interest in magical traditions that they had generated. His follow-up blockbuster *Satanic Rituals* was more explicitly magical, being a self-acknowledged ragbag of magical traditions—'a blend of Gnostic, Cabbalistic, Hermetic, and Masonic elements', with a dash of Lovecraft.[62]

LaVey's works have spawned a whole new generation of diabolic grimoires that are explicitly satanic. Amongst them is Michael W. Ford's *Luciferian Witchcraft* (2005), which, echoing the eighteenth-century *Grand grimoire*, promises 'a talismanic text which presents the medieval concepts of the Black Book being a conjuration itself of the Devil', and contains the added spice of 'forbidden sex magick'. There is also the *Demonic Bible* (2006), which began life on the Internet, and which divulges numerous rituals for conjuring up demons. It is advertised as possibly being 'the most evil book written'. LaVey would probably have been disgusted, amused, and not a little flattered.

EPILOGUE

Much has been written about the Internet heralding the death of the book. As we all become habituated to reading from electronic screens, so the argument goes, print will be usurped by the digital media. The act of writing has certainly been transformed, with the keyboard replacing pen and ink as our main means of putting words on a page. But the book is proving to be resilient and adaptable to the digital age. There is every reason to believe it will continue to play an important role in shaping our world. The book is a companion, an instant portal into other worlds, times, and fantasies. Flipping open a laptop or a multimedia phone and pressing the on button clearly has its own thrill, but the physical pleasure of handling books and turning their pages, of book marking or annotating them, is integral to the absorption and anticipation that a fascinating read inspires. The electronic media is about the here and now, while the book has a venerable history that you share every time you turn the page. Generation after generation has done the same thing. These sensual qualities of the book are essential to the grimoire experience. Those who owned grimoires in the past had a personal relationship with them that went beyond mere ownership. They were added to and annotated, and some even gave their blood to enhance the magic they contained. Some gave their lives.

The history of grimoires, as told in these pages, is not only about the significance of the book in human intellectual development, but also about the desire for knowledge and the enduring impulse to restrict and control it. In this respect the Internet has had a profound and democratic influence. We have seen how in the past the authorities struggled to control print, and today the main battleground over political and religious freedom in undemocratic countries is centred on attempts to control the Internet, to set up virtual borders in cyberspace. The fear of magic has dissipated, of course, though it still remains. Evangelicals have burned Harry Potter books, and Delaurence publications are still banned in Jamaica. But otherwise the Internet now allows billions to have easy access to the magic that two millennia of censorship tried to suppress. Yet, as the continued publication of old and new grimoires across Europe and the Americas shows, people want to *possess* as well as read them. The old bond between magic, writing, and the page has been maintained, and shows no sign of being dissolved.

The final stage in the democratization of grimoires, while connected to the development of new media, is more about social liberation. It has taken over 2,000 years, but women are finally a major force in both the production and the use of grimoires. As in other areas of modern cultural and economic life, this can be traced to the late 1960s and early 1970s, and the rise of feminism and women's central role in the Western counterculture. The goddess worship at the heart of the new religion of Wicca had a potent symbolic attraction to women seeking magical and spiritual empowerment. It is no surprise that modern witchcraft was embraced most enthusiastically in the USA and Britain, where the dominant religion, Protestantism, downplays the centrality of the biblical Marys, and the female saints have little role in devotion. Feminists also looked to the witch trials of the sixteenth and seventeenth centuries as evidence of how misogyny led to the brutal and terrifying attempt to subjugate and control women in the past. Early feminist works and the media bandied about the wildly exaggerated notion that millions of accused witches were executed in the period. This reinforced the conviction that witch hunting was synonymous with woman hunting. Yet, in part through the influence of Wicca a new positive image of the witch was formed in American and British mass culture, one that was empowering and defiant. Witchcraft was no longer defined by such old stereotypes as the illiterate, wrinkled woman who vented her frustrations on a harsh world through simple acts of spiteful magic. Witchcraft was now about magic as a positive form of female expression. Modern witches were reclaiming the inheritance for which their ancestors had died, and that included the books that they were thought to own as independent-minded women who were sacrificed to maintain patriarchal control.

In the USA in the 1970s and early 1980s Anna Riva, the pseudonym of Dorothy Spencer, who ran her own mail order hoodoo supplies company, updated the pre-war pulp genre of short, populist grimoires by appealing to this reformulated conception of the witch, with titles such as *Modern Witchcraft Spellbook* (1973) and *Spellcraft, Hexcraft and Witchcraft* (1977). There were also more familiar titles echoing the Dorene library such as *Candle Burning Magic* (1980), *Powers of the Psalms* (1982), and *Secrets of Magical Seals: A Modern Grimoire* (1975). They have been published regularly ever since for a few dollars. Following in her footsteps is Migene Gonzalez-Wippler, a Puerto Rican academic who has written several respected books on *Santería*. Her awareness of the grimoire tradition has led her down the commercial path and she now successfully writes and markets books of practical magic. She has produced a new edition of the *Sixth and Seventh Books of Moses* as well as a *Book of Shadows*, along with various guides for making amulets, talismans, and spells. The success and influence of both authors is not predicated on their gender. They have rather spotted a commercial opportunity in a market formerly dominated by men, by identifying how magic books could bridge the gap between the old and recent traditions of magic and witchcraft. Anna Riva's books, for instance, have a cultural and geographical appeal beyond the main US market. Her *Power of the Psalms* and *Magic with Incense and Powders* are to be found along with de Claremont's *Seven Keys to Power* on the bookshelves of 'spiritual workers' in Tobago, and her *Voodoo Handbook of Cult Secrets* is sold in Jamaican drug stores.[1] That said, in recent years much of the contemporary grimoire market has been aimed at a Western female teenage audience fascinated by the portrayal of contemporary practical magic and witchcraft in television dramas, rather than histories of witchcraft or the awareness of venerable magical traditions.

The Harry Potter books and films have been blamed by some evangelicals for being responsible for the explosion of teenage interest in practical magic. The story of Hogwarts' child magicians represents a long tradition of fantasy fiction involving youthful wizards, most notably Ursula Le Guin's *Wizard of Earthsea*. Harry Potter may be set in contemporary Britain, but it is a good old-fashioned saga about 'chosen ones' and their role in the universal struggle between good and evil. Teen witches appear to be more inspired by grimoire magic as part of the everyday social reality of urban America, rather than titanic wand-waving battles in remote gothic boarding schools.

The Craft (1996) was an influential template for the female teen witch. The film concerned four girls in a Los Angeles Catholic high school who practise capricious and vengeful magic with unfortunate consequences. Other films followed, such as *Practical Magic* (1998), which borrowed historical themes familiar to millions of high school students taught about the Salem witch trials. It was based on a novel regarding the love lives of a couple of modern-day, hereditary witches in small-town America who cast magic from a grimoire passed down to them through the generations. But it was television that really cemented the grimoire as a cultural artefact in contemporary Western society. Magic books were central to the television series *Charmed* (1998–2006), which concerned three co-habiting sister witches in their twenties who get involved in various supernatural escapades. Like all modern screen witches they also happened to be attractive and glamorous, reversing the old stereotype of the hag-witch. The sisters in *Charmed* derive their power from a leather-bound *Book of Shadows* that, so the plot relates, was first written by an unfortunate female ancestor burned at the stake in the seventeenth century and was then supplemented over the centuries as it passed down the female line. *Buffy the Vampire Slayer* (1997–2003), with its high school setting, was the other influential TV series in inspiring teenagers to explore the possibilities of magic. For the first few seasons the Sunnydale School library, with its old books on magic taken from the British Library, was central to the narrative, while one of the central characters, Willow, became a 'Wiccan', casting spells using her grimoire.[2] It was while Buffy was at its height of popularity that I used to receive periodic e-mails from teenagers, mostly girls from the USA and Britain, asking to know more about witchcraft and how to cast spells. They had seen my personal website presenting my historical studies on witchcraft and magic and assumed I was a practitioner. The flow of e-mails tellingly tailed off once Buffy and Charmed ended.

While undoubtedly inspired by these American dramas the teen witch phenomenon has developed a life of its own, fostered by the social networking possibilities of the Internet, which allow teenagers to form communities outside the school environment. Books still remain fundamental to the teen witch experience though; spells cut-and-pasted from the Web clearly do not have the same appeal. The American author Silver RavenWolf is the queen of teen grimoire writers, and the advertising blurb for her Solitary Witch encapsulates well the appeal of her successful formula, explaining that the book 'relates specifically to today's young adults and their concerns, yet is grounded in the magickal work of centuries past'. Many of the Buffy generation have subsequently lost interest in practical magic, but others have no doubt developed a more lasting spiritual and social interest in magic as a religion, and have graduated from guides written specifically for youth culture to exploring the grimoires of old.

The grimoire continues to have huge cultural currency far beyond those who practise magic or who fantasize about doing so. Several of the largest publishing sensations of the past few years are products of the history of magic books. Apocryphal stories, which were a big influence on the development of grimoires, lie at the heart of the huge success of the Da Vinci Code. The book evidently taps into a continuing popular undercurrent of suspicion that over the centuries the Christian authorities have withheld the true story of Christ, and that ancient secret knowledge equals power. King Solomon and his apocryphal magical reputation continue to intrigue, with rumours abound on the Internet that Dan Brown is writing a book called The Solomon Key. Another international bestseller, Arturo Perez-Reverte's rollicking novel The Club Dumas, and the film adaptation The Ninth Gate, directed by Roman Polanski and starring Johnny Depp, also owe their popularity to the notion that secret diabolic books still circulate amongst us. The story concerns a maverick antiquarian book dealer who finds himself drawn into a dangerous search for the surviving copies of the fictional Book of the Nine Doors of the Kingdom of Shadows, which was printed in the mid-seventeenth century. Its author was burned at the behest of the Inquisition and only three copies were saved from the flames. Together they provide the key to summoning the Devil.

The book dealer's quest leads him to Paris and Toledo, the legendary medieval home of magic. All the elements of this story will be familiar to the reader, and they evidently continue to fascinate today just as they held the attention of readers in earlier centuries.

In her bestseller *Jonathan Strange and Mr Norrell* (2004), Susanna Clarke re-creates an early-nineteenth-century England where learned magic once again becomes a profound force after centuries in the shadows, echoing the real, though decidedly less fantastic world of Francis Barrett, John Denley, and John Parkins. Old magic books are central to her clever, gothic re-imagining of the occult milieu of the period, mentioning titles that sound familiar to the reader but are in fact her own inventions. Clarke even constructs her own history of literary magic, inventing the maxim, 'a book of magic should be written by a practising magician, rather than a theoretical magician or a historian of magic. What could be more reasonable? And yet already we are in difficulties.'[3] This history of grimoires has shown what those difficulties were in the real past.

So grimoires are still with us, not mere historical artefacts but cultural symbols, but what of the magic they contain? Only a small minority in the prosperous Western world still believe in the power of magic let alone practise it. This cannot be explained as a result of education and the consequent spread of rational knowledge. We need only think of the enduring popularity of magic's partner, astrology. Many millions continue to believe in the intercessionary power of angels. Furthermore, literacy has always been the key to the power of grimoires, and their spread actually mirrors the growth of popular education. No, reason has not ended our relationship with magic. It is just that most of us in the West no longer need magic in our lives. Who needs to conjure up spirits to find buried treasure when you can use a metal detector? Seriously, though, much of magic was also about health. Modern medicine can do so much more for us than it could fifty years ago let alone a hundred. Before that it was pretty hopeless at dealing with most major illnesses. Wherever people do not have access to modern medicine today it is understandable that they still depend on magic, on religious faith alone. With sexual liberation, the freedom to divorce, and the pill, few now resort to grimoires to ensure the success of their love lives, though as the popularity of horoscopes and astrological birth signs suggests, many people still place some faith in the occult to try and ensure successful relationships. But grimoire magic was not only put to practical ends. As we have seen, for some intellectual magicians magic was about religious expression and attaining spiritual harmony, and while this impulse might be rare in the context of the main religions these days, it continues to be central to the new Western formulations of the pre-Christian religious world and to syncretic religions elsewhere.

Grimoires have never been more easily available. As we enter uncertain times on a global scale, who knows whether they and their magic, which in the past gave order to a chaotic and unpredictable world, will once again assume wider social importance. If they do, then they are easily at hand. There is no sign of these books being closed for good.

Picture Acknowledgements

In a few instances we have been unable to trace the copyright owner prior to publication. If notified, the publishers will be pleased to amend the acknowledgements in any future edition. © Archives départementales des Landes/Alain Girons: p. 102; The Bodleian Library, University of Oxford (Douce A360): p. 99; © British Library Board. All rights reserved: p. 49 (C40 M 10), p. 51 (719.f.16), p. 103 (RB.23.a.25734), p. 122 (C143 cc 19), p. 133 (P.P.5441.ba, frontispiece); Cambridge University Library: p. 151 (N.2.19), p. 276 (8000.c.144); reprinted from H.P. Hansen, *Kloge Folk* (Copenhagen, 1961), vol. 2, plate 3: p. 130; National Library of Jamaica: p. 228; Steven Wood/North Yorkshire County Council, Skipton Library and Information Centre: p. 58; Wellcome Library, London: p. 125, p. 136

FURTHER READING

Primary sources

Numerous extracts from ancient Greek, Roman, Graeco-Egyptian, and Coptic magic texts can be found in:

Betz, Hans Dieter (ed.), *The Greek Magical Papyri in Translation: Including the Demotic Spells*, 2nd edn (Chicago, 1992).

Meyer, Marvin W., Richard Smith, and Neal Kelsey (eds), *Ancient Christian Magic: Coptic Texts of Ritual Power* (Princeton, [1994] 1999).

Ogden, Daniel, *Magic, Witchcraft, and Ghosts in the Greek and Roman Worlds: A Source Book* (Oxford, 2002).

For extensive extracts from medieval and early modern manuscript grimoires see:

Lecouteux, Claude, *Le livres des grimoires* (Paris, 2002).

Shah, Idries, *The Secret Lore of Magic: Books of the Sorcerers* (London, 1957).

Waite, Arthur Edward, *The Book of Ceremonial Magic* (Ware, [1911] 1992).

Translations of entire manuscripts from the medieval to the nineteenth century include:

Flowers, Stephen E., *The Galdrabók: An Icelandic Book of Magic*, 2nd edn (Smithville, 2005).

Gaster, M., *The Sword of Moses: An Ancient Book of Magic* (London, 1896).

Gollancz, Hermann, *Sepher Maphteah Shelomoh* (*Book of the Key of Solomon*) (Oxford, 1914).

Kieckhefer, Richard, *Forbidden Rites: A Necromancer's Manual of the Fifteenth Century* (University Park/Stroud, 1997).

Mathers, Samuel Liddle MacGregor, *The Book of the Sacred Magic of Abra-Melin the Mage* (London, 1898).

—— *The Key of Solomon the King* (*Clavicula Salomonis*) (London, 1889).

Peterson, Joseph H., *The Lesser Key of Solomon: Lemegeton Clavicula Salomonis* (York Beach, 2001).

Rustad, Mary S., *The Black Books of Elverum* (Lakeville, [1999] 2006).

Skinner, Stephen, and David Rankine, *The Goetia of Dr Rudd* (London, 2007).

Joseph H. Peterson's website http://www.esotericarchives.com and the highly recommended CD he has produced provide numerous transcripts and translations of rare grimoires and books of magic. He is to be congratulated for producing an important resource for scholars and the general public.

Histories of magic

There are few good general surveys of magic covering the entire period of this book. A highly recommended companion is Michael D. Bailey, *Magic and Superstition in Europe: A Concise History from Antiquity to the Present* (Lanham, 2007). The six volumes of the *Athlone History of Witchcraft and Magic in Europe*, under the general editorship of Bengt Ankarloo and Stuart Clark, also provide extensive coverage of the subject from antiquity to the present through lengthy essays of influential historians in the field. My own *Cunning-Folk: Popular Magic in English History* (London, 2003), while primarily concerned with England, also has a chapter on European comparisons. Lynn Thorndike's monumental eight-volume *History of Magic and Experimental Science* (New York, 1923–58) is an essential though expensive resource on the intellectual magical tradition up until the Enlightenment. Mention should also be given to Christopher McIntosh's *The Devil's Bookshelf* (Wellingborough, 1985), which provides a brief, breezy but well-informed introduction to the history of grimoires. Below I provide further suggested reading by period and region. They are just some of the works I have found helpful in understanding the development and significance of grimoires.

Ancient Magic

Bohak, Gideon, *Ancient Jewish Magic: A History* (Cambridge, 2008).

Bremmer, Jan N., and Jan R. Veenstra (eds), *The Metamorphosis of Magic from Late Antiquity to the Early Modern Period* (Leuven, 2002).

Dickie, Matthew W., *Magic and Magicians in the Greco-Roman World* (London, 2001).

Faraone, Christopher A., and Dirk Obbink (eds), *Magika Hiera: Ancient Greek Magic and Religion* (Oxford, 1991).

Klutz, Todd (ed.), *Magic in the Biblical World: From the Rod of Aaron to the Ring of Solomon* (London, 2003).

Mirecki, Paul, and Marvin Meyer (eds), *Magic and Ritual in the Ancient World* (Leiden, 2002).

Pinch, Geraldine, *Magic in Ancient Egypt* (London, [1994] 2006).

Shaked, Shaul (ed.), *Officina Magica: Essays on the Practice of Magic in Antiquity* (Leiden, 2005).

Smith, Morton, *Jesus the Magician* (New York, 1978).

Medieval

Bremmer, Jan N., and Jan R. Veenstra (eds), *The Metamorphosis of Magic from Late Antiquity to the Early Modern Period* (Leuven, 2002).

Burnett, Charles, and W. F. Ryan (eds), *Magic and the Classical Tradition* (London and Turin, 2006).

Fanger, Claire (ed.), *Conjuring Spirits: Texts and Traditions of Medieval Ritual Magic* (Stroud, 1998).

Flint, Valerie, *The Rise of Magic in Early Medieval Europe* (Princeton, 1991).

Jolly, Karen Louise, *Popular Religion in Late Saxon England: Elf Charms in Context* (Chapel Hill, 1996).

Kieckhefer, Richard, *Magic in the Middle Ages* (Cambridge, 1989).

—— *Forbidden Rites: A Necromancer's Manual of the Fifteenth Century* (University Park/ Stroud, 1997).

MacLeod, Mindy, and Bernard Mees, *Runic Amulets and Magic Objects* (Woodbridge, 2006).

Page, Sophie, *Magic in Medieval Manuscripts* (London, 2004).

Ryder, Catherine, *Magic and Impotence in the Middle Ages* (Oxford, 2006).

Skemer, Don C., *Binding Words: Textual Amulets in the Middle Ages* (University Park, 2006).

Trachtenberg, Joshua, *Jewish Magic and Superstition: A Study in Folk Religion* (New York, 1939).

Renaissance to the eighteenth century

Europe

The period of the witch trials, which is an important episode in the story of grimoires, has attracted a huge number of studies. The reader will find accessible overviews of the history of the witch trials and how historians have interpreted them in the likes of Brian Levack, *The Witch-Hunt in Early Modern Europe* (3rd edn, Harlow, 2006), and Jonathan Barry and Owen Davies (eds), *Witchcraft Historiography* (Basingstoke, 2007). Below is a sample of English language histories concerning different types of magical practice and literature in the period.

Barbierato, Federico, 'Magical Literature and the Venice Inquisition from the Sixteenth to the Eighteenth Centuries', in C. Gilly and C. Van Heertum (eds), *Magia, Alchimia, Scienza Dal '400 al '700* (Florence, 2002).

Bever, Edward, *The Realities of Witchcraft and Popular Magic in Early Modern Europe: Culture, Cognition, and Everyday Life* (Basingstoke, 2008).

Butler, Elizabeth M., *Ritual Magic* (Stroud, [1949] 1998).

Eamon, William, *Science and the Secrets of Nature: Books of Secrets in Medieval and Early Modern Culture* (Princeton, 1994).

Kassell, Lauren, *Medicine and Magic in Elizabethan London. Simon Forman: Astrologer, Alchemist and Physician* (Oxford, 2005).

Martin, Ruth, *Witchcraft and the Inquisition in Venice 1550–1650* (Oxford, 1989).

Mollenauer, Lynn Wood, *Strange Revelations: Magic, Poison, and Sacrilege in Louis XIV's France* (University Park, 2007).

Monter, William, *Ritual, Myth and Magic in Early Modern Europe* (Brighton, 1983).

Ruggiero, Guido, *Binding Passions: Tales of Magic, Marriage and Power at the End of the Renaissance* (Oxford, 1993).

Thomas, Keith, *Religion and the Decline of Magic* (London, 1971).

Vickers, Brian (ed.), *Occult and Scientific Mentalities in the Renaissance* (Cambridge, 1984).

Walker, D. P., *Spiritual and Demonic Magic from Ficino to Campanella* (London, 1958).

Wilson, Stephen, *The Magical Universe: Everyday Ritual and Magic in Pre-Modern Europe* (London, 2000).

Yates, Frances A., *The Occult Philosophy in the Elizabethan Age* (London, 1979).

Eighteenth to the twentieth century

Europe

Bachter, Stephan, 'Grimoires and the Transmission of Magical Knowledge', in Owen Davies and Willem de Blécourt (eds), *Beyond the Witch Trials: Witchcraft and Magic in Enlightenment Europe* (Manchester, 2004), 194-207.
—— 'Anleitung zum Aberglauben: Zauberbücher und die Verbreitung magischen "Wissens" seit dem 18. Jahrhundert', PhD, Hamburg (2005). Available online at http://www.sub.uni-hamburg.de/opus/volltexte/2007/3221/pdf/ DissBachter.pdf
Blécourt, Willem de and Owen Davies (eds), *Witchcraft Continued: Popular Magic in Modern Europe* (Manchester, 2004).
Davies, Owen, *Witchcraft, Magic and Culture 1736–1951* (Manchester, 1999).
—— *Murder, Magic, Madness: The Victorian Trials of Dove and the Wizard* (Harlow, 2005).
Devlin, Judith, *The Superstitious Mind: French Peasants and the Supernatural in the Nineteenth Century* (New Haven, 1987).
Doering-Manteuffel, Sabine, 'The Supernatural and the Development of Print Culture', in Owen Davies and Willem de Blécourt (eds), *Beyond the Witch Trials: Witchcraft and Magic in Enlightenment Europe* (Manchester, 2004), 187-94.
Krampl, Ulrike, 'When Witches Became False: *Séducteurs* and *Crédules* Confront the Paris Police at the Beginning of the Eighteenth Century', in Kathryn A. Edwards (ed.), *Werewolves, Witches, and Wandering Spirits: Traditional Belief and Folklore in Early Modern Europe* (Kirksville, 2002), 137-55.
McCalman, Iain, *The Last Alchemist: Count Cagliostro, Master of Magic in the Age of Reason* (New York, 2003).
Midelfort, H. C. Erik, *Exorcism and Enlightenment: Johann Joseph Gassner and the Demons of Eighteenth-Century Germany* (New Haven, 2005).
Stark, Laura, *The Magical Self: Body, Society and the Supernatural in Early Modern Rural Finland* (Helsinki, 2006).
Stokker, Kathleen, *Remedies and Rituals: Folk Medicine in Norway and the New Land* (Minnesota, 2007).
Vicente, Castro, 'El Libro de San Cipriano (I)', *Hibris* 27 (2005), 15-25.

USA

Anderson, Jeffrey E., *Conjure in African American Society* (Baton Rouge, 2005).
Benes, Peter (ed.), *Wonders of the Invisible World: 1600–1800* (Boston, 1995).
Brooke, John L., *The Refiner's Fire: The Making of Mormon Cosmology, 1644–1844* (Cambridge, 1994).
Butler, Jon, *Awash in a Sea of Faith: Christianizing the American People* (Cambridge, MA, 1990).
Chireau, Yvonne P., *Black Magic: Religion and the African American Conjuring Tradition* (Berkeley, 2003).
Ellis, Bill, *Lucifer Ascending: The Occult in Folklore and Popular Culture* (Lexington, 2004).

Godbeer, Richard, *The Devil's Dominion: Magic and Religion in Early New England* (Cambridge, 1992).

Leventhal, Herbert, *In the Shadow of the Enlightenment* (New York, 1976).

Long, Carolyn Morrow, *Spiritual Merchants: Religion, Magic, and Commerce* (Knoxville, 2001).

McGinnis, J. Ross, *Trials of Hex* (Davis/Trinity Publishing Co., 2000).

Quinn, D. Michael, *Early Mormonism and the Magic World View*, 2nd edn (Salt Lake City, 1998).

Versluis, Arthur, *The Esoteric Origins of the American Renaissance* (New York, 2000).

Yoder, Don, *Discovering American Folklife: Essays on Folk Cultures and the Pennsylvania Dutch* (Mechanicsburg, [1990] 2001).

Caribbean, Central and South America

Olmos, Margarite Fernández, and Lizabeth Paravisini-Gelbert, *Creole Religions of the Caribbean* (New York, 2003).

Henningsen, Gustav, 'The Diffusion of European Magic in Colonial America', in Jens Christian V. Johansen, Erling Ladewig Petersen, and Henrik Stevnsborg (eds), *Clashes of Cultures: Essays in Honour of Niels Steensgaard* (Odense, 1992), 160–78.

Houk, James T., *Spirits, Blood, and Drums: The Orisha Religion in Trinidad* (Philadelphia, 1995).

Métraux, Alfred, *Le vaudou haïtien* (Paris, [1958] 1968).

Payne-Jackson, Arvilla and Mervyn C. Alleyne, *Jamaican Folk Medicine* (Kingston, 2004).

Souza, Laura de Mello e, *The Devil and the Land of the Holy Cross: Witchcraft, Slavery, and Popular Religion in Colonial Brazil*, trans. Diane Grosklaus Whitty (Austin, 2003).

Taussig, Michael, *Shamanism, Colonialism, and the Wild Man: A Study in Terror and Healing* (Chicago, 1987).

Modern magic traditions

Berger, Helen A., and Douglas Ezzy, *Teenage Witches: Magical Youth and the Search for the Self* (New Brunswick, 2007).

Evans, Dave, *The History of British Magick after Crowley* (Harpenden, 2007).

Harms, Daniel, and John Wisdom Gonce III, *The Necronomicon Files* (Boston, MA, [1998] 2003).

Howe, Ellic, *Urania's Children* (London, 1967).

Hutton, Ronald, *The Triumph of the Moon: A History of Modern Pagan Witchcraft* (Oxford, 1999).

Johnston, Hannah E., and Peg Aloi (eds), *The New Generation Witches: Teenage Witchcraft in Contemporary Culture* (Aldershot, 2007).

King, Francis, *Modern Ritual Magic: The Rise of Western Occultism* (Bridport, [1970] 1989).

Owen, Alex, *The Place of Enchantment: British Occultism and the Culture of the Modern* (Chicago, 2004).

Ruickbie, Leo, *Witchcraft Out of the Shadows: A Complete History* (London, 2004).

Treitel, Corinna, *A Science for the Soul: Occultism and the Genesis of the German Modern* (Baltimore, 2004).

Uzzel, Robert L., *Éliphas Lévi and the Kabbalah: The Masonic and French Connection of the American Mystery Tradition* (Lafayette, 2006).

Books and literacy

Chartier, Roger, *The Cultural Uses of Print in Early Modern France*, trans. Lydia G. Cochrane (Princeton, 1987).

Chaudenson, Robert, *Creolization of Language and Culture*, revised in collaboration with Salikoko S. Mufwene; trans. Sheri Pargman (London, 2001).

Febvre, Lucien, and Henri-Jean Martin, *The Coming of the Book*, trans. David Gerard (London, [1958] 1976).

Fischer, Steven Roger, *A History of Writing* (London, 2001).

Goody, Jack (ed.), *Literacy in Traditional Societies* (Cambridge, 1968).

Graff, Harvey J., *The Legacies of Literacy: Continuities and Contradictions in Western Culture and Society* (Bloomington/Indianapolis, 1987).

Hayes, Kevin J., *Folklore and Book Culture* (Knoxville, 1997).

Millard, Alan, *Reading and Writing in the Time of Jesus* (New York, 2000).

Street, Brian V. (ed.), *Cross-Cultural Approaches to Literacy* (Cambridge, 1993).

Walsham, Alexandra, and Julia Crick (eds), *The Uses of Script and Print, 1300–1700* (Cambridge, 2004).

NOTES

INTRODUCTION

1. François Noel and M. L. J. Carpentier, *Philologie française* (Paris, 1831), i.742; *Dictionnaire de l'Académie Françoise*, 5th edn (Paris, 1814), i.669; Claude Lecouteux, *Le livre des grimoires* (Paris, 2002), 9.

2. For a good recent discussion see Michael D. Bailey, 'The Meanings of Magic', *Magic, Ritual, and Witchcraft* 1:1 (2006), 1–24.

3. Richard Kieckhefer, *Forbidden Rites: A Necromancer's Manual of the Fifteenth Century* (University Park, 1997), 4.

4. I particularly recommend Michael D. Bailey, *Magic and Superstition in Europe: A Concise History from Antiquity to the Present* (Lanham, 2007), which is an ideal companion to this book.

5. E. M. Loeb, review of Joh. Winkler, *Die Toba-Batak auf Sumatra*, in *American Anthropologist*, NS, 32:4 (1930), 682–7; Harley Harris Bartlett, 'A Batak and Malay Chant on Rice Cultivation, with Introductory Notes on Bilingualism and Acculturation in Indonesia', *Proceedings of the American Philosophical Society* 96:6 (1952), 631.

6. Schuyler Cammann, 'Islamic and Indian Magic Squares. Part 1', *History of Religions* 8:3 (1969), 181–209; David Pingree, 'Indian Planetary Images and the Tradition of Astral Magic', *Journal of the Warburg and Courtauld Institute* 52 (1989), 1–13.

7. See, for example, Keith Thomas, *Religion and the Decline of Magic* (London, 1971), 51–2; David Cressy, 'Books as Totems in Seventeenth-Century England and New England', *Journal of Library History* 21 (1986), 92–106; Stephen Wilson, *The Magical Universe: Everyday Ritual and Magic in Pre-Modern Europe* (London, 2000), *passim*.

8. See, for example, Bengt Sundkler, *Bantu Prophets in South Africa* (London, 1961), 278; Patrick A. Polk, 'Other Books, Other Powers: *The 6th and 7th Books of Moses* in

Afro-Atlantic Folk Belief', *Southern Folklore* 56:2 (1999), 122; Douglas MacRae Taylor, *The Black Carib of British Honduras* (New York, 1951), 136; Caroline H. Bledsoe and Kenneth M. Robey, 'Arabic Literacy and Secrecy among the Mende of Sierre Leone', *Man*, NS, 21:2 (1986), 219.

9. Kenneth Anthony Lum, *Praising His Name in the Dance: Spirit Possession in the Spiritual Baptist Faith and Orisha Work in Trinidad* (Amsterdam, 1999), 120.

10. Don C. Skemer, *Binding Words: Textual Amulets in the Middle Ages* (University Park, 2006), 137, 239; Henry O'Neill, *The Fine Arts and Civilization of Ancient Ireland* (London, 1863), 76; Jack Goody, 'Restricted Literacy in Northern Ghana', in *idem* (ed.), *Literacy in Traditional Societies* (Cambridge 1968), 230–1; Abdullahi Osman El-Tom, 'Drinking the Koran: The Meaning of Koranic Verses in Berti Erasure', *Africa* 55:4 (1985), 414–31; Bartlett, 'A Batak and Malay Chant'.

11. The term was coined in Thomas, *Religion and the Decline of Magic*, 269.

I Ancient and Medieval Grimoires

1. Cited in Daniel Ogden, *Magic, Witchcraft, and Ghosts in the Greek and Roman Worlds: A Source Book* (Oxford, 2002), 41–2.

2. Jonas C. Greenfield and Michael E. Stone, 'The Books of Enoch and the Traditions of Enoch', *Numen* 26 (1979), 89–103; M. Plessner, 'Hermes Trismegistus and Arab Science', *Studia Islamica* 2 (1954), 54; P. S. Alexander, 'Incantations and Books of Magic', in Emil Schürer (ed.), *The History of the Jewish People in the Age of Christ (175 BC–AD135)*, rev. and ed. Geza Vermes, Fergus Millar, and Martin Goodman (Edinburgh, 1986), vol. iii, pt 1, p. 369.

3. Karl H. Dannenfeldt, 'The Pseudo-Zoroastrian Oracles in the Renaissance', *Studies in the Renaissance* 4 (1957), 7–30; George Lyman Kittredge, *Witchcraft in Old and New England* (New York, [1929] 1958), 42; Lynn Thorndike, *History of Magic and Experimental Science*, 8 vols (New York: 1923–58), ii.321; Valerie Flint, *The Rise of Magic in Early Medieval Europe* (Princeton, 1991), 333–8; Benjamin Braude, 'The Sons of Noah and the Construction of Ethnic and Geographical Identities in the Medieval and Early Modern Periods', *The William and Mary Quarterly*, 3rd ser. 54:2 (1997), 103–42. On contradictory legends regarding Zoroaster see Michael Stausberg, *Faszination Zarathustra: Zoraster und die Europäische Religionsgeschichte der Frühen Neuzeit*, 2 vols (Berlin, 1998).

4. Joachim Oelsner, 'Incantations in Southern Mesopotamia—From Clay Tablets to Magical Bowls', in Shaul Shaked (ed.), *Officina Magica: Essays on the Practice of Magic in Antiquity* (Leiden, 2005), 31–3.

5. Jan N. Bremmer, 'Magic in the *Apocryphal Acts of the Apostles*', in Jan N. Bremmer and Jan R. Veenstra (eds), *The Metamorphosis of Magic from Late Antiquity to the Early Modern Period* (Leuven, 2002), 53–4.

6. Georg Luck, *Arcana Mundi* (London, 1987), 11–13; Matthew W. Dickie, *Magic and Magicians in the Greco-Roman World* (London, 2001), 204.

7. Geraldine Pinch, *Magic in Ancient Egypt* (London, [1994] 2006), 160–7.

8. Luois H. Feldman, *Jew and Gentile in the Ancient World* (Princeton, 1993), 285–8; Dickie, *Magic and Magicians*, 223–4, 287–93.

9. See Andreas B. Kilcher, 'The Moses of Sinai and the Moses of Egypt: Moses as Magician in Jewish Literature and Western Esotericism', *Aries* 4:2 (2004), 148–70.

10. Ibid. 158–67; Jan Assmann, *Moses the Egyptian: The Memory of Egypt in Western Monotheism* (Cambridge, MA, 1997).

11. On these and other books attributed to Moses see John G. Gager, *Moses in Greco-Roman Paganism* (Atlanta, 1989), 146–61.

12. Hans Dieter Betz (ed.), *The Greek Magical Papyri in Translation: Including the Demotic Spells*, vol. i: *Texts*, 2nd edn (Chicago, 1992), 189, 195.

13. Kilcher, 'Moses of Sinai', 167.

14. See Gideon Bohak, *Ancient Jewish Magic: A History* (Cambridge, 2008), 175–9; Alexander, 'Incantations and Books of Magic', 350–1; M. Gaster, *The Sword of Moses: An Ancient Book of Magic* (London, 1896), 43.

15. Florian Ebeling, *The Secret History of Hermes Trismegistus: Hermeticism from Ancient to Modern Times*, trans. David Lorton (Ithaca, 2007), 6.

16. Plessner, 'Hermes Trismegistus', 52.

17. William Adler, 'Berossus, Manetho, and "1 Enoch" in the World Chronicle of Panodorus', *Harvard Theological Review* 76:4 (1983), 428–30.

18. Ebeling, *Secret History*, 9.

19. Thorndike, *History of Magic*, ii.226–7; Nicolas Weill-Parot, 'Astral Magic and Intellectual Changes (Twelfth–Fifteenth Centuries)', in Bremmer and Veenstra (eds), *Metamorphosis of Magic*, 170, 172.

20. On Solomon, the *Testament*, and magic see Dennis Durling, 'Solomon, Exorcism, and the Son of David', *Harvard Theological Review* 68:3/4 (1975), 235–52; *idem*, 'The Testament of Solomon: Retrospective and Prospect', *Journal of Pseudepigraphical Studies* 2 (1988), 87–112; Sarah Iles Johnston, 'The *Testament* of Solomon from Late Antiquity to the Renaissance', in Bremmer and Veenstra (eds), *Metamorphosis of Magic*, 36–49; Todd Klutz, *Rewriting the Testament of Solomon: Tradition, Conflict and Identity in a Late Antique Pseudepigraphon* (London, 2005).

21. W. F. Ryan, *The Bathhouse at Midnight: Magic in Russia* (Stroud, 1999), 303.

22. See, for example, Miroslav Marcovich, *Studies in Graeco-Roman Religions and Gnosticism* (Leiden, 1988), 28–47; Walter O. Moeller, *The Mithraic Origin and Meanings of the Rotas-Sator Square* (Leiden, 1973); Bruce Manning Metzger, *New Testament Studies* (Leiden, 1980), 30.

23. Several scholarly editions of the *Testament of Solomon* have been produced. For an overview of their qualities see Klutz, *Rewriting the Testament of Solomon*, 1–4. An online annotated version of one translation is provided at http://www.esotericarchives.com/solomon/testamen.htm.

24. Johnston, 'The *Testament* of Solomon', 43 n. 5.

25. Thorndike, *History of Magic*, ii.280.

26. Jan R. Veenstra, 'The Holy Almandal: Angels and the Intellectual Aims of Magic', in Bremmer and Veenstra (eds), *Metamorphosis of Magic*, 189–229.

27. See Claire Fanger, 'Plundering the Egyptian Treasure: John the Monk's *Book of Visions* and its Relation to the *Ars Notoria* of Solomon', in Claire Fanger (ed.), *Conjuring Spirits: Texts and Traditions of Medieval Ritual Magic* (Stroud, 1998), 217–49; Michael Camille, 'Visual Art in Two Manuscripts of the Ars Notoria', in Fanger (ed.), *Conjuring Spirits*, 110–42; Frank Klaassen, 'English Manuscripts of Magic, 1300–1500: A Preliminary Survey', in Fanger (ed.), *Conjuring Spirits*, 14–19; Benedek Láng, 'Angels around the Crystal: The Prayer Book of King Wladislas and the Treasure Hunts of Henry the Bohemian', *Aries* 5:1 (2005), 6–14.

28. See David L. Wagner (ed.), *The Seven Liberal Arts in the Middle Ages* (Bloomington, 1983).

29. Robert Mathiesen, 'The Key of Solomon: Toward a Typology of the Manuscripts', *Societas Magica Newsletter* 17 (2007), 1–9.

30. Stephen Charles Haar, *Simon Magus: The First Gnostic?* (Berlin, 2003), 158–9; Florent Heintz, *Simon 'Le Magicien': Actes 8, 5–25 et l'accusation de magie contre les prophètes thaumaturges dans l'antiquité* (Paris, 1997), pt. 4.

31. Thorndike, *History of Magic*, i.368–9; Hans-Josef Klauck, *Magic and Paganism in Early Christianity: The World of the Acts of the Apostles* (Edinburgh, 2000), 14–17.

32. See Alberto Ferreiro, *Simon Magus in Patristic, Medieval and Early Modern Traditions* (Leiden, 2005), ch. 10; Flint, *Rise of Magic*, 338–44.

33. Ferreiro, *Simon Magus*, 210–12.

34. See E. P. Sanders, *The Historical Figure of Jesus* (London, 1993), ch. 10; Georg Luck, 'Witches and Sorcerers in Classical Literature', in Valerie Flint, Richard Gordon, Georg Luck, and Daniel Ogden (eds), *Witchcraft and Magic in Europe: Ancient Greece and Rome* (London, 1999), 124–5; Michael D. Bailey, *Magic and Superstition in Europe: A Concise History from Antiquity to the Present* (Lanham, 2007), 46–9; Richard Kieckhefer, *Magic in the Middle Ages* (Cambridge, 1989), 34–6; Carl H. Kraeling, 'Was Jesus Accused of Necromancy?', *Journal of Biblical Literature* 59:2 (1940), 147–57; Justin Meggitt, 'Magic, Healing and Early Christianity: Consumption and Completion', in Amy Wygant (ed.), *The Meanings of Magic from the Bible to Buffalo Bill* (New York, 2006), 89–117. For a full-blown attempt at revealing Jesus as a magician see Morton Smith, *Jesus the Magician* (New York, 1978).

35. Sanders, *Historical Figure of Jesus*, 146–7.

36. Veenstra, 'The Holy Almandal', 201.

37. Ioan P. Culianu, *Eros and Magic in the Renaissance*, trans. Margaret Cook (Chicago, 1987), 167.

38. Hermann Gollancz, *Sepher Maphteah Shelomoh (Book of the Key of Solomon)* (Oxford, 1914); transcript by Joseph H. Peterson online at http://www.esotericarchives.com/

gollancz/mafteahs.htm. On the dating see Claudia Rohrbacher-Sticker, 'Mafteah Shelomoh: A New Acquisition of the British Library', *Jewish Studies Quarterly* 1 (1993/4), 263–70; *eadem*, 'A Hebrew Manuscript of Clavicula Salomonis, Part II', *The British Library Journal* 21 (1995), 128–36.

39. Dickie, *Magic and Magicians*, 72.

40. See David Diringer, *The Book before Printing: Ancient, Medieval and Oriental* (New York, 1982), ch. 4.

41. Samson Eitrem, 'Dreams and Divination in Magical Ritual', in Christopher A. Faraone and Dirk Obbink (eds), *Magika Hiera: Ancient Greek Magic and Religion* (Oxford, 1991), 177, 186 n. 52.

42. Clarence A. Forbes, 'Books for the Burning', *Transactions and Proceedings of the American Philological Association* 67 (1936), 118, 120; A. A. Barb, 'Survival of Magic Arts', in Arnaldo Momigliano (ed.), *The Conflict between Paganism and Christianity in the Fourth Century* (Oxford, 1963), 102; Haig A. Bosmajian, *Burning Books* (Jefferson, 2006), 33-40; Daniel Christopher Sarefield, ' "Burning Knowledge": Studies of Bookburning in Ancient Rome', PhD thesis, Ohio State University (2004), esp. 76–89.

43. Chester C. McCown, 'The Ephesia Grammata in Popular Belief', *Transactions and Proceedings of the American Philological Association* 54 (1923), 128–40; Paul Mirecki and Marvin Meyer, *Magic and Ritual in the Ancient World* (Leiden, 2002), 113–14; Daniel Ogden, 'Binding Spells: Curse Tablets and Voodoo Dolls in the Greek and Roman Worlds', in Flint, Gordon, Luck and Ogden (eds), *Witchcraft and Magic in Europe*, 46–7; Roy Kotansky, 'Incantations and Prayers for Salvation on Inscribed Greek Amulets', in Faraone and Obbink (eds), *Magika Hiera*, 110–12.

44. Paul Tabilco, *The Early Christians in Ephesus from Paul to Ignatius* (Tübingen, 2004), 149–52.

45. Quote taken from an online edition of Chrysotom's *Homilies on the Acts of the Apostles*, Homily 38; http://www.ccel.org/ccel/schaff/npnf111.vi.xxxviii.html; Barb, 'Survival of the Magical Arts', 116.

46. Frank R. Trombley, 'Paganism in the Greek World at the End of the Antiquity: The Case of Rural Anatolia and Greece', *Harvard Theological Review* 78:3/4 (1985), 336.

47. Sarefield, ' "Burning Knowledge" ', 89 n. 158.

48. See Frank R. Trombley, *Hellenic Religion and Christianization, c.330–529*, 2 vols (Leiden, 1993), ii.34–40.

49. Dickie, *Magic and Magicians*, 262.

50. Michael Kulikowski, 'Fronto, the Bishops, and the Crowd: Episcopal Justice and Communal Violence in Fifth-Century Tarraconensis', *Early Medieval Europe* 11:4 (2002), 295–320.

51. Cited in Jennifer M. Corry, *Perceptions of Magic in Medieval Spanish Literature* (Bethlehem, PA, 2005), 38.

52. See Stephen Pollington, *Leechcraft: Early English Charms, Plant Lore, and Healing* (Hockwold-cum-Wilton, 2000), 419–85; Karen Louise Jolly, *Popular Religion in Late*

Saxon England: Elf Charms in Context (Chapel Hill, 1996); Alaric Hall, *Elves in Anglo-Saxon England* (Woodbridge, 2007).

53. Don C. Skemer, *Binding Words: Textual Amulets in the Middle Ages* (University Park, 2006), 76–84; Eamon Duffy, *The Stripping of the Altars: Traditional Religion in England 1400–1580* (New Haven, 1992), 268–87.

54. Kieckhefer, *Magic in the Middle Ages*, 182–3.

55. Steven Roger Fischer, *A History of Writing* (London, 2001), 238, 244; Alan Millard, *Reading and Writing in the Time of Jesus* (New York, 2000), 61–84; J. B. Poole and R. Reed, 'The Preparation of Leather and Parchment by the Dead Sea Scrolls Community', *Technology and Culture* 3:1 (1962), 15–16; Joshua Trachtenberg, *Jewish Magic and Superstition: A Study in Folk Religion* (New York, 1939), 144.

56. Domenico Comparetti, *Vergil in the Middle Ages*, trans. E. F. Benecke (Princeton, [1895] 1997), 273–4, 31–7; John Webster Spargo, *Virgil the Necromancer: Studies in Virgilian Legends* (Cambridge, MA, 1934), 33. See also Mario N. Pavia, 'Virgil as Magician', *The Classical Journal* 46:2 (1950), 61–4.

57. Juliette Wood, 'Virgil and Taliesin: The Concept of the Magician in Medieval Folklore', *Folklore* 94:1 (1983), 91, 94; John Moore, *A View of Society and Manners in Italy* (Paris, 1803), ii.253.

58. For example, David Pingree, 'Learned Magic in the Time of Frederick II', *Micrologus* 2 (1994), 44.

59. See the essays in J. Kraye, W. F. Ryan, and C. B. Schmitt (eds), *Pseudo-Aristotle in the Middle Ages* (London, 1987); Steven J. Williams, *The Secret of Secrets: The Scholarly Career of a Pseudo-Aristotelian Text in the Latin Middle Ages* (Ann Arbor, 2003).

60. Owen Davies, *Witchcraft, Magic and Culture 1736–1951* (Manchester, 1999), 132.

61. David Pingree, 'The Diffusion of Arabic Magical Texts in Western Europe', in *La diffusione delle scienze islamiche nel Medio Evo europeo* (Rome, 1987), 58–102.

62. Richard Kieckhefer, *Forbidden Rites: A Necromancer's Manual of the Fifteenth Century* (University Park/Stroud, 1997), 178.

63. Erica Reiner, 'Astral Magic in Babylonia', *Transactions of the American Philosophical Society* 85:4 (1995), 1–150; David Pingree, 'Indian Planetary Images and the Tradition of Astral Magic', *Journal of the Warburg and Courtauld Institutes* 52 (1989), 1–13.

64. Charles Burnett, 'The Coherence of the Arabic-Latin Translation Program in Toledo in the Twelfth Century', *Science in Context* 14:2 (2001), 249–88; Pingree, 'The Diffusion of Arabic Magical Texts in Western Europe'. See also, Thomas F. Glick, Steven John Livesey, and Faith Wallis, *Medieval Science, Technology, and Medicine: An Encyclopedia* (New York, 2005), 478–81.

65. Quoted in Charles Singer, 'Daniel of Morley: An English Philosopher of the XII Century', *Isis* 3:2 (1920), 264.

66. See David Pingree, 'Some of the Sources of the *Ghāyat al-hakīm*', *Journal of the Warburg and Courtauld Institutes* 43 (1980), 1–15; J. Thomann, 'The Name of Picatrix:

Transcription or Translation?', *Journal of the Warburg and Courtauld Institute* 53 (1990), 289–96.

67. Most recently see Edgar Walter Francis, 'Islamic Symbols and Sufi Rituals for Protection and Healing: Religion and Magic in the Writings of Ahmad ibn Ali al-Buni (d. 622/1225)', PhD thesis, University of California (2005).

68. J. Ferreiro Alemparte, 'La escuela de nigromancia de Toledo', *Anuario de studios medievales* 13 (1983), 208.

69. Ibid. 226–40; Stephan Maksymiuk, *The Court Magician in Medieval German Romance* (Frankfurt, 1996), 139.

70. Jeffrey Burton Russell, *Witchcraft in the Middle Ages* (Ithaca, 1972), 163.

71. Francesco Maria Guazzo, *Compendium Maleficarum*, trans. E. A. Ashwin (New York, [1929] 1988), 194.

72. See François Delpech, 'Grimoires et savoirs souterrains: elements pour une archéo-mythologie du livre magique', in Dominique de Courcelles (ed.), *Le pouvoir des livres à la Renaissance* (Paris, 1998), 23–46; Fernando Ruiz de la Puerta, *La Cueva de Hércules y el Palacio Encantado de Toledo* (Madrid, 1977); Samuel M. Waxman, *Chapters on Magic in Spanish Literature* (Kessinger [1916], 2007), 1–32.

73. Corry, *Perceptions of Magic*, 154–7.

74. Lynette M. F. Bosch, *Art, Liturgy, and Legend in Renaissance Toledo* (Philadelphia, 2000), 24.

75. Waxman, *Chapters on Magic*, 32–42; Martín Del Rio, *Investigations into Magic*, trans and ed. P. G. Maxwell-Stuart (Manchester, 2000), 28.

76. Montague Summers, *Witchcraft and Black Magic* (London, [1946] 1964), 102.

77. Thorndike, *History of Magic*, ii.229–35; Antonio Rigo, 'From Constantinople to the Library of Venice: The Hermetic Books of Late Byzantine Doctors, Astrologers and Magicians', in C. Gilly and C. van Heertum (eds), *Magia, alchimia, scienza dal '400 al '700. L'influsso di Ermete Trismegisto/Magic, Alchemy and Science 15th–18th Centuries* (Florence, 2002), i.77–83; Jeffrey Spier, 'A Revival of Antique Magical Practice in Tenth-Century Constantinople', in Charles Burnett and W. F. Ryan (eds), *Magic and the Classical Tradition* (London/Turin, 2006), 33.

78. See Dov Schwartz, *Studies on Astral Magic in Medieval Jewish Thought* (Leiden, 2004).

79. Bohak, *Ancient Jewish Magic*, 221–4.

80. See Philip S. Alexander, 'Sefer Ha-Razim and the Problem of Black Magic in Early Judaism', in Todd Klutz (ed.), *Magic in the Biblical World: From the Rod of Aaron to the Ring of Solomon* (London, 2003), 170–90.

81. Ibid. 190.

82. See Reimund Leicht, 'Some Observations on the Diffusion of Jewish Magical Texts from Late Antiquity and the Early Middle Ages in Manuscripts from the Cairo Genizah and Ashkenaz', in Shaked (ed.), *Officina Magica*, 213–31; Steven M. Wasserstrom, 'The Unwritten Chapter: Notes towards a Social and Religious History of

Geniza Magic', in Shaked (ed.), *Officina Magica*. On other sources of medieval Jewish magic see Trachtenberg's *Jewish Magic and Superstition*.

83. Jacob Z. Lauterbach, 'Substitutes for the Tetragrammaton', *Proceedings of the American Academy for Jewish Research* 2 (1930–1), 39–67; Skemer, *Binding Words*, 114.

84. Stephen Mitchell, 'Learning Magic in the Sagas', in Geraldine Barnes and Margaret Clunies Ross (eds), *Old Norse Myths, Literature and Society* (Sydney, 2000), 336.

85. Mindy MacLeod and Bernard Mees, *Runic Amulets and Magic Objects* (Woodbridge, 2006), 6.

86. Ibid. 150–1.

87. Kieckhefer, *Magic in the Middle Ages*, 141; Charles Burnett and Marie Stoklund, 'Scandinavian Runes in a Latin Magical Treatise', *Speculum* 58:2 (1983), 419–29.

88. The seminal study is still Theodor Zahn, *Cyprian von Antiochen und die deutsche Faustsage* (Erlangen, 1882). There is a lengthy English review of his theories in *The American Journal of Philology* 3:12 (1882), 470–3.

89. Cited in Flint, *Rise of Magic*, 234.

90. See Martin P. Nilsson, 'Greek Mysteries in the Confession of St. Cyprian', *Harvard Theological Review* 40:3 (1947), 167–76; Edgar J. Goodspeed, 'The Martyrdom of Cyprian and Justa', *American Journal of Semitic Languages and Literatures* 19:2 (1903), 65–82.

91. Fred C. Robinson, ' "The Complaynt off Sanct Cipriane, the Grett Nigromancer": A Poem by Anthony Ascham', *Review of English Studies*, NS 27:107 (1976), 257–65.

92. Marvin W. Meyer, Richard Smith, and Neal Kelsey (eds), *Ancient Christian Magic: Coptic Texts of Ritual Power* (Princeton, [1994] 1999), 155.

93. J. S. Wingate, 'The Scroll of Cyprian: An Armenian Family Amulet', *Folklore* 41:2 (1930), 169–87; Enno Littmann, 'The Magic Book of the Disciples', *Journal of the American Oriental Society* 25 (1904), 1–48.

94. Robert Mathiesen, 'A Thirteenth-Century Ritual to Attain the Beatific Vision from the Sworn Book of Honorius of Thebes', in Fanger (ed.), *Conjuring Spirits*, 147–50; Thorndike, *History of Magic*, ii.284–9.

95. L.-F. Alfred Maury, *La magie et l'astrologie dans l'antiquité et au Moyen Age*, 3rd edn (Paris, 1864), 224.

96. <http://www.librairierossignol.fr/article.php?ref=magieenchiridion>. For early references see Louis Gougaud, 'La prière dite de Charlemagne et les pieces apocryphes apparentées', *Revue d'histoire ecclesiastique* 20 (1924), 233–8; Curt F. Buhler, 'Prayers and Charms in Certain Middle English Scrolls', *Speculum* 39:2 (1964), 271 n. 12. See also Arthur Edward Waite, *The Book of Ceremonial Magic* (Ware, [1911] 1992), 39–45.

97. See Helen L. Parish, *Monks, Miracles and Magic: Reformation Representations of the Medieval Church* (London, 2005), 129–34.

98. See Norman Cohn, *Europe's Inner Demons* (London, 1975), 180–5.

99. John Napier, *A Plaine Discoverie of the Whole Revelation of Saint John* (London, 1594), 44, 48; *The Examination of John Walsh, before Maister Thomas Williams* (London, 1566), preface; Parish, *Monks, Miracles and Magic*, 137.

100. Sophie Page, 'Image-Magic Texts and a Platonic Cosmology at St Augustine's, Canterbury, in the Late Middle Ages', in Burnett and Ryan (eds), *Magic and the Classical Tradition*, 69; Klaassen, 'English Manuscripts of Magic', 9.

101. Edward Peters, *The Magician, The Witch, and the Law* (Philadelphia, 1978), 89–90.

102. Frank Klaassen, 'Learning and Masculinity in Manuscripts of Ritual Magic of the Later Middle Ages and Renaissance', *Sixteenth Century Journal* 38:1 (2007), 60.

103. Kieckhefer, *Magic in the Middle Ages*, 153–6.

104. Culianu, *Eros and Magic*, 167–8.

105. See James Wood Brown, *An Enquiry into the Life and Legend of Michael Scot* (Edinburgh, 1897), esp. 215–19.

106. On the changing reputation of Bacon see Amanda Power, 'A Mirror for Every Age: The Reputation of Roger Bacon', *English Historical Review* 121 (2006), 657–92.

107. Quoted in Thorndike, *History of Magic*, ii.314, 279; William Eamon, *Science and the Secrets of Nature: Books of Secrets in Medieval and Early Modern Culture* (Princeton, 1994), 71.

108. John Bale, *Illustrum Maioris Britanniae Scriptorum* (Gippeswici, 1548), fo. 114v–115; Thomas Wright, *Narratives of Sorcery and Magic* (New York, [1851] 1852), 131; Waite, *Book of Ceremonial Magic*, 23. On Bale's changing attitude towards Bacon see Power, 'A Mirror for Every Age', 661–2.

109. *The famous historie of Fryer Bacon Containing the wonderfull things that he did in his life* (London, 1679), G3v.

110. See Thorndike, *History of Magic*, ii.874–947.

111. Ibid. ii.911–12, 925; Waite, *Book of Ceremonial Magic*, 89–92.

112. *The boke of secretes of Albertus Magnus* (London, 1560), p. ciiiiv.

113. Kittredge, *Witchcraft*, 207; Láng, 'Angels around the Crystal', 23–6.

114. Matteo Duni, *Under the Devil's Spell: Witches, Sorcerers, and the Inquisition in Renaissance Italy* (Florence, 2007), 91.

115. See Kieckhefer, *Forbidden Rites*, 79–91.

116. Cohn, *Europe's Inner Demons*, 194, 196.

117. See Stephen Mitchell, 'Anaphrodisiac Charms in the Nordic Middle Ages: Impotence, Infertility, and Magic', *Norveg. Tidsskrift for folkloristikk* 38 (1998), 19–42; Catherine Ryder, *Magic and Impotence in the Middle Ages* (Oxford, 2006).

118. Ryder, *Magic and Impotence*, 78.

119. Jan R. Veenstra, *Magic and Divination at the Courts of Burgundy and France* (Leiden, 1998), 69–71; Veenstra, 'The Holy Almandal', 193, 197–8.

120. On childbirth charms see Skemer, *Binding Words*, ch. 5.

121. Dickie, *Magic and Magicians*, 180–1, 188.

122. Kittredge, *Witchcraft*, 130.

123. Duni, *Under the Devil's Spell*, 48, 81.

124. Veenstra, *Magic and Divination at the Courts of Burgundy*, 61; Duni, *Under the Devil's Spell*, 47. The Mangialoca case is fully examined in Grazia Biondi, *Benvenuta e l'Inquistitore* (Modena, 1993).

125. Klaassen, 'Learning and Masculinity in Manuscripts of Ritual Magic', 55, 71, 74.

126. Peters, *The Magician*, 91; Kieckhefer, *Magic in the Middle Ages*, 157; Williams, *Secret of Secrets*, 155, 156 n. 41. On the various Church pronouncements on magic see Peters, *The Magician*, 71–81, 98–102, 148–55.

127. For other examples see Kieckhefer, *Forbidden Rites*, 1–2.

128. Benedek Láng, 'Demons in Krakow, and Image Magic in a Magical Handbook', in Éva Pócs and Gábor Klaniczay (eds), *Christian Demonology and Popular Mythology: Demons, Spirits, Witches* (Budapest, 2006), 13, 27–8.

129. Cited in Peters, *The Magician*, 99–100.

130. For these figures and a detailed analysis of the medieval origins of the witch trials see Michael D. Bailey, 'From Sorcery to Witchcraft: Clerical Conceptions of Magic in the Later Middle Ages', *Speculum* 76:4 (2001), 960–90. See also Bailey, *Magic and Superstition*, 126–40.

II THE WAR AGAINST MAGIC

1. Alexandra Walsham and Julia Crick, 'Introduction: Script, Print, and History', in *eaedem* (eds), *The Uses of Script and Print, 1300–1700* (Cambridge, 2004), 1; Susan Brigden, *London and the Reformation*, 2nd edn (Oxford, 1991), 157; Clive Griffin, *Journeymen-Printers, Heresy, and the Inquisition in Sixteenth-Century Spain* (Oxford, 2005), 3.

2. John Rastell, *The Pastyme of People: The cronycles of dyuers realmys and most specyally of the realme of Englond* (London, 1530), B^v.

3. Griffin, *Journeymen-Printers*, 244.

4. J. Martínez de Bujanda (ed.), *Index de L'Inqusition Espagnole 1551, 1554, 1559* (Sherbrooke, 1984), 516. For other examples of this early trade in printed protective charms see Don C. Skemer, *Binding Words: Textual Amulets in the Middle Ages* (University Park, 2006), 222–33.

5. Frank L. Borchardt, 'The *Magus* as Renaissance Man', *Sixteenth Century Journal* 21:1 (1990) 60.

6. For debate on the limited originality of Renaissance magic see, for example, Richard Kieckhefer, 'Did Magic have a Renaissance? An Historiographic Question Revisited', in Charles Burnett and W. F. Ryan (eds), *Magic and the Classical Tradition* (London/Turin, 2006), 199–213; Michael D. Bailey, *Magic and Superstition in Europe:*

A Concise History from Antiquity to the Present (Lanham, 2007), 180–93; D. P. Walker, *Spiritual and Demonic Magic from Ficino to Campanella* (London, 1958); Brian Vickers, 'Introduction', in *idem* (ed.), *Occult and Scientific Mentalities in the Renaissance* (Cambridge, 1984); B. J. Gibbons, *Spirituality and the Occult: From the Renaissance to the Modern Age* (London, 2001), ch. 3, esp. 41.

7. For a clear, concise outline of the Hermitic tradition see D. S. Katz, *The Occult Tradition* (London, 2005), 22–35.

8. See Moshe Idel, 'Jewish Magic from the Renaissance Period to Early Hasidism', in Jacob Neusner, Ernest S. Frerichs, and Paul Virgil McCracken Flesher (eds), *Religion, Science, and Magic: In Concert and in Conflict* (New York, 1989), 82–120.

9. Ben Jonson, *Ben Jonson's Execration against Vulcan* (London, 1640), B2v.

10. Much has been written but for a range of approaches to his work see, for example, Christopher I. Lehrich, *The Language of Demons and Angels: Cornelius Agrippa's Occult Philosophy* (Leiden, 2003); Frances A. Yates, *The Occult Philosophy in the Elizabethan Age* (London, 1979); Donald Tyson (ed.), *Three Books of Occult Philosophy* (St Paul, 1995).

11. See Noel L. Brann, *Trithemius and Magical Theology* (Albany, 1999). For a useful discussion on the way Trithemius's work influenced the grimoire tradition see Stephen Skinner and David Rankine, *The Goetia of Dr Rudd* (London, 2007), 34–6, 55–7.

12. See Ole Peter Grell (ed.), *Paracelsus: The Man and His Reputation, His Ideas and Their Transformations* (Leiden, 1998).

13. Ole Peter Grell, 'Introduction', in *idem* (ed.), *Paracelsus: The Man*, 3.

14. Paracelsus, *Of the supreme mysteries of nature*, 96, 34, 39.

15. See, for example, Allen G. Debus, *The English Paracelsians* (London, 1965), 63, 75; Lynn Thorndike, *History of Magic and Experimental Science*, 8 vols (New York: 1923–58), vi.525.

16. William Foster, *Hoplocrisma-Spongus: Or, A Sponge to Wipe Away the Weapon-Salve* (London, 1631), 32, 34.

17. Much has been written in English and German about the literary and historic Faust. On the historic Faust I have relied on Karl P. Wentersdorf, 'Some Observations on the Historical Faust', *Folklore* 89:2 (1978), 201–23; Frank Baron, 'Which Faustus Died in Staufen? History and Legend in the "Zimmerische Chronik"', *German Studies Review* 6:2 (1983), 185–94.

18. Elizabeth M. Butler's *The Fortunes of Faust* (Cambridge, 1952) remains a formidable account of the various literary versions of the Faust legend. On the *teufelsbücher* see Gerhild Scholz Williams, 'Devil Books', in Richard Golden (ed.), *Encyclopedia of Witchcraft: The Western Tradition*, 4 vols (Santa Barbara, 2006), i.274–5; Robert Muchembled, *A History of the Devil from the Middle Ages to the Present*, trans. Jean Birrell (Cambridge, 2003), 111–24; Lyndal Roper, *Witch Craze: Terror and Fantasy in Baroque Germany* (New Haven, 2006), 253–5; H. C. Erik Midelfort, *Witch Hunting in Southwestern Germany 1562–1684* (Stanford, 1972), 69–70.

19. *Henrici Cornelii Agrippae liber quartus de occulta philosophia* (Marbug, 1559); *Liber quartus De occulta philosophia, seu, De ceremoniis magicis* (Basel, 1565). Some historians cite 1565 or 1567 as the date of the first edition.

20. See Marc van der Poel, *Cornelius Agrippa: The Humanist Theologian and His Declamations* (Leiden, 1997), 82 nn. 41 and 42.

21. See, for example, Richard Argentine, *De Praestigiis et Incantationibus Daemonum et Necromanticorum* (Basel, 1568), 28.

22. Deborah E. Harkness, *John Dee's Conversations with Angels: Cabala, Alchemy, and the End of Nature* (Cambridge, 1999), 128 n. 116.

23. Jean-Michel Sallmann, *Chercheurs de trésors et jeteuses de sorts: La quête du surnatural à Naples au XVIe siècle* (Paris, 1986), 161,166.

24. William Monter, 'Toads and Eucharists: The Male Witches of Normandy, 1564–1660', *French Historical Studies* 20:4 (1997), 587.

25. *The Quacks Academy; Or, The Dunce's Directory* (London, 1678), 5; Richard Baxter, *The Certainty of the World of Spirits* (London, 1691), 62. See also Owen Davies, *Cunning-Folk: Popular Magic in English History* (London, 2003), ch. 5. I have also benefitted from reading drafts of Matthew Green's forthcoming PhD, 'The Publication of and Interest in Occult Literature 1640–1680', University of Hertfordshire.

26. See Carlos Gilly, 'The First Book of White Magic in Germany', in C. Gilly and C. Van Heertum (eds), *Magia, Alchimia, Scienza Dal '400 al '700. L'influsso di Ermete Trismegisto/Magic, Alchemy and Science 15th–18th Centuries* (Florence, 2002), i.209–17.

27. Ibid. 210.

28. Bruce T. Moran, 'Paracelsus, Religion, and Dissent: The Case of Philipp Homagius and Georg Zimmermann', *Ambix* 43:2 (1996), 65–6; Gilly, 'The First Book of White Magic', 214.

29. Grillot de Givry, *Witchcraft, Magic and Alchemy* (New York, [1931] 1971), 102.

30. On the continued importance of manuscript see Walsham and Crick (eds), *The Uses of Script and Print, 1300–1700*.

31. Sofia Messana, *Inquisitori, negromanti e streghe nella Sicilia moderna (1500–1782)* (Palermo, 2007), 430, 432–9. My thanks to Francesca Matteoni for bringing this book to my attention and providing relevant details.

32. David Gentilcore, *From Bishop to Witch: The System of the Sacred in Early Modern Terra d'Otranto* (Manchester, 1992), 228–9.

33. Ruth Martin, *Witchcraft and the Inquisition in Venice 1550–1650* (Oxford, 1989), 96.

34. John Tedeschi, 'The Question of Magic and Witchcraft in Two Unpublished Inquisitorial Manuals of the Seventeenth Century', *Proceedings of the America Philosophical Society* 131:1 (1987), 98; Carmel Cassar, *Witchcraft, Sorcery and the Inquisition: A Study of Cultural Values in Early Modern Malta* (Msida, 1996), 58, 59; Martin, *Witchcraft and the Inquisition*, 89.

35. Guido Ruggiero, *Binding Passions* (Oxford, 1993), 208.

36. Martin, *Witchcraft and the Inquisition*, 89, 91.

37. Úrsula Lamb, 'La Inquisición en Canarias y un Libro de Magia del Siglo XVI', *El Museo Canario* 24 (1963), 113–44. For other Spanish examples see, for instance, Julio Caro Baroja, *Vidas Mágicas e Inquisición* (Madrid, 1992), i.135–51, ii.280, 292; María Tausiet, *Abracadabra Omnipotens: Magia urbana en Zaragoza en la Edad Moderna* (Madrid, 2007), 71, 72; François Delpech, 'Grimoires et savoirs souterrains: elements pour une archéo-mythologie du livre magique', in Dominique de Courcelles (ed.), *Le Pouvoir des livres à la Renaissance* (Paris, 1998), 45.

38. Federico Barbierato, 'Magical Literature and the Venice Inquisition from the Sixteenth to the Eighteenth Centuries', in Gilly and Van Heertum (eds), *Magia, Alchimia, Scienza Dal '400 al '700*, 164.

39. Federico Barbierato, *Nella stanza dei circoli: Clavicula Salomonis e libri di magia a Venezia nei secoli XVII e XVIII* (Milan, 2002), 165.

40. Extracts from one of the French manuscripts are presented in P. L. Jacob, *Curiosités des sciences occultes* (Paris, 1862).

41. J. Buchanan-Brown, 'The Books Presented to the Royal Society by John Aubrey, F.R.S.', *Notes and Records of the Royal Society of London* 28:2 (1974), 192 n. 59.

42. Montague Summers, *Witchcraft and Black Magic* (London, [1946] 1964), 188–9; Elizabeth M. Butler, *Ritual Magic* (Stroud, [1949] 1998), 310.

43. William G. Naphy, *Plagues, Poisons and Potions: Plague-Spreading Conspiracies in the Western Alps c.1530–1640* (Manchester, 2002), 182–4; Barbierato, *Nella stanza dei circoli*, 79–80 n. 222.

44. *The Magick of Kirani King of Persia* (London, 1685), 68.

45. See William Eamon, *Science and the Secrets of Nature: Books of Secrets in Medieval and Early Modern Culture* (Princeton, 1994), 139–47, 252.

46. The best account of Della Porta is ibid. 195–233.

47. Ibid. 199.

48. David Lederer, *Madness, Religion and the State in Early Modern Europe: A Bavarian Beacon* (Cambridge, 2006), 216–18.

49. Henri Boguet, *An Examen of Witches*, trans. E Allen Ashwin (London, [1929] 1971), 180–93.

50. Thorndike, *History of Magic*, vi.556–9; Moshe Sluhovsky, *Believe Not Every Spirit: Possession, Mysticism, and Discernment in Early Modern Catholicism* (Chicago, 2007), 78; Gentilcore, *Bishop to witch*, 107–11.

51. Barbierato, 'Magical Literature', 160.

52. Laura de Mello e Souza, *The Devil and the Land of the Holy Cross: Witchcraft, Slavery, and Popular Religion in Colonial Brazil*, trans. Diane Grosklaus Whitty (Austin, 2003), 109–11, 166. On Brugnoli see Sluhovsky, *Believe Not Every Spirit*, 49.

53. A similar point is made in Sarah Ferber, *Demonic Possession and Exorcism in Early Modern France* (London, 2004), 38–9.

54. K. M. Briggs, 'Some Seventeenth-Century Books of Magic', *Folklore* 64:4 (1953), 445–62; Keith Thomas, *Religion and the Decline of Magic* (London, 1971), 271–3, 727; Barbara A. Mowat, 'Prospero's Book', *Shakespeare Quarterly* 52:1 (2001), 1–33; Davies, *Cunning-Folk*, ch. 5; Diane Purkiss, *Troublesome Things: A History of Fairies and Fairy Stories* (London, 2000), 127–31; Robert Hunter West, *The Invisible World: A Study of Pneumatology in Elizabethan Drama* (Athens, GA, 1939), ch. 7.

55. Butler, *Ritual Magic*, 251.

56. George Lyman Kittredge, *Witchcraft in Old and New England* (New York, [1929] 1958), 208; Briggs, 'Some Seventeenth-Century Books of Magic', 448. 'Andrew Malchus' is probably an anglicization of a spirit named Andromalius found in some versions of the *Lemegeton*; see Mowat, 'Prospero's Book', n. 50.

57. Cited in Mowat, 'Prospero's Book', 14; Briggs, 'Some Seventeenth-Century Books of Magic', 457.

58. William Lilly, *William Lilly's History of His Life and Times from the Year 1602 to 1681*, ed. Elias Ashmole (London, 1721), 108; Katharine Briggs, *A Dictionary of Fairies* (London, 1976), 276.

59. Thomas Jackson, *A Treatise Concerning the Originall of Unbeliefe* (London, 1625), 178–9.

60. Keith Thomas was the first to introduce this idea in his *Religion and the Decline of Magic*.

61. For discussion on clerical educational levels and behaviour see, for example, Reinhold Kiermayr, 'On the Education of the Pre-Reformation Clergy', *Church History* 53:1 (1984), 7–16; R. N. Swanson, 'Problems of the Priesthood in Pre-Reformation England', *English Historical Review* 105:417 (1990), 845–69.

62. Geoffrey Parker, 'Success and Failure during the First Century of the Reformation', *Past and Present* 136 (1992), 55–8.

63. Luise Schorn-Schutte, 'The Christian Clergy in the Early Modern Holy Roman Empire: A Comparative Social Study', *Sixteenth Century Journal* 29:3 (1998), 723; Rosemary O'Day, *The Professions in Early Modern England, 1450–1800: Servants of the Commonweal* (Harlow, 2000), 68–9.

64. Gentilcore, *Bishop to witch*, 42, 131; Mary O'Neill, 'Magical Healing, Love Magic, and the Inquisition in Late Sixteenth Century Italy', in Stephen Haliczer (ed.), *Inquisition and Society in Early Modern Europe* (Totowa, 1987), 88–114, esp. 93.

65. Schorn-Schutte, 'The Christian Clergy', 724.

66. See J. Michael Hayden and Malcolm R. Greenshields, 'The Clergy of Early Seventeenth-Century France: Self-Perception and Society's Perception', *French Historical Studies* 18:1 (1993), 145–72.

67. Sallmann, *Chercheurs*, 145.

68. See, for example, Wilfred Prest (ed.), *The Professions in Early Modern England* (London, 1987).

69. Cassar, *Witchcraft, Sorcery*, 60.

70. See David Pingree (ed.), *Picatrix: The Latin Version of the Ghāyat al-Hakīm* (London, 1986), pp. xix, liii–lv.

71. See Alec Ryrie, *The Sorcerer's Tale: Faith and Fraud in Tudor England* (Oxford, 2008), ch. 4.

72. Lauren Kassell, *Medicine and Magic in Elizabethan London. Simon Forman: Astrologer, Alchemist and Physician* (Oxford, 2005), 215, 216, 218.

73. Bernardo Barreiro de Vazquez Varela, *Brujos y astrólogos de la Inquisicion de Galicia y el famoso libro de San Cipriano* (Madrid, [1885] 1973), 155–60; Tayra M. C. Lanuza-Navarro and Ana Cecilia Ávalos-Flores, 'Astrological Prophecies and the Inquisition in the Iberian World', in M. Kokowski (ed.), *The Global and the Local: The History of Science and the Cultural Integration of Europe* (Cracow, 2006), 684.

74. Robin Briggs, 'Circling the Devil: Witch-Doctors and Magical Healers in Early Modern Lorraine', in Stuart Clark (ed.), *Languages of Witchcraft* (Basingstoke, 2001), 171–2.

75. Paris BN, Ms. fr. 19574, 28–66; *Discoverie admirable d'un magicien de la ville de Moulins* (Paris, 1623); Jean Débordes, *Les Mystères de l'Allier: histories insolite, estranges, criminelles et extraordinaires* (Romagnat, 2001), ch. 11.

76. See, for example, Bruce Tolley, *Pastors and Parishioners in Württemberg during the Late Reformation 1581–1621* (Stanford, 1995), 68, 69; Wolfgang Behringer, *Shaman of Oberstdorf*, trans. H. C. Erik Midelfort (Charlottesville, 1998), esp. 7, 87; Claude et Jacques Seignolle, *Le folklore du Hurepoix* (Paris, 1978), 211–12.

77. Monter, 'Toads and Eucharists'.

78. Ibid. 577.

79. Thomas Tryon, *Miscellania* (London, 1696), 93; David Cressy, *Literacy and the Social Order: Reading and Writing in Tudor and Stuart England* (Cambridge, 1980), 39.

80. Davies, *Cunning-Folk*, 129.

81. Briggs, 'Circling the Devil', 171.

82. Peter A. Morton (ed.), *The Trial of Tempel Anneke*, trans. Barbara Dähms (Peterborough, Ont., 2006), 15, 19, 39, 78.

83. Edward Bever, *The Realities of Witchcraft and Popular Magic in Early Modern Europe: Culture, Cognition and Everyday Life* (Basingstoke, 2008), ch. 6.

84. Davies, *Cunning-Folk*, 73; Thomas, *Religion and the Decline of Magic*, 362.

85. Cassar, *Witchcraft, Sorcery*, 67, 68, 72–3, 98.

86. René Le Tenneur, *Magie, sorcellerie et fantastique en Normandie* (Paris, 1991), 176–7.

87. Martin, *Witchcraft and the Inquisition*, 98,135–6; Matteo Duni, *Under the Devil's Spell: Witches, Sorcerers, and the Inquisition in Renaissance Italy* (Florence, 2007), 56–7.

88. King James I, *Dæmonologie*, Preface.

89. Cited in van der Poel, *Cornelius Agrippa*, 82 n. 42.

90. Nicolas Rémy, *La démonolâtrie*, trans Jean Boës (Nancy, 1997), 196. In the only English translation of the book 'Picatrix' is supplanted by 'Weyer' for some reason: Rémy, *Demonolatry*, trans. E. A. Ashwin (London, 1930), 100.

91. Thorndike, *History of Magic*, viii.556.

92. Martin Del Rio, *Investigations into Magic*, ed. and trans. P.G. Maxwell-Stuart (Manchester, 2000), 76, 77.

93. Del Rio, *Investigations*, 237; Raymond A. Mentzer, 'Heresy Proceedings in Languedoc, 1500–1650', *Transactions of the American Philosophical Society* 74:5 (1984), 37–8.

94. Del Rio, *Investigations*, 27.

95. D. A. Beecher, 'Erotic Love and the Inquisition: Jacques Ferrand and the Tribunal of Toulouse, 1620', *Sixteenth Century Journal* 20:1 (1989), 41–53.

96. Benjamin G. Kohl and H. C. Erik Midelfort (eds), *On Witchcraft: An Abridged Translation of Johann Weyer's* De præstigiis dæmonum, trans. John Shea (Asheville, 1998), 54–8.

97. Ibid. 203; Skinner and Rankine, *The Goetia*, 37.

98. Barbierato, *Nella stanza dei circoli*, 52, 162.

99. Reginald Scot, *The Discoverie of Witchcraft* (London, 1584), 226, 251.

100. Frank Klaassen and Christopher Phillips, 'The Return of Stolen Goods: Reginald Scot, Religious Controversy, and Magic in Bodleian Library, Additional B. 1', *Magic, Ritual, and Witchcraft* 1:2 (2006), 135–77.

101. Davies, *Cunning-Folk*, 125–7, 132, 134, 150–1, 156–9.

102. On the trial of Scottish cunning-folk see Owen Davies, 'A Comparative Perspective on Scottish Cunning-Folk and Charmers', in Julian Goodare, Lauren Martin, and Joyce Miller (eds), *Witchcraft and Belief in Early Modern Scotland* (Basingstoke, 2008), 185–205.

103. Per Sörlin, *'Wicked Arts': Witchcraft and Magic Trials in Southern Sweden, 1635–1754* (Leiden, 1999), 35–6; William Monter, *Witchcraft in France and Switzerland* (Ithaca, 1976), 186–7.

104. Magnús Rafnsson, *Angurgapi: The Witch-Hunts in Iceland* (Hólmavík, 2003), 53; Ólína Fiorvardardóttir, 'Iceland', in Golden (ed.), *Encyclopedia*, ii.533; Kirsten Hastrup, 'Iceland: Sorcerers and Paganism', in Bengt Ankarloo and Gustav Henningsen (eds), *Early Modern European Witchcraft: Centres and Peripheries* (Oxford, 1993), 390.

105. Rafnsson, *Angurgapi*, 56, 58.

106. Stephen E. Flowers, *The Galdrabók: An Icelandic Book of Magic*, 2nd edn (Smithville, 2005), 55; Rafnsson, *Angurgapi*, 46; Hastrup, 'Iceland: Sorcerers and Paganism', 394–5.

107. Fiorvardardóttir, 'Iceland', ii.533.

108. The point is well made in Julian Goodare, 'Introduction', in idem (ed.), *The Scottish Witch-Hunt in Context* (Manchester, 2002), 27.

109. Ibid. 28–9. On concerns over Saami magic see Stephen Mitchell, 'Learning Magic in the Sagas', in Geraldine Barnes and Margaret Clunies Ross (eds), *Old Norse Myths, Literature and Society* (Sydney, 2000), 336.

110. See Harvey J. Graff, *The Legacies of Literacy: Continuities and Contradictions in Western Culture and Society* (Bloomington/Indianapolis, 1987), 227–30.

111. Rafnsson, *Angurgapi*, p. 60.

112. Rafnsson, *Angurgapi*, 23, 60–1.

113. Kevin C. Robbins, 'Magical Emasculation, Popular Anticlericalism, and the Limits of the Reformation in Western France circa 1590', *Journal of Social History* 31:1 (1997), 66. On the French ligature tradition see also Stephen Wilson, *The Magical Universe* (London, 2000), 140.

114. Pierre De Lancre, *On the Inconstancy of Witches*, trans. Harriet Stone and Gerhild Scholz Williams (Tempe, 2006), 510, 506.

115. Monter, 'Toads and Eucharists', 576.

116. See Ferber, *Demonic Possession*, ch. 5.

117. Lucien Febvre and Henri-Jean Martin, *The Coming of the Book*, trans. David Gerard (London, [1958] 1976), 244–5.

118. Thorndike, *History of Magic*, vi.146–58; Paul F. Grendler, *The Roman Inquisition and the Venetian Press, 1540–1605* (Princeton, 1977), *passim*.

119. Barbierato, 'Magical Literature', 159. See also Elizabeth L. Eisenstein, 'Some Conjectures about the Impact of Printing on Western Society and Thought: A Preliminary Report', *Journal of Modern History* 40:1 (1968), 38.

120. Bujanda (ed.), *Index de L'Inquisition Espagnole*, 243–4, 365–6; J. Martínez Bujanda, 'Indices de libros prohibidos del siglo XVI', in Joaquín Pérez Villanueva and Bartolomé Escandell Bonet (eds), *Historia de la Inquisicióon en España y América* (Madrid, 2000), 798, 800.

121. For an overview see Virgilio Pinto Crespo, 'Thought Control in Spain', in Haliczer (ed.), *Inquisition and Society*, 171–88.

122. See Moshe Lazar, 'Scorched Parchments and Tortured Memories: The "Jewishness" of the Anussim (Crypto-Jews)', in Mary Elizabeth Perry and Anne J. Cruz (eds), *Cultural Encounters: The Impact of the Inquisition in Spain and the New World* (Berkeley, 1991), 176–206.

123. See Paul F. Grendler, 'The Destruction of Hebrew Books in Venice, 1568', *Proceedings of the American Academy for Jewish Research* 45 (1978), 103–30.

124. David H. Darst, 'Witchcraft in Spain: The Testimony of Martín de Castañega's Treatise on Superstition and Witchcraft (1529)', *Proceedings of the American Philosophical Society* 123:5 (1979), 319.

125. See Jeffrey Howard, *Between Worlds: Dybukks, Exorcists, and Early Modern Judaism* (Philadelphia, 2003), esp. 64; R. Po-chia Hsia, *The Myth of Ritual Murder: Jews and Magic in Reformation Germany* (New Haven, 1990), 134–5.

126. Georges Mongrédien, *Léonora Galigaï: Un process de sorcellerie sous Louis XIII* (Paris, 1968), 74.

127. Joshua Trachtenberg, *Jewish Magic and Superstition: A Study in Folk Religion* (New York, 1939), 140.

128. Martin, *Witchcraft and the Inquisition*, 98.

129. Pier Cesare Ioly Zorattini, 'Jews, Crypto-Jews, and the Inquisition', in Robert Charles Davis and Benjamin Ravid (eds), *The Jews of Early Modern Venice* (Baltimore, 2001), 114–15.

130. Brian Pullan, *The Jews of Europe and the Inquisition of Venice, 1550–1670* (London, [1983] 1997), 306.

131. Valérie Molero, *Magie et sorcellerie en Espagne au siècle des Lumières 1700–1820* (Paris, 2006), 161.

132. William Monter, *Frontiers of Heresy: The Spanish Inquisition from the Basque Lands to Sicily* (Cambridge, 1990), 214.

133. Cassar, *Witchcraft, Sorcery*, 75.

134. Cited in Henry Kamen, *The Phoenix and the Flame: Catalonia and the Couunter-Reformation* (New Haven, 1985), 219.

135. Ibid. 224, 232–6; Griffin, *Journeymen-Printers*, 10, 12 n. 42; Gustav Henningsen, *The Witches' Advocate: Basque Witchcraft and the Spanish Inquisition* (Reno, 1980), 49.

136. Raymond A. Mentzer, Jr, 'The Legal Response to Heresy in Languedoc, 1500–1560', *Sixteenth Century Journal* 4:1 (1973), 23–4, 26–8; Alfred Soman, 'Press, Pulpit, and Censorship in France before Richelieu', *Proceedings of the American Philosophical Society* 120:6 (1976), 439–63.

137. For a detailed account of the case see Tausiet, *Abracadabra Omnipotens*, 46–57.

138. Ibid. 71; Monter, *Frontiers of Heresy*, 222–3.

139. Henningsen, *Witches' Advocate*, 120–3. On De Lancre and his work see P. G. Maxwell-Stuart, *Witch Hunters* (Stroud, 2005), ch. 2.

140. Jean Bodin, *La Démonomanie des Sorciers* (Paris, 1580), 17v; quote cited in Charlotte Wells, 'Leeches on the Body Politic: Xenophobia and Witchcraft in Early Modern French Political Thought', *French Historical Studies* 22:3 (1999), 363–4.

141. Reproduced in Édouard Fournier (ed.), *Variétés historiques et littéraires* (Paris, 1855), i.90, 91.

142. De Lancre, *On the Inconstancy of Witches*, 361, 362.

143. Barbierato, 'Magical Literature', 161.

144. Kamen, *Phoenix and the Flame*, 389–94.

145. Grendler, *Roman Inquisition*, 186–8; Barbierato, 'Magical Literature', 161.

146. Sally Scully, 'Marriage or a Career?: Witchcraft as an Alternative in Seventeenth-Century Venice', *Journal of Social History* 28:4 (1995), 857–76, esp. 861, 871.

147. Francisco Bethencourt, *O imaginário da magia: Feiticeiras adivinhos e curandeiros em Portugal no século XVI* (São Paulo, [1987] 2004), 169–70.

148. See O'Neill, 'Magical Healing, Love Magic'; Guido Ruggiero, *Binding Passions* (Oxford, 1993), esp. ch. 3; Scully, 'Marriage or a Career?'; Marijke Gijswijt-Hofstra, 'Witchcraft after the Witch-Trials', in Marijke Gijswijt-Hofstra, Brian P. Levack, and Roy Porter (eds), *Witchcraft and Magic in Europe: The Eighteenth and Nineteenth Centuries* (London, 1999), 129–41.

149. Jonathan Walker, 'Gambling and Venetian Noblemen c. 1500–1700', *Past and Present*, 162 (1999), 47.

150. Tedeschi, 'The Question of Magic and Witchcraft in Two Unpublished Inquisitorial Manuals', 100.

151. Maria Pia Fantini, 'Les mots secrets des prostituées (Modène, 1580–1620)', *Parler, chanter, lire, écrire* 11 (2000).

152. Mrs Gutch, 'Saint Martha and the Dragon', *Folklore* 63:4 (1952), 193–203.

153. Olga Lucía Valbuena, 'Sorceresses, Love Magic, and the Inquisition of Linguistic Sorcery in Celestina', *PMLA* 109:2 (1994), 218. For examples of other such saintly love prayers recorded in Inquisition documents see Bartomeu Prohens Perelló, *Inquisició I Bruixeria A Mallorca (1578–1650)* Palma, 1995), 94–6; Martin, *Witchcraft and the Inquisition*, 108–9.

154. Graff, *Legacies of Literacy*, 149; Paul F. Grendler, *Renaissance Education between Religion and Politics* (Aldershot, 2006), 255.

155. Ruggiero, *Binding Passions*, 99–102. A similar tradition existed in Spain and Portugal where they were called *cartas de tocar*, see for the latter country Francisco Bethencourt, 'Portugal: A Scrupulous Inquisition', in Ankarloo and Henningsen (eds), *Early Modern European Witchcraft*, 412, 413.

156. Fantini, 'Les mots secrets', n. 35.

157. Scully, 'Marriage or a Career?', 861. Two of the copies confiscated from Malipiero's house survive and have been analysed in Barbierato, 'Magical Literature', 167–9. Images from them can be found in Barbierato, *Nella stanza dei circoli*, plates between 168 and 169. Barbierato, 'Magical Literature', 173.

158. Cited in Ruggiero, *Binding Passions*, 211.

159. See Roper, *Witch Craze*, ch. 4; François Delpech, 'La "marque" des sorcières: logique (s) de la stigmatisation diabolique', in Nicole Jaques-Chaquin and Maxime Préud (eds), *Le sabbat des sorciers* (Grenoble, 1993), 347–69; Walter Stephens, *Demon Lovers: Witchcraft, Sex, and the Crisis of Belief* (Chicago, 2002), esp. ch. 1.

160. Cited in Francesco Maria Guazzo, *Compendium Maleficarum*, trans. E. A. Ashwin (New York, [1929] 1988), 135. See also Delpech, 'Grimoires et savoirs souterrains', 34.

161. The theological conceptions of most acts of Devil worship were constructed from inversions of Christian worship; see Stuart Clark, *Thinking with Demons: The Idea of Witchcraft in Early Modern Europe* (Oxford, 1997), 80–93. On the Book of Life see, for example, Gregory K. Beale, *The Book of Revelation: A Commentary on the Greek Text* (Grand Rapids, 1999), 281–2.

162. Richard Bernard, *A Guide to Grand-iury Men* (London, 1627), 110.

163. C. L'Estrange Ewen, *Witchcraft and Demonianism* (London, 1933), 280.

164. Cited in Elizabeth Reis, 'Gender and the Meanings of Confession in Early New England', in *eadem* (ed.), *Spellbound: Women and Witchcraft in America* (Wilmington, 1998), 58.

165. Ewen, *Witchcraft and Demonianism*, 274, 300; István György Tóth, *Literacy and Written Culture in Early Modern Central Europe* (Budapest, 2000), 89–91.

166. See Cressy, *Literacy and the Social Order*, 62–103.

167. Edward Vallance, ' "An Holy and Sacramentall Paction": Federal Theology and the Solemn League and Covenant in England', *English Historical Review* 116 (2001), 71–2; Malcolm Gaskill, *Witchfinders: A Seventeenth-Century English Tragedy* (London, 2005), 47–8. On the notion of the witch's book in nineteenth-century folklore see Owen Davies, *Witchcraft, Magic and Culture 1736–1951* (Manchester, 1999), 180–1.

168. *Doctor Lamb revived, or, Witchcraft condemn'd in Anne Bodenham* (London, 1653), 26.

169. Otis H. Green and Irvine A. Leonard, 'On the Mexican Booktrade in 1600: A Chapter in Cultural History', *Hispanic Review* 9:1 (1941), 1–40. On the smuggling of prohibited books see Carmen val Julián, 'Surveiller et punir le livre en Nouvelle-Espagne au XVIe siècle', in de Courcelles (ed.), *Le Pouvoir des livres à la Renaissance*, 100–7.

170. Ana Avalos, 'As Above, So Below: Astrology and the Inquisition in Seventeenth-Century New Spain', PhD thesis, European University Institute (2007), ch. 5.

171. Richard E. Greenleaf, *Zumárraga and the Mexican Inquisition 1536–1543* (Washington, 1961), 117.

172. James E. Wadsworth, 'In the Name of the Inquisition: The Portuguese Inquisition and Delegated Authority in Colonial Pernambuco, Brazil', *The Americas* 61:1 (2004), 47; Carole A. Myscofski, 'The Magic of Brazil: Practice and Prohibition in the Early Colonial Period 1590–1620', *History of Religions* 40:2 (2000), 162–3, 164. For a detailed survey see de Mello e Souza, *The Devil and the Land of the Holy Cross*. For useful comparative overviews of witchcraft, magic and the American Inquisitions see William Monter, *Ritual, Myth and Magic in Early Modern Europe* (Brighton, 1983), ch. 6; Gustav Henningsen, 'The Diffusion of European Magic in Colonial America', in Jens Christian V. Johansen, Erling Ladewig Petersen, and Henrik Stevnsborg (eds), *Clashes of Cultures: Essays in Honour of Niels Steensgaard* (Odense, 1992), 160–78.

173. Teodoro Hampe-Martinez, 'Recent Works on the Inquisition and Peruvian Colonial Society, 1570–1820', *Latin American Research Review*, 31:2 (1996), 44, 45.

174. Paulino Castañeda Delgado and Pilar Hernández Aparicio, *La Inquisición de Lima (1570–1635)* (Madrid, 1989), i.376–7, 380; Henningsen, 'The Diffusion of European Magic', 163; Pedro Sarmiento de Gamboa, *The History of the Incas*, trans. and ed. Brian S. Bauer and Jean-Jacques Decoster (Austin, 2007), 6.

175. Delgado and Aparicio, *La Inquisición de Lima*, 378; Henningsen, 'The Diffusion of European Magic', 164.

176. Donald G. Castanien, 'The Mexican Inquisition Censors: A Private Library, 1655', *Hispanic American Historical Review* 34:3 (1954), 374–92; Avalos, 'As Above, So Below', 211–35.

177. Greenleaf, *Zumárraga and the Mexican Inquisition*, 117–21.

178. Avalos, 'As Above, So Below', 246–54; Myscofski, 'The Magic of Brazil', 164; Lanuza-Navarro and Ávalos-Flores, 'Astrological Prophecies', 685–8.

179. Irene Silverblatt, *Modern Inquisitions: Peru and the Colonial Origins of the Civilized World* (Durham, 2004), 270 n. 18.

180. Henningsen, 'The Diffusion of European Magic', 164.

181. De Mello e Souza, *The Devil and the Land of the Holy Cross*, 98.

182. C. A. Browne, 'Scientific Notes from the Books and Letters of John Winthrop, Jr., (1606–1676)', *Isis* 11:2 (1928), 325–42; Arthur Versluis, *The Esoteric Origins of the American Renaissance* (New York, 2000), 31–6.

183. Jon Butler, 'Thomas Teackle's 333 Books: A Great Library on Virginia's Eastern Shore, 1697', *William and Mary Quarterly* 3rd ser., 49:3 (1992), 449–91.

184. See David D. Hall, *Worlds of Wonder, Days of Judgment: Popular Religious Belief in Early New England* (New York, 1989), 41–61;

185. Richard Godbeer, *The Devil's Dominion: Magic and Religion in Early New England* (Cambridge, 1992), 35–6; William Renwick Riddell, 'Witchcraft in Old New York', *Journal of the American Institute of Criminal Law and Criminology* 19:2 (1928), 252–8.

186. Godbeer, *The Devil's Dominion*, 135–6.

187. John Hale, *A Modest Inquiry into the Nature of Witchcraft* (1702).

188. Paul Boyer and Stephen Nissenbaum, *The Salem Witchcraft Papers* (New York 1977), vol. ii. I have made use of the online edition available at http://etext.virginia.edu/salem/witchcraft/texts/BoySal2.html

189. Hall, *Worlds of Wonder*, 98–9.

190. Peter Benes, 'Fortunetellers, Wise-Men, and Magical Healers in New England, 1644–1850', in idem (ed.), *Wonders of the Invisible World: 1600–1800* (Boston, 1995), 127–42; Godbeer, *Devil's Dominion*, 33–7; John Putnam Demos, *Entertaining Satan: Witchcraft and the Culture of Early Modern England* (Oxford, 1982), 80–4.

191. Reis (ed.), *Spellbound*, p. xv.

192. Mary Beth Norton, *In the Devil's Snare: The Salem Witchcraft Crisis of 1692* (New York, 2002), 52; Michelle Burnham, *Folded Selves: Colonial New England Writing in the World System* (Hanover, NH, 2007), 162. On early American astrological almanacs see Godbeer, *The Devil's Dominion*, ch. 4.

193. Tóth, *Literacy*, 90.

194. Emerson W. Baker, 'Maine Indian Land Speculation and the Essex County Witchcraft Outbreak of 1692', *Maine History* 40:3 (2001), 159–89; Norton, *In the Devil's Snare*, 240.

195. Burnham, *Folded Selves*, 162–4.

196. George Lincoln Burr (ed.), *Narratives of the New England Witchcraft Cases* (Mineola, [1914] 2002), 262–3.

197. F. W. Grubb, 'Growth of Literacy in Colonial America: Longitudinal Patterns, Economic Models, and the Direction of Future Research', *Social Science History* 14:4 (1990), 451–82; Graff, *Legacies of Literacy*, 163–4.

198. See the collected essays in Alfred Soman, *Sorcellerie et justice criminelle: le Parlement de Paris (16e-18e siècles)* (Aldershot, 1992); Brian Levack, 'The Decline and End of

Witchcraft Prosecutions', in Bengt Ankarloo and Stuart Clark (eds), *Witchcraft and Magic in Europe: The Eighteenth and Nineteenth Centuries* (London, 1999), esp. 48–53.

199. The story of the affair is well told in Anne Somerset, *The Affair of the Poisons: Murder, Infanticide and Satanism at the Court of Louis XIV* (London, 2003). On the magical aspects of the affair see Lynn Wood Mollenauer, *Strange Revelations: Magic, Poison, and Sacrilege in Louis XIV's France* (University Park, 2007).

200. François Ravaisson, *Archives de la Bastille*, 19 vols (Paris, 1866–1904), vi.32, 186, 194.

201. Mollenauer, *Strange Revelations*, 104.

202. Ibid. 78.

203. Ravaisson, *Archives de la Bastille*, vi.184.

III ENLIGHTENMENT AND TREASURE

1. H. C. Erik Midelfort, *Exorcism and Enlightenment: Johann Joseph Gassner and the Demons of Eighteenth-Century Germany* (New Haven, 2005), 22.

2. For discussion on the magical activities of Cagliostro and Casanova see respectively, Iain McCalman, *The Last Alchemist: Count Cagliostro, Master of Magic in the Age of Reason* (New York, 2003); Chantal Thomas, 'Giacomo Casanova: Three Episodes from his Life as a Charlatan', *Cultural and Social History* 3:3 (2006), 355–69; Elizabeth M. Butler, *Ritual Magic* (Stroud, [1949] 1998), 129–48.

3. B. J. Gibbons, *Spirituality and the Occult: From the Renaissance to the Modern Age* (London, 2001), 85.

4. Giacomo Casanova, *Memoirs of Jacques Casanova de Seingalt* (London, 1894), vol. v, ch. 21. I have used the version available via Project Gutenberg. See also Butler, *Ritual Magic*, 129–48.

5. See http://levity.com/alchemy/alnwick.html for a list of his manuscripts.

6. See Geneviève Bollème, *La Bible bleue* (Paris, 1975); Lise Andries, *La Bibliothèque bleue au dix-huitème siècle* (Oxford, 1989).

7. Anne Sauvy, *Livres saisis à Paris entre 1678 et 1701* (The Hague, 1972), 13, 321.

8. 'Mémoire de M. d'Argenson sur les associations de faux sorciers à Paris en 1702', reproduced in Robert Mandrou (ed.), *Possession et sorcellerie au XVIIe siècle* (Paris, 1979), 279–328.

9. Ulrike Krampl, 'When Witches Became False: *Séducteurs* and *Crédules* Confront the Paris Police at the Beginning of the Eighteenth Century', in Kathryn A. Edwards (ed.), *Werewolves, Witches, and Wandering Spirits: Traditional Belief and Folklore in Early Modern Europe* (Kirksville, 2002), 138 n. 5.

10. Ibid. 153 n.65.

11. 'Mémoire de M. d'Argenson', 327.

12. François Ravaisson, *Archives de la Bastille*, 19 vols (Paris, 1866–1904), xii.10.

13. Ibid. x.273.

14. 'Mémoire de M. d'Argenson', 292–4.

15. Ibid. 285–6, 292.

16. Ravaisson, *Archives*, x.333. For other references to the Honorius grimoire see also 'Mémoire de M. d'Argenson', 303.

17. Ravaisson, *Archives*, xiii.461.

18. 'Mémoire de M. d'Argenson', 325.

19. Ibid. 297, 310, 303–4,

20. Marc Antoine René de Voyer d'Argenson, *Mélange tires d'une grande bibliothèque. De La Lecture des livres François* (Paris, 1781), 99–104. A survey of his grimoire collection is provided in Grillot de Givry, *Witchcraft, Magic and Alchemy* (New York, [1931] 1971), 102–13.

21. Jane P. Davidson, 'Bordelon, Laurent (1653–1710)', in Richard Golden (ed.), *Encyclopedia of Witchcraft: The Western Tradition*, 4 vols (Santa Barbara, 2006), i.138.

22. *L'Histoire des imaginations extravagantes de Monsieur Oufle* (Amsterdam, 1710), 9.

23. For general accounts see Charles Nisard, *Histoire des livres populaires* (Paris, 1854), vol. i, ch. 3; Charles Lancelin, *La Sorcellerie des campagnes* (Paris, 1911), 341–56. An important source of bibliographic information is Albert Caillet, *Manuel bibliographique des sciences psychiques ou occultes*, 3 vols (Paris, 1912).

24. Daniele Roche, 'Les pratiques de l'écrit dans les villes françaises du XVIIIe siècle', in Roger Chariter (ed.), *Pratiques de la lecture* (Paris, [1985] 2003), 210–11.

25. François Lebrun, *Se soigner autrefois: Médicins, saints et sorciers aux XVIIe et XVIIIe siècles* (Paris, 1995), 100.

26. The name was presumably an allusion to the Beringen Brothers, German printers in sixteenth-century Lyon; see Clive Griffin, *Journeymen-Printers, Heresy, and the Inquisition in Sixteenth-Century Spain* (Oxford, 2005), 121, 122.

27. Geneviève Bollème, *La Bible bleue* (Paris, 1975), 396.

28. 'Mémoire de M. d'Argenson', 325.

29. *Le solide trésor des merveilleux secrets de la magie naturelle et cabalistique* (Geneva, 1704). On the date of the earliest edition see Lise Andries, *Le grand Livre des Secrets: Le colportage en France aux 17e et 18e siècles* (Paris, 1994), 184; Nicolas Prevost and Company, *Duo catalogi librorum* (London, 1730), 48; Jacque-Charles Brunet, *Manuel du libraire et de l'amateur de livres* (Paris, 1860), vol. i, cols 139–40.

30. Jean-Pierre Marby, 'Le prix des choses ordinaries, du travail et du péché: le livre de raison de Ponce Millet, 1673–1725', *Revue d'histoire moderne et contemporaine* 48:4 (2001), 21.

31. M. Ventre, *L'Imprimerie et la librarie en Languedoc au dernier siècle de l'Ancien Régime 1700–1789* (Paris, 1958), 262–3; Jean-Pierre Pinies, *Figures de la sorcellerie* (Paris, 1983), 58.

32. Frank Baker, 'Anthropological Notes on the Human Hand', *American Anthropologist* 1:1 (1888), 55–9. For a list of twentieth-century fictional and cultural references

see the Wikipedia entry for 'Hand of Glory': http://en.wikipedia.org/wiki/Hand_of_Glory.

33. This section in the *Petit Albert* borrows heavily from a French version of the pseudo-Paracelsian work, *Paracelsus of the Supreme Mysteries of Nature* (London, 1655), 64–70.

34. For images of an early-eighteenth-century manuscript version and its publication history see http://www.librairierossignol.fr/catalogue/fiche.php?Rech=reference&param=enchiridion

35. *Les secrets merveilleux de la magie naturelle du Petit Albert* (Paris, 1990), 102.

36. Jules Garinet, *Histoire de la Magie en France* (Paris, 1818), 287.

37. Eloïse Mozzani, *Magie et superstitions de la fin de l'Ancien Régime á la Restauration* (Paris, 1988), 57–8; Gibbons, *Spirituality and the Occult*, 122; Kurt Koch, *Between Christ and Satan* (Grand Rapids, 1962), 132.

38. See Mozzani, *Magie et superstitions.*

39. Nisard, *Histoire des livres populaires*, 175; *Dragon rouge* (Paris, 1866).

40. J.-A.-S. Collin de Plancy, *Dictionnaire des Sciences Occultes* (Paris, 1861), i.487.

41. Thomas Frognall Dibdin, *A Bibliographical, Antiquarian and Picturesque Tour in France and Germany*, 2nd edn (London, 1829), ii.360–1.

42. *Tablettes du clergé et des amis de la religion* (Paris, 1823), iv.257–8.

43. The bookshop purchase of the *Dragon rouge* makes an anachronistic appearance in the adventure novel *Jean le Trouveur* (1849) written by Paul de Musset, brother of the more celebrated writer and librarian Alfred. Set during and after the War of Spanish Succession (1701–14), Jean seeks a copy of the *Clavicules of Solomon* and goes to a bookshop in Montpellier, but is told that the *Clavicule* can only be obtained in Memphis. The bookshop owner suggests instead that he purchase published copies of the *Grand grimoire* and the *Dragon rouge*. Jean buys both immediately and sets out following their instructions.

44. Collin de Plancy, *Dictionnaire des sciences occultes* (1848), cols. 336–7.

45. M. Des Essarts, *Choix de nouvelles causes célebres avec les jugemens* (Paris, 1785), 26–41.

46. Christian Desplat, *Sorcières et diables en Béarn* (Pau, 1988), 218.

47. Jacques-Louis Ménétra, *Journal of My Life*, with an introduction and commentary by Daniel Roche (New York, 1986), 255.

48. *Gremoire du Pape Honorius* (c.1800), 75.

49. See Owen Davies, 'French Healing Charms and Charmers', in Jonathan Roper (ed.), *Charms and Charming in Europe* (Palgrave, 2004), 91–113; Oskar Ebermann, 'Le Médecin des Pauvres', *Zeitschrift des Vereins fur Volkskunde* 2 (1914), 134–62.

50. Des Essarts, *Choix de nouvelles*, vi.347.

51. Ibid. 348.

52. *The Times*, 21 August 1829; Judith Devlin, *The Superstitious Mind: French Peasants and the Supernatural in the Nineteenth Century* (New Haven, 1987), 167, 168.

53. See Daniel Fabre, 'Le livre et sa magie', in Roger Chartier (ed.), *Pratiques de la lecture* (Paris, [1985] 1993), 247–55.

54. *The Times*, 13 August 1884.

55. Pinies, *Figures de la sorcellerie*, 62.

56. *Indice General de Los Libros Prohibidos* (Madrid, 1844), 151, 312.

57. *Catalogo dei Llibri che si Trovano Vendibili presso Giuseppe Molini* (Florence, 1820), 195, 219, 229.

58. Alfons de Cock, 'Tooverboeken en Geestenbezwering', in *Studien en essays over oude Volksvertelsels* (Antwerp, 1919), 239 (thanks to Willem de Blécourt for providing a copy of this chapter); S. C. Curtis, 'Trials for Witchcraft in Guernsey', *Reports and Transactions of La Société Guernesiase* 13 (1937), 9–41; Christine Ozanne, 'Notes on Guernsey Folklore', *Folklore* 26:2 (1915), 195; Marie-Sylvie Dupont-Bouchat, 'Le diable apprivoisé: la sorcellerie revisitée. Magie et sorcellerie au XIXe siècle', in Robert Muchembled (ed.), *Magie et sorcellerie en Europe du moyen âge à nos jours* (Paris, 1994), 239.

59. W. Deonna, 'Superstitions à Genève aux XVIIe et XVIIIe siècles', *Schweizerisches Archiv für Volkskunde* 43 (1946), 367–8.

60. Ibid. 366, 369–70.

61. Ibid. 371–2, 383.

62. *Archives d'Etat*, Geneva, P.C. 12420.

63. Deonna, 'Superstitions à Genève', 359–62.

64. Valérie Molero, *Magie et sorcellerie en Espagne au siècle des Lumières 1700–1820* (Paris, 2006), 174.

65. Ibid. 159.

66. *Indice General de Los Libros Prohibidos* (Madrid, 1848), 18, 276.

67. P. Fontes da Costa, 'Between Fact and Fiction: Narratives of Monsters in Eighteenth-Century Portugal', *Portuguese Studies* 20:1 (2004), 71.

68. Molero, *Magie*, 157.

69. Ibid. 102, 165, 174. For a later example of a French grimoire being brought over, see H. Lafoz, 'El Libro de San Cipriano en la Ribaborza, Sobrare y Somonto', *Primer congreso de Aragón de etnología y antropología* (Zaragoza, 1981), 70. My thanks to Enrique Perdiguero for supplying a copy of the latter.

70. See Zosa Szajkowski, 'Population Problems of Marranos and Sephardim in France, from the 16th to the 20th Centuries', *Proceedings of the American Academy for Jewish Research* 27 (1958), 83–105; Esther Benbassa, *The Jews of France: A History from Antiquity to the Present* (1999), 47–58; Henry Kamen, *The Spanish Inquisition: A Historical Revision* (New Haven, 1998), 301–2.

71. Molero, *Magie*, 237.

72. François Bordes, *Sorciers et sorcieres: Procès de sorcellerie en Gascogne et pays Basque* (Toulouse, 1999), 169, 179–80; idem, 'Le livre des remèdes de Labadie', *Bulletin de la*

Société de Borda (1982), 399–412; D. Chabas, *La sorcellerie et l'insolite dans les Landes et les pays voisins* (Cape Breton, 1983), 95. See also Desplat, *Sorcières et diables*, 124; Bernard Traimond, *Le pouvoir de la maladie: Magie et politique dans les Landes de Gascogne 1750–1826* (Bordeaux, 1988), 183.

73. Chabas, *La sorcellerie*, 84, 95; Bordes, *Sorciers*, 180.

74. Chabas, *La sorcellerie*, 86.

75. Cited in Desplat, *Sorcières et diables*, 164.

76. The case is discussed in Bernard Traimond, *Le pouvoir de la maladie: Magie et politique dans les Landes de Gascogne 1750–1826* (Bordeaux, 1988), 89–153.

77. Ibid. 110; *Gremoire du Pape Honorius (c.*1800 [1995]), 40.

78. Molero, *Magie*, 165, 166.

79. Félix Francisco Castro Vicente, 'El Libro de San Cipriano (I)', *Hibris* 27 (2005), 15.

80. Peter Missler, '*Las hondas raíces del Ciprianillo*. 2ª parte: los grimorios', *Culturas Populares. Revista Electrónica* 3 (Septiembre–Diciembre 2006), fn 6.

81. *Indice General de Los Libros Prohibidos*, 252.

82. Cited in Desplat, *Sorcières et diables*, 63, 64.

83. Bernardo Barreiro de Vazquez Varela, *Brujos y astrólogos de la Inquisicion de Galicia y el famoso libro de San Cipriano* (Madrid, [1885] 1973), 259–88.

84. Devlin, *Superstitious Mind*, 167, 179–80.

85. For its bibliographic history see Vicente, 'El Libro de San Cipriano (I)', 15–25; idem, 'El Libro de San Cipriano (II), *Hibris* 28 (2005), 32–41.

86. Vicente Risco, 'Los tesoros legendarios de Galicia', *Revista de Dialectologia y Tradiciones Populares* 6 (1950), 191; Missler, '*Las hondas raíces del Ciprianillo*'.

87. *Boletin Bibliografico Español y Estrangero* (Madrid, 1847), viii.346.

88. Rosa Seeleman, 'Folklore Elements in Valle-Inclán', *Hispanic Review* 3:2 (1935), 111–12.

89. See Risco, 'Los tesoros legendarios', 185–213, 403–29; H. W. Howes, 'Gallegan Folklore II', *Folklore* 38:4 (1927), 365.

90. Risco, 'Los tesoros legendarios', 202–3, 426.

91. Julio Caro Baroja, *Les falsificaciones en la historia* (Barcelone, 1992), 119–20; Manuel Barrios Aguilera, 'Tesoros moriscos y picaresca', *Espacio, Tiempo y Forma*, 4th ser., 9 (1996), 11–24; Danielle Provansal, 'Tesoros y aparaciones: La prohibición de la Riqueza', *Demófilo, Revista de cultura tradicional de Andalucía* 15 (1995), 37–61.

92. Molero, *Magie*, 179.

93. Benito Jerónimo Feijoo, *Cartas eruditas y curiosa* (Madrid [1750] 1774), 3rd vol., Letter 2, pp. 10–13. I have used the electronic edition available at http://www.filosofia.org/bjf/bjf000.htm

94. Aurelio de Llano Roza de Ampudia, *Del Folklore Asturiano* (Oviedo, [1922] 1977), 144–50.

95. See Peter Missler, 'Tradición y parodia en el *Millonario de San Ciprián*, primer recetario impreso para buscar tesoros en Galicia (Las hondas raíces del *Ciprianillo*: 1ᵃ Parte)', *Culturas Populares. Revista Electrónica* 2 (Mayo–Agosto 2006).

96. Feijoo, *Cartas eruditas y curiosa*, 15–16.

97. Roza de Ampudia, *Del Folklore Asturiano*, 150–1.

98. See 'São Cipriano in Northern Portugal', http://www.caaenglish.com/cipriano_01.htm

99. See, for example, Peter Burke, *Popular Culture in Early Modern Europe* (Aldershot, [1978] 1988), ch. 1, pp. 281–6.

100. See Stephan Bachter, 'Grimoires and the Transmission of Magical Knowledge', in Owen Davies and Willem de Blécourt (eds), *Beyond the Witch Trials: Witchcraft and Magic in Enlightenment Europe* (Manchester, 2004), 194–206; idem, 'Anleitung zum Aberglauben: Zauberbücher und die Verbreitung Magischen "Wissens" seit dem 18. Jahrhundert', PhD Thesis, Hamburg University (2005); idem, 'Wie man Höllenfürsten handsam macht. Zauberbücher und die Tradierung magischen Wissens', in *Geschichte(n) der Wirklichkeit* (Augsburg, 2002), 371–90; My thanks to Stephan for providing copies of some of his published work.

101. Alan Corkhill, 'Charlatanism in Goethe's Faust and Tieck's William Lovell', *Forum for Modern Language Studies* 42:1 (2005), 81–2.

102. Johann Christoph Adelung, *Geschichte der Menschichen Narrheit* (Leipzig, 1789), vii.365–404.

103. John A. Walz, 'An English Faustsplitter', *Modern Language Notes* 42:6 (1927), 353.

104. A. Kuhn and W. Schwarz, *Norddeutsche Sagen, Märchen und Gebräuche* (Leipzig, 1848), 90; translation by D. L. Ashliman, 'Legends from Germany', http://www:pitt.edu/-dash/magicbook.html

105. Frederic Adolphus Ebert, *A General Bibliographical Dictionary, from the German* (Oxford, 1837), iv.1533.

106. Wolfgang Behringer, *Witchcraft Persecutions in Bavaria: Popular Magic, Religious Zealotry, and Reason of State in Early Modern Europe*, trans. J.C. Grayson and David Lederer (Cambridge, 1997), 339–40; David Lederer, 'Living with the Dead: Ghosts in Early Modern Bavaria', in Edwards (ed.), *Werewolves, Witches, and Wandering Spirits*, 48–51.

107. Johannes Dillinger and Petra Feld, 'Treasure-Hunting: A Magical Motif in Law, Folklore, and Mentality, Württemberg, 1606–1770', *German History* 20:2 (2002), 170.

108. Ibid. 167, 175. See also Edward Bever, *The Realities of Witchcraft and Popular Magic in Early Modern Europe: Culture, Cognition and Everyday Life* (Basingstoke, 2008), chs. 5 and 6.

109. Butler, *Ritual Magic*, 190. On Butler's views see her entry in the *DNB*.

110. Manfred Tschaikner, *Schatzgräberei in Vorarlberg und Liechtenstein* (Bludenz, 2006), 56–7, 59–62. My thanks to Manfred Tschaikner for providing me with a copy of his book and Willem de Blécourt for contacting him on my behalf.

111. Ibid. 122.

112. Margarethe Ruff, *Zauberpraktiken als Lebenschilfe: Magie im Alltag vom Mittelalter bis heute* (Frankfurt, 2003), 254–5; Tschaikner, *Schatzgräberei*, 59, 62; Anton Quitzmann, *Die Herdnische Religion der Baiwaren* (Leipzig and Heidelberg, 1860), 124.

113. Bachter, 'Grimoires and the Transmission of Magical Knowledge', 194–5.

114. On the publishing history and content of these two titles see Adolf Spamer, *Romanusbüchlein. Historisch-philologischer Kommentar zu einem deutschen Zauberbuch* (Berlin, 1958); Will-Erich Peuckert, 'Die Egyptischen Geheimnisse', *ARV* 10 (1954), 40–96. Joseph H. Peterson has generously made available English translations of the *Romanusbüchlein* and the *Egyptische Geheimnisse*; (http://www.esotericarchives.com/moses/romanus.htm).

115. Nils Freytag, *Aberglauben im 19. Jahrundert* (Berlin, 2003), 151.

116. Franz Peter, *Die Literatur der Faustsage* (Leipzig, 1851), 17, 18.

117. Freytag, *Aberglauben*, 145.

118. Ibid. 144.

119. See Bachter, 'Anleitung zum Aberglauben', 128–31.

120. The most extensive English account of the grimoires in *Das Kloster* is in Butler, *Ritual Magic*, 154–225.

121. See Bachter, 'Anleitung zum Aberglauben', 95–6. For those who have claimed 1797 as a publication date, see Hans Sebald, 'The 6th and 7th Books of Moses: The Historical and Sociological Vagaries of a Grimoire', *Ethnologia Europæa* 18:1 (1988), 53–8; Karl-Peter Wanderer, *Gedrukter Aberglaube* (Frankfurt, 1976), 51.

122. *Salmonsens konversationsleksikon* (Copenhagen, 1915–30), v.379; Birgitte Rørbye, *Kloge Folk og Skidtfolk* (Copenhagen, 1976), 260.

123. Velle Espeland, *Svartbok* (Oslo, 1974), 23; Carl-Martin Edsman, *Från silverfisken i Skaga till träguden I Silbojokk* (Uppsala, 1996), 348–52.

124. Gustav Henningsen, 'Witch Persecution after the Era of the Witch Trials: A Contribution to Danish Ethnohistory', *ARV* 44 (1988), 134–5.

125. Arne Bugge Amundsen, *Svarteboken fra Borge* (Sarpsborg, 1987), 10.

126. Ferdinand Ohrt, *Danmarks Trylleformler* (Copenhagen, 1917), i.513.

127. Torbjøn Alm, 'Sevenbom Juniperus Sabina i folketradisjonen i Norge', *Blyttia: Norges Botaniske Annales* 61:4 (2003), 187.

128. See, for example, those extracted from black books in Anton Christian Bang, *Norske Hexe-Formularer og Magiske Opskrifte* (Kristiania, [1901–2] 2005), 703–1. On treasure hunting see, for example, John Lindow, 'Swedish Legends of Buried Treasure', *Journal of American Folklore* 95:377 (1982), 257–79.

129. Mary S. Rustad, *The Black Books of Elverum* (Lakeville, [1999] 2006), 5. See also Ronald Grambo, *Djevelens Livshistorie* (Oslo, 1990), 150–1.

130. Tyge Krogh, *Oplysningstiden og det magiske* (Copenhagen, 2000), 124–50; Soili-Maria Olli, *Visioner av världen* (Umeå, 2007); Soili-Maria Olli, 'The Devil's Pact: A Male Strategy', in Davies and de Blécourt, *Beyond the Witch Trials*, 100–17; Per Sörlin,

'*Wicked Arts': Witchcraft and Magic Trials in Southern Sweden, 1635–1754* (Leiden, 1999), 33–5.

131. Bang, *Norske Hexe-Formulare*, pp. xxxviii–xxxix; Kathleen Stokker, *Remedies and Rituals: Folk Medicine in Norway and the New Land* (Minnesota, 2007), 100.

132. Bachter, 'Anleitung zum Aberglauben', 39; Scheible, *Das Kloster*, vol. ii.

133. Amundsen, *Svarteboken*, 17–19.

134. Bang, *Norske Hexe-Formularer*, p. xix.

135. Ravaisson, *Archives*, v.361; vi.185–6, 208.

136. *Pacta und Gelübdnüs dess zu Pignerole gesangen sitzenden Hertzogs von Luxenburg so er mit dem peydigen Satan getroffen (c.*1680). Luxembourg was not in the Bastille in 1659.

137. *A Letter from a Trooper in Flanders, to his Comerade: Shewing, That Luxemburg is a Witch, and deals with the Devil* (London, 1695), 13. See also *The Bargain which the Duke of Luxembourg, General of the Troops of France, made with the Devil, to win battles* (London, 1692).

138. *Den berømte Hertug af Luxemborgs, forrige kongel. Fransk General samt Hofmarskal, hans Pagt of Forbund med Satan* (Copenhagen, 1787).

139. Olli, 'The Devil's Pact', 102; Bang, *Norske Hexe-Formularer*, 710, 712.

140. Lisa Råna, 'Skolelærer Arne Larsen's Svartebok', http://www.aaks.no/FullStory. aspx?m=34&amid=2619; Rustad, *Black Books of Elverum*, p. xxxvii.

141. Ohrt, *Danmarks Trylleformler*, i.99.

142. See Kathleen Stokker, 'Between Sin and Salvation: The Human Condition in Legends of the Black Book Minister', *Scandinavian Studies* 67 (1995), 91–108, esp. 103; Espeland, *Svartbok*, 10, 13; Reimund Kvideland and Henning K. Sehmsdorf (eds), *Scandinavian Folk Belief and Legend* (Minneapolis, 1988), 286–7.

143. Espeland, *Svartbok*, 7–8; Rustad, *Black Books of Elverum*, p. xxxvii.

144. Kvideland and Sehmsdorf (eds), *Scandinavian Folk Belief*, 282; Krogh, *Oplysningstiden*, 130.

145. Stokker, *Remedies*, 70, 82–3.

146. See, for example, Ohrt, *Danmarks Trylleformler*, i.105–7; H. P. Hansen, *Kloge Folk* (Copenhagen, 1961), ii.74–114.

147. For a study of Kokborg and a reprint of his *Syprianus* see H. P. Hansen, *Kloge Folk* (Copenhagen, 1960), i.20–78.

148. Henrik Kokborg, *Mod Forhexelse* (n.d.); *idem, Tre trylleformularerder* (n.d.).

149. Henningsen, 'Witch persecution', 145.

150. Laura Stark, *The Magical Self: Body, Society and the Supernatural in Early Modern Rural Finland* (Helsinki, 2006), 179–80, 248–9.

151. Ülo Valk, *The Black Gentleman: Manifestations of the Devil in Estonian Folk Religion* (Helsinki, 2001), 86–92.

152. See Owen Davies, *Cunning-Folk: Popular Magic in English History* (London, 2003), chs 5 and 6.

153. See Owen Davies, *Witchcraft, Magic and Culture 1736–1951* (Manchester, 1999), ch. 3.

154. See, for example, John Denis, *Denis's Catalogue of Ancient and Modern Books, For 1787* (London, 1787), 179; Nicolas Prevost, *Duo Catalogi Librorum* (London, 1730), 48.

155. Ebenezer Sibly, *A New and Complete Illustration of the Celestial Science of Astrology*, 4 vols (London, 1790), ii.1093–5.

156. Davies, *Cunning-Folk*, 135,

157. E. P. Thompson, *Witness against the Beast* (New York, 1993), p. xiv. On occult London at the time see also Davies, *Witchcraft, Magic and Culture*, 236–50; Owen Davies, 'Angels in Elite and Popular Magic, 1650–1790', in Peter Marshall and Alexandra Walsham (eds), *Angels in the Early Modern World* (Cambridge, 2006), 316–18; A. G. Debus, 'Scientific Truth and Occult Tradition: The Medical World of Ebenezer Sibly (1751–1799)', *Medical History* 26 (1982), 259–78; D. S. Katz, 'The Occult Bible: Hebraic Millenarianism in Eighteenth-Century England', *International Archives of the History of Ideas* 175 (2001), 119–32; J. F. C. Harrison, *The Second Coming: Popular Millenarianism 1780–1850* (London, 1979); Patrick Curry, *Prophecy and Power: Astrology in Early Modern England* (Cambridge, 1989), 134–7.

158. *New DNB*.

159. See Davies, *Cunning-Folk*, 51–2; Francis X. King, *The Flying Sorcerer* (Oxford, 1992), 39–51.

160. For the sketchy details of Barrett's life see King, *Flying Sorcerer*.

161. *Morning Chronicle*, 13 August 1802.

162. Ibid. 16 August 1802; *Caledonian Mercury*, 14 October 1802; *Morning Chronicle*, 19 October 1802.

163. See Alison Butler, 'Beyond Attribution: The Importance of Barrett's Magus', *Journal for the Academic Study of Magic* 1 (2003), 7–33.

164. Francis Barrett, *The Magus* (York Beach, [1801] 2000), p. vi.

165. *The Critical Review*, 34 (1802), 406, 407.

166. *Liverpool Mercury*, 22 June 1857. See also Davies, *Cunning-Folk*, 142–3.

167. Ibid. 115–18.

168. *The Gentleman's Magazine*, 100 (1830), 96.

169. James J. Barnes and Patience P. Barnes, 'Reassessing the Reputation of Thomas Tegg, London Publisher, 1776–1846', *Book History* 3 (2000), 45–60.

170. See Iain McCalman, *Radical Underworld: Prophets, Revolutionaries, and Pornographers in London, 1795–1840* (Oxford, [1988] 2002), ch. 10.

171. Patrick Curry, *A Confusion of Prophets: Victorian and Edwardian Astrology* (London, 1992), 50.

172. Robert Cross Smith, *The Astrologer of the Nineteenth Century* (London, 1825), 230.

173. Curry, *Confusion*, 51.

174. See, for example, Mark Harrison, 'From Medical Astrology to Medical Astronomy: Sol-Lunar and Planetary Theories of Disease in British Medicine, *c.*1700–1850", *British Journal for the History of Science* 33:1 (2000), 25–48.

IV ACROSS THE OCEANS

1. On the continued belief in witchcraft and the activities of cunning-folk during the eighteenth century see Herbert Leventhal, *In the Shadow of the Enlightenment* (New York, 1976); John Putnam Demos, *Entertaining Satan* (Oxford, 1982), 387–94; Peter Benes, 'Fortunetellers, Wise-Men, and Magical Healers in New England, 1644–1850', in *idem* (ed.), *Wonders of the Invisible World: 1600–1800* (Boston, 1995), 127–42; Erik R. Seeman, *Pious Persuasions: Laity and Clergy in Eighteenth Century New England* (Baltimore, 1999), ch. 4; Jon Butler, *Awash in a Sea of Faith: Christianizing the American People* (Cambridge, MA, 1990), ch. 3.

2. William H. Loyd Jr, 'The Courts of Pennsylvania Prior to 1701', *American Law Register* 55:9 (1907), 564.

3. Butler, *Awash in a Sea of Faith*, 77.

4. *Bibliotheca Burnetiana: Being a Catalogue of the Intire Library of his Excellency William Burnet Esq; Deceased* (London, *c.*1730), 33.

5. See Julius Friedrich Sachse, *The German Pietists of Provincial Pennsylvania 1694–1708* (Philadelphia, 1895); Donald F. Durnbaugh, 'Work and Hope: The Spirituality of the Radical Pietist Communitarians', *Church History* 39:1 (1970), 72–90; Elizabeth W. Fischer, ' "Prophecies and Revelations": German Cabbalists in Early Pennsylvania', *Pennsylvania Magazine of History and Biography* 109 (July 1985), 299–333.

6. John Fanning Watson, *Annals of Philadelphia and Pennsylvania* (Philadelphia, 1857), ii.36; Horatio Gates Jones, *The Levering Family* (Philadelphia, 1858), 19.

7. Quoted in Leventhal, *Shadow of the Enlightenment*, 108; Alan W. Armstrong (ed.), *'Forget not Mee & My Garden . . . ': Selected Letter 1725–1768 of Peter Collinson, E.R.S.* (Philadelphia, 2002), 5.

8. Arthur Versluis, *The Esoteric Origins of the American Renaissance* (New York, 2000), 25–8.

9. Ibid.; Jeff Bach, *Voices of the Turtledoves: The Sacred World of Ephrata* (Philadelphia, 2003), esp. ch. 7.

10. *A Catalogue of the Books Belonging to the Library Company of Philadelphia* (Philadelphia, 1835), 188–92.

11. *Catalogue of the New York Society Library* (New York, 1813), 232.

12. *Catalogue of the San Francisco Mercantile Library* (San Francisco, 1854), 153.

13. William D. Stahlman, 'Astrology in Colonial America: An Extended Query', *William and Mary Quarterly*, 3rd ser., 13:4 (1956), 551–63; Leventhal, *Shadow of the Enlightenment*, 23–56; John F. Ross, 'The Character of Poor Richard: Its Source and Alteration',

PMLA 55:3 (1940), 785–94; Henry Phillips, Jr, 'Certain Almanacs Published in Philadelphia between 1705 and 1744', *Proceedings of the American Philosophical Society* 19:108 (1881), 291–7; Butler, *Awash*, 80–2.

14. John McBride, 'Benjamin Franklin as Viewed in France during the Bourbon Restoration (1814–1830)', *Proceedings of the American Philosophical Society* 100:2 (1956), 126; *Gamle Richards Swartkonst-bok* (Karlshamn, 1832).

15. See Victor Neuburg, 'Chapbooks in America: Reconstructing the Popular Reading of Early America', in Cathy N. Davidson (ed.) *Reading in America: Literature and Social History* (Baltimore, 1989), ch. 3; Kevin J. Hayes, *Folklore and Book Culture* (Knoxville, 1997), ch. 1.

16. Cited in Erik R. Seeman, *Pious Persuasions: Laity and Clergy in Eighteenth-Century New England* (Baltimore, 1999), 127.

17. Harry B. Weiss, 'Oneirocritica Americana', *Bulletin of the New York Public Library* 48:6 (1944), 526–9. See also Eric Gardner, '*The Complete Fortune Teller and Dream Book*: An Antebellum Text "By Chloe Russel, A Woman of Colour"', *New England Quarterly* 78:2 (2005), 259–61.

18. *The United States Literary Gazette* 4 (1826), 416.

19. Weiss, 'Oneirocritica Americana', 531.

20. *The History of the wicked life and horrid death of Doctor John Faustus* (Norwich, CT, 1795); *The Surprising life and death of Dr. John Faustus, D.D* (Worcester, MA, 1795); *The Wonderful and surprizing life, and horrid death, of Doctor John Faustus* (Philadelphia, 1797). See also Richard M. Dorson, *Jonathan Draws the Long Bow* (Cambridge, MA, 1946), 55.

21. See Don Yoder, *The Pennsylvania German Broadside: A History and Guide* (Philadelphia, 2005), ch. 8.

22. Thomas Francis Gordon, *The History of Pennsylvania* (Philadelphia, 1829), 579.

23. Watson, *Annals of Philadelphia*, ii.32.

24. Leventhal, *Shadow of the Enlightenment*, 37.

25. Sachse, *German Pietists*, 120–3.

26. See Alan Taylor, 'The Early Republic's Supernatural Economy: Treasure Seeking in the American Northeast, 1780–1830', *American Quarterly* 38:1 (1986), 6–34; Gerard T. Hurley, 'Buried Treasure Tales in America', *Western Folklore* 10:3 (1951), 197–216; Leventhal, *Shadow of the Enlightenment*, 110–18; Dorson, *Jonathan Draws the Long Bow*, 173–87.

27. I have used the online edition of *The Writings of Benjamin Franklin: Philadelphia, 1726–1757*, http://www.historycarper.com/resources/twobf2/bb8.htm; Watson, *Annals of Philadelphia*, 271–2.

28. Andrew Barton, *The Disappointment: or, The Force of Credulity*, 2nd edn (Philadelphia, 1796).

29. Ibid. 10–11.

30. Ibid. 66.

31. Ibid. 53.

32. Watson, *Annals of Philadelphia*, i.268–70. For further background on the authorship and theatrical history of *The Disappointment* see Carolyn Rabson, 'Disappointment Revisited: Unweaving the Tangled Web: Part 1', *American Music* 1:1 (1983), 12–35.

33. Hurley, 'Buried Treasure', 200–1.

34. Ibid. 203. Leventhal assumes that the Moses Book was a key work for the eighteenth-century Pennsylvania Germans, but this is highly unlikely.

35. The literature on the origins of Mormonism is large and often partisan, and I have no wish to provide a full bibliography. As well as those cited, I would also recommend David Persuitte, *Joseph Smith and the Origins of the Book of Mormon*, 2nd edn (Jefferson, 2000); Richard Bushman, *Joseph Smith and the Beginning of Mormonism* (Urbana, 1984); John L. Brooke, *The Refiner's Fire: The Making of Mormon Cosmology, 1644–1844* (Cambridge, 1994); Mark Ashurst-McGee, 'Moroni as Angel and as Treasure Guardian', *FARMS Review* 18 (2006), 34–100.

36. D. Michael Quinn, *Early Mormonism and the Magic World View*, 2nd edn (Salt Lake City, 1998), esp. 194–201, 217–21.

37. On these charms and their derivation see ibid. ch. 4.

38. Ibid. 104.

39. Ibid. 73.

40. Ibid. 84.

41. Ibid. 274.

42. William J. Hamblin, 'That Old Black Magic', *FARMS Review of Books* 12:2 (2000), 2.

43. Ibid. 51.

44. Ibid. 33–4.

45. *Bibliotheca Dramatica. Catalogue of the Theatrical and Miscellaneous Library of the Late William E. Burton* (New York, 1860), 286. On Burton's life see David L. Rinear, *Stage, Page, Scandals, and Vandals: William E. Burton and Nineteenth-Century American Theatre* (Carbondale, IL, 2004).

46. *Bibliotheca Dramatica*, 286; *A Catalogue of Valuable, New and Second-hand Books . . . Willis and Sotheran* (London, 1859), 19.

47. Hamblin, 'That Old Black Magic', 79. He is also wrong to say that the last edition was in 1651.

48. See, for example, David Ogilvy, *A Catalogue of Several Libraries of Books* (London, 1784), 7; John Poole, *Poole's Catalogue, for 1792* (Chester, 1792), 100; Thomas and John Egerton, *A Catalogue of Books* (London, 1787), 92; George Wagstaff, *Wagstaff's New Catalogue of Rare Old Books* (London, 1782), 7; William Collins, *A Catalogue of Books* (London, 1791), 102; Compton, *Bibliotheca elegans & curiosa* (London, 1783), 49; Lackington, Allen, & Co, *Second Volume of Lackington's Catalogue* (London, 1793), 231; Benjamin White, *A Catalogue of the Library of Alexander Thistlethwayte* (London, 1772), 79.

49. Poole, *Poole's Catalogue*, 101; Lackington, *Second Volume of Lackington's Catalogue*, 231.

50. Hamblin, 'That Old Black Magic', 79 n. 174.

51. Ibid. 79.

52. Owen Davies, *Cunning-Folk: Popular Magic in English History* (London, 2003), 155–8. For comparisons of different versions of the symbol of Nalgah see Quinn, *Early Mormonism*, figs. 72–5.

53. W. J. Wintemberg, 'Items of German-Canadian Folk-Lore', *Journal of American Folklore* 12:44 (1899), 50. See also J. Frederick Doering, 'Pennsylvania German Folk Medicine in Waterloo County, Ontario', *Journal of American Folklore* 49:193 (1936), 194–8.

54. See Leslie Choquette, *Frenchmen into Peasants: Modernity and Tradition in the Peopling of French Canada* (Cambridge, MA, 1997); Peter N. Moogk, 'Reluctant Exiles: Emigrants from France in Canada before 1760', *William and Mary Quarterly*, 3rd ser., 46:3 (1989), 463–505; H. Harry Lewis, 'Population of Quebec Province: Its Distribution and National Origins', *Economic Geography* 16:1 (1940), 59–68.

55. Lewis, 'Population of Quebec', 63.

56. Robert-Lionel Séguin, *La sorcellerie au Québec du XVIIᵉ au XIVᵉ siècle* (Ottawa and Paris, 1978), 83–8. On witchcraft in Quebec see also Jonathan L. Pearl, 'Witchcraft in New France in the Seventeenth Century: The Social Aspect', *Historical Reflections* 4:2 (1977), 191–205.

57. C.-Marius Barbeau, 'Anecdotes Populaires du Canada. Premiere Serie', *Journal of American Folklore* 33:129 (1920), 232.

58. Joseph-Norbert Duquet, *Le Véritable Petit-Albert ou secret pour acquérir un trésor* (Quebec, 1861), 5.

59. For literary analyses of the book see Louis Lasnier, *La Magie de Saint-Amand. Essai. Imaginaire et Alchimie dans 'Le Chercheur de trésors' de Philippe Aubert de Gaspé* (Montreal, 1980); Bernard Andrès, 'L'influence des livres: figures de savoir medical chez Pierre de Sales Laterrière et Philippe Aubert de Gaspé fils', *Voix et Images* 19:3 (1994), 466–86.

60. Philippe Aubert de Gaspé, *L'Influence d'un livre*, facsimile edition with introduction by André Senécal (Quebec, [1837] 1984), 18.

61. Ibid. 179–80, 196.

62. Duquet, *Le Véritable Petit-Albert*, 5, 57.

63. Ibid. 41.

64. de Gaspé, *L'Influence d'un livre*, 24.

65. See Mark L. Louden, 'African-Americans and Minority Language Maintenance in the United States', *Journal of Negro History* 85:4 (2000), 223–40. On the complexity of French Louisiana ethnicity see Cécyle Trépanier, 'The Cajunization of French Louisiana: Forging a Regional Identity', *Geographical Journal* 157:2 (1991), 161–71.

66. Robert Chaudenson, *Creolization of Language and Culture* (London, 2001), 258. Original French edition published in 1992.

67. Much has been written on the subject, but for general overviews in English see George Eaton Simpson, *Religious Cults of the Caribbean: Trinidad, Jamaica, and Haiti* (Rio Piedras, 1970); Margarite Fernández Olmos and Lizabeth Paravisini-Gelbert, *Creole Religions of the Caribbean* (New York, 2003); Kean Gibson, *Comfa Religion and Creole Language in a Caribbean Community* (New York, 2001); James T. Houk, *Spirits, Blood, and Drums: The Orisha Religion in Trinidad* (Philadelphia, 1995).

68. See Alasdair Pettinger, 'From Vaudoux to Voodoo', *Forum for Modern Language Studies* 40:4 (2004), 415–25.

69. Laura de Mello e Souza, *The Devil and the Land of the Holy Cross: Witchcraft, Slavery, and Popular Religion in Colonial Brazil*, trans. Diane Grosklaus Whitty (Austin, 2003), 130–41.

70. See Nicole Edelman, *Voyantes, guérisseuses et visionnaires en France 1785–1914* (Paris, 1995), 74–126.

71. Raquel Romberg, 'Whose Spirits Are They? The Political Economy of Syncretism and Authenticity', *Journal of Folklore Research* 35:1 (1998), 71.

72. For English accounts of the rise of Spiritism in Brazil see, for example, Donald Warren Jr, 'Spiritism in Brazil', *Journal of Inter-American Studies* 10:3 (1968), 393–405; David Hess, *Samba in the Night: Spiritism in Brazil* (New York, 1994).

73. Benson Saler, 'Nagual, Witch, and Sorcerer in a Quiché Village', *Ethnology* 3:5 (1964), 319. This was perhaps a reference to the *Sixth and Seventh Books of Moses*.

74. Michael Taussig, *Shamanism, Colonialism, and the Wild Man: A Study in Terror and Healing* (Chicago, 1987). 259.

75. Peter Wogan, 'Magical Literacy: Encountering a Witch's Book in Ecuador', *Anthropological Quarterly* 71:4 (1998), 186–202.

76. Richard Price, 'Fishing Rites and Recipes in a Martiniquan Village', *Caribbean Studies* 1 (1961), 8.

77. Alfred Métraux, *Le vaudou haïtien* (Paris, [1958] 1968), 239; W. B. Seabrook, *The Magic Island* (London, 1929), 308–15.

78. *Philadelphia Press*, 4 August 1885.

79. J. S. Udal, 'Obeah in the West Indies', *Folklore* 26:3 (1915), 294.

80. Anon., 'Concerning Negro Sorcery in the United States', *Journal of American Folklore* 3:11 (1890), 283 n. 2.

81. Ary Ebroïn, *Quimbois, magie noire eti sorcellerie aux Antilles* (Paris, 1977), 113–14.

82. Price, 'Fishing Rites', 5, 8; Ebroïn, *Quimbois*, 155.

83. Udal, 'Obeah in the West Indies', 282–3.

84. U. G. Weatherly, 'The West Indies as a Sociological Laboratory', *American Journal of Sociology* 29:3 (1923), 296, 298.

85. Frank Wesley Pitman, 'Fetishism, Witchcraft, and Christianity among the Slaves', *Journal of Negro History* 11:4 (1926), 651.

86. Pettinger, 'From Vaudoux to Voodoo', 417.

87. Pitman, 'Fetishism, Witchcraft', 652.

88. See the New *DNB*.

89. William W. Newell, 'Myths of Voodoo Worship and Child Sacrifice in Hayti', *Journal of American Folklore* 1:1 (1888), 16–30; *idem*, 'Reports of Voodoo Worship in Hayti and Louisiana', *Journal of American Folklore* 2:4 (1889), 41–7.

90. During the US occupation of Haiti between 1915 and 1934 tales of *Voodoo* and zombies once again became popular news fodder, helping justify the need for the American presence. See Joan Dayan, 'Vodoun, or the Voice of the Gods', in Margarite Fernández Olmos and Lizabeth Paravisini-Gebert (eds), *Sacred Possessions* (New Brunswick, 1997), 14.

91. Spenser St John, *Hayti, or the Black Republic* (London, 1884), 201–2.

92. This account is based on details in *The Gleaner*, 29 October 1904; *The Gleaner*, 12 November 1904; Udal, 'Obeah in the West Indies', 286–93. The latter was based on the trial report in the newspaper *The Voice of St. Lucia*.

93. Jay D. Dobbin, *The Jombee Dance of Montserrat* (Columbus, 1986), 23.

94. *The Times*, 7 August 1884; *Church Times*, 21 December 1928; Montague Summers, *Witchcraft and Black Magic* (London, [1946] 1964), 262.

95. Chaudenson, *Creolization of Language and Culture*, 250, 258.

96. See, for example, Gérard Mouls, *Études sur la sorcellerie a la Réunion* (St-Denis, 1982), 12, 25, 46.

97. Jean Benoist, *Anthropologie médicale en société créole* (Paris, 1993), 60, 141–2. See also Jean Benoist, *Les carnets d'un guérisseur réunionais* (St Denis, 1980), 18.

98. See George M. Foster, 'On the Origin of Humoral Medicine in Latin America', *Medical Anthropology Quarterly*NS 1:4 (1987), 355–93.

99. See, for example, C. H. Browner, 'Criteria for Selecting Herbal Remedies', *Ethnology* 24:1 (1985), 13–22; Arvilla Payne-Jackson and Mervyn c. Alleyne, *Jamaican Folk Medicine* (Kingston, 2004), ch. 2.

100. Foster, 'On the Origin of Humoral Medicine', 365–6.

101. André-Marcel d'Ans, *Haiti: paysage et société* (Paris, 1987), 274; Chaudenson, *Creolization of Language and Culture*, 258.

102. Douglas Taylor, 'Carib Folk-Beliefs and Customs from Dominica, B.W.I.', *Southwestern Journal of Anthropology* 1:4 (1945), 510–11.

103. Jane C. Beck, *To Windward of the Land: The Occult World of Alexander Charles* (Bloomington/London, 1979), 206. See also Payne-Jackson and Alleyne, *Jamaican Folk Medicine*, 116.

104. Dobbin, *The Jombee Dance*, 29.

105. Christiane Bougerol, *Une ethnographie des conflits aux Antilles* (Paris, 1997), 155.

106. Reginald Campbell Thompson, *Semitic Magic: Its Origins and Development* (London, 1908), p. xxxvi.

107. Garnik Asatrian and Victoria Arakelova, 'A Manual of Iranian Folk Magic in the Archive of the Caucasian Centre for Iranian Studies in Yerevan', *Iran and the Caucasus* 3 (1999–2000), 239–42.

108. Gerda Sengers, *Women and Demons: Cult Healing in Islamic Egypt* (Leiden, 2003), 39, 43.

109. Jack Goody, 'Restricted Literacy in Northern Ghana', in *idem* (ed.), *Literacy in Traditional Societies* (Cambridge, 1968), 235 n. 1; Moshe Sharon, 'New Religions and Religious Movements—The Common Heritage', in *idem* (ed.), *Studies in Modern Religions and Religious Movements and the Bābī-Bahā'ī Faiths* (Leiden, 2004), 24–5; A. Fodor, 'The Role of Fir'awn in Popular Islam', *Journal of Egyptian Archaeology* 61 (1975), 238–40; Constant Hamès, 'Taktub ou la magie de l'écriture islamique: Textes soninké à usage magique', *Arabica* 34:3 (1987), 320–2; Nicole B. Hansen, 'Ancient Execration Magic in Coptic and Islamic Egypt', in Paul Mirecki and Marvin Meyer (eds), *Magic and Ritual in the Ancient World* (Leiden, 2002), 427–47; Benjamin J. Kilborne, 'Moroccan Dream Interpretation and Culturally Constituted Defense Mechanisms', *Ethos* 9:4 (1981), 297.

110. See Caroline H. Bledsoe and Kenneth M. Robey, 'Arabic Literacy and Secrecy among the Mende of Sierre Leone', *Man*, NS 21:2 (1986), 202–26.

111. Goody, 'Restricted Literacy in Northern Ghana', 198–241.

112. For examples of Islamic written talismans found in the Caribbean and Latin America see Yvonne P. Chireau, *Black Magic: Religion and the African American Conjuring Tradition* (Berkeley, 2003), 34, 46; Carmen Cerezo Ponte, 'Hallazgo de unos amuletos musulmanes en el interior de dos piezas de la cultura Atacameña', *Anales del Museo de América* 13 (2005), 339–58.

V REDISCOVERING ANCIENT MAGIC

1. Karl H. Dannenfeldt, 'Egyptian Mumia: The Sixteenth Century Experience and Debates', *Sixteenth Century Journal* 16:2 (1985), 163–80.

2. Brian A. Curran, 'The Renaissance Afterlife of Ancient Egypt (1400–1650)', in Peter Ucko and T. C. Champion (eds), *The Wisdom of Egypt: Changing Visions through the Ages* (London, 2003), 119.

3. Zur Shalev, 'Measurer of All Things: John Greaves (1602–1652), the Great Pyramid, and Early Modern Metrology', *Journal of the History of Ideas* 63:4 (2002) 559; Peter N. Miller, 'Peiresc, the Levant and the Mediterranean', in Alastair Hamilton, Maurits H. van den Boogert, and Bart Westerweel (eds), *The Republic of Letters and the Levant* (Leiden, 2005), 117.

4. See Erik Iversen, *The Myth of Egypt and its Hieroglyphs in European Tradition* (1961); Elizabeth L. Eisenstein, 'Some Conjectures about the Impact of Printing on Western Society and Thought: A Preliminary Report', *Journal of Modern History* 40:1 (1968), 10.

5. See Thomas C. Singer, 'Hieroglyphs, Real Characters, and the Idea of Natural Language in English Seventeenth-Century Thought', *Journal of the History of Ideas* 50:1 (1989), 49–70.

6. Erik Hornung, *The Secret Lore of Egypt: Its Impact on the West* (Ithaca, 2001), ch. 14.

7. Iain McCalman, *Last Alchemist: Count Cagliostro, Master of Magic in the Age of Reason* (New York, 2003), 41–2, 52; Henry R. Evans, *Cagliostro and his Egyptian Rite of Freemasonry* (Washington, 1919), 8.

8. Florian Ebeling, *The Secret History of Hermes Trismegistus: Hermeticism from Ancient to Modern Times*, trans. David Lorton (Ithaca, 2007), 121–4.

9. Cited in Fekri Hassan, 'Imperialist Appropriations of Egyptian Obelisks', in David Jeffries (ed.), *Views of Ancient Egypt since Napoleon Bonaparte* (London, 2003), 64. See also Jennifer Hallett, 'Paganism in England 1885–1914', PhD thesis, University of Bristol (2006), 49–57.

10. See, for example, Dominic Montserrat, *Akhenaten: History, Fantasy and Ancient Egypt* (London, 2000), ch. 6; Sally MacDonald and Michael Rice (eds), *Consuming Ancient Egypt* (London, 2003); Susan D. Cowie and Tom Johnson, *The Mummy in Fact, Fiction and Film* (London, 2002).

11. See, for example, Charles Godfrey Leland, *Gypsy Sorcery and Fortune Telling* (London, 1891).

12. Owen Davies, *Witchcraft, Magic and Culture 1736–1951* (Manchester, 1999), 138–9; Maureen Perkins, *The Reform of Time: Magic and Modernity* (London, 2001), 67–9.

13. Charles. W. Roback, *The Mysteries of Astrology, and the Wonders of Magic* (Boston, 1854), pp. xi–xii.

14. Henry Carrington Bolton, 'Fortune-Telling in America To-Day. A Study of Advertisements', *Journal of American Folklore* 8:31 (1895), 305–6.

15. John Ball, 'Remarks on "Lost" Oases of the Libyan Desert', *Geographical Journal* 72:3 (1928), 250–8; E. A. Johnson Pasha, 'Zerzura', *Geographical Journal* 75:1 (1930), 59–61; G. A. Wainwright, 'The Search for Hidden Treasure in Egypt', *Man* 31 (1931), 197; *Livres des Perles Enfouies* (Cairo, 1907), 38; cited in L. V. Grinsell, 'The Folklore of Ancient Egyptian Monuments', *Folklore* 58:4 (1947), 34. See also Okasha El-Daly, *Egyptology: The Missing Millenium: Ancient Egypt in Medieval Arabic Writings* (London, 2005), 32–42.

16. See William Brashear, 'Magical Papyri: Magic in Bookform', in Peter Ganze (ed.), *Das Buch als magisches und als Repräsentationsobjekt* (Wiesbaden, 1992), 25–58; Hans Dieter Betz, 'Introduction to the Greek Magical Papyri', in *idem* (ed.), *The Greek Magical Papyri in Translation: Including the Demotic Spells*, vol. i: *Texts*, 2nd edn (Chicago, 1992), pp. xli–liii.

17. Stephen L. Dyson, *In Pursuit of Ancient Pasts* (New Haven, 2006), 50.

18. On Egyptian–German scholarly relations see Hans Robert Roemer, 'Relations in the Humanities between Germany and Egypt', in *Ägypten, Dauer und Wandel* (Mainz am Rhein, 1985), 1.

19. Cited in Brashear, 'Magical Papyri', 54; Betz, 'Introduction', p. xliii.

20. *The Classical Review*, 8:1/2 (1894), 47.

21. Eustace Haydon, 'Twenty-Five Years of History of Religions', *Journal of Religion* 6:1 (1926), 17.

22. Charles S. Finch, 'The Works of Gerald Massey: Kamite Origins', in Ivan Van Sertima (ed.), *Egypt Revisited* (New Brunswick, 1989), 401–13. See also the *New DNB*.

23. See Scott Trafton, *Egypt Land: Race and Nineteenth-Century American Egyptomania* (Durham, 2004), 33–5.

24. For a good account of the place of Theosophy in the wider occult world of the period see Janet Oppenheim, *The Other World: Spiritualism and Psychical Research in England, 1850–1914* (Cambridge, 1985), ch. 5.

25. I have relied primarily on Robert L. Uzzel, *Éliphas Lévi and the Kabbalah: The Masonic and French Connection of the American Mystery Tradition* (Lafayette, 2006); Paul Chacornac, *Éliphas Lévi (1810–1875)* (Paris, [1926] 1989). See also Christopher McIntosh, *Éliphas Lévi and the French Occult Revival* (London, 1972).

26. Éliphas Lévi, *Magic: A History of its Rites, Rituals and Mysteries* (Mineola, [1860] 2006), 369.

27. Éliphas Lévi, *Transcendental Magic: Its Doctrine and Ritual* (Kila, 1998), 242. First published in French as *Dogme et rituel de la haute magie* (Paris, 1856).

28. Chacornac, *Éliphas Lévi*, 202 n.2.

29. Lévi, *Transcendental Magic*, 242, 341, 291; Lévi, *Magic: A History*, 205.

30. Lévi, *Magic: A History*, 228.

31. Francis King, *Modern Ritual Magic: The Rise of Western Occultism* (Bridport, [1970] 1989), 35–7.

32. Éliphas Lévi, *Mysteries of Magic: A digest of the writings of Éliphas Lévi*, ed. A. E. Waite (London, 1897), 218.

33. Lévi, *Magic: A History*, 119.

34. Jean Du Potet, *La magie dévoilée ou principes des sciences occultes* (Paris, [1852] 1977), 67–84; Roger Gougenot, *des Mousseaux, Moeurs et pratiques des demons* (Paris, 1854), 211–12.

35. Éliphas Lévi, *La clef des grands mystères* (Paris, 1861), 166–7.

36. See Chacornac, *Éliphas Lévi*, 143–60, 194–200.

37. See R. A. Gilbert, ' "The Supposed Rosy Crucian Society": Bulwer-Lytton and the S.R.I.A.', in Richard Caron (ed.), *Esotérisme, gnoses & imaginaire symbolique* (Leuven, 2001), 389–403.

38. John Hamill, *The Rosicrucian Seer: Magical Writings of Frederick Hockley* (Wellingborough, 1986).

39. John Patrick Deveney, *Paschal Beverly Randolph: A Nineteenth-Century Black American Spiritualist, Rosicrucian, and Sex Magician* (New York, 1997).

40. Ibid. 33.

41. Hamill, *The Rosicrucian Seer*; Logie Barrow, *Independent Spirits: Spiritualism and English Plebeians 1850–1910* (London, 1986), ch. 3; Deveney, *Paschal Beverly Randolph*, 33–4, 51–6; Patrick Curry, *A Confusion of Prophets: Victorian and Edwardian Astrology* (London, 1992), ch. 3.

42. Deveney, *Paschal Beverly Randolph*, 69.

43. Cited ibid. 87.

44. See Joscelyn Godwin, Christian Chanel, and John P. Deveney, *The Hermetic Brotherhood of Luxor* (York Beach, 1995).

45. Ibid. 376, 46.

46. Ellic Howe (ed), *The Alchemist of the Golden Dawn: The Letters of the Revd W. A. Ayton to F. L. Gardner and Others, 1886–1905* (Wellingborough, 1985); *New DNB*.

47. See R. A. Gilbert's account of Mathers in the *New DNB*; King, *Modern Ritual Magic*, passim; Ellic Howe, *The Magicians of the Golden Dawn: A Documentary History of a Magical Order* (London, 1972).

48. Samuel Liddle MacGregor Mathers, *The Book of the Sacred magic of Abra-Melin the Mage* (London, 1898), p. xvi.

49. On the dangers of employing the *Sacred Magic of Abra-Melin* see McIntosh, *Devil's Bookshelf*, pp. 117–22.

50. I have relied on Waite's autobiography, *Shadows of Life and Thought* (London, 1938); R. A. Gilbert, *A. E. Waite: A Bibliography* (Wellingborough, 1983); R. A. Gilbert, *A.E. Waite: Magician of Many Parts* (Wellingborough,1987).

51. *The American Anthropologist* 11:2 (1898), 52.

52. Andrew Cunningham, 'Paracelsus Fat and Thin: Thoughts on Reputations and Realities', in Ole Peter Grell (ed.), *Paracelsus: The Man and his Reputation, His Ideas and Their Transformations* (Leiden, 1998), 64–8.

53. Waite, *Shadows*, 137.

54. On his Tarot pack see Juliette Wood, 'The Celtic Tarot and the Secret Tradition: A Study in Modern Legend Making', *Folklore* 109 (1998), 15–24.

55. A. E. Waite, *The Book of Ceremonial Magic* (London, 1910), pp. xii, xi. This was a revised version of the *Book of Black Magic and of Pacts*.

56. Ibid. ix, 92–5. For further speculative discussion on the date of the Abra-Melin text see Bernd Roling, 'The Complete Nature of Christ: Sources and Structures of a Christological Theurgy in the Works of Johannes Reuchlin', in Jan N. Bremmer and Jan R. Veenstra (eds), *The Metamorphosis of Magic from Late Antiquity to the Early Modern Period* (Leuven, 2002), 245–6.

57. See Alex Owen, *The Place of Enchantment: British Occultism and the Culture of the Modern* (Chicago, 2004), ch. 2; Howe, *Magicians of the Golden Dawn*; King, *Modern Ritual Magic*; Ronald Hutton, *The Triumph of the Moon: A History of Modern Pagan Witchcraft*

(Oxford, 1999), 74–81; Alison Butler, 'The Intellectual Origins of Victorian Ritual Magic', PhD thesis, University of Bristol (2003).

58. See Howe, *Magicians of the Golden Dawn*, 1–25.

59. See Butler, 'The Intellectual Origins of Victorian Ritual Magic', esp. ch. 3; Hallett, 'Paganism in England 1885–1914', 184–99.

60. King, *Modern Ritual Magic*, 83.

61. Owen, *Place of Enchantment*, 129–30; Butler, 'The Intellectual Origins of Victorian Ritual Magic', 97.

62. This biography is based on that in the *New DNB*.

63. John Michael Greer, *The New Encyclopedia of the Occult* (St Paul, 2003), 116. Much has been written on Crowley. Most recently see, for example, Lawrence Sutin, *Do What Thou Wilt: A Life of Aleister Crowley* (New York, 2002); Dave Evans, *Aleister Crowley and the 20th Century Synthesis of Magick* (Harpenden, 2007).

64. On the Lemegeton see Joseph H. Peterson, *The Lesser Key of Solomon: Lemegeton Clavicula Salomonis* (York Beach, 2001).

65. Melville J. Herskovits and Frances S. Herskovits, *Trinidad Village* (New York, 1947), 225, 229; Kean Gibson, *Comfa Religion and Creole Language in a Caribbean Community* (New York, 2001), 60; Ralph M. Lewis, *Behold the Sign* (San Jose [1944] 1957), 46.

66. The only published biography of Houssay is by the Martinist Robert Ambelain, *L'abbé Julio (Monseigneur Julien-Ernest Houssay) (1844–1912)* (Paris, 1962). An authoritative article on Houssay's place in the obscure, mystical Catholic and occult movements of the period, '1890 + Ecclesia Gnostica + ', can be found at http://www.rretac. com/docs/1890%20ECCLESIA%20GNOSTICA%20APOSTOLICA%201.pdf. See also http://www.gnostique.net/ecclesia/EG_II.htm.

67. Ambelain, *L'abbé Julio*, 22.

68. The most detailed history of Papus is Marie-Sophie André and Christophe Beaufils, *Papus biographie: la Belle Epoque de l'occultisme* (Paris, 1995).

69. Ibid. 29.

70. Ibid. 38.

71. See also ibid. 124–8.

72. For their use in France see Marcelle Bouteiller, *Medecine populaire d'hier et d'aujourd'hui* (Paris, 1966), 202; Judith Devlin, *The Superstitious Mind: French Peasants and the Supernatural in the Nineteenth Century* (New Haven, 1987), 239 n. 29. In the Caribbean see Richard Price, 'Fishing Rites and Recipes in a Martiniquan Village', *Caribbean Studies* 1 (1961), 8; Christiane Bougerol, *Une ethnographie des conflits aux Antilles* (Paris, 1997), 144; Ary Ebroïn, *Quimbois, magie noire et sorcellerie aux Antilles* (Paris, 1977), 156. Since the mid-twentieth century, Abbé Julio has also been joined by another, albeit fictitious, author of popular exorcisms and prayers named Dom Bernardin. A perusal of occult works on offer in French Antilles' market stalls in the 1970s revealed that Dom Bernardin had become a major influence with titles such as *Les grands exorcisms* and *Les prières dorées*; Ebroïn, *Quimbois*, 156.

73. Laënnec Hurbon, 'Les nouveaux mouvements religieux dans la Caraïbe', in *idem* (ed.), *Le phénomène religieux dans la Caraïbe* (Paris, [1989] 2000), 322.

VI Grimoires USA

1. Henry Carrington Bolton, 'Fortune-Telling in America To-Day. A Study of Advertisements', *Journal of American Folklore* 8:31 (1895), 299.

2. Jeffrey E. Anderson, *Conjure in African American Society* (Baton Rouge, 2005), 120.

3. Carolyn Morrow Long, *A New Orleans Voudou Priestess: The Legend and Reality of Marie Laveau* (Gainesville, 2006), ch. 6; Anderson, *Conjure in African American Society*, 114; Alasdair Pettinger, 'From Vaudoux to Voodoo', *Forum for Modern Language Studies* 40:4 (2004), 425 n. 32.

4. She has attracted considerable academic interest recently. See Ina Johanna Fandrich, *The Mysterious Voodoo Queen, Marie Laveaux: A Study of Powerful Female Leadership in Nineteenth-Century New Orleans* (London, 2005); Long, *A New Orleans Voudou Priestess*.

5. *New Orleans Morning Tribune*, 14 May 1927; cited in Carolyn Morrow Long, *Spiritual Merchants: Religion, Magic, and Commerce* (Knoxville, 2001), 123, 145.

6. See the *Oxford English Dictionary*; A. Monroe Aurand, *The Pow-Wow Book* (Harrisburg, 1929), 20–1.

7. See Don Yoder, *Discovering American Folklife: Essays on Folk Cultures and the Pennsylvania Dutch* (Mechanicsburg, [1990] 2001), 95–103; David W. Kriebel, 'Powwowing: A Persistent Healing Tradition', *Pennsylvanian German Review* (Fall 2001), 14–22; Barbara L. Reimensnyder, *Powwowing in Union County: A Study of Pennsylvania German Folk Medicine in Context* (New York, [1982] 1989).

8. For genealogical details about Lenhart see http://worldconnect.rootsweb.com/cgi-bin/igm.cgi?op=GET&db=gkbopp&id=I942

9. Reimensnyder, *Powwowing in Union County*, 118.

10. Cited in Don Yoder, 'Hohman and Romanus: Origins and Diffusion of the Pennsylvania German Powwow Manual', in Wayland D. Hand (ed.), *American Folk Medicine* (Berkeley, 1976), 243.

11. For the sketchy details of Hohman's career see Carleton F. Brown, 'The Long Hidden Friend', *Journal of American Folklore*, 17:65 (1904), 91–5; Yoder, 'Hohman and Romanus', 236–7; *idem, The Pennsylvania German Broadside* (Philadelphia, 2005), 22–3.

12. Yoder, 'Hohman and Romanus', 236.

13. For a comprehensive list of editions see http://www.luckymojo.com/powwows.html

14. Brown, 'The Long Hidden Friend', 96.

15. John George Hohman, *The Long Lost Friend. A Collection of Mysterious and Invaluable Arts and Remedies* (Harrisburg, 1856), 3. All subsequent quotes are from this edition.

16. Ibid. 5.

17. Ibid. 4.

18. Ibid. 10.

19. Ibid. 29.

20. Ibid. 11.

21. Aurand, *Pow-Wow Book*, 67.

22. *Public Ledger*, 14 May 1904; cited in Brown, 'The Long Hidden Friend', 90.

23. *The Daily Courier*, Connellsville, 22 October 1951.

24. *Public Ledger*, 24 May 1904; cited in Brown, 'The Long Hidden Friend', 91.

25. Yoder, *Discovering American Folklife*, 99; reprinted from an article published in 1972.

26. Hortense Powdermaker, *After Freedom: A Cultural Study in the Deep South* (reprint, Madison, [1939] 1993), 294–5.

27. Loudell F. Snow, *Walkin' over Medicine* (Boulder, 1993), 64.

28. Details of his early life can be found in Måns Hultin, *Doktor Roback eller en Svensk bonde I Amerika* (Stockholm, 1865); *Fallebo Gök eller den sig sjelf så kallande Doktor Roback, handelsman I Döderhultswik* (Westerwik, 1875); Ove Hagelin, 'En falsk svensk doctor i Amerika', *Biblis* 1:2 (1998), 16–29; Barbro Lindgren, *Fallebo göken—den sjunde sonen av en sjudne son* (1998).

29. Charles. W. Roback, *The Mysteries of Astrology, and the Wonders of Magic* (Boston, 1854), p. viii.

30. Ibid. xiii.

31. *The Meteorological Almanac and Spring Quarter Horoscope* (Philadelphia, 1840); *Hague's Christian Almanac* (Philadelphia, 1846); *Hague's Horoscope and Scientific and Prophetic Messenger* (Philadelphia, 1845–8).

32. *Hague's United States' Horoscope* (Philadelphia, 1851), 3.

33. Thomas Hague, *Exposition of C. W. Roback: Alias C. W. Hufeland, in Philadelphia, and William Williams, alias Billy the Sweede, in Baltimore* (Philadelphia, 1851), 9.

34. See also Thorsten Sellin, 'The Philadelphia Years of the Fallebo-Gök', *Yearbook: American Swedish Historical Foundation* (1965), 12–22.

35. *The Tioga Eagle*, 17 July 1850.

36. *New York Daily-Times*, 1 May 1852.

37. *New York Daily-Times*, 31 July 1852.

38. *New York Daily-Times*, 11 September 1852.

39. *New York Daily Times*, 1 October 1853.

40. Francis E. Brewster, *The Philosophy of Human Nature* (1851), 392. See also Charles V. Kraitsir, *Glossology, Being a Treatise on the Nature of Language* (New York, 1852), 52.

41. Charles Wyllys Elliott, *Mysteries; Or Glimpses of the Supernatural* (1852), 249.

42. Lambert A. Wilmer, *Our Press Gang: Or, A Complete Exposition of the Corruption and Crimes of the American Newspapers* (Philadelphia and London, 1859), 160–1.

43. Anon., *Humbug: A Look at Some Popular Impositions* (New York, 1859), 65.

44. *Report of the Penal Code of Massachusetts* (Boston, 1844), ch. 38. See also, Fulmer Mood, 'An Astrologer from Down East', *New England Quarterly* 5:4 (1932), 781.

45. Newspaper report reprinted in Hague, *Exposition*, 1.

46. Ibid. 5.

47. *Laws of the General Assembly of the State of Pennsylvania, Passed at the Session of 1861* (Harrisburg, 1861), 270–1. A slightly revised version of the Act remains on the state's statute books.

48. Roback, *Mysteries*, p. xiii.

49. L. D. Broughton, *Elements of Astrology* (New York, [1898] 1906), pp. xii–xiii.

50. Ibid. xiii. Fragments of Broughton's family history are scattered throughout *Elements of Astrology*. The 1851 census shows Luke working in a chemist's shop in Leeds. For some details regarding the astrological activities of one of his relatives in Leeds see Owen Davies, *Murder, Magic, Madness: The Victorian Trials of Dove and the Wizard* (London, 2005), 35, 39. On Broughton's American career see Mood, 'An Astrologer from Down East', 777–99. For examples of early modern astrologers who provided horoscopes see Herbert Leventhal, *In the Shadow of the Enlightenment* (New York, 1976), ch. 2.

51. D. Michael Quinn, *Early Mormonism and the Magic World View*, 2nd edn (Salt Lake City, 1998), 273.

52. Catalogue of W. Brotherhead, importer of old books, advertised in *American Notes and Queries* 1 (1857). A year earlier a copy was on sale in London for 10s. 6d; *The American Catalogue of Books: Or, English Guide to American Literature* (London, 1856), 56.

53. Donald R. Adam, 'Price and Wages in Antebellum America: The West Virginia Experience', *Journal of Economic History* 52:1 (1992), 210.

54. *New York Daily-Times*, 14 March 1855.

55. Lindgren, *Fallebo göken*, 45.

56. Hultin, *Doktor Roback; Fallebo Gök*.

57. Roback, *Mysteries*, pp. xiii–xiv.

58. *New York Daily-Times*, 11 March 1854.

59. *Fort Wayne Sentinel*, 27 March 1858.

60. See Orm Øverland, *The Western Home: A Literary History of Norwegian America* (Northfield, 1996), 57–8.

61. Kathleen Stokker, 'Narratives of Magic and Healing: *Oldtidens Sortebog* in Norway and the New Land', *Scandinavian Studies* 73 (2001), 411; eadem, *Remedies and Rituals: Folk Medicine in Norway and the New Land* (Minnesota, 2007), 100.

62. See Stokker, 'Narratives' and eadem, *Remedies*, 96, 99–102.

63. Wilhelm Munthe, 'Svarteboka', in Francis Bull and W. P. Sommerfeldt (eds), *Festskrift til Hjalmar Pettersen* (Oslo, 1926), 91; Stokker, 'Narratives', 413.

64. See Kevin J. Hayes, *Folklore and Book Culture* (Knoxville, 1997), 17.

65. *The Bee*, Danville, 11 January 1929.

66. Brown, 'The Long Hidden Friend', 149 n. 119.

67. *Oakland Tribune*, 8 February 1906. On Herrera see Gregory S. Rodriguez, 'Aurelio Herrera, Southern California's First "Mexican" Boxing Legend', http://www.laprensa-sandiego.org/archieve/nov12/greg.htm

68. *The Syracuse Herald*, 15 July 1919. On the malign reputation of the *Sixth and Seventh Books of Moses* in America see also, Hayes, *Folklore and Book Culture*, 22.

69. *The Daily News*, MD, 9 June 1916; *New Oxford Item*, 3 August 1916.

70. The most detailed examination of the case, on which this account is based, is J. Ross McGinnis, *Trials of Hex* (Davis/Trinity Publishing Co., 2000).

71. On press coverage see McGinnis, *Trials of Hex*, 49–63.

72. *The Olean Herald*, 18 March 1929; *Decatur Herald*, 14 April 1929.

73. *Ironwood Daily Globe*, 20 March 1929.

74. *Appleton Post-Crecent*, 21 January 1932; *Dunkirk Evening Observer*, 21 January 1932; *Gettysburg Times*, 24 March 1934. See also A. Monroe Aurand, *The Realness of Witchcraft in America* (Lancaster, PA, 1942), 20–1.

75. Earl F. Robacker, 'Long-Lost Friend', *New York Folklore Quarterly* 12 (1956), 26; Reimensnyder, *Powwowing in Union County*, 129; David Kriebel, 'Powwowing: A Persistent American Esoteric Tradition', http://www.esoteric.msu.edu/VolumeIV/Powwow.htm. Kriebel's PhD research will shortly be published as *Powwowing among the Pennsylvania Dutch*.

76. David Hogan, 'Education and the Making of the Chicago Working Class, 1880–1930', *History of Education Quarterly* 18:3 (1978), 232.

77. Mark H. Haller, 'Historical Roots of Police Behavior: Chicago, 1890–1925', *Law and Society Review* 10:2 (1976), 305.

78. Upton Sinclair, *The Profits of Religion* (New York [1918], 2000), 249.

79. See Catherine Anthony Ohnemus, 'Dr. Cyrus Teed and the Koreshan Unity Movement', *CRM* 9 (2001), 10–12.

80. *Oakland Tribune*, 14 January 1891.

81. Theda Skocpol and Jennifer Lynn Oser, 'Organization Despite Adversity: The Origins and Development of African American Fraternal Associations', *Social Science History* 28:3 (2004), 389–90.

82. Susan Nance, 'Mystery of the Moorish Science Temple: Southern Blacks and American Alternative Spirituality in 1920s Chicago', *Religion and American Culture* 12:2 (2002) 140. See also Herbert Berg, 'Mythmaking in the African American Muslim Context: The Moorish Science Temple, the Nation of Islam, and the American Society of Muslims', *Journal of the American Academy of Religion* 73:3 (2005), 685–703.

83. Erdmann Doane Beynon, 'The Voodoo Cult among Negro Migrants in Detroit', *American Journal of Sociology* 43:6 (1938), 894.

84. Arthur Huff Fauset, *Black Gods of the Metropolis: Negro Religious Cults of the Urban North* (Philadelphia, [1944] 2002), 43.

85. See Nance, 'Mystery of the Moorish Science Temple', 127–34; Abbie White, 'Christian Elements in Negro American Muslim Religious Beliefs', *Phylon* 25:4 (1964), 382–8; Ernest Allen Jr, 'Identity and Destiny: The Formative Views of the Moorish Science Temple and the Nation of Islam', in Yvonne Yazbeck Haddad and John L. Esposito (eds), *Muslims on the Americanization Path?* (Oxford/New York, 1998), 179–80.

86. The *Aquarian Gospel* borrows from Nicholai Notovich's *The Unknown Life of Jesus Christ* (1894).

87. *Drums and Shadows: Survival Studies Among the Georgia Coastal Negroes* (Athens, GA, [1940] 1986), 28.

88. Guy B. Johnson, 'Newspapers Advertisements and Negro Culture', *Journal of Social Forces* 3:4 (1925), 708–9; Yvonne P. Chireau, *Black Magic: Religion and the African American Conjuring Tradition* (Berkeley, 2003), 141–2; Long, *Spiritual Merchants*, 141.

89. Sinclair, *Profits*, 264–5.

90. *The Constitution*, 23 June 1912; *Oakland Tribune*, 10 June 1923.

91. *Fort Wayne Sentinel*, 2 August 1912.

92. See Jacob S. Dorman, '"I Saw You Disappear with My Own Eyes": Hidden Transcripts of New York Black Israelite Bricolage', *Nova Religio* 11:1 (2007), 61–83.

93. Harry Middleton Hyatt, *Hoodoo, Conjuration, Witchcraft, Rootwork*, 5 vols (Hannibal, 1970), i.755. For a useful discussion on the grimoires mentioned by Hyatt's interviewees see Dan Harms, 'The Role of Grimoires in the Conjure Tradition', *Journal for the Academic Study of Magic*, forthcoming.

94. *The Complete Edition of the 6th and 7th Books of Moses: Or Moses' Magical Spirit-Art* (n.p. c.1930s), 146.

95. Hyatt, *Hoodoo*, iv.3186.

96. This account of DeLaurence's life is largely based on information provided during his prosecution in 1919; US National Archives RG 28—U.S. Post Office Records. *Trial of the Delaurence, Scott, and Company Mail Fraud Hearing*. Location: 7E4–10/6/4. Box 29, Folder 77, pp. 112–18. See also Long, *Spiritual Merchants*, 190–1; W. F. Elkins, 'William Lauron DeLaurence and Jamaican Folk Religion', *Folklore* 97:2 (1986), 216.

97. *Trial of the Delaurence, Scott, and Company Mail Fraud Hearing*, 61, 72.

98. Long, *Spiritual Merchants*, 190.

99. *The Evening Times* (Cumberland, Maryland) 21 December 1906.

100. *Trial of the Delaurence, Scott, and Company Mail Fraud Hearing*, 91, 92.

101. Ibid. 8. The plagiarism of *The Magus* was noted in Francis King, *Modern Ritual Magic: The Rise of Western Occultism* (Bridport, [1970] 1989), 195.

102. *De Laurence's Catalog* (Chicago, 1940), 212–14.

103. He was possibly the inspiration for the Sun-worshipping prophet in G. K. Chesterton's Father Brown story 'The Eye of Apollo'.

104. *The Syracuse Herald*, 11 September 1908.

105. 'Reverend Doctor Otoman Zar'Adusht Hanish and His Mazdaznan Movement', available at http://tenets.zoroastrianism.com/ReverendDoctorOtomanZaradusht HanishandhisMazdaznanMovement.pdf

106. *Oakland Tribune*, 17 March 1906.

107. See, for example, *The Syracuse Herald*, 11 September 1908; *The Evening Post*, 27 December 1911.

108. See, for example, *The Daily Review* (Illinois), 6 March 1912; *Oakland Tribune*, 21 November 1913.

109. *The Syracuse Herald*, 11 September 1908.

110. *Chicago Daily Tribune*, 12 and 13 November 1912.

111. *The Syracuse Herald*, 28 October 1912; *Lima News*, 20 October 1912.

112. *Chicago Daily Tribune*, 23 November 1912.

113. See, for example, *The Mansfield News*, 23 December 1923.

114. *Trial of the Delaurence, Scott, and Company Mail Fraud Hearing*, 110.

115. Ibid. 112.

116. Ibid. 69, 102–3, 164–5, 169.

117. James A. Santucci, 'H. N. Stokes and the O.E. Library Critic', *Theosophical History* 1:6 (1986), 129–40.

118. *Trial of the Delaurence, Scott, and Company Mail Fraud Hearing*, 30.

119. Ibid. 43.

120. Ibid. 145.

121. Ibid. 145, 154–5, 144.

122. Frank K. Jensen, *The Story of the Waite-Smith Tarot* (Croydon Hills, 2006); ch. 4; R. A. Gilbert, *A. E. Waite: A Bibliography* (Wellingborough, 1983).

123. Gilbert, *A. E. Waite*, 84.

124. *Trial of the Delaurence, Scott, and Company Mail Fraud Hearing*, 158, 162.

125. Ibid. 127, 140.

126. *Chicago Daily Tribune*, 18 November 1931.

127. Robert Cameron Mitchell, 'Religious Protest and Social Change: The Origins of the Aladura Movement in Western Nigeria', in R. L. Rothberg and A. Mazrui (eds), *Protest and Power in Black Africa* (Oxford, 1970), 478; Elizabeth Isichei, *History of Christianity in Africa* (London, 1995), 295; J. D. Y. Peel, *Aladura: A Religious Movement among the Yoruba* (Oxford, 1968), 128, 142, 170.

128. Peter Probst and Brigitte Bühler, 'Patterns of Control on Medicine, Politics, and Social Change among the Wimbum, Cameroon Grassfields', *Anthropos* 85 (1990), 453.

129. Henry John Drewal, 'Mermaids, Mirrors, and Snake Charmers: Igbo Mami Wata Shrines', *African Arts* 21:2 (1988), 38–45.

130. Daniel Offiong, 'Social Relations and Witch Beliefs among the Ibibio', *Africa* 53:3 (1983), 75.

131. H. W. Turner, *History of an African Independent Church*, 2 vols (Oxford, 1967), ii.74; Peter Probst, 'The Letter and the Spirit: Literacy and Religious Authority in the History of the Aladura Movement in Western Nigeria', in Brian V. Street (ed.), *Cross-cultural Approaches to Literacy* (Cambridge, 1993), 203–10; Robert Cameron Mitchell, review of Turner's *History of an African Independent Church, Journal for the Scientific Study of Religion* 7:2 (1968), 313; Peel, *Aladura*.

132. Neil J. Savishinsky, 'Rastafari in the Promised Land: The Spread of a Jamaican Socioreligious Movement among the Youth of West Africa', *African Studies Review* 37:3 (1994), 37, 47 n. 22.

133. Margaret Field, *Search for Security* (London, 1960), 349, 41–2.

134. Howard French, 'World Fails to End—Again: If It Knew What I Knew, Pepsi Would Never Have Underestimated Ghana's Fascination with Eclipses', *Guardian Online*, 3 April 2006; see http://www.howardwfrench.com/archives/2006/04

135. Robert Pool, 'On the Creation and Dissolution of Ethnomedical Systems in the Medical Ethnography of Africa', *Africa* 64:1 (1994), 13.

136. Hans Debrunner, *Witchcraft in Ghana* (Accra, [1959] 1961), 96.

137. Ibid. 97; Field, *Search for Security*, 41, 350.

138. Roger D. Abrahams, 'Foreword', in Jane C. Beck, *To Windward of the Land: The Occult World of Alexander Charles* (Bloomington/London, 1979), p. xii.; Patrick A. Polk, 'Other Books, Other Powers: *The 6th and 7th Books of Moses* in Afro-Atlantic Folk Belief', *Southern Folklore* 56:2 (1999), 120; Jane C. Beck, 'The Implied Obeah Man', *Western Folklore* 35:1 (1976), 28 n. 6.

139. An envelope stamped in Fort de France, Martinique, with the date 1952, which was sold on eBay a few years ago, was addressed to 'Monsieur De Laurence' at the company's Chicago address. See http://www.luckymojo.com/esoteric/religion/african/diasporic/caribbeanhinduorishaoccult.html

140. Melville J. Herskovits and Frances S. Herskovits, *Trinidad Village* (New York, 1947), 228–9.

141. George Eaton Simpson, 'The Acculturative Process in Trinidadian Shango', *Anthropological Quarterly* 37:1 (1964), 22; *idem*, 'Baptismal, "Mourning," and "Building" Ceremonies of the Shouters in Trinidad', *Journal of American Folklore* 79:314 (1966), 537–50.

142. Kenneth Anthony Lum, *Praising His Name in the Dance: Spirit Possession in the Spiritual Baptist Faith and Orisha Work in Trinidad* (Amsterdam, 1999), 120, 161; Maarit

Laitinen, *Marching to Zion: Creolisation in Spiritual Baptist Rituals and Cosmology* (Helsinki, 2002), 31, 79, 279; Stephen Glazier, ' "Beyond a Boundary": Life, Death, and Cricket in Trinidadian Conceptions of the Afterlife', *Anthropology and Humanism* 31:2 (2006), 180.

143. Robert A. Hill, 'Dread History: Leonard P. Howell and Millenarian Visions in Early Rastafari Religions in Jamaica', *Epoche, Journal of the History of Religions at UCLA* 9 (1981), 69; cited in Polk, 'Other Books, Other Powers', 120.

144. Erna Brodber, 'Brief Notes on De Laurence in Jamaica', *ACIJ Research Review* 4 (1999), 91.

145. Ibid.

146. *The Daily Gleaner*, 20 April 1931.

147. *The Daily Gleaner*, 30 January 1934.

148. *The Daily Gleaner*, 5 February 1934. The book on personal magnetism may have been a copy of *Revelations of a Mysterious Force, Or the Power that Rules the World* by Norman Barclay of Argyll House, Kensington, London. Barclay described himself as a psychologist who had discovered 'the secret of personal magnetism'. I have been unable to trace an extant copy, but in 1915 the author advertised it for sale in *The Gleaner*, to be sent 'under plain sealed cover', along with *The Mystical Oracle or the Complete Fortune-Teller and Dream Book*, a book Barclay claimed was 'written over two hundred years ago' by a Hindu adept. This obscure occultist obviously saw Jamaican *Obeah* practitioners as a prime market for his self-published work on inner forces and telepathic powers, which evidently made no impact in England's crowded psychic market.

149. S. Leslie Thornton, ' "Obeah" in Jamaica', *Journal of the Society of Comparative Legislation*, NS 5:2 (1904), 269.

150. Brodber, 'Brief Notes', 93.

151. E.g. *The Jamaica Gazette*, 14 October 1965; *The Gleaner*, 2 September 1968.

152. Jeffrey W. Mantz, 'Enchanting Panics and Obeah Anxieties: Concealing and Disclosing Eastern Caribbean Witchcraft', *Anthropology and Humanism* 32:1 (2007), 23.

153. Brodber, 'Brief Notes', 96–9. On migration see Dereck W. Cooper, 'Migration from Jamaica in the 1970s: Political Protest or Economic Pull?', *International Migration Review* 19:4 (1985) 728–45.

154. *The Gleaner*, 24 September 1970.

155. *The Gleaner*, 18 February 1973.

156. It also prohibits 'All publications of the Red Star Publishing Company of Chicago in the United States of America relating to divination, magic, occultism or supernatural arts.' The only occult or spiritual publication I have come across from the Red Star Publishing Company, a producer of pulp detective magazines in the 1930s and 1940s, is a book called *Lighted Candles*.

157. Arvilla Payne-Jackson and Mervyn C. Alleyne, *Jamaican Folk Medicine* (Jamaica, 2004), 99, 101, 116, 136.

VII Pulp Magic

1. *The Washington Post*, 30 March 1913.

2. See David C. Smith, 'Wood Pulp and Newspapers, 1867–1900', *Business History Review* 38:3 (1964), 328–45.

3. See Erin A. Smith, *Hard-Boiled: Working-Class Readers and Pulp Magazines* (Philadelphia, 2000).

4. Anita P. Forbes, 'Combating Cheap Magazines', *English Journal* 26:6 (1937), 476–8.

5. Maurice Zolotow, 'The Soothsayer Comes Back', *Saturday Evening Post*, 17 April 1943; cited in Harry B. Weiss, 'Oneirocritica American', *Bulletin of the New York Public Library* 48:6 (1944), 519–20.

6. Lewis de Claremont, *The 7 Keys to Power: The Master's Book of Profound Esoteric Law* (New York, [1936] 1949).

7. Jeffrey E. Anderson, *Conjure in African American Society* (Baton Rouge, 2005), 116–20.

8. *The Charleston Gazette*, 16 December 1929.

9. This account of Dorene is based on Carolyn Morrow Long, *Spiritual Merchants: Religion, Magic, and Commerce* (Knoxville, 2001), 209–10; Catherine Yronwode, 'The Enduring Occult Mystery of Lewis de Claremont, Louis de Clermont, Henri Gamache, Joe Kay, Joseph Spitalnick, Black Herman, Benjamin Rucker, and the Elusive Mr. Young', available at http://www.luckymojo.com/young.html

10. This biography of Rucker is based on Jim Haskins and Kathleen Benson, *Conjure Times: Black Magicians in America* (New York, 2001), ch. 7; Jim Magus, *Magical Heroes: The Lives and Legends of Great African American Magicians* (Marietta, GA, 1995).

11. Charles S. Johnson, 'The Rise of the Negro Magazine', *Journal of Negro History* 13:1 (1928), 19.

12. *Black Herman: Secrets of Magic-Mystery and Legerdemain* (New York, 1938), 8–19.

13. Ibid. 32.

14. Catherine Yronwode, 'Spiritual Cleansing with Chinese Wash', available at http://www.luckymojo.com/chinesewash.html

15. Owen Davies, 'Cunning-Folk in the Medical Market-Place during the Nineteenth Century', *Medical History* 43 (1999), 63.

16. See Long, *Spiritual Merchants*, 229–46; V. E. Tyler, 'The Elusive History of High John the Conqueror Root', *Pharmacy in History* 33:4 (1991), 164–6.

17. Guy B. Johnson, 'Newspapers Advertisements and Negro Culture', *Journal of Social Forces* 3:4 (1925), 707–9.

18. Long, *Spiritual Merchants*, 193–4.

19. *Drums and Shadows: Survival Studies Among the Georgia Coastal Negroes* (Athens, GA, [1940] 1986), 55, 95.

20. Erdmann Doane Beynon, 'The Voodoo Cult among Negro Migrants in Detroit', *American Journal of Sociology* 43:6 (1938), 898.

21. John H. Burma, 'An Analysis of the Present Negro Press', *Social Forces* 26:2 (1947), 172–80; George N. Redd, 'The Educational and Cultural Level of the American Negro', *Journal of Negro Education* 19:2 (1950), 244–52.

22. Yvonne P. Chireau, *Black Magic: Religion and the African American Conjuring Tradition* (Berkeley, 2003), 142–3.

23. George J. McCall, 'Symbiosis: The Case of Hoodoo and the Numbers Racket', *Social Problems* 10:4 (1963), 365; Robert Voeks, 'African Medicine and Magic in the Americas', *Geographical Review* 83:1 (1993), 76.

24. Cited in McCall, 'Symbiosis: The Case of Hoodoo', 365.

25. Ibid. 366.

26. Zora Hurston, 'Hoodoo in America', *Journal of American Folklore* 44 (1931), 411.

27. *The Sixth and Seventh Book of Moses* (n.p., n.d.), 166.

28. I have been unable to find any publication by Duval Spencer, though Young also wrote the following booklet under the name Godfrey Spencer, *The Secret of Numbers Revealed; the Magic Power of Numbers* (New York, c.1942).

29. Yronwode, 'Enduring Occult Mystery of Lewis de Claremont'; Long, *Spiritual Merchants*, 125, 210.

30. Lewis de Claremont, *The 7 Keys to Power: The Master's Book of Profound Esoteric Law* (New York, [1936] 1949), 83. See also pp. 80, 81. Intriguingly in several places in the *7 Keys* the author seems to write as though a British citizen, such as 'In Great Britain we are too materialistic, far too incredulous, to appreciate half the wonders of the world.' This may just be an example of plagiarism though.

31. Loudell F. Snow, 'Mail-Order Magic: The Commercial Exploitation of Folk Belief', *Journal of the Folklore Institute* 16 (1979), 62 n. 17.

32. Yronwode has noted that some of the illustrations in Gamache's work were lifted from OPC catalogues; Yronwode, 'The Enduring Occult Mystery of Lewis de Claremont'.

33. The references are not entirely accurate. In the bibliography of *Mystery of the Long Lost 8th, 9th and 10th Books*, for example, Gamache lists 'Dr Ginsberg: The Kabbalah Unveiled'. He has obviously conflated Christian D. Ginsburg, *The Kabbalah: Its Doctrines, Development and Literature* (London, 1865) with S. L. MacGregor Mathers, *The Kabbalah Unveiled* (London, 1887). Other sources included, Joseph W. Williams, *Hebrewism of West Africa: From the Nile to Niger with the Jews* (London, 1930); Joseph J. Williams, *Psychic Phenomena in Jamaica* (New York, 1934); J. A. Dubois, *Hindu Manners, Customs, and Ceremonies* (Oxford, [1817] 1906); R. S. Rattray, *Religion and Art in Ashanti* (Oxford, 1927).

34. Douglas Taylor, *Black Carib of British Honduras* (New York, 1951), 136.

35. Margarite Fernández Olmos and Lizabeth Paravisini-Gelbert, *Creole Religions of the Caribbean* (New York, 2003), 138; Kean Gibson, *Comfa Religion and Creole Language in a Caribbean Community* (New York, 2001), 60; Maarit Laitinen, *Marching to Zion:*

Creolisation in Spiritual Baptist Rituals and Cosmology (Helsinki, 2002), 31. *Black Herman* also circulated; Christiane Bougerol, *Une ethnographie des conflits aux Antilles* (Paris, 1997), 145.

36. See, for example, *The Daily Gleaner* 7 December 1946; 11 October 1947.

37. Arvilla Payne-Jackson and Mervyn C. Alleyne, *Jamaican Folk Medicine* (Jamaica, 2004), 192. De Claremont's numerology pamphlet, *How to Get Your Winning Number*, which contains a tell-tale 'Master Code' of three-digit numbers, was recently re-reprinted in India for distribution there and in Nepal.

38. Jay D. Dobbin, *The Jombee Dance of Montserrat* (Columbus, 1986), 29.

39. Lewis de Claremont, *Leyendas de la Magia del Incienso Hierbas Y Aceite* (New York, 1938).

40. Francesco Cordasco and Rocco G. Galatioto, 'Ethnic Displacement in the Interstitial Community: The Easy Harlem Experience', *Phylon* 31:3 (1970), 302–12.

41. See, for example, Stanley Fisch, 'Botanicas and Spiritualism in a Metropolis', *Mibank Memorial Fund Quarterly* 46:3 (1968), 377–88.

42. Richard M. Dorson, 'Is There a Folk in the City?', *Journal of American Folklore* 83 (1970), 205–7.

43. Long, *Spiritual Merchants*, 169–70.

44. Anderson, *Conjure in African American Society*, 145.

45. José Madero, 'I Don't Do Black Magic: Mysterious World of Botanicas', *Los Angeles Mission* (December 2004).

46. Joe S. Graham, 'The Role of the Curandero in the Mexican American Folk Medicine System in West Texas', in Wayland D. Hand (ed.), *American Folk Medicine* (Berkeley, 1976), 185–6.

47. For example, *Libro de San Cipriano: libro completo de verdadera magia o sea Tesoro del hechicero* (Barcelona: Maucci, *c*.1920); *El libro infernal: tratado completo de las ciencias ocultas que contiene El Libro de San Cipriano* (Barcelona: Maucci, *c*.1920); *O grande livro de S. Cipriano ou o tesouro do feiticeiropor Cipriano* (Lisbon, 1923); *O verdadeiro livro de S. Cypriano ou o Thesouro da feiticeira* (Lisbon, 1919).

48. R. A. Gomez, 'Spanish Immigration to the United States', *The Americas* 19:1 (1962), 59–78.

49. Lydia Cabrera, *El Monte* (Havana, 1954), 275; Erwan Dianteill and Martha Swearingen, 'From Hierography to Ethnography and Back: Lydia Cabrera's Texts and the Written Tradition in Afro-Cuban Religions', *Journal of American Folklore* 116 (2003), 275; Fernando Ortiz, *Los Negros Brujos* (Miami, [1906] 1973), 164–5.

50. Jerusa Pires Ferreira, *O Livro de São Cipriano: Uma Legenda de Massas* (São Paulo, 1992), 116.

51. On the publication history of the Cyprianus book in twentieth-century Spain see Castro Vicente, 'El Libro de San Cipriano (I)', *Hibris* 27 (2005); *idem*, 'El Libro de San Cipriano (II)', *Hibris* 28 (2005); Alvaro Cunqueiro, *Tesoros y Otras Magias* (Barcelona, 1984), 69–72.

52. Between 1973 and 1975 a New York Spanish-language publisher, Extasis Corps, also put out a series of books on practical occultism, including *El Libro de San Cipriano*.

53. In the past few years publishers in Chile have also produced editions: *Libro de San Cipriano* (Santiago, 2001); *El libro infernal: tratado completo de las ciencias ocultas que contiene el libro de San Cipriano* (Santiago, n.d.).

54. *Ciencias Ocultas: Magia, Hipnotismo y Espiritismo* (Madrid, n.d.), 5, 9.

55. Ferreira, *O Livro de São Cipriano*, 42.

56. Ibid. 149–50.

57. *São Cipriano, o Bruxo* (Rio de Janeiro: Pallas Editora, 2005), 295–315.

58. Diana De G. Brown and Mario Bick, 'Religion, Class, and Context: Continuities and Discontinuities in Brazilian Umbanda', *American Ethnologist* 14:1 (1987), 73–93; Graham M. S. Dann, 'Religion and Cultural Identity: The Case of Umbanda', *Sociological Analysis* 40:3 (1979), 208–25.

59. *O Verdadeiro grande livro de s. Cypriano* (Rio de Janeiro, 1962); *Magia prática sexual; o sexo base da criação, o sexo em tôdas as religiões, a pratica da magia sexual, a magia sexual na Umbanda* (Rio de Janeiro, 1959).

60. Michael Taussig, *Shamanism, Colonialism, and the Wild Man: A Study in Terror and Healing* (Chicago, 1987), 268–9.

61. Ina Rösing, *Die Schliessung des Kreises—Von der Schwarzen Heilung über Grau zum Weiss: Nächtliche Rituale in den Hochanden Boliviens* (Frankfurt, 1991), 255, 263, 320. See also the review in *Current Anthropology* 35:3 (1994), 327–8. On their herbal knowledge see Joseph W. Bastien, *Healers of the Andes: Kallawaya Herbalists and Their Medicinal Plants* (Salt Lake City, 1987). There is no mention of the use of books in the 1917 account of the Kallawaya doctors in G. M. Wrigley, 'The Traveling Doctors of the Andes: The Callahuayas of Bolivia', *Geographical Review* 4:3 (1917), 183–96.

62. Ferreira, *O Livro de São Cipriano*, 45–52.

63. Marlene Dobkin, 'Fortune's Malice: Divination, Psychotherapy, and Folk Medicine in Peru', *Journal of American Folklore* 82, 324 (1969), p. 133, n. 2.

64. 'Editions of the *Sixth and Seventh Books of Moses*', available at http://www.esotericarchives.com/moses/editions.htm

65. John Thompson, 'Santísima Muerte: On the Origin and Development of a Mexican Occult Image', *Journal of the Southwest* 40 (1998), 409, 414.

66. Long, *Spiritual Merchants*, 214–19; http://www.indioproducts.com

67. See Thompson, 'Santísima Muerte'.

68. Madero, 'I Don't Do Black Magic'.

69. See Nicholas Goodrick-Clarke, *The Occult Roots of Nazism* (London and New York, [1985] 1992); Corinna Treitel, *A Science for the Soul: Occultism and the Genesis of the German Modern* (Baltimore, 2004; James Webb, *The Occult Establishment* (La Salle, 1976), ch. 5; Hans-Jürgen Glowka, *Deutsche Okkultgruppen 1875–1937* (Munich, 2003);

Heather Wolfram, 'Supernormal Biology: Vitalism, Parapsychology and the German Crisis of Modernity, c. 1890–1933', *European Legacy* 8:2 (2003), 149–63; Peter-R. König, *Der O.T.O. Phänomen Remix* (Munich, 2001). English translations of some of König's detailed research is available at http://user.cyberlink.ch~koenig

70. Goodrick-Clarke, *The Occult Roots of Nazism*, 27.

71. Quoted in Treitel, *A Science for the Soul*, 75.

72. Glowka, *Deutsche Okkultgruppen*, 81–6.

73. See Adolf Spamer *Romanusbüchlein. Historisch-philologischer Kommentar zu einem deutschen Zauberbuch* (Berlin, 1958), 36–7; Bachter, 'Anleitung zum Aberglauben', 132–3.

74. Adolf Spamer, 'Zauberbuch und Zauberspruch', *Deutsches Jahrbuch für Volkskunde* 1 (1955), 109–126, esp. 122; Bachter, 'Anleitung zum Aberglauben', 134.

75. Bartels, Buchversand Gutenberg, Hülsmann, Max Fischer, and Buchdruckerei Poetzsch.

76. Philipp Schmidt, *Superstition and Magic*, trans. Marie Heffernan and A. J. Peeler (Westminster, MD, [1956] 1963), 227. For a brief account of the case in English see Helmut Lethen, *Cool Conduct: The Culture of Distance in Weimar Germany* (Berkeley, 2002), 206–10.

77. On this belief see Bill Jay, 'Images in the Eyes of the Dead', *British Journal of Photography* 18 (1981); Véronique Campion-Vincent, 'The Tell-Tale Eye', *Folklore* 110 (1999), 13–24.

78. Figure calculated from Herbert Schäfer, *Der Okkulttäter: Hexenbanner-Magischer Heiler-Erdentstrahler* (Hamburg, 1959), pp. x–xi.

79. Johann Kruse, *Hexen Unter Uns? Magic and Zauberglauben in unserer Zeit* (Hamburg, 1951), 26, 137.

80. Treitel, *A Science for the Soul*, 201.

81. See Stephen E. Flowers and Michael Moynihan, *Secret King: Karl Maria Wiligut. Himmler's Lord of the Runes* (Waterbury Center and Smithville, 2001).

82. Treitel, *A Science for the Soul*, 241.

83. Ellic Howe, *Urania's Children* (London, 1967), 114–15.

84. König, *Der O.T.O. Phänomen*; English translation of the relevant chapter from an earlier edition is available online, http://user.cyberlink.ch~koenig/fs1.htm; Christine E. King, 'Strategies for Survival: An Examination of the History of Five Christian Sects in Germany 1933–45', *Journal of Contemporary History* 14:2 (1979), 211–33.

85. Howe, *Urania's Children*, 199 n. 1.

86. Treitel, *A Science for the Soul*, 238–9.

87. One experienced German antiquarian occult bookseller, with an impressive collection of editions, claims to have a copy of the *Sixth and Seventh Books* published around 1935 and another from 1939: http://www.buchversand-mueller.de/mosesalt.html

88. See Gerhard Schormann, *Hexenprozesse in Deutschland* (Göttingen, 1981); Wolfgang Behringer, *Witchcraft Persecutions in Bavaria*, trans. J. C. Grayson and David Lederer (Cambridge, 1997), 37–9.

89. See, for example, James R. Dow and Hannjost Lixfeld (eds), *The Nazification of an Academic Discipline: Folklore in the Third Reich* (Bloomington/Indianapolis, 1994); Christa Kamenetsky, 'Folktale and Ideology in the Third Reich', *Journal of American Folklore* 90 (1977), 168–78; James R. Dow, 'German *Volkskunde* and National Socialism', *Journal of American Folklore* 100:397 (1987), 300–4; Richard F. Szippl, 'Folklore under Political Pressure', *Asian Folklore Studies* 55 (1996), 329–37.

90. Christian Bang, *Norske Hexe-Formularer og Magiske Opskrifte* (Kristiania, [1901–2] 2005).

91. 'Institutions', *Current Anthropology* 4:4 (1963), 370.

92. Hannjost Lixfeld, 'The *Deutsche Forschungsgemeinschaft* and the Umbrella Organisations of German *Volkskunde* during the Third Reich', *Asian Folklore Studies* 50 (1991), 101–3.

93. Spamer, 'Zauberbuch und Zauberspruch'.

94. See, in particular, G. L. Mosse, 'The Mystical Origins of National Socialism', *Journal of the History of Ideas* 22 (1961), 81–96.

95. See Willem de Blécourt, 'The Witch, Her Victim, the Unwitcher and the Researcher: The Continued Existence of Traditional Witchcraft', in Willem de Blécourt, Ronald Hutton, and Jean Sibyl La Fontaine (eds), *Athlone History of Witchcraft and Magic in Europe*, vol. vi: *The Twentieth Century* (London, 1999), 214–15.

96. Harry Bergholz, 'Survey of Book and Music Publishing in Post-War Germany', *Modern Language Journal* 34:8 (1950), 616–25.

97. See, for example, Luke Springman, 'Poisoned Hearts, Diseased Minds, and American Pimps: The Language of Censorship in the *Schund und Schmutz* Debates', *German Quarterly* 68:4 (1995), 408–29.

98. Mary Louise Adams, 'Youth, Corruptibility, and English-Canadian Postwar Campaigns against Indecency, 1948–1955', *Journal of the History of Sexuality* 6:1 (1995), 89–117.

99. Springman, 'Poisoned Hearts', 421.

100. Von A. Eigner and O. Prokop, 'Das sechste und siebente Buch Moses: Zur Frage der Kriminogenität von Büchern und besonders laienmedizinischer Schundliteratur', in O. Prokop (ed.), *Medizinischer Okkultismus* (Jena, 1964), 270.

101. See, for example, Jane Viers, *Wovon eine Frau sonst nicht spricht* (Brunswick, 1950); Marion Stephani, *Schöne Büste—ja aber wie?* (Brunswick, 1957).

102. See Manfred Nagl, 'SF, Occult Sciences, and Nazi Myths', *Science-Fiction Studies* 1:3 (1974), 185–97, esp. n. 25.

103. Schmidt, *Superstition and Magic*, 22.

104. *The Dallas Morning News* 16 June 1963; George Hendricks, 'German Witch Mania', *Western Folklore* 23:2 (1964), 121; Reuters despatch from Bonn in the *Los Angeles*

Times, 31 July 1955; Taras Lukach, 'Witchcraft in Germany', *Western Folklore* 15:1 (1956), 65–6.

105. Schäfer, *Der Okkultäter*, 106, 96.

106. Schmidt, *Superstition and Magic*, 221.

107. Herbert Auhofer, *Aberglaube und Hexenwahn heute: Aus der Unterwelt unserer Zivilisation* (Freiberg, 1960), 9.

108. For discussion on Kruse's views see Joachim Friedrich Baumhauer, *Johann Kruse und der 'neuzeitliche Hexenwahn'* (Neumünster, 1984); Dagmar Unverhau, '"Hexen unter uns?"—Die Vorstellungen eines modernen Kämpfers gegen Hexenwahn aus der Sicht der historischen Hexenforschung', in Dieter Harmening (ed.), *Hexen Heute: Magische Traditionen und neue Zutaten* (Würzburg, 1991), 55–79.

109. Schmidt, *Superstition and Magic*, 219.

110. Baumhauer, *Johann Kruse*, 85.

111. Ibid. 118.

112. *Tagesspiegel*, 30 September 2001.

113. James R. Dow and Hannjost Lixfeld, 'National Socialistic Folklore and Overcoming the Past in the Federal Republic of Germany', *Asian Folklore Studies* 50 (1991), 117–53.

114. Will-Erich Peuckert, 'Die Egyptischen Geheimnisse', *ARV* 10 (1954), 40–96; idem, 'Das 6. and 7. Buch Mosis', *Zeitschrift für deutsche Philologie* 76 (1957), 163–87.

115. For a discussion of this phenomena see de Blécourt, 'The Witch, Her Victim', 156.

116. *Newsweek*, 4 April 1960.

117. Inge Schöck, *Hexenglaube in der Gegenwart* (Tübingen, 1978), 21–2; Baumhauer, *Johann Kruse*, 152–6, 164–7.

118. Will-Erich Peuckert, 'Hexensalben', *Medizinischer Monatsspiegel* 8 (1960), 169–74.

119. *The Times Recorder*, 13 April 1960.

120. Baumhauer, *Johann Kruse*, 87. For a detailed account of the ensuing legal battle see ibid. 83–97.

121. Ibid. 96.

122. See, for example, *Winnipeg Free Press*, 17 August 1957.

123. Kurt E. Koch, *Christian Counselling and Occultism* (Berghausen, 1972), 127.

124. See Bill Ellis, 'Kurt E. Koch and the "Civitas Diaboli": German Folk Healing as Satanic Ritual Abuse of Children', *Western Folklore* 54:2 (1995), 77–94.

125. Kurt Koch, *The Devil's Alphabet* (Grand Rapids, 1969), 12.

126. Ibid. 20.

127. Koch, *Devil's Alphabet*, preface to fourth edition.

128. Koch, *Christian Counselling*, 161–2, 193.

129. Kurt Koch, *Between Christ and Satan* (Grand Rapids, 1962), 131.

130. Ibid. 89.

131. Koch, *Christian Counselling*, 155.

132. Margaret Field, *Search for Security* (London, 1960), 350.

133. Koch, *Christian Counselling*, 161, 162, 133.

134. Kurt Koch, *Gottes Treue: Aus Meinem Liebe, Teil 1* (Lavel, 1980), 20–2; passage translated in Ellis, 'Kurt E. Koch and the "Civitas Diaboli"', 82.

135. Hans Sebald, *Witchcraft: The Heritage of a Heresy* (New York, 1978), 91.

136. Kramer Verlag (1979 and 1984); Schikowski Verlag (1976 and 1980).

VIII LOVECRAFT, SATAN, AND SHADOWS

1. Evelyn Underhill, *The Column of Dust* (London, 1909), 8; Christopher McIntosh, *The Devil's Bookshelf* (Wellingborough, 1985), 132.

2. William Hope Hodgson, *The Casebook of Carnacki the Ghost Finder*, edited with an introduction by David Stuart Davies (Ware, 2006), 45–6.

3. *New DNB*; David Stuart Davies, 'Introduction', in Hodgson, *The Casebook of Carnacki*.

4. See Timothy H. Evans, 'A Last Defense against the Dark: Folklore, Horror, and the Uses of Tradition in the Works of H. P. Lovecraft', *Journal of Folklore Research* 42:1 (2005), 99–135.

5. See H. P. Lovecraft, *The Call of Cthulhu and Other Weird Stories*, edited with an introduction and notes by S. T. Joshi (London, 1999), p. xix.

6. *H. P. Lovecraft: Uncollected Letters* (West Warwick, RI, 1986), 37.

7. For details on these various fictional books see entries in Daniel Harms, *The Encyclopedia Cthulhiana* (1998).

8. On Lovecraft's development of the *Necromonicon* see Lovecraft, *Call of Cthulhu*, 380–1, 387; Daniel Harms and John Wisdom Gonce III, *The Necronomicon Files* (Boston, MA, [1998] 2003), 8–28.

9. Lovecraft, *Call of Cthulhu*, 84.

10. Ibid. 112.

11. H. P. Lovecraft, 'Supernatural Horror in Literature'; available at http://gaslight.mtroyal.ca/superhor.htm

12. See Harms and Gonce, *Necronomicon Files*, 12–15, 98–9.

13. Quoted ibid. 13.

14. Lovecraft, *Call of Cthulhu*, 380–1.

15. *H. P. Lovecraft: Uncollected Letters*, 37.

16. For good accounts of Voynich, his manuscript, and the various theories attached to it see Lawrence and Nancy Goldstone, *The Friar and the Cipher* (New York, 2005); Gerry Kennedy and Rob Churchill, *The Voynich Manuscript* (London, 2004).

17. Lynn Thorndike, review of *The Cipher of Roger Bacon* by William Romaine Newbold, *American Historical Review* 34:2 (1929), 317.

18. Quoted in Harms and Gonce, *Necronomicon Files*, 28.

19. *H. P. Lovecraft: Uncollected Letters*, 37–8.

20. See Dave Evans, *The History of British Magick after Crowley* (Harpenden, 2007), 336–50.

21. This point is well made in Dan Clore, 'The Lurker on the Threshold of Interpretation: Hoax Necronomicons and Paratextual Noise', *Lovecraft Studies* 42–3 (20001), available at http://www.hplovecraft.com/study/articles

22. Montague Summers, *The Grimoire, and Other Supernatural Stories* (London, 1936), 254.

23. On Summers and his views on witchcraft see Juliette Wood, 'The Reality of Witch Cults Reasserted: Fertility and Satanism', in Jonathan Barry and Owen Davies (eds), *Witchcraft Historiography* (Basingstoke, 2007), 76–85; *New DNB*.

24. Summers, *Grimoire*, 265.

25. See Jacqueline Simpson, 'Margaret Murray: Who Believed Her, and Why?', *Folklore* 105 (1994), 89–96; Caroline Oates and Juliette Wood, *A Coven of Scholars: Margaret Murray and Her Working Methods* (London, 1998).

26. Gerald Gardner, *The Meaning of Witchcraft* (New York, [1959] 1988), 10.

27. Ibid. 11.

28. On the debate over the content and origin of Gardner's *Book of Shadows* see Ronald Hutton, *The Triumph of the Moon: A History of Modern Pagan Witchcraft* (Oxford, 1999), 226–36; Doreen Valiente, *The Rebirth of Witchcraft* (London, 1989); Leo Ruickbie, *Witchcraft out of the Shadows: A Complete History* (London, 2004), 106–14; Aidan A. Kelly, *Crafting the Art of Magic* (St Paul, 1991); Philip Heselton, *Gerald Gardner and the Cauldron of Inspiration* (2003); Hudson 'Morgann' Frew, 'Crafting the Art of Magic: A Critical Review', available at http://www.wildideas.net/temple/library/frew.html

29. Hutton, *Triumph of the Moon*, 227.

30. 'Gerald Gardner's Library: Authors D through G', available at http://www.newwiccanchurch.net/gglibrary/dg.htm

31. Hutton, *Triumph of the Moon*, 229–30.

32. See letters transcribed in Morgan Davis, 'From Man to Witch: Gerald Gardner 1946–1949', http://www.geraldgardner.com, 42–3.

33. Frew, 'Crafting the Art of Magic', 12.

34. For a concise breakdown of these influences see Ruickbie, *Witchcraft*, 113.

35. Hutton, *Triumph of the Moon*, 207; Valiente, *Rebirth of Witchcraft*, 41–2.

36. See Jenny Blain and Robert J. Wallis, 'Sites, Texts, Contexts and Inscriptions of Meanings: Investigating Pagan "Authenticities" in a Text-Based Society', *The Pomegranate* 6:2 (2004), 231–52.

37. Linda Jencson, 'Neopaganism and the Great Mother Goddess: Anthropology as Midwife to a New Religion', *Anthropology Today* 5:2 (1989), 4; Tanya Luhrmann, *Persuasions of the Witch's Craft* (Oxford, 1989), 238–9. For a personal reflection on this

see Julian Vayne, 'The Discovery of Witchcraft: An Exploration of the Changing Face of Witchcraft through Contemporary Interview and Personal Reflection', in Hannah E. Johnston and Peg Aloi (eds), *The New Generation of Witches: Teenage Witchcraft in Contemporary Culture* (Aldershot, 2007), ch. 4.

38. See Jencson, 'Neopaganism and the Great Mother Goddess', 4. From a Caribbean perspective see Erwan Dianteill and Martha Swearingen, 'From Hierography to Ethnography and Back: Lydia Cabrera's Texts and the Written Tradition in Afro-Cuban Religions', *Journal of American Folklore* 116 (2003).

39. Daniel Mannix, *The Hell-Fire Club: The Rise and Fall of a Shocking Secret Society* (London, 1959).

40. Massimo Polidoro, 'Blind Alley: The Sad and "Geeky" Life of William Lindsay Gresham—Notes on a Strange World', *Skeptical Inquirer* (July–August, 2003).

41. The facts about LaVey's early life, as far as they can be established, are provided in Michael A. Aquino, *The Church of Satan*, 5th edn (2002), ch. 2. For LaVey's own version of events see Blanche Barton, *The Secret Life of a Satanist* (Los Angeles, 1990). See also http://www.churchofsatan.com/Pages/HistoryMain.html

42. Barton, *Secret Life*, 23.

43. This account of the *Satanic Bible*'s genesis and content is based on that in Aquino, *The Church of Satan*, ch. 5.

44. 'Avon (publishers)', available at http://en.wikipedia.org/wiki/Avon_Books

45. Anton LaVey, *Satanic Bible* (New York, 1970), 53.

46. Ibid. 50.

47. Aquino, *Church of Satan*, 53.

48. Joshua Gunn, 'Prime-Time Satanism: Rumor-Panic and the Work of Iconic Topoi', *Visual Communication* 4 (2005), 102; James R. Lewis, 'Diabolical Authority: Anton LaVey, *The Satanic Bible* and the Satanist "Tradition"', *Marburg Journal of Religion* 7:1 (2002), 9.

49. On the number of practising Satanists and the various groups see Graham Harvey, 'Satanism in Britain Today', *Journal of Contemporary Religion* 10 (1995), 353–66; Jean Sibyl La Fontaine, 'Satanism and Satanic Mythology', in Willem de Blécourt, Ronald Hutton, and Jean Sibyl La Fontaine (eds), *Athlone History of Witchcraft and Magic in Europe*, vol. vi: *The Twentieth Century* (London, 1999), 94–109; James R. Lewis, 'Who Serves Satan? A Demographic and Ideological Profile', *Marburg Journal of Religion* 6:2 (2001), 1–10.

50. William H. Swatos, 'Adolescent Satanism: A Research Note on Exploratory Survey Data', *Review of Religious Research* 34:2 (1992), 161.

51. Lewis, 'Who Serves Satan?', 7.

52. Randy Lippert, 'The Construction of Satanism as a Social Problem in Canada', *Canadian Journal of Sociology* 15:4 (1990), 433.

53. Cited in Diane E. Taub and Lawrence D. Nelson, 'Satanism in Contemporary America: Establishment or Underground?', *Sociological Quarterly* 34:3 (1993), 527.

54. Bill Ellis, *Lucifer Ascending: The Occult in Folklore and Popular Culture* (Lexington, 2004), 87–9.

55. *Satanic Bible*, 136.

56. 'The Sigil of Baphomet', available at http://www.churchofsatan.com/Pages/BaphometSigil.html

57. Gunn, 'Prime-Time Satanism', 105. A recent Brazilian edition of the Cipriano contains a version of the Baphomet symbol on the cover; *O Tradicional Livro Negro de São Cipriano* (Pallas Editora; Rio de Janeiro, 2006).

58. *Satanic Bible*, 21.

59. Anton LaVey, 'The Church of Satan, Cosmic Joy Buzzer', reprinted in Barton, *Secret Life*, 248.

60. *The Cloven Hoof* 3:9 (1971).

61. *Satanic Bible*, 103; Barton, *Secret Life*, 248.

62. Anton LaVey, *The Satanic Rituals: Companion to the 'Satanic Bible'* (New York, 1998), 21.

EPILOGUE

1. Maarit Laitinen, *Marching to Zion: Creolisation in Spiritual Baptist Rituals and Cosmology* (Helsinki, 2002), 31; Arvilla Payne-Jackson and Mervyn C. Alleyne, *Jamaican Folk Medicine* (Jamaica, 2004), 192. On the influence of Gonzalez Wippler's populist works see, for example, Donald J. Cosentino, 'Repossession: Ogun in Folklore and Literature', in Sandra T. Barnes (ed.), *Africa's Ogun: Old World and New* (Bloomington, 1989), 297.

2. Tanya Krzywinska, 'Hubble-Bubble, Herbs, and Grimoires: Magic, Manichaeanism and Witchcraft in Buffy', in Rhonda Wilcox (ed.), *Fighting the Forces: What's at Stake in Buffy the Vampire Slayer* (Lanham, 2002), 192. On the influence of these series amongst teen witches see Helen A. Berger and Douglas Ezzy, *Teenage Witches: Magical Youth and the Search for the Self* (New Brunswick, 2007), 39–40; Hannah E. Johnston and Peg Aloi (eds), *The New Generation Witches: Teenage Witchcraft in Contemporary Culture* (Aldershot, 2007). On the historical context and cultural ramifications of the screen presentation of witches see Marion Gibson, *Witchcraft: Myths in American Culture* (London, 2007), 216–23.

3. Susanna Clarke, *Jonathan Strange and Mr Norrell* (London, 2004), 14.

INDEX

Illustrations are indicated in *italic*